Culture Through Time

Contributors

PETER BURKE

JAMES W. FERNANDEZ

DON HANDELMAN

EDMUND LEACH

EMIKO OHNUKI-TIERNEY

SHERRY B. ORTNER

JAMES L. PEACOCK

MARSHALL SAHLINS

LEA SHAMGAR-HANDELMAN

VALERIO VALERI

Culture Through Time

Anthropological Approaches

Edited by Emiko Ohnuki-Tierney

 STANFORD UNIVERSITY PRESS

Stanford, California

Stanford University Press, Stanford, California
© 1990 by the Board of Trustees of the
Leland Stanford Junior University
Printed in the United States of America
CIP data appear at the end of the book

To EDMUND LEACH,
a towering intellect and a modest man

Preface

The idea for this volume was conceived during a conversation with Sue Allen Mills, former editor at Cambridge University Press. We agreed that although historical interests have surged strongly in anthropology in recent years, no single volume contains works representing various approaches by so-called symbolists with historical interests. My initial idea was to publish a single volume of articles by those scholars who are pioneers in the field of historical symbolism, so that the major directions in the field could be readily gleaned.

But at an early stage of the project, some of the contributors suggested a conference. With generous support, both financial and intellectual, from the Wenner-Gren Foundation for Anthropological Research, we held a conference entitled "Symbolism Through Time" in the historical city of Fez, Morocco, from January 13 to January 20, 1986. The participants were James Boon, Lee Drummond, James W. Fernandez, Don Handelman, Bruce Kapferer, Kazuhiko Komatsu, Edmund Leach, Noboru Miyata, Emiko Ohnuki-Tierney, Sherry B. Ortner, James L. Peacock, Paul Rabinow, Marshall Sahlins, and Valerio Valeri; the discussants were Karen Blu, Peter Burke, James Clifford, and Clifford Geertz. At the conference we all agreed that we should revise the papers pursuant to our discussions there, but in a few cases the contributors could not find time to do that, and their papers are not included in this volume. Peter Burke, one of the discussants, had prepared a written text that he subsequently revised for inclusion in the volume. Thus the papers in this volume are by those who were at the conference and were able to meet the initial deadline for the submission of their papers.

Although the conference experience was invaluable for all of us, this project started as a publication project and remained such. There-fore, this volume does not incorporate the extensive discussions pur-sued at the conference; neither the tapes nor the records were readily available, so the discussion could not be usefully incorporated into the text. The contributors have, however, had ample time to reflect the discussion in their revisions.

Many other scholars have made significant contributions to the field; although it has not been possible to include their work, their accomplishments, much prized by all of us, appear as references in the individual papers.

This volume is dedicated to the late Sir Edmund Leach, who was most supportive of the project from beginning to end. He was a tow-ering intellect but a humble man, always ready to learn. His openness led him to take several turns in his career, rather than dogmatically guarding one approach. His many works tackled perennial problems in anthropology, and he did so often in the vanguard. "Culture and the individual" and "structure and practice" were the central issues in his *Political Systems of Highland Burma* (1954), a classic in an-thropology. His "Magical Hair" (1958) and his "Anthropological As-pects of Language" (1964) began a long series of writings on anomaly and ambiguity. His *Culture and Communication* (1976) is a bril-liantly articulate exposition of anthropology as a semiotic study, and his "Virgin Birth" (1967), like his paper in the present volume, is an eloquent and forceful postmodern statement. His legacy—of having ushered in the golden age of anthropology—will remain with us al-ways. I cherish the memory of this great man, who with warmth and gentleness laughed as he explained to us in Morocco how he always overstocked groceries for his wife, Celia, lest she run out of food while he was gone. His was a formidable presence, precisely because he both had a powerful mind and was a fine human being.

As the organizer of the conference and the editor of this volume, I want to thank, on behalf of all the participants, three officials of the Wenner-Gren Foundation for Anthropological Research: Lita Os-mundsen, then director; Nina Watson, the conference coordinator; and Fatima DaSilva. Ours was the 100th Wenner-Gren conference, and it was indeed a memorable occasion.

E.O.-T.

Contents

Contributors

PETER BURKE, Reader in Cultural History, Cambridge University and Fellow, Emmanuel College.

JAMES W. FERNANDEZ, Professor, Department of Anthropology, University of Chicago

DON HANDELMAN, Professor, Department of Sociology and Social Anthropology, The Hebrew University of Jerusalem

SIR EDMUND LEACH, Provost, King's College, Cambridge (1966–79); Professor of Social Anthropology, University of Cambridge (1972–78)

EMIKO OHNUKI-TIERNEY, Vilas Research Professor, Department of Anthropology, University of Wisconsin, Madison

SHERRY B. ORTNER, Professor, Department of Anthropology, University of Michigan, Ann Arbor

JAMES L. PEACOCK, Kenan Professor, Department of Anthropology, University of North Carolina, Chapel Hill

MARSHALL SAHLINS, Charles F. Grey Distinguished Service Professor, Department of Anthropology, University of Chicago

LEA SHAMGAR-HANDELMAN, Senior Lecturer, Departments of Sociology and Social Anthropology, and Education, The Hebrew University of Jerusalem

VALERIO VALERI, Professor, Department of Anthropology, University of Chicago

Culture Through Time

I

Introduction: The Historicization of Anthropology

EMIKO OHNUKI-TIERNEY

Today an unprecedented degree of reflexivity is seen in the work not only of anthropologists but also of scholars in many other disciplines. Epistemologies of all textures and degrees—structuralism, Marxism, hermeneutics, and phenomenology (with all the variants within each), to name only a few—are alive in most disciplines, creating a fertile if uneven landscape of competing and complementary theories and methodologies. Scholars no longer have a dominant paradigm to hang on to. Even more important, much of the academic reflexivity we are seeing arises from the ending of the political and intellectual hegemony of the West and the consequent reexamination of the "*situation coloniale*," to use Balandier's well-known phrase. Some say this phenomenon is an expression of a crisis in anthropology in particular and in academia in general. Yet in many ways what we are seeing is the exciting beginning of a new era for anthropology. A major thrust in this new era is the incorporation of historical dimensions in research, a result in part of the realization that there has never been a culture without history and in part of a more serious attempt by anthropologists to study so-called complex societies with long historical traditions.

The Historicization of Anthropology

The rapprochement between history and anthropology is natural, since the two disciplines share "the distancing of self" as a basic tenet. Three decades ago, Braudel wrote: "With regard to the present, the past too is a way of distancing yourself" (1980: 37). The past makes us think about the present reflexively. And with an understanding of the past, the contours of the present suddenly become clearer. Thus, the "other" that historians traditionally study has been temporally, if not also spatially, distanced from the investigator's culture. A historian's other, though, has often been situated within his or her own cultural tradition: an English historian, for example, studies the history of another European society. The other that anthropologists study is not only spatially distanced from themselves (see Cohn 1980, 1981) but also, usually, in a totally different cultural tradition. Scholars in both disciplines choose the cultural other as their object of investigation, and their work often results in the reflexive examination of self.[1]

To juxtapose historians and anthropologists, however, is simply to reify an artificial boundary and to negate the "blurred genres" of the contemporary academic scene (Geertz 1983). Even fieldwork, once the unique province of anthropologists, has been effectively practiced by historians, as exemplified by the work of Marc Bloch. If anthropologists have stressed "proctological history," to borrow from Bernard S. Cohn (1980), so have contemporary historians, as expressed in E. P. Thompson's (1974) notion of plebeian culture. Furthermore, we find no longer tenable such contrasts between the two disciplines as the historians' emphasis on the exhaustive study of primary sources before arriving at generalizations and the anthropologists' eagerness for analyses and interpretations to uncover patterns and structures. Geertzian or not, anthropologists strive for "thick description," just as many historians are eager for generalizations.

Although mutual interest between anthropology and history is long-standing, the recent interest in historicizing anthropology is phenomenal in its intensity and promises to be a lasting development. A new type of historicized anthropology arises from the epistemological reexamination of theories and methods undertaken in the current climate of postcolonialism and postscientism. The shifting geopolitics and the shifting paradigms are part and parcel of a phenomenon that has affected both disciplines. In hindsight, anthropologists' previous failure to tackle history seriously was due primarily to their colonial *mentalité*. Perhaps not deliberately but nonetheless persistently, they shared the Eurocentric belief that "nonliterate" peoples did not really have a history. Lévi-Strauss's well-known distinction

---

[1] For the view that anthropology is a quest for the self through the study of the other, see Lévi-Strauss 1967: 17; Lévi-Strauss 1983: 36.

between rapidly transforming "hot" societies and slow-moving "cold" societies can easily translate to mean hot societies have history and cold societies do not. A corollary assumption is that colonial contacts produced the first drastic cultural or historical changes in these cold societies, which presumably had had peaceful and unchanging cultures for the preceding millennia.

Anthropologists are confronting the histories both of peoples who had writing systems before colonial contacts and of those who did not.[2] In the forefront in this endeavor are such figures as Vansina, who has worked relentlessly to abolish "the zero-time fiction" (1970: 165) by using oral tradition, art, and other such cultural institutions as historical records (Vansina 1965, 1984, 1985). Furthermore, anthropologists no longer specialize in nonliterate societies or in the cold pockets of hot societies. Many have started to work in societies that have had historical records for thousands of years. As a result, historical information (or their experience with it) "recast[s] fieldwork from a descriptive and conditional into a reflective and subjunctive mode," as Fernandez puts it in his paper in this volume. In the case of literate peoples, anthropologists must also confront histories that have been interpreted not only by native laypeople but by native scholars, native historical schools, and native intellectual traditions as well. The picture is, or should be, no longer that of a lone anthropologist and his or her informants (or the infamous "my people") standing, or sitting, in a stark landscape devoid of intellectual traditions.[3] Anthropologists now see the omission was theirs.

If anthropologists have shifted gears, so have historians. The concept of history, like fieldwork and anthropological representations in

[2] Some anthropologists reject a sharp distinction between the histories of nonliterate and literate peoples. Others find the degree of difference in the availability of historical sources to create significant differences between the two types of history. At any rate, the *longue durée* is not easily accessible for histories of nonliterate peoples.

[3] I add *should* here because of my disappointment that those at the forefront of this reflexive endeavor reify the picture of anthropology as a Western discipline through almost complete neglect of the intellectual traditions other than those of Western Europe—primarily French, British, and German—and through failure to more seriously incorporate native intellectual traditions and native anthropologists. By *native*, I do not wish to incur a false image of those "pure and uncontaminated Natives" plucked out from some imagined remote or well-marked society. The world has been too dynamic and fluid to equate culture with society, and only the latter is a bounded political entity.

This reservation aside, postmodernism has made a major contribution to anthropology. For a critical overview of the field, see Geertz 1988. See also Clifford 1983.

general, has been placed under epistemological scrutiny. Left behind is history "in the raw" and Ranke's dictum of "*wie es eigentlich gewesen ist*" (how things really were); now confronted are the "forms of life" (Wittgenstein 1968) and "local knowledge" (Geertz 1983). Such polarities as history from below versus history from above, event history versus serial history, the native view of history versus the outsider's view of history all point to the complexity and multiplicity of what we call history. Today anthropologists and historians alike emphasize "plebeian culture," or "proctological history" (Cohn 1980), without altogether negating the historical significance of events and power holders (cf. Sahlins 1983).

As Edmund Leach illustrates in his paper in this volume, "records do not become a part of history simply by happening to survive." The flow of time is continuous, while historical events, constructed by people and professionals, punctuate it to create discontinuous "history." Historical records themselves result from the subjective and cultural sifting of perspectives, insights, and "facts." Any attempt at historical representation, then, must take into account the subjectivity of those who made the record, written or oral, and the role of memory, along with other problems associated with such records of the past (Vansina 1985).

In addition, historicity, or historical consciousness[4]—the culturally patterned way or ways of experiencing and understanding history—also plays an important role in constructing and representing history.

The same subjective and cultural factors inherent in historical texts—verbal and nonverbal—affect their interpretations, and both historians and anthropologists are often unknowingly constrained by their membership in a particular society at a particular period in history, by their gender, age, and class, and, most important, by the power inequality that often exists between the observed and the interpreters of history.[5] Historiography in any intellectual tradition is

[4] Although the term *historical consciousness* has been used more widely than the term *historicity*, I use the latter to avoid the inference that how people think of and experience history is always conscious.

[5] Although recent literature focuses on the power inequality between Western colonial states and the colonized, it is well to remember that there are or have been other colonial powers in the world, such as Japan, and that power inequality is also present within every society (for a detailed historical treatment of the so-called outcastes in Japanese society in historical perspective see Ohnuki-Tierney 1987).

not an objective science but is constrained by the same subjective, cultural, and political factors.

In sum, any historical construction only partially represents the multiplicity inherent in any culture in the past, and such constructions are constrained by forces beyond the control of those who left the records of the past, on the one hand, or of historians and anthropologists, on the other.

Although anthropologists of all persuasions have become involved in historical studies of cultures, so-called Marxists and neo-Marxists have been most active in this area. Recently, works by those who are (for better or worse) called symbolic or semiotic anthropologists have received particular attention, both within and outside anthropology.[6] What the reader will find in this volume is evidence of the dynamic complexity of "culture and history"—as presented by major figures in symbolic/semiotic anthropology. It is well, however, not to make a clear distinction between Marxists and symbolists, since, for example, Raymond Williams, E. P. Thompson, Bourdieu, and Gramsci are as symbolist as Sahlins is Marxist.

Each paper in this volume, not to mention the volume as a whole, raises important issues and offers clear directions for further research on culture mediated by history and history mediated by culture—a new field of inquiry that transcends both history and anthropology. No artificial unity—theoretical, thematic, or epistemological—has been imposed on the articles. The articles, each in its own way, offer an array of possibilities and different answers to the question of how to historicize anthropology and anthropologize history. The strength of the volume derives from a complementary diversity and tension. Each paper, drawing on a particular culture, offers an original way of penetrating that culture's historical dimensions.

Within the diversity, however, certain concerns recur. Consequently, the articles fall into two major categories: those concerned with the historical representations and constructions of a particular people and those concerned with epistemological questions of historicity and historiography. Since the selection of the articles was

---

[6] This field used to be, and by some continues to be, called symbolic anthropology, a term originally proposed by Peacock, a contributor to this volume. Other competing labels include semiotic anthropology. While that label has the advantage of stressing culture as a system of communication, it too is very broad, and practitioners represent a wide variety of methodological and theoretical perspectives.

based on theoretical concerns, a balanced representation of the world's geographic areas was accorded no priority. I am aware of the potential problems raised by this decision, since certain theories often arise from the ethnographic and historical knowledge of particular geographic areas. On that premise, a balanced theoretical representation cannot be divorced from a balanced geographic representation. In addition, the problem of possible differences between the historical representations and constructions of people with written records and those without could have been addressed more directly than they were. The papers lean slightly more toward structuralism than toward other persuasions. This slant occurs not by intention but because of the pragmatic need to include only those papers completed in time. Again, however, the theoretical and epistemological frameworks of the authors are too complex to pigeonhole.

Without pretending to provide an overview of the field of culture and history,[7] the remainder of this Introduction delineates some of the important issues in the field while introducing the major themes discussed in the individual papers that follow. The last paper in this volume is by Peter Burke, a social historian by profession, whose work is as familiar to anthropologists as theirs is to him. After introducing a history of unsuccessful attempts for rapprochement between anthropology and history, he discusses, with a particular emphasis on studies of "symbols," fruitful interactions between the two disciplines in the recent past.

Throughout this Introduction, the term *history* is used to refer to an interpretation or construction that attempts to represent the past on the basis of information from the past.

Historical "Transformations" and Processes

There are two basic questions in any historical study. First, in what way does a culture change over time, and in what way does it remain stable? Second, how does a culture change? What is the process that

---

[7] As expected, different reviewers asked why I did not discuss Evans-Pritchard's work, the Birmingham school, and so forth. This field is enormous in scope and growing rapidly. There are innumerable publications in anthropology, social history, geography, and other traditional academic disciplines, including a number of journals: *Ethnohistory* (whose articles tend to discuss historicity, rather than historical process) and *Comparative Studies in Society and History*, to mention only two.

drives the historical transformation of a society or a culture? I shall address these two issues here while introducing the papers by Sahlins, Ortner, Fernandez, and myself.

Levels of change. When treating the question of change versus stability in a society, it is important to identify the level at which changes take place, that is, to distinguish between changes or transformations at the basic level and those at a more superficial level. This quest is closely related to the time frame given to a historical investigation. During a short period of time, changes at the basic level are almost never discernible. If they are, they often misdirect assessments of enduring changes, which can be identified only if the investigator examines historical processes over a very long period of time—that is, over a time qualitatively long enough for the particular case under study; quantitatively, the time period will differ from case to case.

This question obviously relates to Braudel's distinction between "surface oscillations" and "long-term transformations." Braudel, Bloch, Le Roy Ladurie, and most scholars of the Annales school stress the enduring nature of the structure of society and culture. Structure for these historians endures through a long period of time. Thus, for Braudel, as for others, the basic structure is not only deep but is also, by definition, of *longue durée* (Braudel 1980) or motionless (Le Roy Ladurie 1977). Ironically, on this point the Annales scholars depart radically from Lévi-Strauss, under whose influence they became "practicing structuralists" (Skinner 1985). For Lévi-Strauss, whose structure is synchronic, history is "irrational," and there are in historical changes only "structural or structurable islands" that "bathe in an ocean of random phenomena not amenable to structural analysis" (quoted in Bucher 1985: 363).

Because of the primacy of the temporal duration, Braudel defined the "structure of the long run," or *longue durée*, in contrast to two shorter spans: the conjuncture, which covers a decade or up to a century, and the event, which entails only a short span of time when "surface oscillations" are most conspicuous (Braudel 1980; see also Furet 1972: especially 54–55; Le Goff 1972). His well-known triadic scheme is divided on the basis of temporal duration. The specific nature of the historical changes involved in the *longue durée*, the conjuncture, and the event, respectively, is therefore a corollary. Thus, the perennial question in anthropology and history of whether the structure can "transcend the individual and the particular event" (Braudel 1980: 6–11) hinges on the magnitude of different time scales.

Studying a culture over a long period of time allows the strategic advantage of examining the question of change versus stability, often phrased as the problem of *plus ça change, plus c'est la même chose.* For some scholars, such a study is the only way to determine whether short-term changes are really powerful enough to change the structure(s) of meaning in a culture. As Ricoeur forcefully stated, "History characterized by short, rapid, nervous oscillations" is "richest in humanity" although "the most dangerous" (1980: 11). It is dangerous, that is, if the oscillations are mistaken for enduring basic changes.

Systematic studies of historical changes over long periods of time, though limited in number,[8] point to the stability of the basic structure of a culture. In a study of the Balinese state, Clifford Geertz, an avowed antistructuralist, emphasizes the "transcriptions of a fixed ideal" for a period of nearly 600 years. In fact, in *Negara*, his major historical work, Geertz is willing to see regularities and patterns. Thus, he explains that in the new approach to history, historical changes are seen to consist of "a low but patterned alteration" and to be "the formal, or structural patterns of cumulative activity" (1980: 5). A collaborative work by De Creamer, Vansina, and Fox (1976) indicates that Central African cultural patterns have been flexible but stable and that the common religion has been remarkably stable, likely for millennia. In a general statement about history, Braudel writes that "the social content can renew itself almost completely without ever reaching certain deep-seated structural characteristics" and that "some structures" become "stable elements for an infinite number of generations" (Braudel 1980: 12, 31).

Whatever one's basic stance, such studies involve considerable time depth and pose a difficult problem in research, requiring a strategic focus on certain key issues. Of particular importance is the micro-macro linkage—a window, as I call it. It is a specific cultural activity—a symbol, a ritual, or a trade, for example—that enables a researcher to tap into the essentials of macro changes in the given culture and society, as Keith Thomas (1971) did by focusing on the mi-

[8]Besides such scholars as Boon (1977) and Hunt (1977), anthropologists who deal with long periods of time have tended to be so-called Marxian and neo-Marxian anthropologists, with their emphasis on historical materialism. They include Mintz (1986), Schneider (1978), and Wolf (1982).

crophenomenon of witches to reach an understanding of the macro-phenomenon of the decline of magic in general.

The authors of the first four papers in this volume all address the question of structural transformations: Sahlins for Hawaii, Ortner for Nepal, Fernandez for Spain, and myself for Japan. Each chooses a strategic window to examine significant aspects of changes: Sahlins chooses trade; Ortner, monastery founding; Fernandez, "enclosure" metaphors; and myself, the monkey as metaphor of self.

Sahlins tackles the question of structural transformations by strategically focusing on a dramatic period of Hawaiian history (1810–30), when "the moment of a structural break" took place. Rather than treating Hawaii as a closed system, Sahlins situates it within the context of international commerce and the development of Western capitalism and its expansion into the rest of the world. Thus, "the structure of conjuncture" involves the Hawaiians, the British, and the Americans, as well as the Chinese and the Native Americans of the Pacific Northwest. Sahlins sees in the conjuncture a "mythopraxis," whereby a cosmological scheme meets the pragmatics at a critical historical conjuncture.

The strategy taken by Ortner in her long-term study of the culture of the Nepalese Sherpas is to examine "key scenarios," which she defines as "preorganized schemes of action, symbolic programs for the staging and playing out of standard social interactions in a particular culture." According to her interpretation, the key scenario, with its major characteristics, is invoked and acted upon in a variety of contexts and over a long time—definitely since the eighteenth century—right down to the present. Key scenarios are not a straitjacket imposed by culture. Like Sahlins's mythopraxis, they are enacted in practice. For example, during the twentieth-century founding of the monasteries the two actors followed the key scenario while treating the world system as a resource.

The papers by Fernandez and myself most directly address the question of the symbolic *longue durée*. Both of us choose dominant metaphors of the self defined in relation to the other in the respective culture and then link changes in the form and meaning of these metaphors to macrochanges in culture and society—privatization for Fernandez and secularization for myself—over a long period of time. Fernandez anchors his problem of long-term macrochanges—"the great Western European shift toward agrarian individualism" as manifested in rural Spain—in specific symbolic forms (a key to a house, a dooryard, a field gate, field markers, and the public pasturage in the mountain passes) that represent markers between the self and the other. Thus, the changing meaning of the symbols sensitively expresses the great waves of modernity—increasing privatization and loss of communal rights—which indeed transformed these symbols into metaphors of "enclosures" in Marx's sense. The objects are deeply involved in the changes that are simultaneously symbolic-conceptual and economic-political-social.

A similar interest in understanding a culture through a long period motivated me to study the monkey metaphor in Japanese culture from the eighth century to the present. My choice of a micro scene is the meaning of the monkey, which is a reflexive symbol for the Japanese that sensitively registers macrochanges in Japanese culture and society, which in turn have undergone changes as a result of series of conjunctures, earlier with northeast China and later with the world at large.

To effectively study the long-term changes of culture, anthropologists need a tighter concept of "transformation." My theoretical concern is how to understand structural transformations as diachrony. I use the term *diachrony* to refer to historical changes, as originally used by the Prague school, rather than to temporal sequences in speech, as used by Lévi-Strauss.[9] Structural principles provide only possible directions for change, but they do not dictate a particular type of transformation. Therefore, by focusing on the question of why a particular transformation takes place at a particular historical period and then comparing this type of transformation with another, one can approach the question of structural transformation as historical change. Put the other way, we must distinguish structural reproductions from structural transformations in which we can identify such historical changes as modernization and secularization that are nonetheless structural transformations.

These four papers offer three divergent research strategies for long-term changes in culture. Sahlins targets a historical moment of structural break. Ortner examines the recurrence of key scenarios. Fernandez and I focus on a dominant metaphor that offers a key to the

---

[9] For an incisive analysis of the concept of transformation in linguistics and a critique of its use by Lévi-Strauss, see Ingold 1986; Turner 1977.

order of meaning in a given culture and trace its changing forms and meanings. All four papers point to the long-term continuity of the structure of a culture while recognizing the continuous process of its transformations. Whether an author talks about "structure," "order," "scenario," or even "transcriptions of a fixed ideal," anthropological studies of a culture over the long run seem to point to a certain, and at times high, degree of regularity in historical processes.

Dimensions of culture and causal agents. Even though historical transformations may manifest some regularity, structural transformations are historical processes, not a pile of paradigms produced by collapsed syntagmatic chains. The next question, then, is how these changes take place—the problem often referred to as historical causality, prefiguration, or periodicity. I choose the term *historical process* to avoid the inference of an a priori assumption about the mechanisms involved.

Any discussion of historical process must refer to a number of issues. These include the identification of the primacy of a certain principle of culture in the sequence of change, the evaluation of the relative weight of the structure vis-à-vis historical events, since structure affects historical changes, and the examination of historical actors as causal agents, although these polarities dissolve in practice, as already shown.

Because of the plethora of publications on the subject, no summary is needed here of the debates over the primacy of the base structure over the superstructure of classical historical materialism and subsequent reformulations, such as Gramsci's hegemony or Althusser's overdetermination (see Bloch 1977; Ortner 1984; Smith 1984), not to mention conceptual formulations by E. P. Thompson and Raymond Williams. Anthropologists too have made significant contributions to these debates (see note 7). I should like to stress here that it is becoming increasingly meaningless to pitch scholars into different, and by inference opposing, camps.

Geertz's thesis on incongruity, mentioned by Burke in his paper, raises another issue about the different cultural dimensions involved in historical processes. Using a Javanese funeral as an example, Geertz argues that the incongruity between these people's urban social organization, characterized by causal-functional integration, and their folk cultural systems, characterized by logico-meaningful integration, is pivotal for historical changes. His position, however, is different from the neo-Durkheimian position, which gives primacy to the social structure and views other dimensions of culture as epiphenomena or, at best, as by-products of the social structure.

What is rarely pointed out in discussions on this subject is that scholars' propositions on historical causality often derive from their basic position on culture or society. Historical materialists and Durkheimian scholars share the view that one particular dimension of culture is both dominant and determining: production for the former and social structure for the latter. Structural Marxists, too, fall into this camp, but they are less committed and careful in their qualification about the extent to which production is determining and dominant (for Althusser's position see, for example, Skinner 1985). Geertz, in contrast, does not see any one particular dimension of culture as primary. He views culture as an octopus: Its tentacles are separately integrated with a barely developed brain that centrally controls all the tentacles (Geertz 1973: 407–8). Since different dimensions of culture are interdependent and yet only loosely interrelated, according to his view, the discontinuity can become greater; his incongruity theory is a corollary to his concept of culture.

Lévi-Strauss and Sahlins (for the latter, see especially 1976) are the most articulate proponents of the third view. For them, the structure of thought constitutes the core from which different dimensions of culture derive. Thus, according to Sahlins (1976: 211), in the West the locus of symbolic production is the economy, whereas in "tribal" societies, it is kinship relations.[10] For these scholars, then, changes in economic activities are changes in the structure of meaning.

In addition to the question of which dimension of culture is the primary mover in historical processes, debates over historical process often center on whether internal or external agents are precipitators of historical change. However scholars approach historical process, they realize now that they were wrong in the past to assume that any culture has ever been isolated from the rest of the world. Most, if not all, historical transformations are directly or indirectly related to forces outside the boundary of the society. Leach (e.g. 1965: 282;

[10] Although my position on the issue is close to Sahlins's, I strongly disagree with his dichotomy between Western and tribal. Not only is the term *tribal* problematic, but this false dichotomy denies the existence of other types of "civilization" in the world. The symbolic dominance of economic activities also may be confined to a few societies within the so-called West.

1982: 41–43) has repeatedly reminded his colleagues that they cannot think of a culture in the same sense as they think of a society, which is a bounded political unit. Culture, in contrast to society, is never bounded. Whether the agent of change is the development of capitalism, the growth of worldwide trade, or the spread of a religion, it travels across political boundaries. Thus, historical processes in most parts of the world have been, in Braudel's sense, stories of conjunctures.

The interconnections between societies and the consequent interconnections between historical changes in different cultures of the world do not, however, translate into the unilinear development of cultures into a world culture. Affected though cultures may be, "primitive" or not, they are far more resilient than the Wallersteinian world system would have it. Sahlins's paper in this volume takes on the world-system theory and turns it upside down. Denying the hegemonic power that world-system theorists assign to the Western capitalist economy, he shows how Western market forces acquired power only as market forces were determined, not by the material forms, but by the cultural schemes, of the recipient cultures—Hawaiian, Chinese, and Kwakiutl. All three cultures, in his analyses, weave their own tapestries, rather than simply being absorbed into the world system. Ortner's findings also show how historical actors used the products of the world system—accumulation of wealth—to enact their own scenarios, rather than becoming the puppets of the rising capitalistic economy.

External forces may be seen in terms of "modernization,"[11] of which "secularization" is often an aspect. This is an area of investigation that somehow has become less popular among anthropologists but continues to attract historians' attention (see Burke's paper in this volume). The model for the universal historical development of secularization still tends to derive from Western European societies, although some macrosociologists, such as Bellah and Eisenstadt, have studied this process in Japan, China, and elsewhere. Yet,

[11] Social scientists of modernization theory have split. The unilinear or universal camp interprets modernization as a monolithic-universal phenomenon, whereas the opposing, relativist camp holds that each culture patterns the modernizing process in that society. Among anthropologists, most of whom belong to the latter camp, interest in modernization has subsided considerably. However, among historians there has been a growing interest in the problem, with a particular emphasis on secularizatior as exemplified in the work by Peter Burke and Keith Thomas.

the "disenchantment of the world" (Weber), "the decline of magic" (Keith Thomas), "the mechanization of the world picture" (Dijksterhuis), and "the order of things" (Foucault) take on very different contours, even within the Judeo-Christian tradition, if one looks at their folk counterparts. For example, many of Japan's religious beliefs and practices are "magical" in nature. Contemporary Japanese carry amulets to their hospital beds when they undergo surgery, and today's young educated owners of automobiles flock to shrines and temples on New Year's Day to have their cars purified (Ohnuki-Tierney 1984: 125–26). Yet, a profusion of what I call "urban magic" in Japan today (pp. 144, 224–25) is far more secular than the Japanese religions, for example, during the medieval period, suggesting the culture-specific nature of Japanese secularization.

In our papers, Fernandez and I offer a relatively new approach to the question of modernization.[12] As I mentioned earlier, both of us focus on the concept of self and how it has changed through history. As privatization has encroached on rural Spain, the meaning of the same symbolic form of the key, along with other symbols that represent the boundary of the self, has undergone transformation. Similarly, in my work, the monkey's transformation from mediator to scapegoat to clown indicates a subtle but decisive secularization and increased reflexivity in the concept of the Japanese self.

The course of modernization, especially secularization, is not necessarily unilinear and unidirectional. During the postindustrial era of the twentieth century, modernization seems to have taken a complex course. In many societies of the world, we see the simultaneous presence of secularization and religious revival, or of cultural homogenization and ethnic assertion or nationalism. The phenomenon may represent a temporal and surface-level change within the longer-term trend of modernization, or it may indicate a basic change in the direction of modernization in some areas of thought and activities. The picture seems complex as well as fluctuant. Without assuming a smooth unidirectional path—from magic to religion to science—researchers must take into account the complex nature of modernization, both as a local phenomenon and as a universal development, while distinguishing between surface changes and enduring ones.

---

[12]Compare Tuan (1982), who focuses on the concept of self in his comparative historical study of spatial segmentation.

Furthermore, studies of modernization in general and secularization in particular must include other areas of investigation besides the traditional categories of religion and magic and explore such concepts as self and other, as well as various other thought processes that are important in all cultures, and how the concepts have changed in the face of the universal force of modernization, however it may be defined.

The dialectic between historical actors and the structure of culture is another area of major concern. To pose the question in terms of actors versus structure only reinforces the false polarity that does not exist in practice. An individual's intentions are always construed culturally to a great degree; and culture, or the structure of meaning, values, and ideology, is always expressed in the thoughts and behavior of individuals, who reinterpret them to a greater or lesser degree. According to Ortner's analysis, the key scenario is the cultural structure that serves not only as an interpretive frame but as a schema for action. Thus, she argues for a culturally or symbolically ordered causality. Her cultural scenarios involve both freedom and constraint, though they often privilege a certain course of action over other courses by providing it with meaning and value. Ortner maintains that the outcome of a situation is often not what the actors sought or chose, although there is always some set of people for whom the change is a product of their intention. Emphasizing the difference between his "conjuncture" and Braudel's, Sahlins explains that a historical event is a "*relation* between a happening and a structure (or structures)," and a "structure of the conjuncture" is the situational synthesis of the two, which is expressed in "the interested action of the historical agents" (1985: xiv; italics in original). His scheme shows the question of structure versus either the individual or historical events to be a false dichotomy. The intricate and intertwined nature of structure and praxis is also convincingly argued in Valeri's paper. He demonstrates the reciprocal nature of the being and the becoming of kingship, as we shall see later.

Thomas S. Kuhn, Foucault, and others have argued that a structure or an order becomes *the* paradigm, not because it stands the test of falsifiability or whatever other "test" a society can exercise, but as a result of control—only that which is allowed to be "knowledge" can constitute a paradigm. What is important for us here is to examine the hegemony of a particular structure of meaning over alternatives within a culture and the way this process of gaining hegemony has taken place. Although an extensive discussion of Foucaultian power inequality is not included in the papers in this volume, there is no question that the social position of historical actors makes an enormous difference in their ability to affect the operations of their society. The "invention of tradition" (Hobsbawm and Ranger 1986), or the naturalization of the arbitrariness of a system (Bourdieu 1982), takes place more easily if the historical agents are at the center of power—political, economic, and intellectual. Furthermore, powerful institutionalized mechanisms, such as formal education, facilitate hegemony (cf. Bourdieu and Passeron 1977).

What seems to me most dangerous, however, is to evaluate power in a shortsighted way or to focus only on the most obvious power. The power exercised by the politically peripheral, the metaphysical power of a clown, for example, may never be expressed in a dramatic form like a revolution. Yet it may steadily affect the course of history; without its presence the history of that society might have gone in a different direction (for details of this argument see Ohnuki-Tierney 1987). The power of the politically peripheral to change the course of history is usually not obvious. I suggest that students of transformation take into account various kinds of negative evidence, such as how the presence of some people without power steadily upholds alternative paradigms and inverted structures and keeps the moment of opposition going.

The question of the role of historical actors becomes subtle and complex when we examine the related problem of how historical actors are cognizant of the meaning of their actions as anthropologists would interpret them. Fernandez discusses this question in terms of "primary process"—a process whereby a deep metaphorical meaning surfaces in the minds of individuals at certain times in their experience. Through these primary processes the system of meaning becomes the lived experience of historical actors. An examination of the primary process, therefore, enables us to avoid the pitfall many students of the *longue durée* step into; as their critics have accused, they often fail to confront the "humanities" involved in the dynamic process of historical transformation. Similarly, I have examined the degree to which monkey trainers, as historical actors, are cognizant of the meanings assigned to their profession and to the monkeys and of their symbolic power (Ohnuki-Tierney 1987). In neither case are the historical actors completely unconscious in their thoughts and behavior; rather, they are partially aware of the meaning of their actions and their power.[13]

But Fernandez's interpretation of the Spanish case and my own of the Japanese case diverge considerably with regard to the effect of symbolic communication upon the course of history. The symbols in Fernandez's discussion are liminal symbols; each represents a passage from one dispensation to another—a passage during which paradoxes, pivotal in precipitating changes, are dominant (see also Fernandez 1982, 1986).

In contrast, I emphasize various factors that prevent historical change. They arise from the ambiguity and complexity involved in symbolic communication. Most symbols, verbal or nonverbal, are polysemic, giving rise to situations in which historical actors read different meanings into the same symbols without realizing that they are talking past each other. The actors may go on without scrutinizing and challenging the structure of meaning because they fail to see the presence of paradoxes or the absence of communication. Thus, polysemes have two mechanisms that are diametrically opposed in their effect upon historical change. On the one hand, polysemes have an embedded mechanism that facilitates historical change, since they allow the same form to readily take on another meaning as the dominant meaning. On the other hand, the same mechanism can prevent change by allowing different readings of the meanings without the actors ever realizing they are not reading the same meaning into the symbol. Another possible factor preventing historical change is what I refer to as the routinization of meaning. It takes place when actors take a meaning or a form for granted and do not examine its relevance to their conscious thinking. A form or a meaning may even be placed in a time capsule and remain unchanged while the *mentalité* of the people undergoes significant transformations.

I have also applied the concept of symbolic marginality, or anomaly, to historical processes, viewing it as a built-in mechanism for his-

---

[13] Compare Lévi-Strauss, who sees a distinction between history and anthropology. He states: "History organizes its data in relation to conscious expressions of social life, while anthropology proceeds by examining its unconscious foundations" (1967: 19). As elaborated in the text, I do not make a clear distinction between history and anthropology. Also, I see varying degrees of articulateness in the actor's perception of the meaning of a symbol.

torical transformation. Scholars of symbolic anthropology have emphasized that a being or an object that does not fit into any class in a classificatory system is often assigned a dual quality and power—both a marginal, negative meaning and a positive power and nature. This duality is expressed in the ability to traverse categorical boundaries, an ability that is not accorded to full-fledged members of the class. Thus, it provides the conceptual basis for a marginal, peripheral, or anomalous being or object to become the clown, the trickster, or the prophet—one who can stand outside the system to comment critically on it and even rejuvenate it with new meaning or energy. Although this definition of structural marginality is a standard argument in symbolic anthropology (for details, see Ohnuki-Tierney 1981: 119–29), from the perspective of historical change, marginality can also be seen as a built-in mechanism for the change and transformation of a symbolic system; only these figures can be critical of the existing system, thereby, under the right circumstances, changing it.

In sum, studying historical changes through symbols requires careful scrutiny. The primary process in some situations provides an opportunity for actors to be fully or partially aware of the meaning of an action or of a given symbol. In some situations, however, the primary process may never take place. Symbols can facilitate change, and yet they can also be time-binding and ahistorical. Needed in future research are close examinations, both theoretical and ethnographic, of symbols as lived experience.

Historical Constructions and Representations: Epistemological Issues

If culture is mediated by history, history is also mediated by culture. Since historical processes are not objectively there to be recorded, the first task is to understand "historical consciousness," or "historicity"—the collective experience and understanding of history—which plays a crucial role in the construction and representation of history. Understanding historicity is essential in a hermeneutic reading of historical texts, interpreting them in their historical-cultural contexts, or in a reading of the appropriate "forms of life" (Wittgenstein 1968: 8–12, 226) of the authors or the observed, who usually belong to a culture that is different spatially and/or temporally from the interpreter's. Likewise, it is essential to understand historiography, including its underlying political and epistemological underpinnings, which play an important role in the construction of history.

In this section I introduce two papers on historicity—Valeri's on Hawaiian historicity and Handelman and Shamgar-Handelman's on Jewish historicity. A discussion of Leach's paper on historiography and its political underpinnings then follows, and I conclude with Peacock's paper on the epistemological question posed by Gadamer.

Historicity: native constructions. Valeri's article on ancient Hawaiian culture explores historical representations, or cultural modes of articulating past and present, and the relationship between the past and the present. He emphasizes that there are two distinct and yet intimately interrelated modes of historical representation. The Hawaiian narrative history of genealogies expresses the paradigmatic mode of historical representation in which the past and the present are analogically determined in relation to each other through either similarity or contrast. The genealogical chants, on the other hand, express the syntagmatic mode of historical representation, in which the past and the present are determined in a metonymic mode so that history represents a cumulative process. Far from being static structural principles, the two modes of ancient Hawaiian historical representation are richly played out in practice, as Valeri demonstrates through his analysis of 'Umi's successful accession to the throne. This is accomplished on the basis of the legitimization of divine election through the demonstration of analogical achievements between 'Umi (the new king) and his ancestors and through the establishment of genealogical legitimacy. The *being* of kingship must be sanctioned by the performative *becoming* of kingship, and vice versa.

Close to Valeri's work on Hawaiian concepts of historical representation is the work by Handelman and Shamgar-Handelman on Jewish historicity. The authors analyze the process whereby the seven-branched lampstand, the menorah, was finally chosen as the emblem of the new nation of Israel. Their work is about visual representations and the iconographic encoding of historicity. It is therefore about time through a symbol. In the Jewish notion of history, as with the Hawaiian, the existential and experiential conditions of present and past inform one another. Crucial is the Jewish notion of redemption, for the return to Zion represented a return—spatial, temporal, and moral—to the sacred space and the ancient time of God. The structures of historicity, therefore, consist of a series of dyads—spatial, temporal, and cosmological. What is striking about Jewish historicity, as articulated in the process of selecting an emblem for the new state, is that some of the familiar historical events are either unimportant or completely absent. For example, the long period of diaspora, during which the Jews lived in gentile lands and in gentile time, does not enter their history; they had been expelled from their history and were waiting to reenter it. Nor is the immediate-past catastrophe of the Holocaust, vitally important for the Jews in almost all other contexts, included; it took place during the nonhistorical time and hence does not enter into their history either.

Both the works by Valeri and by Handelman and Shamgar-Handelman illustrate that historicity is not at all a static given in a culture. It involves the active involvement of historical actors—they use, select, and create their own understanding of history as they act upon the collective notion of historicity.[14]

In sum, Hawaiian and Jewish concepts and experiences of history offer important insights into historicity and have broad implications. First, historicity tends to be highly selective, at times deliberately so, which points to the crucial importance of understanding historicity in any historical representation. Second, the historicity of a particular people contains multiple representations of history. We no longer can talk about *the* Hawaiian historicity, just as we cannot talk about *the* Hawaiian history. Third, in historicity, the past and the present are interdependent and interdetermined through metaphorical and metonymic relationships. Fourth, the "structuration" of the past (or history) is often mitigated by the intentionality and motivation of the people who construct the history. Leaving out unnecessary details may be done as a way to legitimize an aspiring Hawaiian chief. Or, through the choice of the emblem, the Jews in Israel chose to focus on ontological continuity and stability in the midst of upheaval. In historicity, we see "rich humanity" and the powerful role played by historical actors. These four factors that characterize the nature of historicity, therefore, compel us to consider carefully the role of historicity in the constructions and representations of history, which always involves historicity.

[14] We recall Blu's (1980) work on the Lumbee and how they "constructed" their own history as well as their "ethnic" identity.

Native and nonnative historiography. In the representation of history, the historicity of the investigator's culture also plays an important role. First, nonnative scholars risk superimposing the historicity of both their own culture and their professional culture—historiography—upon the one they are studying. For example, Western historiography has been dominated by chronological history, which is based on the notion of a linear progression in time. If scholars from this tradition are not reflexive about their own historicity, they can easily misunderstand the historical texts of a people whose concept of history is cyclical (see Errington 1979; Siegel 1979). Second, anthropologists and historians have recently recognized the problem of representations that involve power inequality between informants and scholars, be they native or nonnative. These representations often involve explicit or implicit "Orientalism" (Said 1978). It is imperative to identify the locus of power, political and intellectual, within the society of their study and in the international political economy, since any representation is constrained by forces beyond the individuals involved. Third, the nature of the relationship between the scholar and the historical texts involves a number of epistemological issues, as we shall see below in Peacock's paper.

In a 1967 article, "Virgin Birth," Leach astutely foreshadowed the reflexivity of the late 1970's and 1980's, calling attention to the fact that anthropologists call their own practice religion but assert that other peoples practice magic. In the present volume he presents the dramatic case of the fabrication of the Aryan invasion, which shows how profoundly the seemingly objective academic endeavors are affected by the *mentalité* of the culture to which they belong. Leach describes how cherished but erroneous assumptions in linguistics and anthropology were accepted without question. If the *mentalité* of the academic culture was in part responsible for the fabrication, geopolitics was even more responsible for upholding the Aryan invasion as history. The theory fit the Western or British vision of their place in the world at the time. The conquest of Asian civilization needed a mythical charter to serve as the moral justification for colonial expansion. Convenient, if not consciously acknowledged, was the Aryan invasion by a fair-skinned people, speaking the so-called Proto-Indo-European language, militarily conquering the dark-skinned, peasant Dasa (Dasyu), who spoke a non-European language and with whom the conquerors lived, as Leach puts it, in a "system of sexual apartheid." The first civilization in India, thus, was built by the Aryan invaders. A remarkable case of Orientalism indeed.

One of the new developments arising from anthropologists' reflexivity about historical and ethnographic representations is a series of questions about the nature of ethnography and the role of anthropologists in fieldwork and ethnographic writing (see Geertz 1988 for a detailed and critical overview). Often invoked in recent discussions of these issues is Gadamer, whose position Peacock critically evaluates in his paper. Peacock compares his three fieldwork experiences in Indonesia: on *ludruk*, a working-class drama, which he studied as a graduate student in the early 1960's; on Muhammadijah, a fundamentalist movement of the Muslim middle class, which he studied in 1970 as an assistant professor; and on Sumarah, a meditation club allied with the upper class, which he studied in 1979 as a department chair.

These three different movements involved three different Javanese social classes and took place in three distinct eras of recent Indonesian history. The three forms of movement are, in Peacock's view, quintessentially Javanese. They are "objective patterns" expressing three different aspects of Javanese culture and three phases in modern Indonesian history. They also happen to coincide with the three stages of Peacock's professional career. According to Peacock, no native scholar has put the three together. Making sense out of a particular combination of these three forms is up to Peacock.

In his interpretation of Indonesian history, Peacock, then, rejects Gadamer's central proposition—the fusion of the horizons of the text with the interpreter. In historical as well as ethnographic interpretations, according to Peacock, the process of interpretation is controlled by the interpreter, for whose interpretation detachment from the "horizon" of any one form is required. Still, Peacock emphatically points out that Indonesian culture goes on whether he is there or not. He concludes his paper with a statement that "the sort of historical interpretation that ethnographers do remains method; only romantically can it be considered ontology."

Summary

Although the historicization of anthropology and the anthropologization of history have already made significant contributions to the way anthropologists and historians try to understand a culture historically, this new and exciting era is still at the opening stages. In this volume a number of anthropologists and a social historian whose concern has been culture in its broad sense offer directions and research strategies in this endeavor.

Any historical endeavor must be tripartite, at least in perspective. It must consider historical processes, historicity, and historiography. Although there is no objective history out there to be reconstructed, historicity—or, even more accurately, historicities—must be carefully taken into account in any historical representation, which is almost always partial, forcing us to recognize the pluralistic nature of any history. Histories, structures, and meanings not only are all multiple but are also all contested by historical actors. The dynamics of historical practice become unveiled when histories are seen as processes and historicities are seen as the lived experience of historical actors.

In any historical study, it is necessary to be aware that changes take place at different levels, just as some dimensions of culture change more rapidly than others. An investigator must choose the time frame accordingly. As a general rule of thumb, a longer time period is needed for discerning changes at deeper levels, although quantitatively the time frame differs from culture to culture and from situation to situation. The choice of a window, as I call it, that offers an insight into broader scenes or historical processes at deeper levels is crucial as a research strategy. The window can be a pivotal historical event, a trade, the founding of a monastery, a dominant symbol. Each can offer insights into the order of meaning, cultural scenarios, the structure of self and other, and other important conceptual principles.

Whatever we do, we can no longer view any society as an isolated island. A healthy approach to future endeavors will be to place the local and the contingent within the broad world context. The local cannot be fully understood without reference to its broader context, be it the world system, modernization, or the development of colonialism—German, French, American, Chinese, or Japanese. At the same time, universality is an empty proposition without the specificity of a particular culture.

Whatever one's theoretical or ideological perspective, historical processes must be thought of as multicausal and mutually influential.

That is, as Bloch and others of the Annales school have emphasized, there seldom is a first cause for any complex social phenomenon, and rarely is there a single organizing principle. Althusser's overdetermination, originally a concept from Freud, is one attempt to fine-tune the notion of causality by distinguishing "determinant" and "dominant" instances of social formation. In addition, changes in a particular dimension of culture often affect other dimensions of culture, and vice versa. Changes can be seen to have a spiral form. Most important, any assessment of historical causality must be evaluated in terms of a long period of time.

When we reject the monocausal notion of historical process, we begin to move away from the idea that a particular dimension or principle of culture acts as the pivotal or causal agent for historical changes. And moving away from the structural-functional position to assume an "integration" of the different dimensions of a culture, we can see various inherent bases for culture change: contradictions and other types of incongruity at the cultural level; anomaly and marginality at the symbolic level; and paradoxes in the minds of individuals. These represent built-in mechanisms for change.

Some of the old dichotomies, such as structure versus event, structure versus individuals, and external versus internal causal agents, are no longer tenable. Structure and practice are not antithetical. Each is inherent in the other, and each affects the other in the ongoing processes of historical developments. Similarly, no island of history is unconnected to the rest of the world; every historical study must be situated in the context of the world.

Acknowledgments

Most of the research and writing for this Introduction was undertaken during the 1986–87 academic year at the Institute for Advanced Study in Princeton and during the 1988–89 academic year at the Center for Advanced Study in the Behavioral Sciences at Stanford. I am most grateful to these institutions and to the National Endowment for the Humanities and the National Science Foundation (#BNS87-00864) for their support of my stay at the institute and the Center, respectively. I am also indebted to the Wenner-Gren Foundation for Anthropological Research for supporting me as a senior scholar during the 1986–87 academic year. Jan Vansina's comments and criticism of the first draft of this Introduction were extremely helpful in revising the draft. Yi-Fu Tuan read a draft close to the final version and offered me invaluable comments and suggestions. All weaknesses in this article, needless to say, must be laid to my own shortcomings.

2

The Political Economy of Grandeur in Hawaii from 1810 to 1830

MARSHALL SAHLINS

This is about a brief time, from 1810 to 1830 or thereabouts, in the early modern history of the Hawaiian kingdom. The choice might seem inspired by the usual anthropological *esprit de clocher*, given thus to weighty reflections on parochial events, were it not that, marked by the meteoric development of a commercial trade in sandalwood with go-getting Yankees, this period saw the great Hawaiian chiefs engage in heroic feats of invidious consumption rarely matched in any history, including even recent American assaults on the world records for economic narcissism. A few contemporary notices of the life-style of *le tout* Honolulu will give a preliminary sense of the phenomenon:

Not contented with the comforts of life, they [the Hawaiian ruling chiefs] latterly sought its luxuries, and even indulged in its extravagances. Kahumana [Ka'ahumanu, so-called regent] filled chests with the most costly silks of China, and actually expended four thousand dollars upon the cargo of one vessel. Boki [governor of O'ahu] paid one thousand dollars for a service of plate as a present for the king, notwithstanding he had other services in his possession, one of which was of expensively cut glass from Pellat and Green of London. (Beechey 1832: 350–51)

The chiefs invariably wear a complete and reputable English dress; and those among them who hold offices of authority assume a neat uniform of blue broadcloth, resembling the undress of British military and naval officers. Their wives, also, envelop their colossal persons in European manufactures of a very superior description, and upon every fresh importation of novelties in dress are usually purchasers to a large amount. It sometimes occurs that a chiefess will engross an entire investment of a favorite silk or riband rather than that any portion of it should be worn by a female of inferior rank. (F. D. Bennett 1840, 1: 210–11)

The members of the royal family [i.e. the high chiefs of Ka'ahumanu's kindred] and the ruler himself have become accustomed to the luxuries of the civilized world and they don't want to be second to the missionaries and the foreign merchants in these things. They drink our expensive wines which sell for an enormous price. . . . Through the extensive trade in sandalwood . . . the high Allis [chiefs] and the King accumulated great sums of money. These are all gone now but the recipients have not wanted to give up their adopted luxuries. We need only refer to the facts which Mr. Beechey presented so excellently to illustrate the excessive luxury of a royal family which rules over a land of naked inhabitants. They have wasted thousands of piastres on the most useless things. (Meyen 1981: 75–76)

The texts have the added historical virtue of showing that Western observers of the time could still be scandalized by this carnival of self-indulgence. Modern scholars are sometimes too ready to understand the like as normal economic behavior: the transparent "effect" of exposure to the temptations of the capitalist market economy, if not also the natural tendency of the human species when freed from constraints of a traditional "subsistence" economy. Yet reference to the addictive character of market commodities—let alone to human nature—will never be a sufficient explanation of the economic habits acquired by the Hawaiian aristocracy, since this kind of relation to the World System has not been general even among Pacific-island peoples. On the contrary, a comparative ethnography of capitalism in the South Seas since the eighteenth century would easily prove the historical cum cultural relativity of the Hawaiian experience.

Western sandalwood traders often had difficulties in Melanesia developing any sort of demand for European commodities, or at least a demand sufficient to induce local labor to cut and haul the timber (Shineberg 1967). Hawaiians themselves had analogous problems when they mounted a sandalwood expedition in 1829 to Eromanga in the New Hebrides to pay off the debts to American merchants that the chiefs had incurred by their extravagances (G. Bennett 1832).[1] But

[1] The story of Boki's expedition to the New Hebrides can be followed in standard Hawaiian histories (e.g. Daws 1968: 82–83; Kuykendall 1968: 97–98). Bennett's report indicates that Boki had imperial designs on the New Hebrides and that the Hawaiians who did manage to get there, under the chief Manuia, showed little compassion for the "natives": "The whole endeavours of the Sandwich Islanders seem to have been to carry on war against the aborigines—not to conciliate them: thus putting in practice their original intent of taking permanent possession of the island, and exterminating the original possessors. On the least alarm of an approach of the aborigines they began discharging their artillery, whether the alarm was false or not" (G. Bennett 1832: 128).

then the acquisitive impulses of the Hawaiian ruling chiefs, their individual and competitive appropriation of foreign luxuries with an eye to the last word in military uniforms or fast sailing ships, could only be matched by the kind of consumptionitis that has broken out since the 1960's in certain "advanced" sectors of the island societies. Even so, it has taken a century or more of Christianity, colonial rule, and other sustained attacks on the indigenous social nexus to generate such refinements of material self-interest. But in Hawaii the material avarice was an indigenous organization of the global imperialism.

The Conjuncture

Not to claim that Hawaiian history was simply reproducing the ancient cultural order. On the contrary, we enter at the moment of a structural break in the course of events. The onset of the sandalwood boom coincides with the establishment of a unified Sandwich Islands kingdom. In 1810 the famous Kamehameha, who began his career as a ranking chief of Hawai'i Island,[2] guardian of the war god for the royal cousin he soon deposes and replaces, now receives the surrender of his last remaining adversary, the ruler of Kaua'i Island, Kaumuali'i. So ends a long prehistory of independent chiefdoms and internecine conflicts—and begins a new era of political strife on another level. In the ensuing decades Hawaiian history will be marked by the confrontation between the king and an oligarchy of great *ali'i* ("chiefs"), who themselves came into power and control of their large estates as beneficiaries of Kamehameha's conquests. While this rivalry repeats certain conflicts of old, it does so now in the context of the unified state and largely in the transposed register of a commercial warfare. The main interest of the remaining historical continuity is that it helps account for such changes, as by giving us some access to the cultural structures of the shift from military to commercial prowess.

Already in the course of Kamehameha's victories, success in trade and war had been pragmatically linked—by way of a common Hawaiian cosmology of foreign places and divine powers. Alone among the several ruling chiefs, Kamehameha could claim a privileged re-

[2] To avoid confusion, we mark the name of Hawai'i Island with the appropriate glottal stop, while using the modern spelling, Hawaii, without the glottal stop, to refer to the entire archipelago.

lationship to the manes of Captain James Cook, which he also knew how to turn into a differential advantage in intercourse with the European ships that followed in the explorer's wake (cf. Sahlins 1981). Cook had "discovered" Hawaii in 1778 on the same voyage that also disclosed the possibilities of carrying furs for superprofits from the American Northwest Coast to the China market. By the end of the century, Hawaii would be described as "a great caravansary" on the Northwest Coast–Canton trade route (Fleurieu in Bradley 1968: 22). The fur traders stopped in the islands for "refreshments," leaving Western goods in exchange, most notably muskets, powder, and ball. And Kamehameha was soon famous among the traders for the security offered in his domains as well as for the supplies obtainable there. Yet more than cunning was involved in the chief's enlightened policies. Consider that the commercial behavior of his main enemies—Kahekili, chief of Maui, and his son Kalanikapule, ruler of O'ahu—was comparatively erratic and frequently violent, although they had no less strategic interest in the trade than Kamehameha. But they were too often tempted by the advantages of raid over trade. These chiefs were known as much for their larceny as for their generosity, while their own territories, unlike Kamehameha's, were often found wanting in provision for trade. Here is where the dead Cook figures.[3]

In the later years of Kamehameha's reign, Cook's (purported) bones were paraded in the annual rites of kingship and world renewal called Makahiki: period of the appearance of the god Lono and the appropriation by the king of his fertilizing powers (cf. Valeri 1985; Sahlins 1981, 1985b, 1989a). Kamehameha had long considered his relationship to Cook, and through Cook to England, a condition of

[3] For notes on the comparative violence of Kamehameha's rival chiefs toward European shipping, and on the insufficiencies of trade in O'ahu and Maui, see Kirch and Sahlins, forthcoming. Or see, for example, Dixon 1789: 119, 161–67, 253; Meares 1790: 279, 341, 348–49, 352f; Ingraham 1918: 20f; Kuykendall 1923; and Vancouver 1801, 1: 361–62, 3, among the published documents. Bradley summarizes Kamehameha's contrasting policy, which he understands as a way of living down the death of Cook at Hawai'i: "For fifteen years after the death of Cook, cautious seamen believed it necessary to exercise special care to guard against surprise attacks while at the Hawaiian Islands. The scrupulous protection which Kamehameha provided for all visiting vessels presently dispelled the fears of visitors while within the territory controlled by the great Hawaiian king. After the extension of his rule to Maui and Oahu [i.e. 1795], there was no part of the Islands—with the possible exception of Kauai and Niihau—where traders might not anchor with confidence that they were as safe as in any part of the world" (1968: 21–22).

his own legitimacy. King George he considered his own "brother" (Bell 1929–30, 2 (2): 119; Franchère 1969: 63). Ralph Kuykendall summarizes the Hawaiians' enduring British connection:

From the time of Vancouver's last visit to Hawaii [1794] until 1825, Great Britain held the highest place in the thought of Hawaiians about foreign countries; they considered themselves under the protection of that nation and frequently referred to themselves as "kanaka no Beritane" ("men of Britain"). (1968: 206; cf. Sahlins 1981: 27–28; Sahlins 1982)

In fact Kamehameha had the English colors flying from his royal residence and canoe even before he ceded his home island of Hawai'i to Vancouver in 1794 (Bell 1929–30, 2 (1): 80, 81). For in conquering the island, Kamehameha had also appropriated the sacrifice of Captain James Cook.

Avatar of the year-god Lono, Cook was killed at Kealakekua in 1779 and then offered in sacrifice by the king: an act that inscribed the Englishman historically in the sovereign powers of Hawai'i paramounts, in the same way that every year the god Lono was appropriated ritually. Kamehameha's cession of Hawai'i, incidentally, was not accepted by His Britannic Majesty. But this did not prevent Kamehameha, or his son Liholiho after him, from supposing that he held his own domain of "King George" (whether III or IV).[4] In the emerging state fashioned by Kamehameha, the cult of Cook and the English could assume strategic-political values, among other reasons, just because of the traditional relationship between the appearance of Lono and the cessation of warfare (cf. Valeri 1985; Sahlins 1985b). At the same time, in external affairs the dead Cook mediated between the Hawaiian king and European ships' captains, whose own reverence for the Great Navigator—as culture hero of commercial expansion— was hardly less developed (Smith 1979). For Hawaiians, Lono had always represented their link to Kahiki—the overseas and celestial islands whence came divine kings, ritual knowledge, and all kinds of cultural good things.

[4] In 1822 Liholiho "professes openly to hold his dominions under the King of England" (Tyerman and Bennet 1831, 1: 472); or as he told another British visitor, "his islands belonged to the King of Great Britain" (Mathison 1825: 366). As we shall see, this special relation of the Hawaiian king to the British Crown continued to shape the Islands through the early nineteenth century in ways that were all out of proportion to the actual power mounted by the British and long after they had been surpassed and displaced commercially by Americans.

Still Hawaii would only have this modern history because the Chinese had virtually the opposite sense of the value of things and persons British. Ever since the opening of direct trade with the West in the early sixteenth century, the Chinese had been profoundly unimpressed with European manufactures. Indeed, they confined the barbarian merchants to an economic and cultural quarantine, mainly in Canton. And even when the English industrial revolution was in full swing, the Chinese would take little else but precious silver for their own goods, now in such fashion among Westerners: silks, nankeens, porcelains, and especially the teas to which the British and British colonials became addicted in the eighteenth century. But the ensuing flow of silver to the Orient was in the European view a violation of sound mercantilist principles, even if the bullion was available—which was not always the case for Americans. Hence the search for alternative goods for the China market, leading to the successive exploitation of furs in the American Northwest and sandalwood in Hawaii. The displacement of British merchants by Americans in this Pacific trade around 1800 was correlated with the success of the Honorable East India Company in finding alternative means of overcoming the unfavorable trade balance contracted from the British tea habit: by dumping manufactured woolens at Canton for a loss (to get exchange credits), by exporting raw cotton from India, and finally by inflicting an even greater addiction on the Chinese in the form of India-grown opium. On the other hand, Yankees had got into the Canton trade in the first place because their access to the British West Indies was cut off after the Revolutionary War (1783). They were soon as interested in Northwest Coast furs as the British were indifferent. And when the profits on the maritime fur trade began to decline in the first decade of the new century, the American merchants increasingly found Hawaiian sandalwood an attractive proposition.[5]

For their part the Chinese had been acquiring sandalwood from India and the Indies since the T'ang dynasty (A.D. 618–906). At that time the aromatic odors of the wood were helping to disseminate the whiff of an increasingly influential Buddhism: "the divinely sweet

---

[5] A more extensive discussion and documentation of this history of commerce in the Pacific can be found in Sahlins 1989b. The history of the sandalwood in Hawaii has been ably documented by Bradley (1968), Kuykendall (1968), Morgan (1948), and Thrum (1904).

odor of the sandal expressed to the senses the antidemonic properties concealed within its godlike body" (Schafer 1963: 137). In addition to ritual incense and religious images, the wood was employed by the Chinese medicinally, in sumptuary architecture, and for finely carved *objets d'art*. A thousand years later, by virtues of powers undreamed of in this philosophy, the mystic properties concealed in sandalwood trees of the New Hebrides, Fiji, and the Hawaiian Islands, used to drive out Chinese demons, could thereby be transformed into teas and other chinoiserie that, in turn, brought profits to American entrepreneurs at whatever the cost to whom it might concern.

Whom it did concern in Hawaii, the principal *dramatis personae* in the organization of trade, shifted in the course of the sandalwood business, particularly after Kamehameha's death in 1819. Until then sandalwood was a royal monopoly, although not so restricted as some historians have claimed. Afterward a group of high ali'i who had come into land and power with the conquest seized *de facto* control of the sandalwood and the state. The brief reign of Liholiho as Kamehameha II (1819–24) thus marks a decisive transition in the kingship. Indeed the story of his death condenses the developing correlation of forces. The young king died of measles in London, where he had gone to solicit the aid of his father's brother, King George (now IV), against the coterie of *arriviste* chiefs who were undermining his royal powers. Asserting stronger and stronger claims to land and labor, they would turn the sandalwood trade to their own account, at the expense of the king's revenues. Among these notables, a certain kindred of own and collateral siblings called the Ka'ahumanu-folks (Ka'ahumanu *ma*) were the dominant force (Fig. 2.1). Ka'ahumanu, the oldest and the head, had been the favored wife of Kamehameha. Adoptive mother of Liholiho, she became the coruler—or so-called regent (*kuhina nui*)—in an interesting mother-son diarchy that remained in effect when Liholiho was succeeded by his younger brother, Kauikeaouli, as Kamehameha III (1825–54).[6]

Ka'ahumanu was the most prominent advocate of the famous abolition of the tabus: a spectacular *coup de théâtre* presided over by Liholiho on November 1, 1819, officially abolishing the ancient

[6] Likewise Ka'ahumanu was succeeded as "mother" to the king by high-ranking women related to Kamehameha; they were called the king's mother, although on genealogical grounds the designation would be dubious (see Kirch and Sahlins, forthcoming).

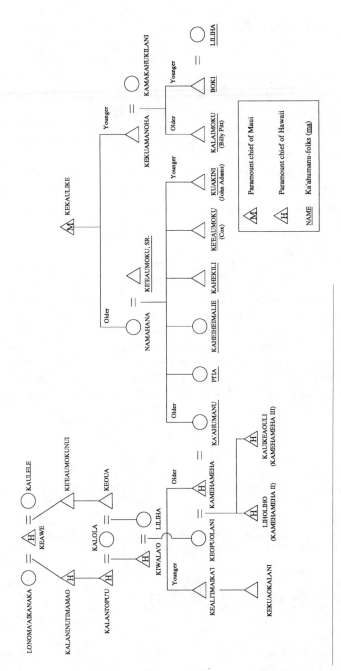

Fig. 2.1. The Kaʻahumanu-folks (*ma*) and Kamehameha.

forms of worship.[7] Ka'ahumanu's role was a rehearsal for the part she played in the spiritual reform that followed a few years after, when Protestant Christianity introduced by American missionaries enjoyed a sudden success. Until then the missionaries, who first landed in April 1820, had had little effect, even though they were apparently presented with the spectacle of "a nation without any religion" (Dibble 1909: 136). After Liholiho's death, however, Ka'ahumanu and her people made the propagation of the new faith their special cause. In the interregnum of 1823–25, when Liholiho went to England, Ka'ahumanu was becoming a model of Christian piety and propriety: "the new Ka'ahumanu," the missionaries called her, or else "Ka'ahumanu the Good." Then she and her immediate kin, the *de facto* ruling group, revived the tabu system that had in effect been suspended since Kamehameha's mortuary rites—except now it was in the translated form of a puritanical Protestantism. Along with church construction and the establishment of schools, they made the strict Sabbatarianism and the lugubrious blue laws of the New England missionaries the signs and means of their own sovereignty.[8] Their enthusiasm never went so far as the Protestant Ethic in the Weberian sense of work as a calling. Nor did they ever learn to mortify their own flesh—which was mountainous, as in the traditional aesthetics of Polynesian nobility. Indeed the self-indulgence of the ali'i went quite beyond their prodigious appetites for food.

It was now, through the 1820's, that the ruling chiefs turned to an

[7] For analyses of the tabu revolution see, among others, Alexander 1917, Davenport 1969, and Daws 1968: 53–60. An Hawaiian account appears in Kahananui (1984: 216–22). Important descriptive material collected from Hawaiians and Europeans said to have been present at the event appears in the *Missionary Herald* (*MH* 1820: 166–68, 282; *MH* 1821: 172–73; *MH* 1827: 257; see also Dibble 1909: 120–21).

[8] See Alfons Korn (1983: 22) on the use of Christian "tabus" by the new ruling class. The continuation of the old religion, especially such aspects as had political value, in early Hawaiian Protestantism is remarkable. Among other continuities were the circuits made by ruling chiefs dedicating churches and announcing religious prohibitions, and the construction of churches by the chiefs themselves, without benefit of missionary initiative. Such churches were called *luakini*, after the main temples of the old regime. Ka'ahumanu's brother Kuakini (John Adams) built one such at Kailua in 1823: "as erected by a heathen ruler on heathen ground, encircled by the ruins of a fallen *Heiau* (temple), where so lately were offered human victims, it wants neither gold nor carved work to induce the benevolent mind to contemplate it with interest" (*MH* 1825: 98). The construction or reconstruction of a major temple, followed by a royal circuit in the course of which other temples were rededicated, was an annual feature of the traditional kingship system (Valeri 1985).

unrestrained competition in conspicuous consumption. In this endeavor they had the full cooperation of a growing number of resident traders, mainly from Boston firms. Urged on by the complementary competition between the American merchants, the ali'i decked themselves in every shape and form of Polynesian flash that could be devised from the deluxe imports of China, New England, and Europe. The effects were fairly disastrous for everything and everyone concerned: the supply of sandalwood, which gave out by 1830; the production of food, which suffered because of the deployment of labor to sandalwood operations; the population, which declined by 20–25 percent in twenty years; the economic condition of the merchants, the king, the chiefs, and—of course, more than anyone else—the ordinary people, who in time to come would still be working to pay off the debts owed by the chiefs on all those years of the good life. Things had been different in Kamehameha's time.

In Kamehameha's Time, 1810–19

Having taken some Hawaiian sandalwood to Canton in 1811, partly on the king's account, a small consortium of Boston ship captains (the Winship brothers and W. H. Davis) entered into an agreement with Kamehameha to monopolize sandalwood exports from the Islands (Gast and Conrad 1973: 40–41; Phelps Ms.). The agreement was to last ten years, Kamehameha receiving 25 percent of the profits. But only one cargo was taken to China before the contract was abrogated, the Hawaiians claiming bad faith on the Americans' part. Through the Anglo-American war of 1812–14, the trade continued to falter, in part owing to harassment by British ships of war. But it was renewed thereafter on a much larger scale—and on a different commercial basis.

Kamehameha reverted to his older policies of negotiations with all *Haole* comers.[9] The king still dominated the trade on the Hawaiian side, to the extent that he was largely able to shape the supply of foreign commodities by his own political ambitions. In comparison to the vainglories of his aristocratic successors, these ambitions remained firmly grounded in the pragmatics of conquest and rule. But Kamehameha could not completely cut off the lofty aspirations of the

[9] The term *Haole*, latterly signifying "white man" in Hawaiian, is here capitalized for use as an ethnic name.

chiefs, any more than he could completely engross the trade. The last years of his reign were troubled by a crisis of power, foretelling a shift to a political economy of personal grandeur.

Kamehameha had occupied O'ahu since 1804 with a view toward invading Kaua'i. Having secured the submission of the latter island without battle, he returned to Hawai'i in 1812, to Kailua, Kona, where he remained until his death. During these last years, Kamehameha ran the sandalwood business out of Kailua, including the important commerce of O'ahu, using techniques he had studied during the years of the fur trade. Contracts with *Haole* merchants were often negotiated at Hawai'i for delivery at O'ahu, where the transaction would be supervised by chiefs left in charge by the king. Some of these ali'i were Whites who had entered Kamehameha's service. At first their Hawaiian counterparts were men of relatively modest status, hence, like the White chiefs, dependent on the king, with relatively modest political pretensions of their own.[10] But in 1815–16 agents of the Russian-American Company were entering into conspiratorial arrangements with the ruling chief of Kaua'i (Kaumuali'i) and posing a political threat to O'ahu; in response, Kamehameha sent his trusted *Haole* chief, John Young, and the so-called prime minister, "Billy Pitt" Kalaimoku, to Honolulu with orders to construct a fort. From that time, Kalaimoku, his brother Boki, or his collateral brother Ke'eaumoku "Cox"—all members of the Ka'ahumanu kindred—had primary charge of O'ahu. Ke'eaumoku was also sometime "governor" of Maui and another brother, Kuakini, was prominent on Hawai'i (which he formally governed after 1819). Sons of Kamehameha's trusted companion of the conquest, the senior Ke'eaumoku, these chiefs held substantial amounts of land scattered throughout the archipelago.[11] And as they thereby controlled the labor of the people on

---

[10] The Hawaiian chiefs in charge of O'ahu before 1816 included, at various times, Kahanaumaika'i and Kuihelani (cf. I'i 1959: 94, 105). Kahanaumaika'i lived until mid-century, appearing in the O'ahu records of the Lands Commission as the holder of a considerable estate in Waikiki (LC/FT 5: 167; LC/NT 10: 158). For the procedures by which trade was arranged with Kamehameha in Hawai'i, the contracts to be filled in O'ahu, see, for example, Corney 1896; Kotzebue 1821, 1: 313–14; or Golovnin 1979: 183.

[11] The process by which the high chiefs secured rights in perpetuity to their estates, overcoming the king's traditional prerogatives of redistributing the land at his accession or on the demise of the chiefly holder, is documented in Kirch and Sahlins, forthcoming.

the land, the chiefs appropriated a certain share of the so-called royal monopoly in sandalwood.

True, in principle Kamehameha was the lord of all lands, with preemptive claims to the tributes as well as to the labor services of the farming people (*maka'āinana*). But on the lands held of the king by the greater ali'i such privileges were exercised through the intermediacy of these chiefs—as in fact has always been true of royal dues. Thus when Kamehameha agreed in 1817 to purchase the brig *Columbia* from certain Americans, at the price of twice the ship's full in sandalwood, the wood was furnished by the chiefs holding lands in Kaua'i and certain divisions of O'ahu (Corney 1896). This was the defect in Kamehameha's "monopoly." As in the ancient system, a certain share of the tributes fell to the chiefs of the infeudated lands. In Weberian terms, the Hawaiian kingship was coupled to an estate type of patrimonial domination, enabling those with seigneurial rights "to conclude compromises with the ruler."[12]

We cannot be sure of the precise arrangements between Kamehameha and the great chiefs with regard to their respective shares of the sandalwood commerce. According to a later recollection of one of the chiefs (Kanaina), during the rule of Kamehameha's successors in the 1820's the landed ali'i retained six shares in ten of the sandalwood proceeds, the king getting only four (Wyllie 1856: 25). In fact, the chiefs were then engaged in depriving the king of his customary rights; Liholiho (Kamehameha II) or Kauikeaouli (Kamehameha III) would have been fortunate to secure four shares in ten. Even in Kamehameha's time it is clear that, having concluded their "compromises with the ruler," the chiefs were concluding their own deals with the foreigner.

European traders' records from Kamehameha's last years show several important ali'i trafficking in sandalwood on their own accounts, including the aforementioned Billy Pitt Kalaimoku, Boki, Ke'eaumoku Cox, Ka'ahumanu, and others. The transactions of one William French with "Gov. Boka" [Boki'] and "Crymacoo" [Kalaimoku] were particularly substantial: goods advanced by French to the value of $25,078 and $53,790, respectively, although a large part

---

[12] Rocquefeuil, for example, describes the situation in 1819: "Beside the commerce in this precious wood [sandalwood], Taméaméa generally reserves to himself all traffic of importance; only certain of his favorites obtain permission to trade with foreigners" (1823, 2: 361).

of these transactions was probably trade for the king (French, Accts.). Still Kalaimoku had already bought a schooner for himself (apparently around 1813: LC/FT, 1: 127; cf. Chamisso in Kotzebue 1821, 3: 240–41), whereas Ke'eaumoku Cox was purchasing Irish linens from James Hunnewell, for which he paid more than $1,500 in sandalwood over three days in January 1818 (HC/Journal: Jan. 19–21, 1818). French's records, incidentally, show that in March 1819 Kamehameha received "guns, powder, [and] shot" to the nominal value of $8,000 besides the 34 casks of powder, 80 muskets, flints, and shot entered against Liholiho's account in May. Kamehameha's death was imminent—he died on May 8—and apparently the fears for the safety of his heir were growing. Probably these armaments were used in battle in December 1819, when Liholiho's forces, led by Kalaimoku, put down the rebellion of the new king's cousin, Kekuaokalani. Brother's son to Kamehameha, Kekuaokalani claimed the inheritance of the ancient god of war, but he as well as the *Ancien Régime* died in the December battle. The timing was fitting: the period of the New Year (Makahiki), when the king ritually affirmed his sovereignty by the sacrifice of the original god Lono (cf. Valeri 1985; Sahlins 1985a, b).

Organized with a mind to further conquest and potential sedition, the foreign trade of Kamehameha's declining years offers a certain contrast to the orgies of consumption in which the high chiefs engaged after his death. Not to say that the king deprived himself of luxuries. A surviving invoice of the China goods Kamehameha received in 1812 (from his initial dealings with the Winship brothers) is fair enough testimony to his own royal tastes: chairs, lamps, tables, fireworks, velvets, satins, silks, 50 paper parasols, 50 silk hats, 135 pounds of large glass beads, and the like (Marin, Invoice).[13] The Hawaiian ruler, however, had a considerable income at his disposal,

[13] The relatively modest costume of assorted foreign pieces assumed by Kamehameha when he visited the *Tonquin* in 1811 (Ross 1849: 35) or greeted Golovnin in 1818 (Golovnin 1973: 181–82) was characteristic of his official attire; otherwise, he wore a loincloth (*malo*). Golovnin also provided an inventory of furnishings in the king's "dining hall" (thus his *mua*, or domestic shrine), where he held audience with important foreign visitors: a huge trunk containing hand weapons, a mahogany bureau, two mahogany tables—on one a tablecloth, a quart of rum, a half-decanter of red wine, and some glasses—two ordinary mirrors ("worth not more than five rubles apiece"), several guns, cutlasses and spears, a ship's cast-iron stove, and an assortment of dishes (pp. 182–83).

from his own as well as the chiefs' lands, including the large annual offerings of the Makahiki, or New Year, ceremonies delivered on ships—sometimes those of passing Europeans—from the other islands to Hawai'i (cf. Corney 1896: 84; Barnard 1829: 94–95; Kotzebue 1821, 1: 324; Gast and Conrad 1973). Only some minor fraction of the king's resources was going into his personal consumption.

If there was royal excess, it was in Kamehameha's military and monetary acquisitions. During his residence in O'ahu Kamehameha established a shipyard that turned out a small fleet of ships of European type (Campbell 1822: 111–12; Cox 1832: 45). This affair was reestablished upon Kamehameha's return to Hawai'i in 1812. The French explorer Freycinet described the "royal naval yards" at Kailua in August 1819, a few months after the old king's death (Freycinet 1978: 8, 87). Manned by 170 carpenters (including some *Haole*), the workshops continued to produce ships of European design, besides "a prodigious number of canoes" (Arago 1823: 60). By Freycinet's reckoning, the Hawaiian fleet (exclusive of canoes) consisted of five brigs of 90–100 tons, five schooners of 60–70 tons, and ten cutters of 20 tons, the schooners and cutters being locally built (1978: 91). To the end of his life, Kamehameha was also accumulating arms and ammunition, as we have noted, including 40 to 60 cannon, some as large as 32 caliber, and "several thousand muskets" (Rocquefeuil 1823, 2: 342–43). But ships were the royal passion, along with specie. And the ships had more than military value. They cruised the archipelago collecting sandalwood or transporting food and other tributes to Hawai'i. In 1817 Kamehameha sent one of his own vessels to China with a cargo of sandalwood. The voyage was not a commercial success, partly because of high port charges—upon learning of which the Hawaiian king promptly instituted the same at Honolulu.

All of Kamehameha's larger ships, two- and three-masters, had been acquired in sandalwood barters with Americans. Between 1816 and 1818 he so purchased six substantial vessels. Yet in marked contrast to the later business ethics of the Hawaiian ali'i, Kamehameha paid for them all on time. Indeed the two shiploads of sandalwood promised for the *Columbia* were delivered more than a month in advance of the six-month term called for in the agreement (Corney 1896: 90). Kamehameha did not run up his trading debts. Even so, he still had something left over for his old age: a treasure of $200,000 to $300,000 in Spanish dollars at the time he died, according to the reports (no doubt exaggerated) circulating among the foreigners (Freycinet 1978: 90; Rocquefeuil 1823, 2: 341n; Khlebnikov 1976: 67; Golovnin 1979: 196).

Foreign residents and passing visitors were also hearing tell, sometimes from the lips of the chiefs concerned, that the great ali'i intended to seize and divide up the islands just as soon as Kamehameha died (Whitman 1979: 89; Chamisso 1981: 431–32; Rocquefeuil 1823, 2: 342n; Dobel 1842: 237). The Ka'ahumanu-folks, affines to the king, were notably implicated. In this respect the rebellion that did break out following the abolition of the tabus, led by Kamehameha's brother's son, Kekuaokalani, represented certain counterclaims of the Hawai'i ruling line and thus the politics as well as the spirit of the old regime. Indeed, Kamehameha's problems with the Ka'ahumanu-folks and their ilk also go back a long time. According to the recollections of John Papa I'i, the Ka'ahumanu people were urging the assassination of the king when he was still on O'ahu (1959: 51). According to I'i's fellow historian Samuel Kamakau, the reason Kamehameha left O'ahu for Hawai'i in 1812 was the dangerous buildup of arms, followers, and wealth among the great landed chiefs:

It was Kamehameha's wish to remain on Oahu and end his days there, but he was afraid of conspiracies in his old age; he observed that the chiefs were increasing their households and cultivating large tracts in Ko'olaupoko, Ko'olauloa, Waialua and 'Ewa to feed their followers. They were also storing guns and powder bought from foreigners. (1961: 197)

Kamakau goes on to relate the tradition that, by a clever maneuver, Kamehameha used the move to Hawai'i as a way of seizing the chiefs' armaments. He also retails the story that the Ka'ahumanu kindred was suspected in 1819 of having caused Kamehameha's death by sorcery, an accusation that would imply royal pretensions of their own (p. 214; cf. Valeri 1985). As we know, Liholiho nonetheless succeeded his father *de jure*, while from the beginning of his reign the Ka'ahumanu crowd, as predicted, controlled the several islands *de facto* (cf. Barrère and Sahlins 1979: 25). But to understand this crisis of the Hawaiian kingship, as well as the sequel in the sandalwood business, we have to take note of just who these would-be usurpers took themselves to be. The ruler of O'ahu, and also "prime minister" of the kingdom, was *Billy Pitt* Kalaimoku; the sometime governor of Maui was Ke'eaumoku *Cox*; while his brother, *John Adams* Kuakini, ruled Hawai'i Island. These were not just sobriquets laid on the Hawaiian ali'i in a mocking way by passing Europeans; the chiefs delighted in their European names and often insisted on being known by them.

In 1793, the same year the Chinese emperor was telling the English ambassador, Lord Macartney, that the Celestial Kingdom had no need of British manufactures, while also commending the tributary English king for showing the proper reverence to the Son of Heaven—by this same year three of the most powerful Hawaiian ruling chiefs had named their own heirs "King George" (Bell 1929–30 1 (5): 64; cf. Cranmer-Byng 1962). Hawaiian chiefs were also anxious to know of their European visitors if they did not live just as well as, or even just like, King George. Yet the chiefs' avidity for things European was not confined to material goods, which they indeed considered generally superior to their own. They wanted the *identity* of the European great, whose names as well as habits they adopted as signs of their own dignity. I have elsewhere cited the remarks to this effect of an American fur trader, describing the Honolulu sporting scene in 1812: at a race staged near the village, Billy Pitt, George Washington, and Billy Cobbet were seen "walking together in the most familiar manner . . . while in the center of another group, Charley Fox, Thomas Jefferson, James Madison, Bonnepart and Tom Paine were seen on equally friendly terms with each other" (Cox in Sahlins 1981: 29).

From foreign lands lying in the skies beyond the horizon, from the mythical Kahiki, have come powerful dynasties, cults of order and human sacrifice, chiefly regalia, and wealth in general. At the climax of the New Year ritual (the Makahiki) the Hawaiian king and his warriors, rehearsing the great Polynesian tradition of the "stranger-king," wade ashore to battle the partisans of the ancient and popular god Lono. Lono had himself returned from celestial realms to fertilize the land, and now the king would violently encompass the god's sovereignty and productive work. Yet the continuing interest of Hawaiian ruling chiefs in the names, goods, and other signs of overseas powers represented something more than the customary prestige or even the divinity of the "foreign" in the Hawaiian categorical scheme. It reflected also a political structure that continually reproduced the necessity for such distinction. Here again is a common Polynesian problem, compounded, as Valeri shows, of a double indeterminacy: an uncertainty regarding genealogical rank and an uncertain relation between ancestral rank and actual force. Hence the issue: "*comment créer une discontinuité satisfaisante du point de vue politique?"* (how to create a satisfactory discontinuity from the political point of view?)—or more precisely, *"comment se créer une discontinuité qui est fonction des lignes de force d'une société?"* (how is a discontinuity created that corresponds to the lines of force of a society?) (Valeri 1972: 37).

If Hawaiian chiefs competed with each other by taking on European identities, in this way modernizing an ancient geography of cosmic powers, it was because they confronted each other as perpetual rivals who in divinity were virtual doubles. Alike in their ancestral claims to sacred life-giving powers, the sources of reproduction in every form, the several great chiefs too had their similar tabus, signs of their own consecrated status. Ultimately the sacred ancestral sources were one, converging on the same original. The sacred ali'i were thus united in a universal genealogy that indeed included the species of nature alongside the forebears of humanity—and the older brothers of mankind, who were great gods. Yet just as Hawaiians in myth and ritual knew how to challenge the gods and secure their powers for human use, so could rising chiefs in practice capture high ancestry and sacred tabus, notably by marrying ranking women, and thereby defy the established ali'i of senior lineage and divine pretension. Marital politics was a privileged means of reconciling real discontinuities of force with ideal differences in rank, as Valeri (1972) shows. In the event, the political reality appears as a humanized version of heroic legend (cf. Sahlins 1985b). It would only be necessary to conclude the struggle by the sacrifice of one's royal adversary in order to reproduce as history the theory of sovereignty that Hawaiians annually reenacted in the Makahiki ceremonies: the theory of usurpation by the upstart warrior, who is archetypally a stranger and whose victory over the god or king of ancient lineage involves also the capture of his predecessor's sacred woman. But then, the genealogical-political conflict is isomorphic with the most general cosmogonic myths: an iconic realization in the mode of social relations of the appropriation of the bearing earth (= the wife) from the god (= the chief of the senior line) by and for humankind (= the usurper, the warrior). The problem was that this apparent harmony of act and myth led to struggles without end.

For the effect of these marital and martial tactics was a kind of entropy in the relations of hierarchy: a tendency to move always toward an undifferentiated state, since by one genealogical line or another an ambitious chief could always make claims of seniority against political rivals who on similar grounds supposed themselves superior to him. Generations of intermarriage had resulted in the convergence of noble lines at numerous points. Contending chiefs were all able to trace their descent—one way or another, that is, bilaterally—to the same godly sources. Hence a parvenu chief rich in lands and followers could fairly hope to turn such assets into a legitimate claim to authority. But as so transposed into practice, the competition for divine honors among the Hawaiian ali'i became at once permanent and indecisive.[14]

Kamehameha was junior by descent (FyBS) to his royal cousin Kiwala'o, but this did not prevent him from sacrificing the latter and then marrying his daughter to produce the royal heir, Liholiho. Despite the tabus this bestowed on Liholiho, the time would come when the Ka'ahumanu crowd dared to match their own wealth and power to his—as an English traveler recounts, for example, of Ka'ahumanu's brother "Cox" in 1822:

He is worth twenty or thirty thousand dollars and derives an increasing yearly income from the sale of sandalwood, which grows upon his land. He is very covetous and fond of money withal, and knows how to drive a hard bargain. The mention of his wealth and power as very great, gives him infinite satisfaction, and when some one had the boldness to say, that in real importance he was superior to the King, his vanity seemed not a little gratified. (Mathison 1825: 408–9)

In the context of universal powers to which all contenders had claim, politics became the pursuit of distinction. Consider that the Ka'ahumanu people, although they descended from many of the same Hawai'i greats as Kamehameha and Liholiho, had consistently preferred to set themselves apart as "Maui chiefs," demanding that island also as their special province (Bingham 1969: 77–80; Vancouver 1801 3: 270–71, 5: 92). They thus made genealogical reference to famous royal forebears of Maui, people who had long despised the

---

[14] In Polynesian conical clan systems, even normal succession is a kind of usurpation, since by distance from divine ancestors sons are lesser beings than their fathers, hence inheritance is again a victory of the humanized over the divine (relatively speaking). If in Hawaii the participation of the son in the mother's rank, or the inheritance of tabus through the mother, also becomes possible, this merely exacerbates the oedipal drama. It is notable that the children of high-ranking Hawaiian chiefs were characteristically raised apart from their fathers. Early on, the Ka'ahumanu crowd tried to come to power by inciting the child Liholiho to sanction the killing of his father, Kamehameha (I'i 1959: 50).

Hawai'i ali'i for mixing their blood with commoners'. Even their attempts to dismember Kamehameha's centralized rule had analogies under the ancient regime—struggles that had periodically resulted in the segmentation of islandwide chiefdoms (Sahlins 1972: 141–42; Valeri 1972). But at Kamehameha's death in 1819, this Polynesian political cycle came into conjunction with an equally classic capitalist cycle, a business crisis in America—and the combined effect launched the ruling ali'i on their brilliant careers of conspicuous consumption.

1820–30: "They consume without cease, and never pay up"

In 1818–19 America was in the grip of a financial crisis. Taken together with the declining returns in the maritime fur trade, the shortage of specie among New England merchants put a premium on Hawaiian sandalwood as a means of carrying on the China trade. As the historian Kuykendall observes, the Americans thereupon

descended upon the islands in a swarm, bringing with them everything from pins, scissors, clothing, and kitchen utensils to carriages, billiard tables, house frames, and sailing ships, and doing their utmost to keep the speculating spirit at a fever heat among the Hawaiian chiefs. And the chiefs were not slow about buying; if they had no sandalwood at hand to pay for the goods, they gave promissory notes. (1968: 89; cf. Bradley 1968: 60–61)

The chiefs were not slow about buying, but these "mild temper'd villains" were very slow about paying, as the exasperated James Hunnewell wrote from Honolulu (HC/Letters: Jan. 13, 1823). "No one takes account of the goods furnished them," observes a French visitor; "they consume without cease, and never pay up" (Morineau, Ms.). A great international division of labor was here coming together in unlikely subtropical tableaux: these high Polynesian notables decked out in variegated costumes of fine Chinese silks and English broadcloths being hauled through the dusty lanes of Honolulu in elegant pony chaises (or perhaps just wheelbarrows) by straining menials (themselves clothed in loincloths) to fancy dinners in thatched houses at teak tables set with silver and crystal—all the good things imported on the never-never.

The consumption fever was being fueled by two intersecting systems of rivalry: on one side, the White merchants competing with each other for custom; on the other, the Hawaiian chiefs with the custom of competing with each other. Honolulu agents of Boston firms would advance extravagant goods against future sandalwood deliveries. By constant dunning, the merchant might sooner or later collect more or less of the wood owed him. But just as often he would find it had been loaded on the ship of some other trader, who had been able to convince the chief in question by offering even more extravagant things on the spot—without failing to deprecate the goods already received from his competitor. "Till now," John C. Jones wrote home to Boston, "I never knew the rascality of mankind, every one here is ready to cut his neighbor's throat, truth is never spoken, treachery is the order of the day. I am disgusted with my fellow [White] man" (ML/Jones: July 6, 1821). "That infamous scoundrel of a Blanchard has been of the greatest injury to our cause, he has circulated the most infamous, base and unprincipled falsehoods concerning yourselves . . . etc., etc." (Nov. 20, 1821; Hammatt, Journal: Aug. 3, 1823; Bradley 1968: 61, etc., etc.). And all the while the traders were thus undercutting each other, they were exacerbating the divisions among the chiefs by appealing to their emulative spirit of self-regard. In 1823 Kaikioewa, a high ali'i and sometime guardian of the future Kamehameha III, wanted to buy a ship from Charles Hammatt of Bryant and Sturgis (Boston), ostensibly for his royal ward but really for himself. When the ruling chiefs Kalaimoku and Ka'ahumanu objected, Hammatt asked Kaikioewa "if he was the servant of Krymokoo [Kalaimoku] and the old woman [Ka'ahumanu], if he was bound to obey their orders, or was himself a chief at liberty to do as he pleased. He said he was a chief & wanted to be a chief, that he would keep the vessel & did not care for Krymokoo or any of them" (Hammatt, Journal: Aug. 9, 1825).

By the close of 1821, according to trader Jones, the Hawaiian king and chiefs owned "Ten large & elegant Brigs, besides a large number of Sloops & Schooners, all of which they have purchased from Americans" (UCSD: Dec. 31, 1821). This would include *Cleopatra's Barge*, a luxuriously fitted and leaky vessel sent out by a Boston firm to dazzle the local nobility, which King Liholiho agreed to buy for $90,000 in sandalwood[15]—that the local agent Charles B. Bullard

---

[15] The purchase price was 9,000 piculs of sandalwood. A picul is a Chinese measure, equivalent to 133⅓ pounds. Through most of the sandalwood period in Hawaii, a picul of sandalwood had the nominal value of 10 Spanish dollars, though it might trade in Canton for as high as $14.00 or $15.00—or around 1830, as low as $3.00

could not collect (Bullard, Letters). Adopting a metaphor that seems curiously appropriate, Bullard wrote to Boston: "If you want to know how religion stands in the Islands, I can tell you; all sects are tolerated and the King worships The Barge" (Nov. 1, 1821). The tabus had been broken, but not the spiritual self-consciousness of the Hawaiian ali'i, who were thus testifying to the divinity in their own nature, derived from an overseas homeland (Kahiki), by rivaling each other in the material signs of a foreign *mana* (cf. Sahlins 1981).

There was an Hawaiian tradition too in the chiefs' appreciation of Western distinctions between "fancy" and "plain" goods. Send out "articles of a showy kind," a resident trader wrote to Boston. "Everything new and elegant will sell at a profit, coarse articles are of no use" (ML/Jones: Mar. 9, 1823; May 31, 1823). The Hawaiian ali'i were thus appropriating the categorical differences among mercantile commodities to a correspondence between brilliance and *mana* whose grounds are set forth in founding myths and chiefly practices, or indeed the descent of kings from the legendary Wakea, personification of the sun at high noon. Like the sun, chiefs could not be directly seen without injury—they were *lani*, "heavenly ones," and commoners *makawela*, or "burnt eyes"—while their passage made all things visible, caused them to appear (cf. Beckwith 1970; Sahlins 1985a; Valeri 1985). "You'd be surprised how fast these people are advancing towards civilization," Jones reports to Boston, telling how just the other day Billy Pitt Kalaimoku asked him for three gold-adorned carriages (ML/Jones: May 31, 1823).

Jones's instructions in the 1820's to the parent firm of Marshall and Wildes concerning "items wanted" in the Islands amounts to an entire catalog of current Polynesian splendors, from "superfine broadcloth and cassimere," "large size different patterns of silk," "first quality calicoes," and "muslins gold and silver sprigg'd"; through writing desks, mirrors, trunks covered with red leather, "ladies dresses, large and small sizes, first quality materials & showy," "handsome feathers," and material for house construction and naval supplies; to the steamboat for which "the King and Pitt would give anything" (ML/Jones: various dates from 1821).

---

or less. Unless otherwise specified, I will use the $10.00-for-one-picul rate in this discussion. Foreign commercial goods (as well as ships) were usually paid for at this rate, though the valuation of these goods in dollars was (of course) what the traffic would bear, thus yielding profits as high as 300–400 percent.

In catering to such demands, the capitalist global economy allowed itself to be organized locally by values of another kind, by a Polynesian mentality of objects—which of course did not faze the *Haole* merchants since in their own system of fetishism the commodities at issue were merely exchange-values. If anything, the market and political events widened the scope of Polynesian use-values by allowing such people as the Ka'ahumanu crowd to so express royal aspirations, despite their limited traditional credentials (by tabu status). Nor need we assume that the development of the kingdom had made the old-time wars of chiefs out of date. Twice after Kamehameha's death there were armed conflicts: one following the abolition of the tabus in 1819 and another rebellion at Kaua'i in 1824. Thereafter bloodshed was often threatened and sometimes only narrowly averted.[16] The first decade of Kauikeaouli's reign as Kamehameha III, from 1825 to 1834, was marked by strife over royal powers; more than once factional parties mobilized for an armed showdown. The main protagonists of the violence were in general the same as those making ostentatious display of themselves in the swank trappings of foreign elites. But of course commercial and military success would have the same practical grounds: both were based on control of lands and of large followings of subchiefs and cultivators. Conspicuous consumption was thus an expression of potential force, even as the code of object-properties signified, in the novel medium of *Haole* commodities, the cosmic qualities of ancient victories. All this helps explain why violence and venality appear as historical alternatives of the Hawaiian cultural order, either one capable of passing into the other, although of course in the longer run and the larger world order, business was destined to replace war as the competitive means of choice. Trade was the continuation of war by other means.

We can see that the process was not simply dictated by the foreign trading class. On the contrary, the Hawaiians developed complex relations to the forces of imperial domination in ways that harnessed the divisions among *Haole*—between traders and missionaries, British and Americans, Protestants and Catholics—to their own political projects. For much of the 1820's Hawaiian politics turned on a classic dissension between senior and junior kinsmen of the Ka'ahumanu

---

[16]Bloodshed was averted no thanks to *Haole* merchants such as Jones, who had muskets to sell and did not then scruple to add to the rumors of armed conflict between chiefs for control of the kingdom (e.g. ML/Jones: Dec. 1822).

group, the parties to which were quick to exploit equally traditional schisms among the resident foreigners. Ka'ahumanu and her immediate siblings, now in *de facto* control of the Islands, were being undermined by the sometime governor of O'ahu, Boki, and his wife, Liliha. The boy-king Kauikeaouli figured in this dispute, at least as its object. Boki was his formal guardian (*kahu*) and the Boki faction claimed to defend the interests of the king against the usurpations of the Ka'ahumanu crowd. The foreign parties were opposed to each other on other grounds, of course. But when they were respectively engaged by the contending chiefs, the effect was a complex set of chiasmic structures, acting to redouble the intensity of competition among *Haole* and Hawaiians alike. The energies of one set of differences were thus added to the interests of another.

Guardian to the Hawaiian king, Boki was also special friend to the White traders, particularly one Richard Charlton, the British consul. In the event, this coalition developed not only as the party of the king but of the traditional kingship—which had been linked to the British since Cook. The coalition was opposed to the pious Ka'ahumanu chiefs, who for their part were thick with the American missionaries. The rivalry between the king and the landed ali'i was thus calqued on the international rivalry of British and Americans. Nor had the traders on the king's side much liking for the missionary friends of the chiefs, whom they accused of enlightening the natives too well in commercial affairs and diverting Hawaiian labor from cutting sandalwood to building churches.[17] So when Catholic priests arrived in 1826–27, their cause was supported by Boki and certain merchants (notably Charlton and Jones), as against the chiefs and Protestant missionaries who would rid the Islands of "Papists." We need not go into the further details of this involved "structure of the conjuncture." It is enough to note its contribution to the Hobbesian quest for power

[17] A characteristic blast at missionaries comes from the pen of the merchant John C. Jones: "Trade will never again flourish at these Islands until these emissaries from the Andover mill are recalled. They are continually telling the King & Chiefs that the White traders are cheating and imposing on them, consequently [they] have dissipated the value of most articles. I believe it is a fact generally acknowledged by all here, that the natives are fifty percent worse in every vice since the missionaries began their hypocritical labour here; these blood suckers of the community had much better be in their native country gaining their living by the sweat of their brow, than living like lords in this luxurious land, distracting the minds of these children of Nature with the idea that they are to be eternally damned unless they think and act as they do: O that Providence would put a whip in every honest hand to lash such rascals naked through the world" (ML/Jones: Jan. 1823).

after power now raging among the Hawaiian elite, which meant a greater and greater commitment to the economy of grandeur. "The chiefs," as Kamakau says, "were all bent at this time on securing honors for themselves" (1961: 265). But then, given the traditional indeterminacies of such honors, each one felt compelled to prove in the new medium of commercial prowess that he or she was equal to *and* better than, the same as *and* different from, the others.

The elite economy was an arena of differential and differentiating consumption. Hence the endless pursuit of novelty, the passion for fashion. The resident trader James Hunnewell writes to his suppliers that having sold fifteen bedsteads at $50 each, he had exhausted the Honolulu market, since "they are all alike." "Your best silks are but little wanted," he adds, because silks of the same pattern had already come out on a competitor's ship, "and they [the chiefs] want such patterns as they have never seen before" (HC/Letters: Dec. 30, 1829). Hunnewell was writing at the end of the sandalwood era, but of course the pursuit of individual distinction had been running strong since Kamehameha's death: "Everyone that comes brings better and better goods, and such as they have not seen will sell when common ones will not" (Bullard, Letters: July 4, 1821).

The accumulation of deluxe items outran any possibility of personal consumption. The objective was thesaurization as much as display. The chiefs hoarded up the exotic returns of the sandalwood trade—quite to the point of waste. Fine cloths and Chinese curios were accumulated in unusable quantities; they lay moldering away in the storehouses until perhaps at the chief's death they were ritually set adrift in the ocean. Even if the goods were needed for some current purpose, the ali'i showed a certain disinclination to make any inroads on their stocks-on-hand, as if this could be taken as a sign of failing powers. They preferred in such cases to make additional purchases of the kinds of things they already possessed in superfluity:

these people have an incurable reluctance to part with anything they have stored away. There is now an immense amount of property stowed away in caves & dirty houses which is rotting away, but which the chiefs will not take out of their repositories even to use themselves. The King [Liholiho] some time ago was in want of duck [cloth] when it was scarce, & bought a few bolts at a very high price, when at the same time he had two or three hundred bolts which was stored away rotting. (Hammatt, Journal: Aug. 18, 1823)

The "caves & dirty houses" no doubt include the houses of subchiefs and retainers, to whom the great ali'i consigned some of their treasures (cf. Kekauluohi, Journal).[18] The guardianship of the chief's goods, like the guardianship of the chief's child, appears to have constituted a certain hierarchical bond, involving some participation in the chief's person or substance. It was usually correlated with the retainer's right to supervise some part of the ali'i's land (together with the cultivators thereon). Since the distribution of large tracts of conquered land in Kamehameha's time, the number of these supervisory people (*konohiki*) was growing disproportionately to the population at large. Indeed, their numbers grew absolutely while the farming population declined, both by mortality and by migration to the ports of Honolulu and Lahaina. The great landed chiefs, moreover, were competing to place konohiki land agents on their respective estates. In turn these retainers might bring relatives in their train, perhaps as *luna*, or "overseers," of specific tracts (*'ili 'āina*). All these dependents cum petty landholders made a welcome addition to the potential force of the superior ali'i, if an unwelcome imposition on the underlying people. For the maka'āinana, or farming people, the involution of the tenure system—by infeudation and subinfeudation—meant a growing number of notables "above," all with claims on the products of their lands and the service of their bodies. In addition to "taxes" in kind, the cultivators were subject to *corvée* labor on behalf of the greater and lesser powers that be.

By such means of coerced labor the people participated in a sandalwood trade that the great ali'i differentially controlled and enjoyed. Technically the common people's labor was a ground rent or due owed the chief in return for rights to cultivable land—which in most cases had been in the possession of the cultivators' families for generations. Hence the ali'i seem to have felt no obligation to remunerate the work, though they were ready to dispossess the commoner who failed to respond to the sandalwood *corvée* (cf. Mathison 1825: 384–85). Nor did the people see any share of the proceeds, except for a very limited "trickle-down" of stuff, or from the very occasional permission to cut a small amount of sandalwood on their own after they had met the chief's requisitions (cf. Bullard, Letters: Oct. 25, 1821; Dec. 10, 1822; Kuykendall 1968: 92). As a rule the common people were simply excluded from the sandalwood busi-

[18] In Kekauluohi's journal, there is a 40-page inventory of the estate of Hoapiliwahine, an important ali'i. It lists real and chattel goods in the hands of some 79 different persons, many of whom held both land and property of the deceased.

ness, except in this capacity of labor. They were underpaid or unpaid, and sometimes sent to the mountains for weeks on end in sustained campaigns of logging sandalwood. The diversion of labor from agriculture is said to have caused food shortages, even as the sandalwood cutters in the uplands were reduced to eating wild roots (Kotzebue 1821, 2: 200; Bullard, Letters: Oct. 25, 1821; Beechey 1832: 202; Judd 1966: 35; Kuykendall 1968: 90).

In April 1821, according to the Russian naval commander Vasilyev, Liholiho brought about 5,000 men from Maui to Honolulu, "for felling and pulling down from the mountains the sandalwood, unmindful as to how they should maintain themselves" (quoted in Tumarkin, mimeo). On occasion Liholiho's predecessor, Kamehameha, and his successor, Kauikeaouli, are supposed to have concerned themselves more with the subsistence of the people collecting sandalwood for them (Kamakau 1961: 204, 278–79). And once Billy Pitt Kalaimoku distributed 300 blankets received in trade to his followers—his immediate retainers?—an event so notable that it was repeated in travelers' accounts for decades as evidence of this chief's generosity. More characteristic, however, is the notice in 1822 by the LMS missionaries Daniel Tyerman and George Bennet of 2,000 men carrying sandalwood down to the royal storehouses at Kailua, Hawai'i, "wearied with their unpaid labors, yet unmurmuring at their bondage" (1831, 1: 415). Hence also the frequent comment on the "abject misery" of the common people's existence, especially by comparison with the opulence affected by the chiefs (cf. Ralston 1984).

In the 1820's and 1830's, the king, the Ka'ahumanu-folks, and other powerful chiefs maintained in Honolulu or Lahaina their "civilized houses." Constructed preferably in European style and graced with assorted Chinese and American furnishings, these houses were rarely used, except to receive foreign dignitaries (*MH* 1825: 276; Korn 1983: 14, 17; Judd 1966: 14, 21; Jarves 1843: 127–28, 172; Stewart 1831, 2: 135–36). Here again we are confronted with the material translation of a ritual system that had ostensibly been done away with. In its location at the front of a larger domestic compound, as in functions and connotations, the civilized house was a modern form of the ancient *mua* or domestic shrine cum men's eating house, also customarily used as a place of reception. The chiefs, moreover, inaugurated their civilized houses as was formerly done for certain temples, demanding offerings from all their followers for the privilege of entering (cf. Valeri 1985: 181–82). Only now the prescribed offerings were in cash. Liholiho is said to have cleared upward of $5,000 when he opened his civilized house, collected from resident Europeans as well as Hawaiians (Bingham 1969: 188; Ellis 1828: 427–28; Ellis, Ms. Journal: Apr. 28, 1823; *MH* 1824: 209; Stewart 1830: 132).

Besides the civilized house, in the high chief's compound other signs of his or her acquisitive powers were on display: the numerous dependents and hangers-on living about, usually in meaner huts of Hawaiian style, and generally in idleness. The missionary Charles Stewart describes these establishments at some length: households of both the great and the not-so-great, with a company of 30 to 100 attendants, who all

> seem to enjoy a perpetual saturnalia. . . . This portion of the inhabitants spend their lives principally in eating and drinking, lounging and sleeping; in the sports of the surf, and various games of the country; at cards, which have long been introduced; in hearing the songs of the musicians . . . and in witnessing the performances of the dancers. (1830: 138; cf. Corney 1896: 105; Judd 1966: 21; Morineau 1826–29)

The ali'i kept their domestic retainers in food drawn from their extensive estates and in pieces of cloth from the proceeds of their trade. The food the chiefs commanded was considerable, sometimes staggering.[19]

Yet then, by their own great bulk, the great chiefs "were easily distinguishable from the common people" (Stewart 1830: 133). In this respect the Ka'ahumanu chiefs have been particularly remarked in European annals. John Adams Kuakini was six feet three inches tall and in 1825 weighed in at 361 or 392 pounds (Bloxam, Ms. Nar-

---

[19] John B. Whitman records the annual "rents" from a district in Ko'olau, O'ahu, paid to the high priest who owned it before 1815: 200 large salted fish, 2 hogs of the largest size, 5 "suits" of tapa, 5 women's tapa skirts, 10 loincloths (1979: 79). This would be a regular offering sent to the "lord of the land" (*haku'āina*) living elsewhere; it does not include irregular levies, nor would it be typical of the demands made by the elite on more accessible lands. When visiting district estates, the chiefs were tendered very large offerings (*ho'okupu*). We have a record, kept by the Tahitian teacher Auna, of such gifts given to Ka'ahumanu when she went in a train of hundreds on a visit to west Maui, Moloka'i, and various divisions of Hawai'i in 1822. The total enumerated goods received was 54 "bundles" of tapa, 610 "pieces" of tapa, 1,306 dogs, 144 calabashes of poi, 18 hogs, 222 fish, 3 feather cloaks, and 4 canoes. This list does not include the amounts of poi, sweet potatoes, fish, tapa, mats, dogs, fowl, and various other unspecified foods also mentioned by Auna but not enumerated (Auna, Journal).

rative: May 15, 1825; Dampier 1971: 48). Ka'ahumanu herself was compared by one French visitor to "the celebrated Elisa, the obligatory ornament of all the *fêtes* of Paris and its environs, where one could for the small price of three sols or fifteen centimes, contemplate her 150 kilograms of flesh at leisure" (Lafond 1843–44, 4: 25). The magnitude of Ka'ahumanu's sister Pi'ia frequently evoked special comment even in comparison to other big chiefs: "without exception," Bloxam says, "the largest woman I ever saw" (Ms. Narrative: May 28, 1825) and, according to Kotzebue, "the greatest appetite that ever came under my observation" (1830, 2: 223; cf. Dampier 1971: 48; Bingham 1969: 244). Yet Pi'ia was only living up to a general ideal. "To attain to this so much desired corpulence, nothing can be better than the mode of living in vogue with the chiefs. They pass their lives, so to speak, reclining on their mats; very seldom do they take a walk, and they eat from morning to night" (Barrot 1978: 28).

One is reminded of the reply of the Tongan islander to the apparently naive question of the ethnographer: "Can't you see he is a chief? See how big he is" (Gifford 1929: 124). The embonpoint of the Hawaiian ali'i was not just a final extravagance but something of their noble essence. Or at least it was the self-evidence of chiefship, the obvious sign of control over people and land, at once in the real-political sense and in terms of the divine powers (*mana*) that made these flourish. Precisely, then, superiority consists in the enlargement of the chief's persona to include other people, objects of wealth, and even nature itself in his or her own existence. Trade goods thus appear as glorious artificial extensions of sacred chiefly bodies that were already stretched to their organic limits. Fashionable clothing and swank domestic furnishings are metonymic extensions of the chiefs themselves; indeed traditionally, the sacred ali'i's houses and personalities were tabu to the touch of commoners, in the same way as his body. And the enlarged household economy, with its dozens of people ministering to the wants and pleasures of the chiefly body, carries this same organic system to a higher social level. The chief's retinue functions as a kind of superorganism, its disjoined members acting to sustain the one life with which all are identified.[20] Or again, we have seen

[20] There are no corporate group designations or even proper names for the followers of a given chief. They would be hierarchically (inclusively) known as So-and-so *ma*, as in Ka'ahumanu *ma*.

the chiefly substance extended even further by the distribution of the ali'i's personal treasures among landholding subchiefs. Over and over in all these forms, the same relationship appears between personal grandeur and the inclusion of others.

So the chiefs' singular concern with the people's labor was their own accumulation of consumption goods. And such was the competition between them that they preferred to sustain their interest by going into debt rather than restrain it by more prudent expenditures. A few of the higher ali'i developed a more bourgeois relation to their resources. Boki apparently had a share in several public houses in Honolulu, including one with the British consul Charlton; he and others made some desultory attempts at starting sugar or coffee plantations; and there were a few trading voyages to California and the Northwest Coast. But as Adam Smith said, the great proprietor is seldom a great improver: the chiefs' enterprises came to very little, if they were not dead losses (Beechey 1832: 352, 360; Morineau, Ms.; Judd 1966: 67n; J. N. Reynolds 1835; BCP/Charlton: Nov. 28, 1829). Even if the chiefs had been inclined to productive investments, they were for the most part too deeply in debt—which the common people were losing interest in paying off even faster than they were losing the manpower to do so. The chiefs showed a much greater ability to accumulate goods than they did to make others pay for them. Estimates of the collective chiefly deficit in 1824—reflecting the splurge that followed Kamehameha's death—run as high as $300,000 (USCD/Crocker: Sept. 15, 1824; cf. HC/Letters: Jan. 29, 1822; on the collective debt of 1826, see Kuykendall 1968: 91–92, 434–36). Yet at the same time the ali'i were running up debts, some of them at least were accumulating cash, which they preferred to hoard rather than apply to their accounts. Ka'ahumanu, it is said, was good for as much as $40,000 in specie, while Ke'eaumoku Cox is reported to have had $30,000 when he died in 1824 (Morineau, Ms.; Ellis, Ms. Journal: Nov. 20, 1823; Mathison 1825: 408; S. Reynolds, Journal: May 5, 1825). "They thought they could pay in sandalwood," as one chief explained many years later during an official inquiry into the debt; "the chiefs thought it would never come to an end" (Wyllie 1856: 23).

But the sandalwood trade, which had already known its ups (1821–22, 1827) and downs (1823–24), virtually collapsed in 1829–30. Large supplies of Indian and Pacific sandalwood drove the Canton price to a fraction of what it had been; more importantly, the

Hawaiian forests were exhausted. "We get little other than Chips," wrote the discouraged Hunnewell, "the gleanings of the mountains, the refuse of better days" (HC/Letters: Aug. 31, 1830). Even this did not put an end to the chiefs' acquisitive habits. They lived on as they had before, as if it could never come to an end. It is a fair question, wrote a leading *Haole* merchant in 1835, "whether the value of all the marketable produce of these Islands, is equal in amount to the known expenditures of the chiefs" (Ladd 1838: 73).

The ruling chiefs could not now hope to compete with advancing capitalist modes of exploiting the Islands' resources. Indeed the great ali'i were rapidly dying out, which is the reason usually given for their surrender of political authority to White Men. But the explanation is too simple. It ignores that the Hawaiian aristocracy failed to make use of available social means for recruitment. If the chiefs died out, it was because they were obsolete as a ruling class.

This decadence of the Hawaiian aristocracy, which soon enough brought about the quasi-total collapse of Hawaiian culture, was no simple reflex of the capitalist world economy.[21] If anything, the history of Hawaii since the late eighteenth century—beginning with the treatment of Cook as a divine visitation—has been marked by a certain disproportion between the nature of the materialist forces and their local-historical consequences. By giving these forces direction, value, and cultural effect, the Hawaiian system succeeded in amplifying the "impact" of the World System. The history recounted here has not obeyed the laws of physics, not even as translated in the terms of a "cultural materialism." That is because, as translated in the terms of an Hawaiian culture, the Western market forces took on powers that could never be determined from their material forms.

[21] Elsewhere (Sahlins 1989b) I contrast the response of Hawaiians and Kwakiutl to the world-capitalist economy, a comparison all the more pertinent since many of the same ships and European personnel were initially involved with both these peoples. Reducing the comparison to an abusive simplicity: where the Hawaiians accumulated different kinds of goods, the Kwakiutl elite demanded more and more of the same good (the Hudson's Bay blanket), which, moreover, they distributed widely in the famous potlatch system. The differences are correlates of different cosmologies cum sociologies of power. The Northwest Indian lineages claimed distinct and incommensurable ancestral powers; their problem was how to compare them, or turn qualitative into quantitative distinctions. Whereas, of course, for Hawaiian ali'i the problem was how to differentiate their claims to a universal power, to turn quantitative differences in standing into qualitative distinctions.

3

Patterns of History: Cultural Schemas in the Foundings of Sherpa Religious Institutions

SHERRY B. ORTNER

The lines are being drawn in the debate over the role of culture in history. On one side there is a set of authors denying culture anything other than a minor representational role. For them, culture operates largely as a set of markers *of* social phenomena (particularly as markers of group identity) but rarely as models *for* social phenomena, shapers of the social and historical process. On the other side there is a set of authors insisting that culture, in the form of complex templates for thought, feeling, and action, plays a strong role not simply in representing the world but also in shaping its ongoing historical emergence.

The anticultural position has been articulated most forcefully by Richard G. Fox in a recent study of Sikh history. Fox opens with the question, "Can anthropologists be defined as otherwise intelligent human beings who nevertheless believe in the concept of culture?" (1985:xi). Aligning himself with a set of theorists who are in fact claimed by the other side as well (Raymond Williams, E. P. Thompson, Pierre Bourdieu), Fox caricatures a position that he calls "culturology." In the culturology perspective, according to Fox, culture is "inertial and coercive" (p. xiv). It has a "tyrannical" role vis-à-vis the people being studied, and feeds racism and orientalism among academics and administrators: "Is it possible that to some degree the anthropological concept of culture prepares the ground for these misuses [orientalism, racism]? Does placing human behavior under the tyranny of culture license such stereotyping and homogenizing 'explanations' of the human condition in different societies?" (p. xii). Concluding his preface with an angry and unhappy discussion of Indira Gandhi's assassination and the violence against Sikhs that followed, Fox once again blames the concept of culture and the anthropologists who give it play:

This false cultural determinism obscures real history. While it pretends to explain human action in another society, it actually only feeds current prejudices that culture keeps India and other poor countries backward. Whereas individuals are said to move society in the West, people in India are merely carriers of communal traditions, which, once recognized as cultural and therefore presumed to be above history and beyond easy change, need little investigation. . . . 'the people without history,' as Eric Wolf calls the colonial and neocolonial world, remain so because they are said to have culture instead. (p. xv)

Let me ignore the mud-slinging quality of these comments, and simply make the substantive point that Fox is confusing a view that culture may be constraining with a notion that such constraints always operate in a politically conservative direction. This mistake then allows him to align the intellectual position that accords a strong modeling role to culture with a political position that blames the victim (they are as they are only because of their culture) and that thus fosters, among other things, racism and ethnic violence.

This double slippage in Fox's argument—from an analytic view of cultural constraints to an analytic view of cultural conservatism, and from an analytic view of cultural conservatism to a prejudiced position of political conservatism—is in turn possible because Fox ignores several large bodies of literature on the dynamics of culture. For example, he cites Max Weber's views on the conservatism of Hinduism, first published in the 1920's and translated in the 1950's. But he never refers to the many contemporary publications by sociologists and anthropologists that question and modify Weber's views on the historical conservatism of Asian religions, yet that nonetheless accept Weber's general position that cultural forces, including especially religious ideologies, play a powerful role in shaping history. Similarly, Fox ignores most of the post-1970's literature in symbolic anthropology and structuralism that accepts many of his own Marxist emphases on class, conflict, and domination, but that nonetheless insists on the force of culture (for a discussion of this body of literature, see Ortner 1984). It is thus simply false to state, as Fox does, that an intellectual commitment to understanding culture as a powerful and dynamic component of the social and historical process commits an author to attributing conservatism to culture, or to adopting a politically conservative (blame the victim) analytic stance.

Fox's grounds for denying the active role of culture in history are thus largely spurious. Proceeding inappropriately from those arguments, however, he then sets up what he takes to be the alternative position, in which culture plays a largely passive role in historical change. This position is shared by a number of other anthropologists and must be examined a bit more closely here.

The position is that culture—a body of symbols and meanings in play in a given society at a given time—operates largely as a pool of symbolic resources upon which people draw, and over which people struggle, in the course of social and political differentiation and conflict: "Society is a battleground over beliefs, [and] social relations are specific engagements" (Fox 1985: xii). Eric Wolf stresses selection rather than battle, but the general point is the same: "If a mode of production gives rise to idea-systems, these are multiple and often contradictory. They form an 'ecology' of collective representations, and the construction of ideology takes place within a field of ideological options in which groups delineate their positions in a complex process of selection among alternatives" (1982: 390).

Let me state at once that I would not actually disagree with this position, at least as a partial representation of the reality of the social process. Yet I would immediately point out that if culture is a desirable or contested resource, there must be some reason for people and groups to struggle over its control. The notion of ideological choice or struggle can only have meaning if one assumes precisely the point that this position seeks to deny—that culture (symbols, meanings, ideological systems) is extremely powerful. Culture can be a passive object of politics only if it is also an active force in history; it must be selected and shaped precisely because it has selecting and shaping force. Or in other words, one must appreciate the power of culture if one is to appreciate the politics of culture.

Wolf himself recognizes at least an aspect of this point, although he never follows up on it analytically:

The ability to bestow meanings—to "name" things, acts, and ideas—is a source of power. Control of communications allows the managers of ideology to lay down the categories through which reality is to be perceived. Conversely, this entails the ability to deny the existence of alternative categories, to assign them to the realm of disorder and chaos, to render them socially and symbolically invisible. (p. 388)

In the interest of depolemicizing the argument, then, especially since I do not disagree with many other aspects of Wolf's (or Fox's) perspective, let me say that in this paper I shall simply pick up on this undeveloped part of Wolf's position. I shall try to show that if people struggle over definitions, over ideology, over culture, they do so because culture indeed defines the categories through which people experience, and more importantly, act on, the world. My ultimate intent is to illustrate, contrary to Fox's charges, the possibility of a social and historical theory that is at once cultural and critical.

Cultural Schemas

In a 1973 paper (based in turn on a 1970 dissertation), I sketched a concept of "key scenarios." These were defined as preorganized schemes of action, symbolic programs for the staging and playing out of standard social interactions in a particular culture. The point was that every culture contains not just bundles of symbols, and not even just bundles of larger propositions about the universe ("ideologies"), but also organized schemas for enacting (culturally typical) relations and situations.

I argued further that these schemas (as I now prefer to call them) often take on an ordering function, achieving a degree of generality and transferability across a variety of social situations. Thus I showed that the Sherpas of Nepal use a scenario, or schema, of hospitality to structure a wide variety of social encounters: ordinary social interactions, where the host or hostess is simply "being social"; pressure transactions, where the purpose is to get a favor; shamanistic séances for curing the sick; rituals of offerings to the gods for community well-being. In all these contexts, the interaction is structured as a hospitality event, with the sponsoring person(s) defined as the host(s), the recipient(s) of the largesse as the guest(s), and with food and drink served as if the event were a party. Hospitality here is an ordering schema, shaping these interactions in particular ways, endowing them with particular meanings, and setting them up to unfold along more or less predictable lines (Ortner 1970).

The same general idea appeared in that same era in Edward Schieffelin's *The Sorrow of the Lonely and the Burning of the Dancers* (1976), in which the author explored a "cultural scenario" of reciprocity and opposition among the Kaluli of New Guinea, and showed the degree to which the scenario orders a range of social and ritual interactions. Perhaps the most complex work centered on this sort of idea was Victor Turner's *Dramas, Fields, and Metaphors* (1974), in which Turner showed the persistent force of what he called "root paradigms" (such as martyrdom in Christianity) in various religious traditions.[1]

These earlier writings on cultural schemas of various sorts are stamped with the preoccupations of their intellectual era. For one thing, they are synchronic. In both Schieffelin's and my writings on the subject, there is virtually no history. Scenarios are shown to order action across cultural domains, but not across time. Since Turner looks at European history, his work has a slightly more historical flavor, but it too is essentially synchronic, since he concentrates on historical moments, rather than on processes of change.

Further, the works tend not to question the sources of reproduction of the schemas, leaving them floating in a Platonic realm of ideal forms. We see what the schemas structure, but we rarely see what structures (and potentially changes) the schemas.

And finally, it does seem to be the case (as Fox et al. would charge) that these earlier writings present an overly constraining and deterministic view of key scenarios or root paradigms, almost as if they produced a programming effect on actors. On the surface, Turner seems more contemporary on this point. He specifically denies seeing "social dynamics as a set of 'performances' produced by 'program'" and sounds at times much like the modern political economists in claiming that "if there is order, it is seldom preordained (though transiently bayonets may underpin some political schema); it is achieved—the result of conflicting or concurring wills and intelligences" (p. 14). Yet for him, as for the others, the cultural schemas seem to stamp themselves upon social action in a somewhat mysterious but mechanical manner.

The whole idea of cultural schemas went dormant for a while, but it has recently resurfaced in a number of specifically historical studies,

[1] See also Fernandez's discussion of rituals as "scenarios" for the enactment and realization of metaphoric predication (1974).

with the argument that the events of history may be structured by cultural schemas in much the same way as social behavior is across synchronic contexts. In both Clifford Geertz's *Negara* (1980) and Marshall Sahlins's *Historical Metaphors and Mythical Realities* (1981) we find the notion that there are cultural patterns of action, cultural dramas or scenarios, that reappear over time, and that seem to order the ways in which people play out both conventional and historically novel social encounters. In *Negara*, Geertz talks of the reconstruction of forms, and the "transcriptions of a fixed ideal." He shows the way in which the shape of the Balinese state was fixed by a cultural schema over a period of nearly 600 years:

> Over larger periods of time or over larger stretches of space, major shifts in political fortune could and did, of course, take place. . . . But for all that, the characteristic form seems to have reconstructed itself continually, as Balinese theory claims that it should; new courts modeled themselves on vanished ones, reemerging under different names and in different places as but further transcriptions of a fixed ideal. . . . The scale of things varied, and their brilliance, but not, so far as I can see, between, say, 1343 and 1906, what they were all about. (1980: 134)

As for Sahlins, he writes of "structures of the long run" (Braudel's [1980] phrase), and of the replaying of "a cosmological drama." He specifically sets about showing that a cultural script, embodied in myth and ritual, ordered the ways in which Hawaiians dealt with certain novel historical events:

> At the great annual Makahiki festival, the concept of political usurpation is set in the context of a cosmological drama. The lost god-chief Lono returns to renew the fertility of the land, reclaiming it as his own, to be superseded again by the ruling chief and the sacrificial cult of Ku. Now Captain Cook's second visit to the Islands coincided with the annual return of Lono, and the treatment Hawaiians accorded him corresponded to the prescribed sequence of ritual events in the Makahiki Festival. (1981: 17)

Geertz and Sahlins thus effectively respond to the critique that a cultural schema perspective is ahistorical. Indeed, the main point is to show that a significant part of history itself is ordered by these sorts of cultural forms. This will be one of the main points of the present paper as well.

But the other two charges remain unanswered, and I shall try to tackle them in this essay. Thus I shall try to show that cultural schemas are grounded in particular practices, that they are as much structured as structuring. My view of the reproduction of schemas through practice parallels Bourdieu's (1977) on the reproduction of *habitus*, although the notion of a schema is less formalistic than the notion of *habitus*.

The third charge concerns the overly deterministic or "programming" view of cultural schemas—clearly the most problematic aspect of the concept from the standpoint of Fox, Wolf, and company. My position here is that a cultural schema represents a hegemonic selection, ordering, and "freezing" of a variety of cultural practices into a particular narrative shape, by virtue of their representation in cultural stories—myths, legends, folktales, histories, and so forth. Moreover, schemas represent a positive valuation of that particular ordering of those practices, by virtue of the fact that the stories are about heroism, about the accomplishment of culturally important deeds. Schemas do form, to use Wolf's term, a symbolic ecology within which people operate. But it is an ordered and weighted ecology, not a realm of free symbolic choices ordered only after the fact by the interests of the moment. In the end, then, my conception of schemas will give actors more room for choice and agency than they seemed to have in the older versions of this concept, but less than Fox and Wolf want to assume. Actors *both* manipulate their culture *and* are constrained by it.

The Political Economy of Monastery Founding

In the second decade of the twentieth century, the Sherpas of Nepal began building celibate Buddhist monasteries. Although they had always practiced a folk form of Tibetan Buddhism, they had never, until the twentieth century, had these more orthodox institutions. In the larger project of which this paper is a part (Ortner 1989 and n.d.), I consider both sides of the problem: the forces behind the foundings of the monasteries on the one hand, and the consequences of the foundings—many of them unintended—on the other.[2] The present

[2] Oral history interviewing was conducted for five months in 1979 in Khumbu, Solu, and Kathmandu, Nepal, with support from a National Science Foundation research grant and from the University of Michigan. The historical work in turn builds upon 21 months of ethnographic fieldwork in 1966–68 and 1976. I thank His Majesty's Government of Nepal, and the Center for Nepal and Asian Studies of Tribhuwan University, for permission to carry out the research.

essay considers only the first half of the problem—why and how the monasteries came to be founded—and then emphasizes only the cultural dimension of that problem. But this emphasis does not deny, and indeed complements, political-economic considerations, which must be surveyed all too quickly here.

The Sherpas are a Tibeto-Burman-speaking ethnic group now numbering about 23,000 people. Over half of them reside in their home area in northeast Nepal, in the immediate environs of Mount Everest. They inhabit two connected regions—an upper, colder, higher region called Khumbu, and a (slightly) warmer, lower, and more fertile region called Solu. Their ancestors are thought to have left Kham in eastern Tibet in 1480–90, and to have moved into their present region of Solu-Khumbu, Nepal, around 1533 (Oppitz 1968: 78). In terms of language, religion, and general cultural patterns they remain closely related to Tibetans, and distinct from the Indo-European-speaking Hindu Nepalese who are the dominant ethnic group in Nepal.

The Sherpa economy includes agriculture (mostly wheat and potatoes), herding (mostly yak and cow), some trading with Tibet (much diminished since the 1959 Chinese occupation of Tibet), and cash labor for western mountaineering and tourism expeditions. Economic production is based in the nuclear family, which owns its own land and herds. There is no formal system of stratification of any sort, nor any formal political organization. There are, however, wealthy "big people," who make most of their money through external trade.[3] In the past, including the period covered here, the "big" sector also supplied the tax collectors for the Nepal state, and the tax collecting constituted a form of extraction of wealth (used primarily to capitalize trade), thus playing a significant role in keeping the "big people" big and the "small people" small.[4]

Before considering the political economy of the foundings of the first monasteries, it is important to convey just how novel the found-

[3] For more on the role of "big people" in Sherpa and Tibetan politics, see Samuel 1982.
[4] The point about taxes and trade is drawn from a model of the Sherpa political economy developed in Ortner 1989. For more details on Sherpa production and wealth, apart from political relations, see von Fürer-Haimendorf 1975; other general works on the Sherpas include Funke 1969; von Fürer-Haimendorf 1964, 1984; Oppitz 1968; Ortner 1970, 1978; Paul 1970, 1982.

ings were in relation to the existing religious system. The folk or popular form of Sherpa religion consisted, and still does, of the performance of a variety of rituals in households and in village temples, by religious specialists called lamas. The village lamas are married, have families, and support themselves in the same way as any other villager. (They do get fees for performing rituals, but this supplements, rather than replaces, their own subsistence production.)

Monastic religion is very different from village religion. In contrast to the married lamas, based in villages and focusing their ritual activities in village temples for the well-being of the lay people, monks in monasteries are celibate, do no subsistence labor, and are supported by others (among the Sherpas, usually by their natal families). They orient their religious activities first toward their own salvation, second toward the well-being of the monastic order, and only last toward the well-being of the people at large. Further, monastic religion, with its emphasis on celibacy and on a more stringent morality oriented toward rebirth and salvation, has much greater prestige than village religion. The foundings of monasteries thus represented a major reordering of the Sherpa religious landscape, in terms of both its organization and the greater prestige of monastic (otherworldly) values.

The historical background to the foundings of the monasteries begins in the mid-nineteenth century, in north India and central Nepal.[5] In India after the mutiny of 1857, the British crown took over direct control of the colony, and the period 1858–1920 was one of rapidly expanding economic development (as well as repeated and severe famines). A relevant instance of such development, for present purposes, was the expansion of tea plantations in the Darjeeling area, 100 miles east of the Sherpa region in Nepal. Further, in the Darjeeling area, as throughout much of the rest of the country, the British began building the infrastructure of development—roads and railroads (Dozey 1922). Although Sherpas do not appear to have got

[5] I especially thank Lindsay French, then graduate student in anthropology at the University of Michigan, for preparing preliminary bibliographies and issue papers for me on mid-nineteenth-century Nepal and the Darjeeling-Kalimpong region of India with reference to the historical implications for the Sherpas. In general the research for the entire project involved oral sources (oral history, ethnography) and published sources, rather than archival work. This decision is explained in some detail in Ortner 1989 but the short version is that there were no apparent archival resources to turn to.

much involved in tea plantation labor, some Sherpas went to the Dar-jeeling area and made money either as laborers or as labor contractors for the British construction projects.

In addition to generating income directly, the development activity in north India created something of an economic boom in southeast and east Nepal (Regmi 1978: 190). The expansion in the economies in both the southeast and east would have created very favorable con-ditions for Sherpa traders operating, as they had been for several cen-turies, between their own high, cold region in northeast Nepal, the warmer and more fertile regions of south and southeast Nepal, and the Tibetan plateau on the other side of the Himalayas.[6]

One other aspect of the British presence on the subcontinent af-fected the Sherpa economy: The Sherpas got the first seed tubers for what is now their staple crop, the potato, from the British Resident's garden in either Kathmandu or Sikkim in about 1850 (von Fürer-Haimendorf 1964: 9). The potato, originally an Andean crop, took well to the high altitudes of the upper Sherpa region of Khumbu, and further contributed to the general expansion of the economy that be-gan taking place at this time.

To the west of the Sherpa area, in central Nepal, other develop-ments of importance for our story took place (see especially Burghart 1984; English 1985; Regmi 1978; Rose and Scholtz 1980). In the mid-nineteenth century a family called Rana, which had been pro-viding prime ministers to the kings of Nepal, took all effective power from the king and installed its own people as hereditary rulers. Ap-parently this move was part of a large complex of reactions to the Brit-ish presence in India and represented a successful attempt to secure Nepal against British occupation. The Ranas began to rationalize tax collections throughout the country, largely for the purpose of lining their own pockets more effectively. The taxation system was a variety of tax farming, or tax contracting, which allows collectors to keep whatever they can collect over and above the assessments for the pay-ers on their list. Such a system, as has been widely observed, fre-quently works to enrich the local collectors (e.g. Regmi 1978).

---

[6] The primary commodity imported from Tibet by the Sherpa traders was salt. Wool, cattle, and horses were also brought down. The primary Sherpa export com-modities were iron (mined not far from the Sherpa area until the 1930's) and lowland grains (mostly from southern Nepal)—rice, maize, and millet. Many lesser commod-ities also traveled both ways (von Fürer-Haimendorf 1975: ch. 3).

Among the Sherpas, the collectors tended to be the big traders who were apparently doing well anyway as a result of the economic expansion in south and southeast Nepal generated by British activity in north India.

The first two Sherpa monasteries were founded in the context of these events. The first, called Tengboche, was founded in 1916, and the second, called Chiwong, was founded in 1923.[7] At the very least, the economic changes described would have provided some of the material conditions for the foundings. The general increase in wealth brought about by the introduction of the potato created some of the surplus necessary to build them (von Fürer-Haimendorf 1964: 10). The dramatic increase in the wealth of the traders and tax collectors would have had the same effect, and would have perhaps been even more important than the potato in the long run. Sherpa monks are supported primarily by their families, rather than by begging (the orthodox method) or by taxation (the standard means of support in Tibet). Monks therefore tend to come from the wealthier families, and the growth of wealth of these families in the late nineteenth and early twentieth centuries would have allowed them to more easily support their sons in lifelong monastic careers.

But the rapidly expanding economic situation of the Sherpas as a whole and the big people in particular did more than facilitate the monastery foundings; arguably, it motivated them. Here one must sort out the points of view of the various sectors of Sherpa society involved: the high religious leaders, the "big people," the "small people," and the young monks and nuns. Obviously all of these groups cannot be covered in this paper; I will concentrate here on the perspective and role of the big people.

The big people put up most of the money for the foundings (the religious people put up ideas and leadership; the small people put up mostly labor). I noted earlier that throughout much of Sherpa history, some of the wealthy big people became tax collectors (the Sherpa term used was *pembu*, "governor") for the Nepal state. While not all big

---

[7] For Chiwong, David Snellgrove implies 1915–17 (1957: 217). Sangye Tenzing gives 1917, or the Tibetan year *me dul*, or Fire Snake (1971: 31); he was also emphatic about this date in conversation in the field. A document at the monastery gives 1917. Despite all this authority, however, I have concluded that the monastery was actually begun in 1923, as Kathryn March (1977, 1979) also suggests. See Ortner 1989 for the arguments.

people became pembu, many of them did, and in any event all pembu came from this sector of Sherpa society. In fact, three of the four main sponsors of the first two monasteries were pembu tax collectors.

The late nineteenth century had contradictory implications for the political situation of the big people. On the one hand, as we have seen, they were getting wealthier, in many cases dramatically so. On the other hand, their political position actually began to deteriorate. The many reasons for decline can only be sketched in the briefest of lines here: Their growing wealth was itself a negative factor in the eyes of others; the Rana regime in Kathmandu was doing its best to keep them from gaining too much power and hence too much autonomy from the state; the wage-earning small people coming back from Dar-jeeling now had independent economic means and new ideas, and so forth. In short, the big people were having a growing problem of le-gitimacy in the Sherpa community.

Founding a religious institution in turn has enormous legitimating capacity in Sherpa culture. Virtually nothing is more morally worthy than expending one's own material resources on an institution de-signed for the benefit of all members of society, and indeed, for "all sentient beings." Although in practice, most monks were to come from the better-off families, in principle the monasteries were and are open to all and, by adhering to high moral standards, generate vast amounts of merit for all. Other, and deeper, aspects of legitimation are beyond the scope of this discussion, but even at this level it is clear that monasteries could offer powerful solutions to the legitimacy problems of the big people.

The rising wealth and declining legitimacy of the big people, and the brilliant way in which monastery founding can convert excess money into positive social esteem, constitutes one strand of the political-economic argument about why (and how and when and by whom) the Sherpa monasteries got founded. There is absolutely noth-ing wrong with an argument couched in these terms, and indeed I hope and assume that the argument is right in both its general form and its specific linkages. Yet, as I shall try to show for the remainder of the paper, the argument is incomplete and in many ways impov-erished. Missing are both the human element—the stories of real people in real relationships—and the cultural element—the symbolic frames through which these people understood and responded to events.

Let me start with the cultural material before getting to the individuals. A large body of cultural data, ignored by this analysis, reveals that the Sherpas have their own notions of why and how religious institutions (including monasteries) get founded. These do not exclude the motives of prestige and legitimation, and in that sense are not radically divergent from the anthropologist's analytic perspective. But they systematically recontextualize the significance of outside forces (like British economics and Rana politics), and they reveal a much more complex and profound relationship between politics and religion than is grasped by an account that is, like the one just given, essentially rational and instrumental.

The Cultural Schema of Political-Religious Triumph

The foundings of the ancient noncelibate temples. The cultural materials in question are a set of stories of the foundings of the first noncelibate temples in the late seventeenth and early eighteenth centuries.[8] The foundings of these temples were in certain ways analogous to the foundings of the monasteries in the twentieth century in terms of overall social import. Although it is difficult to get a clear picture of early Sherpa religion, it appears that, prior to the foundings of the early temples, popular religion was largely household and clan based. When the temples were founded, on the other hand, they appear to have stood outside the kinship structure, being based on a more voluntaristic patron-client relationship between the lamas and the affiliated families. The temples thus stood, at least initially, outside the established order, much as the monasteries would later do. In addition, a prestige differential apparently pertained, in that the lamas associated with the temples (like the monks of the monasteries today) were viewed as having greater ritual potency than the local village lamas.

If the foundings of the temples represented doctrinal or sectarian changes, these are not apparent. Nonetheless, the foundings of the first noncelibate temples were clearly major cultural events, since they were enshrined in a fairly extensive body of folklore that is still told

---

[8] The dates are contested. Again see Ortner 1989 for a justification of this choice among the proposed alternatives.

today. And it is from this body of folklore about early temple found-ings that I will extract what may be called a cultural schema of re-ligious institution founding. I will first show that these stories unfold in a certain fixed pattern. I will then suggest that the pattern reappears in certain ritual and social (inheritance, political succession) prac-tices, and may be considered to be grounded in those practices. Finally I will show that the pattern or schema reappears in, and seems to be structuring, much of the activity that culminates in the foundings of the celibate monasteries in the early twentieth century.

The story I will use here is the story of the founding of the temple in what is now Zhung, a village in the lower valley of Solu. Three other early Sherpa temples, built in the same period, have similar stories about their foundings, so the tale of the Zhung temple is by no means atypical. Here is a condensed version of the tale, put together from several different, but not conflicting, versions collected in the field.

The villain of the tale is a certain Lama Gombu, a practicing re-ligious specialist and also a pembu, in the lower Sherpa region of Solu. Lama Gombu is described as "rich and famous." The hero is a younger man, Dorje Zangbu, described as "not rich, but talented and clever," and apparently aspiring to "big" status himself. After young Dorje Zangbu's father dies, the pembu Lama Gombu sees Dorje Zangbu as a future competitor, and works out an elaborate plan to kill him by causing him to fall from a cliff. (The cliff is at Chiwong, later to be the site of the twentieth-century monastery.) Dorje Zangbu foils the plan and escapes to Tibet, where he studies religion and be-comes a powerful lama. On his way back to Solu-Khumbu, he meets a high reincarnate lama who gives him a powerful tutelary god in the form of a very sacred idol, and who says to Dorje Zangbu, "Now you can do anything. Now you can triumph."

Dorje Zangbu then returns to the home of his mother's brother, who is described as "very rich." The mother's brother devises a plan to humiliate and defeat Lama Gombu, who had tried to kill his sister's son earlier. The mother's brother invites Lama Gombu to his house to perform a certain ritual, but when Lama Gombu performs the ritual, he fails to achieve the necessary psychospiritual state. Meanwhile, Dorje Zangbu has been sitting silently in the lowest status position in the room, disguised as a beggar. Here I will translate, with only minor editorial changes, a piece of the text recorded on one occasion.

And Lama Gombu sang and danced and beat his drum but did not have any success in achieving identification with the gods. The mother's brother said to him, "You're supposed to be such a powerful lama, but you can't do anything. Shame on you. Whoever is more powerful, you or a certain person of my sister's husband's clan [Dorje Zangbu]—only under him will we place ourselves." Then he said, "Lama Gombu, you sit down, and now you, beggar, get up." Lama Gombu did not know that the beggar was the certain person in question. "Today we will find out who has a bad heart and who has a good one," said Dorje Zangbu. Then he began dancing. And [he had so much power that] the central offering cake on the altar danced with him. Then Lama Gombu recognized Dorje Zangbu, and was ashamed, and ran away with all his retinue.

Now Dorje Zangbu was elevated, and Lama Gombu was brought low. Before this, Dorje Zangbu was not very famous. But because he made the offering cake dance and did many other magical feats, his reputation became great, like the moon or the sun. Lama Gombu could no longer stay in the Zhung area; he could not stand Dorje Zangbu's success, and he felt great jealousy. Today his lineage is found in villages to the west of Zhung, in Changma and Gyama. And because Lama Gombu actually left, Dorje Zangbu's reputation became even greater.

Dorje Zangbu then moved down from his father's village, and went to Zhung and built the temple.

This is only the stripped-down version of the story. I have left out not only many details of the portion summarized here but also further episodes that take place after the temple is founded, involving in some cases much greater levels of violence than we saw when Lama Gombu tried to kill Dorje Zangbu. (Alexander Macdonald has called the tale "mafia-like" [1980: 145].) Still, the shortened version will be enough for our immediate purposes.

Now let me sketch what I see as the skeletal structure, or the basic plot-schema, of the story, in the form of a series of steps.

Rivalry. An initial pair of characters, whom I will call Ego and Rival, engage in violent, even mortal, competition for political dominance: In this case Lama Gombu (Rival) tries to kill Dorje Zangbu (Ego), whom he sees as potentially displacing him.[9]

[9] According to a version of the tale published by Sangye Tenzing (1971: 33–47), the plot to kill Dorje Zangbu was initiated and carried out not by Lama Gombu himself, but by one of his followers. The follower had heard Lama Gombu and another lama complaining about Dorje Zangbu's rising reputation, and trying to think of ways to discredit him. Lama Gombu tried to dissuade the follower from trying to kill Dorje Zangbu, not on moral grounds, but on the grounds that Dorje Zangbu was too powerful. The follower, however, insisted that he could take care of the matter, and Lama

Departure and the acquisition of a protector. Early on, Ego appears
to be losing. He then goes away and gets a powerful protector:
Dorje Zangbu acquires first the protection of the high reincarnate
lama in Tibet, then that of the god-idol given him by the lama, and
finally that of his rich mother's brother.

Defeat of the rival. With all this protection and patronage, Ego defeats Rival, acquires his subjects—remember Dorje Zangbu's
mother's brother saying that he and his people will place themselves under whoever wins the magical contest—and becomes the
pembu.

Departure of the loser. The loser leaves the area and settles elsewhere: In this case Lama Gombu goes west to the Changma area.

Founding of a temple. Ego builds a religious institution—in this case,
the (noncelibate) Zhung temple.

In addition to appearing in other tales of ancient temple founding,
a variant of the complete plot-schema also appears in certain frequently performed rituals of Sherpa religious practice. These rituals
must be discussed, both to demonstrate the generality of the schema
beyond the folktales of temple founding, and to open the question of
the grounding of the schema in practice.

Rituals for gaining the protection of the gods. The rituals in
question, which we may simply call offering rituals, are performed
with variations with great regularity in Sherpa communities—in
households, village temples, and monasteries.[10] They are performed
at prescribed calendrical times, as well as on occasions of life
crises, especially and extensively at death. The longest, most elaborate, and most dramatic versions of them are enacted annually in
monasteries, in the form of festivals called Mani Rimdu (see Jerstad 1969; Paul 1982). But although the monastic versions are the
most dramatic of the performances, it is important to realize how
often, and in how many contexts, these rituals are performed. They
are part of fundamental Tibetan Buddhist practice, common to the
whole greater Tibetan area, and performed by Sherpas as much

Gombu tacitly agreed to let him try. (Patrick Pranke and Clair [Sandy] Huntington,
graduate students in Buddhist Studies at the University of Michigan, did a working
translation of the Sangye Tenzing book for me. See also Macdonald 1980 for a summary of Sangye Tenzing's version.)

[10]I have dealt with these rituals at length elsewhere: Ortner 1975; Ortner 1978:
ch. 6.

when the early temples were founded in the seventeenth and eighteenth centuries as when the monasteries were founded in the twentieth.[11]

Let us consider how the rituals follow the schema seen in the temple-founding tales.

Rivalry. The basic assumption of the rituals is that people are constantly encroached upon by demons and other evil forces that wish to harm and destroy the world. The antagonistic relationship between people and demons is at least loosely analogous to the relationship between Ego and Rival in the temple-founding tales.

Acquisition of a protector. The rituals further assume that people can only defeat demons by acquiring powerful protectors—the gods. The solicitation of the gods' protection is the very core of the work of the ritual, as the people, through the mediation of religious specialists, lavish the gods with offerings in order to bring them into battle against the demons on the side of humanity.

Defeat of the rival. Since the demons are intrinsically bloody and violent, the gods must adopt violent tactics as well, and when this part of the scenario is fully dramatized (rather than merely recited), the gods, through the vehicles of the lamas and/or monks, violently stab, eviscerate, and chop up representations of the evil forces. At the end of the ritual the demons have been temporarily defeated.

Departure of the loser. The demons cannot actually be killed or wiped out since they are part of the eternal order of existence. They have simply been forced to leave the area, only to infiltrate again later and so to require further ritual struggles.

Here then in the rituals is the basic schema that we saw in the tales: an initial relationship of enduring antagonism, the acquisition of protection that allows the good side to triumph, and the departure of the loser. There is even a link with the temple-founding step of the schema in these rituals, as there is in the case of the oral folklore. The link is present in two ways. First, the altar of the offering ritual is constructed on the same cosmic plan (the mandala) as the space of a temple. Indeed, the altar is said to be, among other things, a temporary temple

[11] That rituals are ancient can no longer be facilely assumed. We now recognize that some supposedly timeless rituals were only recently invented (see Hobsbawm and Ranger 1983). On the other hand, historical research is also beginning to demonstrate the extraordinary durability of at least some rituals (see, for example, Bloch 1986).

(also palace and heaven) for the gods called in for the occasion. Since a new altar is constructed for each performance of the ritual, every performance is also a symbolic temple founding. Perhaps more importantly, offering rituals are said to have originated in the context of the founding of a religious institution. Thus it is told in another tale, widely known among both Tibetans and Sherpas, that the ritual was originally taught to people when they were trying to build Samye, the very first Buddhist monastery in Tibet, in the eighth century.[12] According to a version of the legend told by a Solu lama, the people would work hard all day on the building, but at night the demons would come and tear down all their work. The people appealed to the Guru Rimpoche, the founder of Tibetan Buddhism, for help. He replied, in effect, "Of course you are having trouble, for you have not got the gods on your side." So he taught them how to perform the offering rituals to acquire the gods' protection, and then with the gods' help the demons were kept at bay and the monastery was finished very quickly (Ortner 1978: 85–86). Once again, then, the offering rituals, structured on the same cultural schema as the temple-founding folklore, are also themselves legendarily connected with the founding of a temple.[13]

Several points may be drawn from this brief discussion. First, the parallels between the plot structure of the rituals and the plot structure of the temple-founding tales strongly support the claim that a generalized cultural schema is at work here. Second, we may take the performance of the rituals as one of several ways in which the schema is grounded in practice, that is to say, in real, sensuous activity. Of course, telling the tales of the foundings is itself a form of practice. Yet one must perhaps privilege the rituals over the storytelling as a major locus of reproduction, for several reasons. First, the rituals are far more frequently and regularly performed than the stories are told. Second, the rituals are more materially consequential. If the rituals are not done, evil consequences (crop failure, etc.) may follow,

[12] Samye is famous for its perfect mandala shape.

[13] A Tibetan version given by L. Austine Waddell begins with the Guru Rimpoche performing the ritual in the presence of the royal sponsor of the monastery, King Thi-Srong Detsan. The "devils" then assist with the building of the temple. The king is astonished to see the demons so pacified, whereupon the Guru Rimpoche performs the ritual again, in such a way as to enable the king to see and feel directly the fearful power of the gods as mobilized by the ritual (1959: 266–67n).

whereas if the stories are not told, no consequences are said to ensue. And finally, the rituals are often (though not always) performed under circumstances of heightened emotional sensitivity, during funerals, for example, and during festivals. For all these reasons, then, one must take the rituals as one of several crucial loci of the reproduction of this very general—and apparently very durable—cultural schema.

The social grounding of the schema. Beyond the realm of religious legend and ritual, the schema does not appear in complete form. Yet its components, and specifically its patterns of rivalrous interaction, appear in other aspects of Sherpa social life. These too must be taken as sites in which the cultural schema is at least in part reproduced as a meaningful mode of organizing social relations and historical action.

Chronic rivalry has been a continuing feature of both sibling relations and political relations in Sherpa society. Taking siblingship first, according to inheritance rules, all brothers are supposed to get equal shares of the parental estate—land and herds. When applied rigorously over time, this rule tends to produce excessive land fragmentation, with parcels too small to support a family. Thus in some cases a brother simply has to go away and find other means of support. Moreover, the equal inheritance rule creates many opportunities for fraternal friction, even when there is enough land to go around. To give each brother a precisely equal share is difficult, creating frequent occasions for a given (usually middle) brother to feel less favored. Once again, then, the solution has been for the discontented brother to go away, both to make a better stake for himself and to escape the strained relationship with his brothers. From the point of view of fraternal relations, then, the schema of rivalry seen in folklore and ritual would make sense.

We see a similar pattern in Sherpa political relations. Succession to political position was (and still is, to a great extent) a do-it-yourself affair. Individuals from the big sector competitively sought to set themselves up as pembu, with rights to collect gifts, labor, and taxes. Although an existing pembu might try to pass his position down to his son, and might succeed in doing so if serious contenders were lacking, in general patrilineal succession was not a well-established principle, and anyone who felt he had the power to succeed could mount a challenge. Thus the political order, like the kinship/inheritance order, was inherently generative of competition and rivalry. Moreover, the key to success was, more obviously than in the case of fraternal relations, to gain the backing of a powerful protector. When the Sherpas were under state control, the successful pembu was the person who succeeded in gaining the backing of the state. Lamas who became pembu claimed superior supernatural protection as well, from tutelary gods who helped them defeat their rivals. The secular or supernatural protection that allowed a pembu to defeat his rival in turn allowed him to claim that he was offering his clients superior protection from whatever ills they feared—worse pembu, worse state officials, worse gods.

Most of the components of the temple-founding narrative—recurrent rivalries, protectors who help the hero to triumph, defeats that cause the loser to leave the area—are thus grounded in recognizable practices of ordinary social life. The organization of fraternal relations, particularly concerning inheritance, produces inequities and rivalries for which the best solution appears to be the departure of the losing brother. The organization of political relations also produces chronic rivalry and competitive challenge, and here again losers tend to leave. Political actors also count heavily on the acquisition of protectors, both for support in defeating a rival and for buttressing claims of one's value to one's clients.

Of course if these practices can be said to ground the cultural schema of political-religious triumph, they are at the same time shaped by that schema. For both inheritance and succession, alternative arrangements were possible and were part of local knowledge. Brothers could have shared property (in Tibet polyandrous brothers held undivided estates); leadership could have been (and sometimes was) passed on through patrilineal succession. The particular patterns that have emerged thus reflect choices that have been ordered as much by culture as by any material necessity. In other words, the cultural schema shapes the practices as much as the practices ground the schema.

I think this circularity is real and must be recognized analytically. Any effort to posit a permanent "base" and a permanent "superstructure," and thus to mechanize cultural interpretation and analysis, is doomed to failure. At the same time we must be able to talk about the grounding of abstract structures in human experience and human practices. These practices may be "economic," or "political," or "religious," or whatever, but their common feature is that they are modes of actors' experience and activity in the world.

Put in other words, cultural schemas (structures, scenarios, paradigms, etc.) must be recognized as real on the one hand, and demystified on the other. They are real in that they operate as generalizable ordering principles in a given culture: People find them useful, sensible, "natural" ways of understanding and acting. One may even say that schemas are "in people's heads." Yet ultimately they get "into people's heads" and become part of people's repertoires for ordering, experiencing, and acting on the world, as a result of their enactment in real lived forms—in stories that are told, rituals that are performed, kinship and political relations that are practiced. (See also Bourdieu's discussion of the "dialectic of the internalization of externality and the externalization of internality" [1977: 72].)

Whether some practices in turn are more crucial than others to the reproduction of a given cultural schema at a given historical moment is largely an empirical question. I noted earlier that in this case rituals have probably been more important than stories (and on a par with fraternal and political practices), since they are more regularly performed than stories, often in more emotional contexts, and in principle more materially consequential. But this situation may well be changing. The folklore of temple founding has become more important in recent years within a discourse of the value of "old" and "historical" things, generated largely in response to touristic and scholarly questioning. Thus these stories are being more frequently told and are acquiring material consequence (in terms of touristic donations to religious institutions), while the performance of the rituals may well be declining in frequency.

And now we must return to the twentieth-century monastery foundings. I will show that this same cultural schema seemed to be operating even in the context of very novel historical circumstances—the heightened development activity in north India of the British raj, and the increased efficiency of the Rana state apparatus in Kathmandu—and that the schema played a significant role in shaping the events culminating in the foundings of the monasteries. Here I will also deal with the final question concerning the use of this approach: How can we recognize that actors may be constrained in certain ways by cultural schemas and yet not be "tyrannized" by them?

The Foundings of the Twentieth-Century Monasteries

The world-system situation surrounding Solu-Khumbu, was profoundly different at the turn of the twentieth century from what it had been at the turn of the eighteenth. I indicated earlier that the British raj and the Rana-run state were creating conditions that were dramatically enriching the Sherpa big people of Solu-Khumbu, yet at the same time undermining their legitimacy in various ways. The British were generating improved economic opportunities for the small people as well, a fact that was indirectly having a destabilizing effect on big people–small people relations. The big people's sponsorship of the foundings of the monasteries can easily be seen as a practical attempt to firm up their weakening legitimacy.

This argument, I also said, is not necessarily wrong, but it is thin. Emphasizing social sectors (big people, small people), it loses specific actors and their complex intentionalities. Further, it does not attend to the cultural frames within which the people themselves understood and acted upon their situation. Most of the people involved are now dead and cannot be asked about their understandings and intentions. Yet we may look carefully at their actions during the events in question, and we may interpret from those actions at least some of the assumptions upon which they were operating. And when we do look at their actions, we find an interesting pattern: The big men of the twentieth century appear to have followed a course of conduct based on the same schema that underlay the foundings of the Zhung and other noncelibate temples in the eighteenth century. In this section, then, I will show as far as possible the structuring effect of the cultural schema on the general patterning of events surrounding the foundings of the monasteries. In the following section I will confront the "tyranny" question, and attempt to lay out the ways a structuring effect may operate without rendering actors cultural puppets.

Tengboche, the first monastery, was founded in 1916. There were three primary lay sponsors, all of whom were quite wealthy. The senior figure of the group was a man called Karma, who was the eldest son of a tax collector, and who inherited the collectorship from his father. In addition, Karma was given another government post by the Rana regime, the stewardship of a government cattle farm in his home region of Solu. Karma was also very clever at trade, devising novel strategies for getting around certain trading restrictions in order to eliminate middlemen and maximize his own profit. Although his father (a married lama as well as a tax collector) is described as having been moderately well off, Karma built up a much larger fortune in the late nineteenth century.

The other two men involved in the founding of Tengboche were also traders who had built up substantial wealth. One of them, called Kusang, married Karma's daughter. The other, called Tsepal, was both a successful trader and a tax collector, ultimately becoming the head tax collector (*gembu*) for the entire Sherpa region.[14]

The second monastery, Chiwong, had a single major sponsor, Karma's younger brother Sangye. Sangye went off to Darjeeling as a young man and made a great deal of money contracting labor for British road-building projects. He returned to the Solu area, where he did some trade for a while, but then took over his older brother's positions as tax collector and as steward of the government cattle farm. According to most informants (although some of Sangye's and Karma's most influential descendants deny it), the two were extremely competitive with one another, and Sangye actively sought to undermine his older brother's position by getting the two government jobs transferred to himself.[15] Sangye made the biggest fortune of all during this period and singlehandedly sponsored the founding of Chiwong, a move itself taken to be a competitive response to Karma's founding of Tengboche.

Most informants take the rivalry between the brothers Karma and Sangye to be central to the stories of the foundings. Sangye's political displacement of his older brother in effect triggered the whole history, since it was after Karma's "defeat" that he went off to a meditation retreat in Khumbu, where he connected with the lamas who drew him and his wealth into the scheme to found Tengboche.

The rivalry between Karma and Sangye was largely irrelevant to the political-economic interpretation of the foundings of the mon-

[14] Most of these actors were also involved in the founding of Devuche, the first Sherpa nunnery, in 1925. Devuche was conceived as a branch of Tengboche. See Ortner 1983.

[15] I especially thank Dr. Harka Gurung for arranging and facilitating interviews with two of these influential descendants (Ang Dandi Lama and Tsering Tenzing Lama) for me.

asteries, but it turns up repeatedly in the microlevel stories of the foundings and indeed was forecast by the ancient temple-founding stories examined earlier. In those stories, as in these events, the foundings of religious institutions begin with political rivalry and conflict. As I will now try to show, both the story of the founding of Tengboche and the story of the founding of Chiwong can appear as virtual reenactments, with only minor transformations, of the story of the founding of the Zhung temple, and more generally of the cultural schema of political conflict and temple founding.

We begin with the founding of Tengboche. Told first with Karma as Ego, the story goes like this. Karma and Sangye were apparently on good terms in their early life. Together they sponsored the founding of a residence hall for Sherpa monks at the Tibetan monastery at Tashilhunpo. But they came into conflict later over Karma's government positions. In his later life, Karma became more actively and personally religious. He moved to the meditation retreat created by a Khumbu lama named Lama Gulu and apparently undertook some religious training and spiritual exercises. When Lama Gulu was approached by a Tibetan lama (the Zatul Rimpoche, about whom more below) to found the first celibate monastery in Solu-Khumbu, Lama Gulu in turn asked the wealthy Karma to become a financial sponsor, and Karma eagerly agreed.

The story has all the elements of the temple-founding schema discussed earlier.

Rivalry. There is an initial rivalrous relationship between Ego (here Karma) and Rival (here Sangye). Sangye attempts to displace Karma through devious means, cultivating Karma's political contacts in Kathmandu and getting Karma's positions transferred to himself.

Acquisition of a protector. Karma goes off to Lama Gulu's retreat. While studying there, he develops a close relationship with the lama, thereby acquiring the protection of the lama's religious teacher, the revered and religiously powerful Zatul Rimpoche.

Defeat of the rival. Under the Zatul Rimpoche's protection, Karma stages a triumph of prestige over his younger brother Sangye, by sponsoring the founding of the first Sherpa monastery.

Founding of a religious institution. Karma founds Tengboche.

Departure of the loser. Sangye founds Chiwong in response to Karma's founding of Tengboche, then builds himself a house near the monastery. He thus moves away from his and Karma's natal village and never returns.

The events of the founding of Tengboche thus seem to fit the schema laid out earlier. Most of the classic elements are present: the rivalry between political figures who are also brothers; the role of the protector in the triumph of one over the other; the founding of a religious institution; the departure of the loser.

If we look at the roles of the religious figures involved in the Tengboche founding, the pattern appears again. We may begin with Lama Gulu. Lama Gulu was a married lama who had had an unhappy marital career. Late in life, after the death of his wife, he decided to take monastic vows and went over the Tibetan border to Rumbu monastery to do so. The head of the monastery was the Zatul Rimpoche, by all accounts a man of extraordinary energy, zeal, and charisma. He himself had founded the monastery at Rumbu only a decade or so earlier, in 1902, on a site on the lower north slope of Mount Everest, where until then only a few meditation huts had stood. He had also built up a large following in the surrounding D'ing-ri region, although he was only 26 years old when he founded the monastery (Aziz 1978: 209–15).

Though himself a Tibetan, the Zatul Rimpoche now suggested to the Sherpa Lama Gulu that the Sherpas needed, and could afford to have, their own monasteries in their own Solu-Khumbu region, and he told Lama Gulu to found one. The apparently modest Lama Gulu at first resisted, feeling that the task was beyond him, but eventually he was persuaded by the Zatul Rimpoche (see also von Fürer-Haimendorf 1964).

The first monks of Tengboche were four Sherpa men who had, like Lama Gulu, taken vows at Rumbu monastery. How they came to form the first cohort of Tengboche monks provides another important piece of the story. It seems that there had been another Sherpa man who had taken vows in Tibet (but not apparently at Rumbu), a monk called the Zamte Lama. The Zamte Lama had returned to Khumbu and gathered about himself a small celibate community, with the four monks in question as his first disciples. He was of both higher social status and higher religious status than Lama Gulu, and in retrospect was a more likely candidate than Lama Gulu to head the first Sherpa monastery. Unlike Lama Gulu, however, he did not have the backing of the revered Zatul Rimpoche, and so—it seems—was passed over.

His four monks joined the new Tengboche community, and he himself left the Sherpa area, dropping veiled threats of supernatural retribution. He is said to have become the personal lama of the king of Sikkim, and he never returned to Solu-Khumbu.

Now let us recast these events in the terms of the schema.

Rivalry. Lama Gulu, the Ego of the story in this context, is a modest but respected religious man whose reputation is on the rise. The Zamte Lama, here in the position of Rival, is from a higher-status family and is Lama Gulu's senior in religious terms since he took his monastic vows earlier than Lama Gulu. Although not directly antagonistic, the two are in implicit competition for the leadership of the newly emerging monastic community in the region at the time.

Acquisition of a protector. Although Lama Gulu does not depart in any way that is significant for the story, he does acquire a powerful protector—the Zatul Rimpoche—while the Zamte Lama does not.

Defeat of the rival. Lama Gulu defeats the Zamte Lama by being chosen to become the founder and head of the first Sherpa monastery, Tengboche. There is even an element here that we have not seen since the story of the founding of the Zhung temple: In defeating the Zamte Lama, Lama Gulu takes over all the Zamte Lama's "subjects"—the four Zamte disciples, who now become the first four Tengboche monks.

Founding of a religious institution. Lama Gulu founds Tengboche.

Departure of the loser. The Zamte Lama leaves the area and never returns.

Once again events seem to parallel the cultural schema seen in the early temple-founding stories and in the offering rituals. But before discussing the ways in which this fit happens, we have one more founding to consider—the founding of Chiwong. We have already given all the elements of the narrative, and may simply show here once again the apparent conformity to the cultural schema.

Rivalry. For Chiwong, we now have Sangye in the position of Ego, with Karma as his Rival. With this inversion, Karma appears as the reigning big man, "rich and powerful," much like Lama Gombu in the Zhung-temple tale. Sangye appears as the rising hero-challenger, much like Dorje Zangbu in the same tale.

Departure. Sangye goes off to Darjeeling, does labor contracting for
the British, and becomes wealthy.

Acquisition of a protector. Sangye returns with his wealth and establishes a relationship with the Rana general in charge of the Solu-
Khumbu region, thus gaining a protector.

Defeat of the rival. The Rana general transfers Karma's offices to
Sangye, who thereby achieves a political defeat of his older
brother.

Departure of the loser. It is apparently at this point that Karma
moves up to Lama Gulu's meditation retreat.

Founding of a religious institution. Sangye undertakes the reconstruction of the noncelibate temple in his home village of Zhung—
his initial triumphant temple founding. Karma founds Tengboche,
a result of a partially separate chain of events. Sangye takes the
founding as a new prestige move on Karma's part and founds Chiwong in return.

Except for the triple temple founding at the end, the story is a virtually
perfect replay of the tale of the Zhung temple founding in the early
eighteenth century. There is a rivalry; Sangye appears to be losing; he
goes away; he gains a protector; he defeats Karma; Karma leaves;
Sangye founds a temple (actually two temples).

The cultural schema of religious-institution founding thus seems
to account for the unfolding of relations among both lay and religious
actors in the events surrounding the foundings of the first monasteries
in Solu-Khumbu. Again and again we see the same pattern of relations played out—of political rivalry and defeat, of antagonism and
protection, of bad losers who leave and big winners who build temples or monasteries. Each actor in effect becomes the hero of the
schema. Karma as Ego gets the Zatul Rimpoche's protection, defeats
his younger brother Sangye, and founds Tengboche monastery. Lama
Gulu as Ego gets the protection of the Zatul Rimpoche as well, defeats
the Zamte Lama, and also founds Tengboche. Sangye as Ego gets
Rana-family protection, defeats his older brother Karma, and founds
Chiwong. From the foundings of the early noncelibate Zhung temple
in the eighteenth century to the foundings of the celibate monasteries
in the twentieth, the same cultural structure appears to be operating,
and to play a powerful role in ordering people's relationships, interpretations, and actions.

Yet if this is indeed the case, then we must face the charges against "culturology": If actors appear to be following a cultural script, have we in effect deprived them of their own agency and intentionality? In order to answer this question, we must consider the way in which a cultural structure comes to do its work.

Modes of Structuring

Understanding how structures structure is vital to the continued theoretical health of various forms of cultural and structural analysis. Without such understanding, interpretations that claim to see reiterated cultural patterning in social and historical events remain open to the charge that such patterning is imposed by the observer, or alternatively that it is an aesthetic frill. If one wishes to argue to the contrary that such patterning not only exists, but may have a historical force of its own on a par with other forces (individual interest, the inner logic of a social formation, adaptation to environmental conditions, etc.) that are said to shape and drive history, then one must show that there is a comprehensible mechanism by means of which cultural patterning comes to manifest itself in events.

The positions on this question form a continuum. At one end is what may be called the "soft" or external position, concerning the way in which cultural structures operate in social interaction. Here the structures exist as "models" or "symbolic resources" external to actors, on which actors may draw in the course of social action. This is essentially the position outlined earlier for Wolf, Fox, and others. At the other end is the "hard" or internal position. Here actors acquire a kind of internal programming, which in turn generates their behavior, or at least the parameters of their behavior. This is essentially Bourdieu's position concerning the *habitus*. And then there is an intermediate position, in which actors may internalize a schema under certain conditions and thus be constrained by its forms, but under other conditions may reestablish a distance between themselves and the schema.

The stories of the foundings of the monasteries illustrate all these possibilities. I will thus discuss each position in a bit more detail, and illustrate the discussion with the stories. As may be surmised, I consider the intermediate position the most reasonable and realistic.

The soft/external position. The general line here is that people are acting on motives that are commonsensically understandable to the analyst, normally (but not always) some form of rational self-interest. The way in which people enact a particular event thus has little to do with a cultural schema like the one discussed here. Insofar as a cultural schema does seem to be operating, its operation is the result of one or another after-the-fact use of the schema—to describe what has happened, for example, or to legitimate what has happened.

The founding of Tengboche told from Karma's point of view fits this description relatively well. It is not clear that Karma ever sought to undermine his brother Sangye, though Sangye clearly thought that Karma did. Moreover, when Karma went off to Lama Gulu's meditation retreat, he was not likely seeking to enhance his powers, gain a protector, and come back to overwhelm Sangye. His engagement to found Tengboche (which Sangye took to be a move of this nature) seems to have been largely accidental, since he was approached by the Zatul Rimpoche and Lama Gulu, rather than having approached them. Thus at no point does it appear that Karma was following the schema. Why then does the story seem to fit the schema as well as it does?

Here we must first remember that a cultural schema is a narrative linkage of cultural bits that may, but need not, co-occur. The narrative gives their co-occurrence a necessity that it does not necessarily have, and gives meaning to the bits in juxtaposition that they do not have alone. Thus, for example, fraternal and/or political rivalry is commonplace among the Sherpas, but it does not always eventuate in monastery founding; similarly, monastery founding does not necessarily presuppose political rivalry. Where there is monastery founding, however, prior rivalries very likely existed, since monastery founding is an activity of big people, and big people tend to be very competitive and rivalrous with one another. In other words, there is a statistical tendency for monastery founding to be preceded by political conflict, and there are also cultural stories that act as if there is a necessary connection between the two. Moreover these stories implicitly ascribe a meaning to the statistical connection: that the founder is expressing triumph and/or dominance at having beaten the rival.

Given the availability of the schema, then, Karma's involvement in the founding of Tengboche, however fortuitous from his point of view, would have suggested to others that a prior conflict existed, in relation to which the founding was an act, and a statement, of winning. Leaving aside for a moment that the founding implied conflict not only to passive observers (who later became the anthropologist's informants) but also to actors directly involved in the events, one may say here that in this context the schema remains entirely external to the events, operating at most to structure people's stories of what happened, but not to structure what actually happened.

A variant of the external position would emphasize that participants themselves may, either during or after the fact, utilize the schema to legitimate their activities to others, without actually being motivated in any internal way by the interactional dynamics of the schema. There is evidence for this position as well. It appears that Sangye intentionally sought to align himself with Dorje Zangbu, the hero of the founding of the Zhung temple, after undermining his brother Karma by taking over Karma's political positions. Thus Sangye's first act of temple building, after Karma left Zhung, was the reconstruction of the Zhung temple itself.[16] Then, when he later decided to found a celibate monastery, he chose the site at Chiwong, where the villain Lama Gombu had tried to trick Dorje Zangbu into falling from a cliff, and where Dorje Zangbu had done the first of his clever and powerful deeds. Though these connections could be accidental, it does not seem too farfetched to suggest that Sangye may have been intentionally linking himself to Dorje Zangbu and his heroism, thereby seeking to legitimate his own newly established dominance of Solu. These legitimating moves in turn would feed the perception among others that prior events (including the foundings) were all generated by the schema, when in fact they may have been generated by a variety of unconnected motives and accidents.

The hard/internal position. The internal position holds that cultural schemas may become deeply embedded in actors' identities as a result of actors' growing up within a particular cultural milieu, and as a result of practices (social, ritual, etc.) that repeatedly nourish the schema and its place within the self. In consequence, actors will tend to "do the cultural thing" under most circumstances, and even sometimes under inappropriate circumstances. This is the position that Fox seems to be attacking, or rather, it is the untheorized psycho-

---

[16] He even rebuilt it twice, since something was wrong with the construction and the temple collapsed the first time it was built. People were discouraged after the collapse, but Sangye managed to rekindle their enthusiasm and get them to build it again.

logical underpinnings of that position. My own view is that none of the writers who appear to hold it—Bourdieu (1977), Geertz (e.g. 1973a, b), Sahlins (1981), myself (1978)— would want to agree that they hold it in this form.[17] Yet in failing to theorize it, that is, in failing to explicate how structures may constrain action and events without programming actors, they allow it to stand as an interpretation of their views. I will sketch such an explanation in a moment, but first I should note that there is some evidence for the hard position as well. A good example seems again to be the story of Sangye.

Sangye, more than any of the others, appears to be driven by the schema. He seems determined to construe his relationship with Karma as rivalrous, even though Karma does not seem to construe it that way (Karma, in fact, makes various efforts at fraternal solidarity, including giving Sangye a position at the government cattle farm). Further, when Sangye returns from Darjeeling with his fortune, he actively seeks the political protection of the Rana general, and it is hard to escape the sense that he has competitive intentions. Next, in competing with Karma he seems determined not only to win, but to win utterly, by taking away not one but both of Karma's positions: the stewardship of the cattle farm (which may have seemed legitimately open to competitive bidding, since it had not been in the family before) as well as the tax collector position (to which Karma, as eldest son, was reasonably entitled). Finally, when Sangye does win, he performs the famous act of triumph: He founds a temple. Then when Karma one-ups him (which seems to be the way Sangye viewed the founding of Tengboche), Sangye simply founds another one, and with a far bigger endowment than Tengboche or any other Sherpa monastery would ever have.

Sangye, then, seems to identify deeply with the culturally heroic role of political victor and religious benefactor, as constructed by the schema. (This view, by the way, somewhat recontextualizes his apparently rational manipulation of the cultural schema for legitima-

[17]Claude Lévi-Strauss is the only one who has explicitly taken a position close to this one, as in this famous passage from *The Raw and the Cooked*: "I therefore claim to show, not how men think in myths, but how myths operate in men's minds without their being aware of the fact. . . . It would perhaps be better to go still further and, disregarding the thinking subject entirely, proceed as if the thinking process were taking place in the myths, in their reflection upon themselves, and their interrelation" (1969: 12).

tion purposes discussed above. But the two modes of relationship to the schema are not necessarily contradictory.) It does not seem implausible to argue that the schema is ordering Sangye's behavior, and thus shaping real events.

The internal/external position. This is a combination of several aspects of the other two positions. We begin with the point, assumed in the external position as well, that people may act for a variety of motives—rational self-interest, genuine spiritual desires, and so forth—with no particular intentions (or compulsions) to enact a cultural schema and no particular tendency to assume that others are doing so either. As with Karma in the first example, they may simply be going about their business.

Now, I said with respect to the "external" position that even if people are not enacting a cultural schema, given the fact that the schema is a widely held and pervasively grounded frame of interpretation, others will tend to interpret events as though the actors had in fact been following the schema—hence, for example, the assumption that if the Zamte Lama went away permanently after his monks moved to Tengboche, he must have felt defeated and angry. But—and this is the key point of the middle position—if observers will tend to interpret events in that way, so of course would at least some of the participants: the Zamte Lama (and there is evidence for this) probably *was* angry. Thus the schema may not initially be part of the events: Lama Gulu was almost certainly not operating on it, and in the Zamte Lama's earlier life he does not appear to have been doing so either. But insofar as the schema becomes part of a participant's interpretations, it enters the event and begins to shape it: The Zamte Lama decided he had been defeated and actually left the area.

To consider further aspects of this suggestion, let us take again the case of the relationship between Karma and Sangye. The case is interesting because some informants claim the brothers were rivalrous while others deny it. The evidence indicates that they were not rivalrous when young but that they likely were when older. As young men, they cooperated in building the Sherpa college at Tashilhunpo, and the young Karma gave Sangye a position at the government cattle farm. Only later are they said by some informants to have had at least one personal confrontation, and of course to have engaged in competitive monastery founding. In other words, at some earlier point they were not operating within the framework of fraternal rivalry, and at some later point they were.

Exactly what happened is probably unknowable. But at some point either Karma or Sangye did something—achieved too much political power, made too much money—that had the feel of competition and potential defeat to the other. One or the other (or both, for that matter) decided that more was at stake now than had previously been assumed, and that they were now in a recognizable mode of serious competitive relations. With that shift in perception, the cultural schema is appropriated, and further moves—particularly the acquisition of a protector—appear as the rational next step. In effect, the cultural schema has been moved by an actor from an external to an internal position, from an abstract model of deeds done by ancient heroes and ritual participants to a personal program for understanding what is happening to one right now, and for acting upon it.

In this view, as in the external view, there is a distance between actors' selves and their cultural models, in the sense that not all of a culture's repertoire of symbolic frames make sense to all actors at all times. Much of the time a cultural story like that of the founding of the Zhung temple will seem to any given Sherpa to be just a story, with little relevance for his or her life. Yet at moments in the course of events the story seems to make sense of a person's circumstances and is thus appropriated and internalized. (As Bourdieu has emphasized, such moments are not infrequent, since the shape of life in the culture and the shape of cultural stories have at least in part evolved together.) At that point it is no longer "just a story"; it is part of the action and takes on structuring force.

Yet the notion of distance, or at least loose fit, between the structure of the self and the structure of cultural models means that a cultural frame that has been taken into the self can also be put out again—when others fail to react in expected ways, for example, or when circumstances change, or simply when a person matures. It means too that no two actors will necessarily have the same relationship to the schema, and that while one (like Sangye) is moved by it, another (like Karma) could take it or leave it. (This kind of variation would explain the divergence of views about whether the brothers were rivalrous.) Given such differences between actors' relationships to the schema, in turn, other factors will come into play in determining whether events will have the schema's shape. Thus a wealthy and powerful actor may in effect coerce another player to respond in ways consistent with the schema. Alternatively, a rhetorically skillful actor may persuade another that the schema is valid and meaningful and should guide his or her actions. Under such circumstances, everyone is drawn in, in one way or the other, although not necessarily in the same way.

To summarize: The suggestion here is that one way in which structures structure events is that actors find them personally meaningful in a given context, internalize them or in some other way make a link between them and the self, and enact them such that the cultural schema becomes a vehicle of personal agency. No permanent linkage is made, no one is programmed, as it were, yet in the particular context in which the connection is operating, the structure has for the actor a certain naturalness, and realism, and hence coerciveness. The actor will thus tend to enact the schema, and depending on his or her wealth, power, and charisma, may pull others along as well.

Operating in this way, and reproduced at the same time through multiple social and ritual practices, a cultural schema may thus structure events consistently over a long period of a society's history. Yet the critical point here is the recognition of a kind of elastic distance between actors' selves and cultural schemas. This means that actors can, as in Fox's position, manipulate schemas instrumentally under certain circumstances. They can also appropriate them more intimately, and forge a kind of merger with them, that has a subjective meaningfulness and urgency. Yet finally, under other circumstances, they can in principle reestablish distance, rendering the schema once again a relatively abstract part of their symbolic ecology.

Conclusions

I have been arguing that there is a culturally or symbolically ordered causality, as well as an economic and political causality, behind the founding of the Sherpa monasteries in the early twentieth century. In an accumulating series of cases (Bali [Geertz 1980], Hawaii [Sahlins 1981], and now the Sherpas), it has been relatively easy to show that there is cultural patterning in the process of social change and institutional evolution, just as there is in cultural continuity and stability. Some of the standard tools of the anthropological trade, though worked out in synchronic modes of analysis, are clearly applicable to a more historical-minded anthropology. The patterned and structured nature of culture that anthropologists have brought to light over the past 50 years is not relegated to darkness with the shift to historical considerations.

Rather, it can be shown that there is pattern in history itself: Cultural modes of constructing and interpreting relations may, in complex ways, constrain the forms that historical change will take. Such patterning or structure, moreover, intervenes between material causes (such as those generated by the activities of the British and the Ranas) and institutional outcomes (such as the founding of Tengboche and Chiwong). Indeed such symbolic patterning is itself part of the causal sequence, without which one cannot fully understand why events took the particular course they did.

I have also tried to show that cultural schemas do not have a Platonic existence. While I do not think that any of the writers who have worked with the concept hold such a position, the grounding and continuous reproduction of schemas in social life has perhaps been insufficiently emphasized. Like everything else in the human social process, schemas can only be reproduced and carried across generations through some form of human activity. Thus I have emphasized that the schema of religious institution founding is carried by, and reproduced for all Sherpas through participation in, a variety of culturally organized actions and interactions: in real-world political relations, in kinship/inheritance relations, and in ritual practices.

The final problem addressed is the one with which I began the paper: To the extent that one emphasizes structural or symbolic constraints on history, is one in danger of rendering the actors of one's account mere players in a scripted drama on which they can leave no mark? Have I placed Sherpa actors under the "tyranny of culture," robbing them of choice, agency, and intentionality?

I have tried to answer these questions through a consideration of the ways in which, if cultural schemas exist, they must operate to structure events. This can only be through the actions of real actors, and the question thus becomes, what is the relationship between actors and their culture repertoire? But this question brings us full circle to the positions laid out at the beginning: Are actors free to treat their cultural models as basketsful of options, or are actors heavily programmed to follow cultural modes of operation? The first position seems too loose for me (although obviously people make conscious tactical choices some of the time), and the second position seems too tight (although some instances of apparent cultural programming can be adduced). I thus proposed a position in which a certain distance is analytically assumed to obtain between actors and their cultural repertoire. This is to say that actors have enough cultural shaping so that much of their cultural repertoire will seem reasonable, but not always necessarily deeply meaningful and compelling. Under certain circumstances, however, actors may connect with a particular cultural schema, which may then assume intense meaningfulness. They will take it, or equally, it will take them. Then the schema may acquire potential structuring force: The actor will actually use it to order his or her interpretations and actions. Even under these conditions, it will not *necessarily* take on structuring force; whether it does or not depends on a multitude of real-world factors (the actor's money, luck, social clout, the degree to which the other parties can be enlisted to play their parts, and so forth).

At this point I may appear to be describing a cultural tyranny, since the actor is said to be under the sway of the schema's interpretations, meanings, and prescriptions. Yet I could just as well say the reverse—that the actor has made the culture an instrument of the self's agency. Either way, however, it must be borne in mind that this connection is only a moment in the overall social process. It is a consequential moment, because it brings about a historically visible enactment of the schema, thereby contributing powerfully to its reproduction. And it is consequential because it makes durable things—temples and monasteries are founded, and the social landscape is reordered in major ways. Yet actors may also disconnect from the schema and reestablish the distance that, under other circumstances, might allow them to look critically upon their culture and possibly seek to change it.

Acknowledgments

This chapter was first outlined as a talk in 1983 at the Center for Advanced Study in the Behavioral Sciences, where I had fellowship support from the center (NSF Grant BNS 8206304) and from the John Simon Guggenheim Memorial Foundation. Both sources of support are gratefully acknowledged. A new paper ("Culture Making") was written for the Wenner-Gren conference from which this volume derives, but the arguments of that paper required more data than could be fitted into its space. The paper will thus be subsumed within *The Monks' Campaign* (Ortner n.d.). For detailed comments on the present paper, I would like to thank Salvatore Cucchiari, Richard G. Fox, Thomas Fricke, Raymond Kelly, Michael Peletz, Edward L. Schieffelin, and Harriet Whitehead. William Malandra and Bruce Lincoln, organizers of an excellent symposium, "Religion and Power," at the University of Minnesota, also provided helpful responses. Of the Morocco group, Emiko Ohnuki-Tierney and James W. Fernandez saw a draft of this paper and made useful suggestions. Rachael Cohen provided excellent technical and editorial support. I thank them all.

4

Enclosures: Boundary Maintenance and Its Representations over Time in Asturian Mountain Villages (Spain)

JAMES W. FERNANDEZ

> For when man understands, he extends his mind and takes in the things; but when he does not understand, he makes the things out of himself and becomes them by transforming himself into them.
>
> Vico, *Scienzia Nuova*

> To the ethnologist the most trifling features of social life are important because they are expressions of historical happenings. They are part of the data from which the past has to be reconstructed.
>
> Franz Boas, "The Aims of Ethnology"

Let us recall that classic Charles Addams cartoon in the *New Yorker* of a New Yorker attending to the battery of locks, dead bolts, bars, and chains that secure his apartment door. At the same moment, surreptitiously, a small white valentine with a red heart is being slipped in beneath the door. Why not begin with this cartoon and its pithy comment both on enclosure and on the modern, or at least urban, condition, so different from the condition of the country men and women I will be discussing here? Our academic canons, however, are not so restrictive as to lock out from consideration such heartfelt, if macabre, little messages. Given only a half-minute of anyone's time the cartoonist has to be a master, as Addams surely is, of the argument of images, the display of symbols. The cartoon is almost all visual, and next to nothing needs to be said. There may be something salutary for us academicians in this, lest we be content in our lucubrations to offer no images at all but rather a skein of abstractions, imageless ideas.[1] In the rural milieux in which my wife and I have worked, communication is abbreviated and is characterized by such images and symbols as the cartoonist Addams employs.

Locking In and Holding Out

The cartoon image frames appropriately the subject matter of this essay, which has to do with some aspects of the evolution of enclosures in those Asturian mountain villages of northern Spain whose meaning worlds have been the locus of our fieldwork. More particularly it has to do with the changing symbolism over time of some utilitarian instruments and arenas of enclosure: fences and gates and field stones, locks and keys, plazas and portals, high-altitude passes and pastures. Enclosures and the instruments of enclosure are evocative images practically anywhere, one would suppose, to the degree that people are concerned with boundary maintenance and proprietorship. But they need not be symbolic. The focus here will be, as with Vico and Boas, on the conditions that make practical artifacts and arenas, and the signals and signs of coordinated human interaction, into evocative symbols with some historic resonance. I will focus, that is, on the enduring problem of symbol formation, on the historical problem of how things become resonant, pass into history and out of it, and go through phases in doing so.

I will be anchoring this inquiry in several revelatory incidents that arose in our fieldwork or in the archives we consulted. Then I will use these incidents and the concrete symbols characteristic of them to reflect upon symbolization over time.

"The Imponderabilia of Actual Life" and the Attributes of Asturianity

Let me first say something in general about symbols. Symbols as emblems of identity abound in provincial life.[2] They are the objects

---

[1] Richard Werbner (1985) discusses insightfully the dynamic interplay of images and accepted realities in cultural revitalization, and the responsibility of the anthropologist to the study of images.

[2] By "emblems" is meant that class of signs standing for or representing a social group that in some way claims to distinguish its identity (in part by means of the em-

or events that occur naturally in Asturias, that are felt to belong to the provincial way of life, and that have thus come to represent it. Such symbols—the apple, cider, the provincial way of pouring cider, the use of butter and lard, the bagpipe, the cow, the bear, provincial dress, provincial dances, the provincial "deepsong" (*asturianadas*), the wooden granaries (*hórreos*), the spiked wooden shoes (*madreñas*), the umbrella, the miner's lamp, the Virgin of the Sanctuary of Covadonga, etc.—are all characteristic of traditional Asturian lifeways, and their presence is felt to give character to the province, although for some, it is true, in a superficial, stereotypic way. These symbols characterize the province and its personality and contrast it with other, particularly the contiguous, provinces of Spain, whose citizens do not grow apples and drink cider, eat butter, play the bagpipe, sing intense melismatic airs, walk behind cows in spiked wooden shoes, or devote themselves to the Virgin of Covadonga.

Now these emblems are akin to the state birds or trees or flowers of the various states of the American union, which are felt to belong to the state and contrast it with other states. To be sure, many of the "natural" symbols of the American states seem to be constructed or invented and either shared with other states or of questionable local provenance. The Asturian symbols, however, are almost all natural and endemic. That is, a stereotypical Asturian male has the look of a cider drinker, a bagpipe player, a wooden-shoe wearer, a devotee of the Virgin of Covadonga, and stores his grain in wooden granaries. Or put another way, certain objects and actions, indices of the presence of Asturias where they are found, can all become icons of Asturianity. Other Spaniards, or Asturians themselves, being asked to construct an image of the Asturian would likely construct that image out of the attributes I have listed. Indeed, in the popular culture of provincial comics, humorous histories, and monologues, the comic or stage figure of the Asturian is accompanied by many or all of these attributes.

The question arises: How do certain objects and activities come to represent the lifeways and character of a given social group, whether that be a province or a village? Of all the objects and actions present in a given lifeway, how do some come to stand for that life-

---

blems themselves) from other groups. See the discussion of emblems in Singer 1984: ch. 5. Essentially what lies behind the emblem are matters of intensity of interaction (contiguity) and felt resemblance (iconicity).

way? The answer seems obvious enough. Given competing claims about distinct personality and possessions, such objects and actions are selected because they have the property of contrast: Cider contrasts with the wine drunk elsewhere in Spain; butter contrasts with the olive oil used elsewhere; the cow contrasts with the bull of bullfights; umbrellas contrast with parasols. These contrasts enable the claim of distinct provincial character. Such objects and actions enable effective boundary maintenance.

A structural answer, the kind of answer that is satisfied with the discovery of a structure of contrasts, will not, however, be sufficient for the argument here. The deeper question is how these particular entities and actions enter into and depart from awareness—enter and leave history, as it were. Malinowski called these objects and actions "the imponderabilia of actual life" (1984: ch. 1),[3] and they lie at the very heart of the historical process. How culture or tradition is suddenly brought into consciousness, invented, or discovered is a persistent question in anthropology.[4] These discoveries, these "historical (or micro historical) happenings" (1940: 632), to use Boas's phrase, will be probed here. I will do so primarily in a village and not in a provincial context. Needless to say, these resonant entities are incapable of being weighed or evaluated with precision. But anthropologists know by "being there" how vital they are in the human experience.

The Lady of the Keys: The Key as Symbol

Let us, then, ground this inquiry into "enclosures" and raise major questions with a series of incidents that arose in our first month of fieldwork in the mountains of southern Asturias, municipality of Aller, northern Spain. The incidents were attendant to my seeking access to an abandoned and decrepit quarter of a former *casona* (great house) to set up an office. This great house, actually called La

---

[3] See especially the discussion in Malinowski 1936, 1: app. 2. "Confessions of Ignorance and Failure," 2. Method of Collecting Information.

[4] The underlying question of innovation in culture is an old one in anthropology and, between the two world wars, was central to the concerns of both the diffusionists and those interested in acculturation. It has recently come back into focus with a greater sense of the intentionality involved in the "invention of culture" (Wagner 1981) or the "invention of tradition" (Hobsbawm and Ranger 1983).

Casona, was located in the neighboring village of El Pino, quite close to our focal village, Felechosa. El Pino was the parish seat, and though now a village much in decline—"muy degenerado," in the villagers' view—it had a history of seignorial residence. There were four casonas in this village and none in Felechosa, the town in which we were living and an otherwise (though recently) prosperous head-of-the-valley watering spot.

The particular casona in question, in fact all four, had belonged to the family of "los Ordoñez," a seignorial line dating from the Middle Ages and popularly thought to be linked with the three Ordoños, kings of Asturias and León in the ninth and tenth centuries. Los Ordoñez were those members of the Asturian nobility particularly identified with the municipality of Aller, especially with El Pino. Indeed, the grandee title, count of Ordoñez del Pino, was conceded by Felipe V in 1708 to Lorenzo, a member of another noble family, the Bernaldo de Quirós—one of the most important in Asturias—which was related to the Ordoñez family. El Pino was widely recognized as the seat of several of the main branches of the Asturian nobility. But all this splendor, such as it was, had fallen into a state of disrepair and abandon—"muy degenerado."

In the first half of the nineteenth century los Ordoñez had sold La Casona to the Argüelles, a newly rich Asturian family that was later, at the end of the century, ennobled through a purchased title. The Argüelles had in turn, in the late 1880's or early 1890's, sold the casona and its associated lands to two rich "Indianos," local men who had gone to the New World, the brothers Manuel and Ceferino Díaz Tejón, and who were newly returned with significant wealth from Cuba. The Indianos, unlike the increasingly urbanized aristocracy, still had a rural orientation. The fate of the great house from then on was tied to the vicissitudes of their descendants—their grandnephews and grandnieces—who held the key to that quarter of the house in which I was interested.

The actual key, however, was entrusted to a daughter of a grandniece of the two Indianos. This young woman, Puri (Purificación by name), was married to a miner and thought to have the acumen to deal with strangers. As a great-grandniece, she had little power of decision making herself and had to wait while the four siblings made up their minds. At the same time she found herself acting to calm my growing impatience. It seemed to me that the decision to definitively pass over the key was unconscionably delayed—over a month—for I had been more or less assured of the availability of the rooms. That these quarters were otherwise useless, or appeared so, that my stay would only be temporary, and that the rent offered was generous argued for a quick decision. But one was not forthcoming. Since I was anxious to install my boxed books, I made frequent inquiries.

Inevitably, there being no other news to report, we—that is, Puri and I—began to focus upon the key itself as a symbol of these prolonged and increasingly awkward proceedings. Essentially a delegate of her elders, Puri had little material interest in the matter and, discomfited by the delay in her relatives' decision, became increasingly aware of *my* discomfiture. No doubt my research timetable made me more importunate than any Asturian would have been under the circumstances. Puri began to feel embarrassed about her control of the key and let me know on several occasions that as far as she was concerned, it was my key already: "Just be patient."

The key became, therefore, the object of a playful and inevitably gendered interchange of male need and female resistance. Nothing overtly boisterous or bawdy was said, since the interchange was between generations, between social classes, and between near strangers. There was just a sly recognition that something more than the use of a house could be in negotiation in such a situation. And there was perhaps the recognition that, as has often been argued for domestic space in Spain, the house is female in character (in contrast to the street)[5]—a female dispensation to be properly opened only to authorized males. As frequently happens, the situation became one of those in which some practical activity or object becomes decontextualized and removed from its normal routine and associations. It becomes transformed and weighted with untoward meanings. Like

[5] This association is plentifully represented in the proverb corpus. In mild form it begins with the house requirement of every newly married woman: "la que se casa a su casa" (she who marries straightaway to her house). But it continues in stronger form: "La mujer casada. La pierna quebrada y en casa" (The married woman with a broken leg and in her house). The woman, as administrator, controls the house as hers and, in fact, without her it is nothing: "Casa sin mujer, cuerpo sin alma" (House without a woman, body without a soul). The outside/inside, street/house identification is part of the association: "El hombre en la plaza y la mujer en casa" (Men in the plaza and women in the house). And of course there is the identification between the woman's body, particularly the private parts, and her house. See Cela 1971, 1: 769. See also Fernandez 1985.

any sign or signal out of place, it becomes a symbol (see Fernandez 1985).

If the key was developing these "primary process" meanings between Puri and me, it may well have had a more lofty significance for her. She may have been aware that keys figure prominently on the coat of arms of the marquesses of Camposagrado, prominent property-holders in Aller, a branch of whose family had built a hunting lodge (now fallen in) in her own village of Felechosa in the first decade of the present century. Their coat of arms had been displayed there, and the noble family was otherwise well known to the villagers.

The Camposagrados were a branch of the Bernaldo de Quirós family (also related to los Ordoñez), and theirs was one of the few Asturian coats of arms to carry keys as heraldic bearings.[6] These were the keys of St. Peter and recalled the contribution of the house of Quirós to the papacy in the triumphant battles of Pope Stephen III against the Lombards in the eighth century, which led to the establishment of the Papal States. This seems to be an apochryphal reference, for the house of Quirós is late medieval rather than early medieval in origin. Nevertheless, the referent of the keys—that as Christ gave the keys of the kingdom of heaven and earth to Peter, so the Quirós were among those who gave the keys of his earthly kingdom to the Pope—is in its overweening pride perfectly compatible with the motto of this family: "Después de Dios la casa de Quirós" (After God comes the house of Quirós). (See Figs. 4.1 and 4.2.)

Puri would not have been aware of all this history bound up in heraldic symbolism. She would just have been aware that keys were, in some way, seignorial attributes—they figured on coats of arms—and means of access to a special dispensation that was not to be taken lightly, whatever playful meanings might emerge. The dispensation was of course that which the rich Indianos might have aspired to have access to when they purchased La Casona. Just as Christ's handing of the keys over to Peter is usually read as a symbolic representation of Peter's coming into the New or Christian Dispensation, so the granting of the key by Puri and her family represented for them, in

---

[6] Keys are unusual in Asturian heraldry and are primarily associated with the house of Quirós. Sarandeses 1966, the standard reference, lists and pictures 1,783 coats of arms. Of those, 54 carry keys as heraldic bearings; 32 of the 54 are directly associated with the house of Quirós: 19 belong to the house of Quirós proper, and 13 to family offshoots.

Fig. 4.1. Coats of arms of the house of Quirós (middle two rows).

Fig. 4.2. Coat of arms of the Bernaldo de Quirós.

some vague way, my admission to a dispensation or especially favored condition that the now dissipated wealth of their Indiano forebears had obtained for them.

The key and its handing over, which in any brief negotiation would have simply signified agreement over rent and access to occupancy, came, in the exceptionally long negotiation, to symbolize much more: some "creative libidinous force denied or dallied with," as psycho-

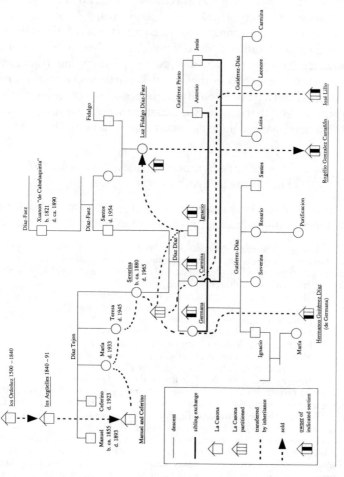

Fig. 4.3. Proprietors of La Casona, 1500-1986.

analysis might put it,[7] or access to a special historical dispensation. But while the key came to have something of that complex significance in my relationship with Puri, a focus upon meanings, archetypically analytic or purely historical and thus transcendent, takes us away from the changing meaning of the key and other instruments of enclosure in my particular circumstances and the circumstances of Asturian society and culture. Rather than confirming an archetype by such transcendence, it is upon the vicissitudes of this present symbol that I wish to concentrate. I wish to see the Casona key in the social context of the house itself and its succession of proprietors—once noble but now rural proletarians, that is, miners and country people. Needed here is the kinship chart mapped upon the ownership of the house (Fig. 4.3).

Degenerated Symbolic Structures: The House as Symbol

In our visits to the desired quarters Puri referred to the house several times, with some chagrin and quite expressively, as "muy de-

---

[7] Carl Jung (1956: 124–25) evokes a passage from Goethe's *Faust*: "The phallus also working in darkness begets a living being; and the key unlocks the mysterious forbidden door behind which some wonderful thing awaits discovery." One thinks in this connection of "The Mothers" in *Faust*:

> *Mephistopheles*. Congratulations, before you part from me!
> You know the devil that is plain to see. Here, take this key.
> *Faust*. This little thing! But why?
> *Mephistopheles*. First grasp it; it is nothing to decry.
> *Faust*. It glows, it shines, increases in my hand!
> *Mephistopheles*. How great its worth you soon shall understand.
> The key shall smell the right place from all others:
> Follow it down; it leads you to the Mothers!" (Goethe 1951: 177)

Sigmund Freud, in *The Interpretation of Dreams*, gives approximately the same reading to keys (1965: 389–90) and refers the reader to Dora's first dream, in which her mother locks the dining room of their house against her father and then gives the key to Dora to lock her own bedroom door (1963: 81–85).

More apposite would be evidence from Spanish culture. See here Camilio José Cela's two compendiums of erotica (1971, 1982), particularly his *Diccionario Secreto*, where, among other references, he makes mention of a cartoon from a 1912 Madrid demimonde magazine picturing a man and woman before a door that the man is intent on opening: "But my good man," the woman remarks, "every night you have the same problem with the key, you never succeed in inserting it!" (1971, 2: 421). Joan Frigole Reixach ("La casa y el espacio doméstico tradicional y su sistema de representaciones," unpub. ms., 1986) gives a Murcian song-verse collected by P. Díaz Cassou (1980, 143): "Quien se fia de mujeres / d'este mundo poco sabe; / no hay que fiar de una puerta / que tos tenemos la llave!" (Who puts faith in women / Knows little of the world; / Put no trust in a door / To which everyone has a key!).

generada," a phrase that occurred with some frequency in conversations with the Asturian villagers in the early stages of our acquaintance, when they were evaluating my reiterated intention to study authentic Asturian culture in the high mountain valley. The quarter of the house I was interested in was certainly decrepit. But more than that seemed to be involved in her remark. The chart shows some reason for it. What was in the eighteenth century and earlier just one of the four great houses in the village belonging to the Ordoñez family had become by the mid-twentieth century a house divided into three parts belonging to three different families only distantly related, if related at all. The casona had degenerated into a house with three small apartments and with the possibility of a fourth. The same thing had happened to the other great houses of the village.

For the rural aristocracy the building of casonas had symbolized family greatness (cf. Lisón Tolosana 1973). It is not surprising that, in comparison, country men and women like Puri found the breakdown of the casonas into parts, and of family perpetuity into family squabbling, to be a symbol of degeneration: An undisputed great house had become a disputed apartment house. Let us address the inheritance disputes which resonated in La Casona in the twentieth century and which were part of Puri's sense of degeneration—of the inability of her class of country people to maintain the seignorial status of the house.

We know first that the truly ancient line of rural aristocrats associated with El Pino, los Ordoñez, sold the casona and its lands in the early nineteenth century to a newly wealthy, eventually to be ennobled, family of industrialists, the Argüelles. The Argüelles, in turn, more oriented to the city than to country seats, like most of the nineteenth-century aristocracy, sold the house and lands to the returned Indianos, the villagers Manuel and Ceferino Díaz Tejón, around 1890. Manuel died in 1893, and his half of the casona passed to his brother, who in turn passed this half in usufruct (*llevanza*) to his married younger sister Severina. When Ceferino died in 1923, Severina gained full title to that half, while her unmarried older sister, María, inherited lifetime usufruct to the other half. The two sisters seem to have disputed this inheritance arrangement. (The sister Teresa was mentally impaired and not involved in these matters.) In any event, on María's death in the early 1930's full possession passed to Severina and her descendants. It was the degeneration into disputes between these descendants that dissipated the seignorial equanimity and self-control that a casona should manifest.

Upon Severina's death, her three children, Ignacio, Carmina, and Germana, inherited the house, now divided into three parts. Already, this arrangement had engendered some disputes because Germana's share (the quarters I was interested in), though slightly smaller in living space, also comprised the stable, hayloft, and chicken yard. Although the principle of partible inheritance should have applied, the three children were somewhat unhappy about the division of the house. As it happened, Ignacio quickly sold his third to his paternal aunt, Luz Fidalgo, to satisfy a debt. He later had second thoughts about the equity of this transfer and attempted to reclaim his portion of the house. But his aunt resisted the claim and sold her third in the 1950's to Rogélio González Castañón, the present proprietor. The dispute between Ignacio and his aunt is remembered whenever the Casona is talked about.

The part of the house in which I was interested, Germana's share, and the other third passed from Carmina and Germana, each of whom had four children, to those children without sale. The children of Carmina, then living in a downriver town, rapidly went to *suertes*, a drawing of equal parts, to resolve the inheritance. Their Casona part went to Leonore, who sold it forthwith to José Lillo of El Pino, a distant relative, the present occupant. The division of Germana's inheritance—she died more recently in any case—was not easily resolved, so her portion was held without going to suertes, in part because two of the siblings were *sub normales*. One was something of an *inocente*, and the other an unmarried woman of promiscuous lifestyle with two children born out of wedlock.

The indeterminate nature of Germana's inheritance, which comprised lands as well as a third of the casona, posed the difficulty in respect to my rental offer. It raised the question of the need to go to suertes. Also, while my rental monies could be divided four ways, my residence posed a problem for Ignacio's daughter, María, who was marrying a miner and envisioned eventually setting up house in that third of the casona. She and her father wanted to be sure that my stay would not last longer than a year and a half, as promised. And they wanted to be sure a precedent was not established that would prevent her buying out her aunts and uncles, or a specific aunt or uncle, if they decided to go to suertes and the house fell to other than her father.

Thus the casona, or that part of it in negotiation, came to symbolize all these inheritance disputes, and a degeneration into disputatiousness in place of seignorial equanimity, although the family had attempted to maintain this equanimity and mastery in the face of the constant potential for squabbling over inheritance. Puri's feelings of degeneration arose in part because of the high value placed on those qualities, because of a sense that things might have been managed better, as, for example, in the marriage of her grandmother, Germana, and grandaunt, Carmina, to two brothers, António Gutiérrez Prieto and Jesús Gutiérrez Prieto. This marriage of brothers and sisters, *casarse a trueque* in the Asturian phrase, was understood, whatever other natural attractions of courtship might bring it about, to be a way of avoiding the dispersion of family lands and possessions and maintaining equanimity and mastery of the temporal vicissitudes of inheritance. A family that had practiced casarse a trueque in the generation immediately antecedent to the presently disputing generation was likely to feel the divisive degeneration of family affairs the more strongly, as Puri apparently did.

Now let me tie these family matters and the symbolism of the seignorial house into the question of enclosure. The coats of arms that the casonas regularly carried and that all of the casonas in El Pino once carried were the discrete signs placed upon them to symbolize family greatness, understood as perpetuity, equanimity, possessions, abundance of descendants, influence, and so forth. The coats of arms were signs upon the house indicating an enclosure of these qualities in family form. The house was a symbol of these family qualities and at the same time a literal enclosure of them. But the casona I was negotiating for had become a hollow shell enclosing family decline through alienation of resources and perpetual squabbling over inheritance. Puri, like many villagers, was acutely aware of how the great house had changed its meaning over time. And while the former seignorial occupants might themselves have undergone a similar decline into fractiousness, as far as Puri was concerned, the great houses, which should have been enclosures of great families, had become enclosures of degenerated families. The house as symbol had changed so over time.

The Ambiguous Boundaries of House and Field as Symbols: The *Antoxanu*

The key and the house to which it gives entrance, we have seen, are changing symbols. The privacy they give access to has changed, in local views, from something full of promise and possibility to something fraught with the dispute and distrust of inheritance. Though I have made this case for a casona, it is also true of most villagers' houses where partible inheritance obtains, as is typical of most parts of Asturias. It is likewise true that villagers thinking upon the past, even though they have no casona in the family, romanticize that past, believing that once their family was united but now it has fallen into rancorous dispute. Access to a house, therefore, is often access to a knowledge of that debilitating family discord. Part of the resistance to giving out a key is a resistance to giving a stranger access to disagreeable facts about the family romance—the dirty linen. But let us turn from the maintenance or defense of boundaries against such private facts becoming public knowledge to one aspect of the negotiation of house boundaries negotiated vis-à-vis the neighborhood (*vecindad*).

In reading through municipal archives, particularly the proceedings of the municipal council, one notes the frequency with which one householder denounces another or the community denounces a household for infringement of a neighbor's property or a public right-of-way.[8] Within the village these denunciations have largely to do with the space lying before the house, the dooryard, known as the *antojana* or *antoxanu* (Fig. 4.4). This rectangular space, partially confined by the house walls, which extend to sustain the second story and upper porch, and partially protruding several meters beyond the walls, is the arena of negotiation between private and public property and is correspondingly a potentially symbolically evocative arena. It is a symbol that has also undergone, in the villagers' view, a transformation: Villager and municipal functionary alike often lament how much more people dispute over this space these days than formerly. What is, in part, symbolized when the antoxanu is brought into

[8] In the Aller Libro de Actas for March 7, 1936 (24: 50), for example, is an order that María Lobo of Casomera retire from the public way her woodpile, which was exceeding the limits of her "antoxu."

Fig. 4.4. Dooryard, or *antoxanu*.

discussion is loss of moral community and cooperative neighborliness, *vecindad*.

The antoxanu has long been a contentious arena in Asturian village life, belying present views that litigation of this century symbolizes loss of community. Obligations vis-à-vis the treatment of this
space are explicitly stated in the village ordinances drawn up in the
late eighteenth and early nineteenth centuries, before village and parochial administration was displaced by more centralized municipal

government in the mid-nineteenth century.[9] Changes in provincial
and village life have, however, made this space more subject to symbolization, which is to say a center of contention. Let us review each
of these pressures with an eye toward their effect on the symbolization
of the antoxanu.

First, houses have tended to conglomerate in settlements, con-
travening an older and still widespread pattern in many parts of Asturias of living in separated or isolated farmsteads, *quintanas* or *case-
rios*. In this increasing conglomeration—although, to be sure, a pattern dating back to the Middle Ages[10] in many parts of Asturias, such
as Aller—friction as regards the antoxanu has intensified, and personal and house identity and neighborhood rights have become
bound up in this liminal space.

Second, with the establishment of effective municipal government
in the nineteenth century, control over these public-private spaces, as
well as over practically all aspects of village life, has shifted from local
village government, the Parochial and Neighborhood Councils, Jun-
tas Vecinales, to municipal councils in other towns.[11] This shift in-
duced a greater abuse of this space since the supervisory authorities
were now much removed and litigation was likely to be lengthy and
impersonal rather than immediate and among neighbors. This distancing and prolongation of dispute acted to symbolize the antoxanu

    [9] See the Ordenanzas of the village of Bello as discussed by R. Prieto Bances (1977,
1: 413). Prieto Bances is making use of the Ordenanzas collected by the secretary of the
municipality of Aller, Benjamin García Alvarez. See the Ordenanzas of the town of
Bello (1846): "Ningún vecino podrá abreviar los caminos o calles del pueblo con made-
ras ni otras cosas dejando tres baras libres sin embarazo alguno. Así mismo tendrá sus
antojanos limpios y despedregados cortadas las canas de los árboles que impedían las
procesiones y otras cualesquiera cosas y el que faltare a esto el regidor la castigara en
dos reales por la primera y después doblando" (No citizen can intrude upon the alleys
or streets of the town with wood or other material and must leave three yards clear for
passage without any impediment. In the same fashion one must maintain one's court-
yard clean and smooth, with tree branches cut that might impede public passage and
other related impediments whatever removed, and he who fails at this the supervisor
will punish with fines of two reales for the first offense and thereafter double [García
Alvarez 1963: 212]).
    [10] The impetus toward this settlement pattern in some parts of Asturias in the Mid-
dle Ages is well examined in Ruiz de la Peña 1981.
    [11] In the north of Spain, in contrast to the center and south, municipalities are made
up of a number of parishes, each composed of several villages. The municipality of Aller
is made up of 17 different towns and villages. There is considerable competition between them, and the municipal seat cannot easily represent them all equally.

in two ways. The surfeit of antoxanu complaints in municipal councils in twentieth-century meetings and the onerousness of attending to them caused administrators to look upon the complaints as representative of the rancor of village life and the failure of neighborliness that characterized it. Municipal secretaries and other functionaries drew my attention to these complaints as something that would give insight into what village life was all about. For the villagers themselves the delay in attending to their complaints, coupled with the challenging necessity of presenting these complaints in legal form to the municipal government, clothed the complaints with transcendent meanings associated with frustrated waiting for resolution on the one hand and the willfulness and unpredictability of bureaucracy on the other. Normal everyday things bound up in frustrating and unpredictable situations became, as we have seen, symbolic by such associations.

Third, with the increasing affluence of the countryside in the last two decades the antoxanu has become a depository of more goods than it can easily accommodate without infringements on others' spaces. This affluence, in other words, has given the antoxanu a spillover effect on the public right-of-way and adjacent property. Where disputes about the antoxanu were formerly confined to the overflow of woodpiles and manure piles at its two edges, in recent decades its use for tractors and automobiles, and, even more, the attempt to fence it in for such purposes, has been a main cause of complaint. The litigation provoked has become so widespread that provincial lawyers now dedicate themselves to the complicated legal status of this space and its relationship to the house and to its neighborhood (in particular the *corrala*), as well as its divisibility and inheritability independent of the house (Fonseca González 1984).

Fourth, the percentage of houses held in rent within seignorial estates has declined. Problems of the antoxanu that were once problems to be referred for resolution to the local administrators of these large estates have become problems of the houseowners themselves. This is just the inverse of the problem of the increase, at the village level, of municipal authority at the expense of village authority.

Last, there has been that change within which all these other changes have taken place: the steady movement in Asturian life, as in Western Europe generally, toward privatization of the public and communal. This has affected not only land but these house-associated properties as well.

Although the antoxanu has long been of concern in village life and is manifest in village ordinances of the eighteenth century, the creation of municipal administration removed these disputes from direct resolution by fellow villagers to municipal councils, few members of which were local villagers or even members of the same parish. The antoxanu, then, for a complex of reasons has come to represent that space in which private and public are negotiated and that space in which the private, the casa, is likely to intrude on the most immediate public space, the plaza of the quarter, or corrala.

La Portietsa

If Asturians of these valleys think the antoxanu symbolizes the rancorous and proprietary spirit that has come to dominate village life, they are plentifully aware of the same dominating spirit in their agricultural and pastoral life in the fields and meadows. Here are two revelatory incidents from municipal and provincial archives. The first is selected from a long series of documents (Fig. 4.5) from the provincial notarial archives of 1776 to 1778 concerning the opening and closing of a field gate, *portilla* or *portietsa* in the local dialect.[12] One Andrés Muñiz Santos seeks to enjoin some of his fellow villagers and the village officials, to desist from their lax ways in both closing one of these gates too early in June and opening it too late in the fall. What is in contest here is *derrota*, the communal right of pasturage over stubble after fall harvest and until spring planting. The plaintiff is resisting a tendency in his fellow villagers to expand their private rights over against the public rights of stubble grazing. The plaintiff's cattle had been seized (*prindado*) against costs for infringement of private property, and in any case he had been impeded in his and the public's right of passing through to pasturage. In the document on display the judge gives reason to Muñiz Santos's complaint.

A similar case, although advanced by a plaintiff with a different perspective, appears nearly two centuries later, in the municipal ar-

[12]This extended litigation can be found in the Archivo Histórico Provincial, Oviedo, in the notarial records, Box 1001, 1770–80, compiled by the notary Francisco Javier González. See particularly the records for 1778.

chives for 1958 from the neighboring upper-valley village of Villar de Casomera.[13] This time the secretary of the municipality, in response to villagers' complaints, writes to one Doña Rogelia Lobo Baizán requesting that she remove all the fruits of her field, Finca Orana, before November 1 and open the gate so that the field will be available for stubble grazing by village cattle. She replies as an aggrieved plaintiff before the court citing various twentieth-century laws that permit her to keep her fields closed to stubble grazing. Besides, she adds, the Asturian climate, particularly the weather of 1958, has prevented full harvesting of her corn, beans, and beets before November 1. She should be due, she argues, some compensation for opening her fields and losing some of those crops. The matter comes before the municipal council in 1958.[14] The municipal secretary provides a white paper on *jus fruendi* recommending that the municipality should defend this immemorial right in this case. The barrio mayor of Villar, *alcalde pedaneo*, also presents testimony arguing that all the citizens of the village have enjoyed stubble-grazing rights (*segundo pelo* or *toñá*) on this land as an ancient custom and that such rights should continue to be respected with no monetary obligation to villagers. The council supports both the secretary and their alcalde pedaneo.

In both these cases the authorities sought to uphold communal rights over privatization. But in both cases litigation continued. And despite these particular rulings, the massive historical shift in the last two centuries has been toward increasing privatization and the loss of stubble-grazing rights. In the central part of Asturias this old right of derrota has almost disappeared, but in the eastern part of Asturias large stretches of land privately held in plots (sometimes for planting and harvesting but mainly for haymaking), yet subject to communal usufruct, are still present although the area involved is in decline. The negotiations of many centuries of the communal and the private are still going on there (see Fernandez 1981).

But the purpose here is to focus on the field gate, *portietsa*, itself the focus of the disputes, as their symbol. These legal documents are in fact sometimes termed "the affair of the gate." While the gate might be, as an instrument of boundary maintenance, symbolic in itself in

[13] Libro de Actos, Ayuntamiento de Aller, Asuntos Especiales, Caja 1860, Asunto 26.
[14] Ibid.

any context, the historical context examined here of the struggle over the communal and the private has become a crucial part of its meaning. The great Western European shift toward agrarian individualism is symbolized in it. Villagers frequently went out of their way to call our attention—the attention of these strangers seeking to learn about Asturian life—to the portietsa. In these upper valleys the gate is usually a light and skillfully woven barrier of hazel branches, but its easy movability contrasts humorously and perhaps defiantly in villagers' minds with the embittered struggle that has gone on over the centuries, mostly downvalley and among bureaucrats, over its permanent emplacement—the attempt to make of it something heavy that could not be easily moved. Some villagers have eagerly sought, others have acquiesced in, that privatization. Still, they seemed to recognize the field gate as embodying historical struggle and historical change—the passage from one dispensation, one moral community, one "moral economy," to another. To say that it carries that import is not to deny its libidinal qualities as well (cf. Fernandez 1975).

Los Puertos: Property and Pasturage in the Mountain Passes

The final symbolic arena I wish to examine is the public pasturage in the mountain passes, *los puertos*, between Asturias and León. Three revelatory documents disclose the vicissitudes of this high-altitude pasturage and what it represents to villagers. Indeed, claims and rights over these passes have been a central preoccupation of upper-valley life for centuries. Many upland fights between parishes over pasturage are recalled in local life histories.

Two documents demonstrate the perdurance of these disputes. The first (Fig. 4.6) comes from the archives of los Condes de Luna, an old Leonese noble family, dated February 1, 1530. In this, the king, Carlos I, enjoins the municipal officials and citizens (*vecinos*) of Caso to appear at the royal audience sitting in Valladolid to appeal their complaint against the Conde de Luna, Claudio Fernández de Quiñones, in respect to his claim over the Puerto de San Isidro, the mountain pass lying between León and the municipalities of Caso and Aller in Asturias. The citizens of Caso are claiming their ancient pasturage rights in the puerto over against the seignorial claim of the Conde de Luna. They claim that the puerto depends directly upon the king, is *re-*

Fig. 4.5 *(left)*. *La portilla*, a complaint by Andrés Muñiz against Toribio and Bartolomeo Muñiz concerning their closing of a gate to the free passage of cattle.

Fig. 4.6 *(lower left)*. Invitation from Carlos I to the citizens of Caso to appeal their claim to Puerto de San Isidro, dated February 1, 1530.

Fig. 4.7 *(lower right)*. Agreement between the villages of Felechosa, in Aller, and Caleao, in Caso, to close their pastures near the Puerto de San Isidro for revegetation, dated April 10, 1984.

Reunidos en la Casa Consistorial de Pola de Laviana, a las doce horas del día diez de abril de mil novecientos ochenta y cuatro, de una parte el Sr. Alcalde del Ayuntamiento de Aller y el representante del pueblo de Felechosa en dicho consejo, y de la otra el Sr. Alcalde del Ayuntamiento de Caso y el Presidente de la Entidad Local Menor de Caleao (Caso),

ACUERDAN:

Que ambas partes, Ayuntamiento de Aller y pueblo de Felechosa, Ayuntamiento de Caso y E.L.M. de Caleao, manifiestan su conformidad en que se lleve a efecto el cierre de los pastos limítrofes de ambos concejos, pertenecientes a las parroquias de Felechosa y Caleao, por el Instituto Nacional para la Conservación de la Naturaleza (I.C.O.N.A.), respetando el Acta de Deslinde vigente del Instituto Geográfico y Catastral, de fecha 9 de septiembre de 1.941.

Por el Ayto. de ALLER
El Sr. Alcalde.
Fdo.: Gabriel Pérez Villalta

Por el Ayto. de CASO
El Sr. Alcalde.
Fdo.: Juan Manuel Estrada Álvarez

Juan M. Cal

Por el pueblo de Felechosa con la condición de que la operación de cierre se lleve a efecto con presencia de los representantes del pueblo de Felechosa para comprobar que se ajuste al deslinde de 1.941.

Por el pueblo de Caleao
El Pte. de la E.L.M.
Fdo.: Juan Manuel Calvo

José Fernández

EL ALCALDE DE BARRIO DE FELECHOSA
D. JOSE FERNANDEZ RODRIGUEZ.

alengo, and not a seignorial dependency. Though the citizens of Aller, and in particular the parish of El Pino, do not appear together with Caso in this petition, they surely shared the same attitude toward their ancient rights over pasturage in this puerto.

The other document (Fig. 4.7), from 1984, is an agreement between the villages of Felechosa, in Aller, and Caleáo, in Caso, to temporarily close their mountain pastures adjacent to the Puerto de San Isidro for revegetation. In effect, it is a reestablishment of the pasturage boundaries between these two villages, for in the previous several years they had been in dispute about pasturage. Thus the agreement is accompanied by the delimitation agreement of 1941, Acta de Deslinde, which established the field markers, *moyones*, between the two villages by actual visitation. Several of these stones also mark the limits, in the Puerto de San Isidro, between Asturias and León, so this document addresses the same contested area as the document from 1530.

Rights over high mountain pasturage in Puerto de San Isidro have thus been periodically in dispute for at least four and a half centuries. Since the use of the puertos for summer pasturage seems to have been a practice since Celtic times and even before, in the first and second millennia B.C., no doubt these disputes are much more ancient. But in the last four centuries municipalities have struggled against seignorial claims by seeking direct dependency upon the king. For the monarch, direct sovereignty was advantageous for tax purposes; hence there were also struggles between sovereign and nobility, as well as rival claims among the aristocrats themselves. And of course there are disputes, the disputes of interest here, between the various villages and parishes about rights over pasturage. These disputes over the actual demarcation by field markers seem never to be finally resolved from one generation to another. At this level of governance, given fields that are not permanent, the suspicion endures that one's neighbors, whether in one's village or in the next parish or municipality, are moving the boundaries, centimeter by centimeter, in their own favor.

With the creation of the first truly centralized municipalities in the early mid-nineteenth century (the 1840's), the control over these mountain pasturages was definitively though gradually taken away from local villages and parishes and given over to municipal hands to administer from the municipal seat downvalley. But it was not taken without a fight. Indeed, the municipal minutes for Aller for 1902 and 1903 detail a conflict between the villages of Felechosa and the municipal authorities concerning the passage of cattle from downriver parishes to the high pasturage of Braña in Puerto de San Isidro.[15] In both years villagers argue that pasturage is theirs alone, and they seek to block the passage of other cattle. Even the mayor is insulted and threatened when he makes a visit of inspection. Women and children throw mud, manure, and sticks at him. Finally, a detachment of the Civil Guard is established in the village to prevent further disorder and to guarantee safe passage for downriver cattle.

By the end of the nineteenth century, of course, there had also been some privatization of pasturage in the puerto because church lands and some seignorial holdings held there had been purchased in the disentailments of the 1830's and 1840's (called Mendizabel) and the 1860's and 1870's (called Madóz). The purchases and consequent enclosure of fields, aimed toward rationalized land use, had also acted to keep villagers from exercising their old privileges of pasturage and usufruct at a minimal fee and fed the resentment that erupted in the unrest of 1902–3. The final chapter in the history of Puerto de San Isidro began in the 1970's, when the province of León began to develop a ski resort in its half of the pass and the municipality of Aller then began to sell plots of ground for building private mountain vacation houses.

What, given this history, can we say about the puerto as a symbol through time? Let us take into account the meaning of the term itself: port or harbor, that is, a place of coming in and going out. That the word is used for a mountain pass is commented on by Asturians themselves and other Spaniards. For the fact that a mountain pass and an ocean port carry the same name suggests to the villagers that when one is adrift in the mountains in a dense fog, it is the puerto that will lead one home, to harbor.

But I want to go beyond that folk meaning to suggest that the puerto, like any harbor, is a boundary place where one can pass into a new dispensation. Of course, more information than is obtained by a review of the usufruct claims over pasturage is needed to understand that meaning. It is necessary to understand how, in a lifeway of semi-transhumance, removal to a summerlong residence in the cabañas

[15] Libro de Actas, Ayuntamiento de Aller, Asuntos Especiales, Caja 1860, Asunto 26. See particularly the Sessiones del Pleno of May 23, 1901; May 31, 1901; May 16, 1902; Aug. 8, 1902; Dec. 16, 1902; May 2, 1903; July 25, 1903; Aug. 16, 1903.

was a revitalizing change. One left the compressions of village life in the narrow valleys for life in the scattered cabañas of the wide open uplands, for a more relaxed life, free of the rancorous rub of the village. It was an easily romanticized life more directly keyed to the peaceable, ruminating rhythms of the cattle themselves—a life of cheese making, spinning, long evenings of storytelling around hearth fires, courtship. Whole families lived together in close quarters with the animals and slept together in the large cabaña beds. So the puerto life did offer a new dispensation and did represent qualities of life that the village could not offer. Nowadays, to be sure, villagers, though they may still keep cattle, rarely go to the puerto for those extended revitalizing stays. They have become almost entirely village oriented, and increasingly the puerto has come to be the playground of the middle classes and the well-to-do, themselves seeking revitalization from urban lives. It has increasingly become a leisure land for those who can afford it.

The boundary disputes over pasturage rights, then, have made the puerto a frontier between the autochthony of local life and those larger forces, seignorial, provincial, municipal, and state, that would intrude upon it and seek to appropriate it. So the puerto represents at once the autochthony of the pastoral lifeway, the dispensation that lies in transhumance, and the perennial threats to autochthony that would alienate it and make it into something controlled by other hegemonic forces.

Alienation, indeed, has taken place since the civil war (1939), for a changing economy has brought a shift in village life from a dependence on cattle to a dependence on tourism. Families that used to move back and forth between the two dispensations of village life and pastoral transhumance, between winter houses and summer cabañas, have opened bars and stores to cater to the tourists now going to the puerto. They are thus held in the perpetual responsibility of storekeepers to their clients—clients who have insinuated the needs of the resort world into the villagers' ancient claim on those high mountain harbors for their cattle and for themselves.

Circumstances Alter Cases: History and the New Science in Anthropology

I have made a point of including facsimiles of some of the archival documents pertaining to the artifacts and arenas scrutinized here.

These documents have a special—indeed symbolic—meaning for Asturian country people, who often treasure copies in trunks and safe-deposit boxes because they testify to former rights and privileges won or defended and to property inherited.

But they also have symbolic meaning for anthropologists—at least anthropologists like myself who have moved from the study of non-literate African societies with minimal archives to a rural Western European society awash in unconsulted documents at the parish level, not to mention all the administrative documents of the sometimes negligent, sometimes encompassing, state. Documents alter the circumstances of fieldwork and make the fieldworkers aware of the deep roots of their case studies. Documents recast fieldwork from a descriptive and conditional into a reflective and subjunctive mode, for they can never all be consulted, and the vast majority are subject to variable interpretation. So the documents symbolize the inescapability of the subjunctive mode in fieldwork among European country men and women. They symbolize the way that introducing deep time into case histories alters one's view of one's subjects.

Raising the question of the shift in research from nonliterate African societies to rural European societies rich in religious and administrative archives points up one further difference: The African societies all experienced the impact of the more or less sudden arrival of colonialism. Indeed, their attempt to maintain traditional integrities and viable boundaries in the face of this imposed and destabilizing dispensation is of great interest (see Fernandez 1982, 1978). The Asturian mountain villages did not experience any such changes of dispensation so drastic as the imposition of Pax Britannica or Pax Gallica.

Thus I have concentrated here on symbolic arenas—houses and dooryards, fields subject to derrota, mountain meadows and passes—and their symbolic accoutrements—keys and locks, gates and field markers—which have been part of the structure of daily life and daily routine for a very long time. I have examined the changing dispensations at a microlevel as villagers were involved in the perennial shifting back and forth between street and house, between neighborhood corral and private house and dooryard, between public and communal pasture and pasture "closed over against itself" by private interests and between parochial grazing rights and the municipal, provincial, seignorial, and state uses of the upland meadows. The documents indicate that the parameters of these microshifts of arena and struggles over them are of a *longue durée*, to use Braudel's term. Indeed, in the first years of our research, particularly our reconnaissance in these villages in the mid-1960's, most villagers were, in respect to material life, still living in that condition of "inflexibility, inertia, and slow motion," of "autonomy" vis-à-vis the larger world, of which Braudel speaks. Of course he also speaks, in the same breath, of two worlds side by side, of a "market oriented economy and an expanding capitalism [spreading out] and gradually creating and prefiguring the very world in which we live" (Braudel 1977: 5).

So although there is something perennial and durable in our archive materials, surely at the microlevel there is also the insidious working away of other ideas and other structures of relationship that have brought significant change over the centuries—the change of rationalization and privatization—to these villagers. This working away has been particularly rapid in the last several decades.[16] It is the symbolics of this change that we have also sought to address. For it is in the working out in the political economy of this "great idea" of rationalization and privatization that the symbols discussed here, however perennial in one sense, have inevitably been shaped. For the mountain vacation-home owner the field marker is the same kind of boundary maintenance entity as for the cattle keeper, yet different. It symbolizes personal more than communal rights of pasturage.

Insisting on sameness in difference recognizes how often social scientists end up with arguments of the *plus ça change* variety. Here I simply want to affirm that in the study of cultural evolution we have to see things, that is, symbols, as working at different levels—specific and general perhaps—and that if we do so, there is, at once, something perennial and something dynamic, something opening up and something closing down over time, in our materials. For men and women, wherever they are studied, both understand and do not understand, and their lives are made up of the dynamic of such paradoxical states. In fact, revitalization processes themselves are based upon such paradoxes.

[16]See Susan Harding's study of Ibieca (1984), in which she shows how insidiously and yet rapidly the Francoist political economy of the 1960's and early 1970's created a much different life world for villagers by the "invisible hand" of market capitalism than that of their former peasant agriculture.

Open Fields and Dead Hands

There is a larger context for this symbolism of open and closed fields. Spain, though more isolated, was no different from any other part of Europe in respect to the ideas of rationalized agriculture that, for example, accompanied, if not led to, the enclosure movement in England (see Fernandez 1981). In Spain, however, these Enlightenment ideas arrived later and only began to be expressed in the late eighteenth century by statesmen, "los Illustrados," like the Asturian Melchor G. Jovellanos.[17] If Jovellanos symbolized the land tenure and agricultural practices of the Old Regime with the synecdochic "dead hands," so Marx, in an opposite vein, chose "enclosure" as a classic illustration—can I say symbol?—of the privatization process by which the exploitive capitalist ethos imposed itself upon the countryside, divorcing the producer from the means of production and eradicating the more tolerant, if not more generous, balance of private rights and community obligations that had prevailed there.[18] Indeed, chapter 27 of *Capital*, "Expropriation of the Agricultural Population from the Land," is, in my judgment, the most expressive, not to say symbolic, part of the work.[19]

If, for Marx, enclosure came to stand for the classic and most representative form of expropriation and accumulation, so in Spain disentailment and its offshoots, such as the suppression of derrota, has, at least for the intellectual elite, come to stand for, to symbolize, those fundamentally preoccupying changes in the countryside that, in some

[17] See Jovellanos 1753. The nub of the argument is "individual interest is the first tool of agricultural prosperity" (p. 163).

[18] "To understand its march [the transformation of feudal exploitation into capitalist exploitation] we need not go back very far. In the history of primitive accumulation all revolutions are epoch making that act as levers for the capitalist class in the course of formation, but above all, those movements when great masses of men are suddenly and forcibly torn from their means of subsistence and hurled as free and 'unattached' proletarians on the labour market. The expropriation of the agricultural producer, of the peasant from the soil, is the basis of the whole process" (Marx 1946: 787).

[19] "The spoliation of the churches' property, the fraudulent alienation of the State domains, the robbery of the common lands, the usurpation of feudal and clan property, and its transformation into modern private property under circumstances of reckless terrorism, were just so many idyllic methods of primitive accumulation. They conquered the field for capitalistic agriculture, made the soil part and parcel of capital, and created for the town industries the necessary supply of a 'free' and outlawed proletariat" (Marx 1946: 805).

views, led to its necessary rationalization and, in other views, to the drastic loss of the moral community. There has thus been a long debate in Spain about disentailment and the attendant privatization of real property, with the figure of Joaquín Costa (1902) being the classic antagonist of the iniquities of that privatization if Jovellanos is the classic protagonist. But in historiographic terms that is little different from the debate about enclosure in England between those such as the Hammonds, who in *The Village Labourer* (1911) eloquently espoused the essentials of Marx's views, and a succession of others who have taken revisionist views. Michael Turner has identified three phases in English historiography of the enclosure movement, from Marxist pessimism about the results of enclosure, to revisionist optimism, to the present counterrevisionism (1984: 12–15). In all these studies open fields have a primordial symbolic quality.

To localize these large-scale historical matters and make them more pertinent, let me mention here a series of interviews I had with a former (1940's and 1950's) secretary of the municipality of Aller, Benjamín García Alvarez (interviews that would have eventuated in a life history had he not died). He was the secretary who contributed the white paper on *jus fruendi* to the municipal council in the case of Rogelia Lobo Baizán of the Paramo of Villar. He was a conservative by temper and conviction, though not a Falangist or a Francoist.

Thematic and recurrent in our discussions was his regret over the loss of community in the various parishes and villages of Aller. As a secretary of the municipality for many years, the principal functionary in charge of the administration of its various villages, he knew that lack of community only too well. He blamed Spanish decadence upon it, since a strong state cannot be built on such weak foundations. Although a civil administrator himself, whose very job was created by the municipal reforms and municipal centralization of the nineteenth century, he felt that the reforms had only compounded the exaggerated individualism and loss of collective identity in village and parish produced by the disentailments of that century. As was typical of his sort of conservative, he blamed the Cádiz Parliament of 1812 and the French-influenced liberalism of the period that led to the reforms. The reforms, by removing the economic role of the church in local life, had abolished the moral community that the church and seignorial obligation had created at that level through their power to instill a sense of disciplined and responsible hierarchy.[20] As a consequence, the communities had lost the ability to manage their own affairs, while their inertia made management from the municipal center very difficult.

The former secretary was also alert to the issue of symbolism and frequently referred to the church's use of symbols to instill respect in country people for the ultimate values of this life and the next. With disentailment the church lost, in his view, its symbolic power over the imaginations of many of its rural parishioners. A preoccupation with sheer acquisitiveness followed. García Alvarez had reflected also on the "dead hands" metaphor and argued its inappropriateness. Jovellanos was wrong. It was not the church that had dead hands, he said, but those who can work only for themselves and who do not know how to work for their community.

Symbol Formation and Human Relatedness in a Rural Milieu

Only a rare villager knows enough of the history of disentailment to take a position on it or would, like García Alvarez himself, debate the aptness of the "dead hands" metaphor.[21] Nevertheless, the way that the accompaniments of enclosure or disentailment, whether open fields, field gates, or field markers, are formed into symbols and come to have highly charged associations is essentially no different for villager, historiographer, or administrator. Perhaps the only difference lies in the fact that the historiographer, ensconced in an office or archive, will have no direct tactile or visual experience of a field gate or a field marker—will never have propped the one open or nudged the other over a centimeter. But the main contested currents of Western European history, about which the historiographer or the political economist debates and parts of which have come to symbolize those currents and those debates, have their resonance, as I have tried to show, in this rural world of meaning.

[20] García Alvarez's preoccupations led him to collect village Ordenanzas drawn up previous to municipal reorganization and centralization. These, in his view, testified to the capacity for local self-rule before disentailment. See note 9 for reference to his collection of Ordenanzas.

[21] I am speaking about villagers who have maintained their residence in the village. Asturian mountain villages and towns have regularly produced members of the province's and the nation's educated elite, including García Alvarez himself.

I have tried to show how in contested milieux—milieux of social interactions, in which parties are in amiable or acrimonious contest—certain accompaniments that are a part of the contested whole (keys and field markers) or the whole itself (houses and puertos) will come to stand for that contest. They will come to be invested with the tension of significant differences, with the ongoing negotiation of human relatedness in that milieu. They will come to be an expression of that contest.

Such observations need axioms! I take as primordial and beyond contest in the revitalization theory I have in mind,[22] first, that human relations come in and out of contest; that is to say, people pass from routine states, which are more or less well organized and efficacious for everyday purposes and projects, to states in which they are fractious and frustrated and increasingly aware of differences in respect to such things as the division of labor (sexual and otherwise), modes of production, or distribution of surpluses. Second, the most often contested questions are (1) questions of use rights over things and people, which is to say, contest over primordial and pronomial questions of what is mine and yours, ours and theirs, yours and mine and his, and (2) related questions of confinement and exclusion or enclosure, that is, questions in the broadest sense having to do with what is within our (mine or yours, or mine and yours) sphere of use rights and what is beyond it. Third, in such contested situations, certain arenas or objects can be seen to be the focus of these elemental contests and hence become symbolic, that is, expressive of them in the subsequent revitalization scenarios, the practical culture-changing activities that such human contest produces. Fourth, these symbols are not simply expressive or representative of the contests but have a life of their own and thus influence the situation of action in which they arise.

In a sense, all of Western European history has long been preoccupied with questions of enclosure. In this paper I have sought to identify objects and arenas in the rural milieu that have come to represent aspects of this prolonged contest. I have sought to study these symbols, and changes in their weighting, in increasingly wider social and political networks: keys within the framework of the relation be-

---

[22] That would be A. F. C. Wallace's (1957) revitalization theory grounded in the vicissitudes of pronouns as played out in the predicative process by means of tropes. See Fernandez 1986.

tween the sexes and the dispensation that the one has to offer the other; houses in their dialogue with the street and within the framework of the inheritance dilemmas of extended family relations; dooryards within the framework of agitated neighborhood life; field gates within the framework of acrimony between village neighborhoods and between villages; field markers, mountain meadows, and passes within the framework of interparish and intermunicipal disputes about grazing rights. The study of symbols over time, therefore, is directly related to the study of the vicissitudes of contest in human relationships. Symbols, whether dream symbols or political symbols, are formed out of that problematic and come to stand for it as a way of thinking about it and managing the threats to order implicit in it.

Cycles of Revitalization and the Parameters of Enclosure

Two words have recurred here: dispensation and degeneration. Dispensation has preoccupied us, in part, because the symbols addressed—keys, dooryards, field gates, field markers, and mountain passes—not only symbolize contested arenas but are all liminal symbols of passage from one state of being, one dispensation, to another. But dispensation has been a key word here also because in the revitalization scenario generated by human contest there so often arises the question of new dispensations and old dispensations, of redemption by radical restoration or by radical eradication. In Spain the struggle over dispensations, the struggle over redemption, has been particularly acute, as is especially seen in the rhetoric of the civil war and the subsequent repression of the late 1930's (*depuración* in Spanish).

The word dispensation is often accompanied by the word degeneration, for which it is seen to be an antidote. It has been frequently used in Spain as part of the literature and general preoccupation with Spanish decline. It is in use in the villages as well, although with parochial and not national meaning, where collapsing great houses are bought by suddenly affluent country people and are then filled with acrimonious contest over inheritance, and where struggles over the public and the private and over usufruct have convinced many villagers that their life in community is "muy degenerado" in comparison with former times.

This sense of the degeneration of community inevitably invests with that meaning the symbols scrutinized here. Most were at that point in the revitalization cycle in which, rather than standing for access to a new dispensation, they remind many villagers of loss in the quality of life and of loss in the richness in their meaning world. Of course some villagers, whose views I have not presented, have responded with alacrity and to their benefit to the world that rationalization and privatization have opened to them. As storekeepers or barkeepers, as small entrepreneurs, they have tied themselves profitably to the modern world and the opportunities that trends like tourism make available. They find themselves optimistically riding the up phases of a cycle and do not feel themselves or their situation to be in decline. The new dispensation shines upon them. It is a time of "fat cows" (*vacas gordas*). These villagers understand how to reach out and take in and use the things that a rationalized, privatized world offers to them. But for the pastoralists and for the pastoralists-turned-miners who are the bulk of the parish population, the situation is often enough one of a dimming dispensation, of "thin cows." And this is brought to mind whenever they think about, or dream about, keys and houses, dooryards or field gates, field markers or high-altitude meadows and passes. They feel locked out and/or locked in, and they are left to make the world out of themselves, transforming themselves into those things of their world discussed here.

I use the term cycle both because I want to tie the idea of symbols through time into revitalization theory and also because I have Vico's "new science" in mind, with its emphasis not only on reflexive historiography but also upon the cycles of poetic wisdom and reason in history—cycles, that is (and to recall the epigraph), of reaching out and taking in or of turning in and making things out of oneself and transforming oneself into them. In the end any of the observations on symbols through time must be made in relation to historical cycles of revitalization, always with the caution in mind that in this pluralistic, intercommunicated world in which Western Europeans live, even villagers of the smallest and most isolated hamlets will not be perfectly "coeval," finding themselves in the same time and place upon the cycle.[23] They will find themselves in different figurative times

[23] See Johannes Fabian's (1983) discussion of the challenge of coevality to truly intersubjective anthropological fieldwork. His argument presumes that one's informants are coeval among themselves.

and places vis-à-vis the major symbols of their lives. For some the cows are fat, and for others thin. But for all, whatever the cows' transitory weight, the same symbols have persisted for hundreds of years.

Acknowledgments

This research has been supported by grants from the National Science Foundation and the Spanish–North American Joint Committee administered by the Fulbright Program. As always I am grateful to Renate Lellep Fernandez for supplying me with data and insights from her rich ethnographic knowledge of these Asturian mountain valleys and their society and culture. I have been fortunate also in working and consulting with students, now colleagues, exceptionally well informed about rural Spain: Ruth Behar, Richard Detweiler, David Frye, John Holmquist, Peter Sahlins, and Joseba Zulaika. This is a version of a paper presented at the Wenner-Gren conference "Symbolism Through Time," in January 1986 in Fez, Morocco. Let me express my gratitude to Emiko Ohnuki-Tierney for organizing the conference and especially for her important paper "Phases in Human Perception/Conception/Symbolization Processes" (1981), which raises in a trenchant and original way this issue of symbols through time.

5

The Monkey as Self in Japanese Culture

EMIKO OHNUKI-TIERNEY

My concern in this article is the Japanese contemplation of the self via the metaphor of the monkey. I am interested in how the concept of self in Japanese culture has changed through time, and in pursuit of that question I attempt to trace the meaning of the monkey—a dominant metaphor for the self in Japanese culture—from the time of the first written records during the early part of the eighth century to the present.[1] Throughout history, the Japanese have used monkeys to deliberate about themselves. Culturally construed meanings assigned to the monkey in different historical periods, therefore, succinctly reveal the Japanese answer to the question, Who are we as humans vis-à-vis animals and as Japanese vis-à-vis foreigners? In short, the monkey has served as a mirror in which the Japanese have seen themselves, sometimes positively and other times negatively.

More specifically, the monkey has been a polysemic symbol, assigned the meanings of mediator, scapegoat, and clown, each occupying a significant place in the reflexive structure of the Japanese. Although all of these meanings have been present throughout history, the *dominant* meaning has gradually changed. Between the latter half of the Medieval period (1185–1603) and the outset of the Early Modern period (1603–1868), that is, from roughly the mid-thirteenth century to the beginning of the seventeenth century, the dominant meaning of the monkey changed from mediator, represented in the belief that it was the messenger of the deities, to scapegoat, although during the transitional period the two meanings were equally dominant. The second shift in meaning is now taking place in contemporary Japan. Though the meaning of scapegoat still exists, another meaning—that

---

[1] For a discussion of metaphor within the context of trope theory, see Ohnuki-Tierney 1990.

of clown—is gradually emerging. These two changes in the meaning of the monkey coincide with the two major periods of transition in Japanese history.

Fully recognizing the weaknesses inherent in a macrostudy, I have ventured to consider the entire period of recorded history in Japan— from the beginning of the eighth century to the present—in order to accord my assessment of Japanese culture a sufficient duration of time. This seemingly impossible task is undertaken with the assumption that only by giving a structure of meaning enough time to work itself out through historical events can we assess the nature of transformation. Put another way, people's interpretation of a historical event is almost always mediated, at least partially, by the structure of meaning. But historical changes do not automatically reproduce that structure. The enduring nature of structure that emerges from the dialectic between structure and process must therefore be determined long after "vivid oscillations" caused by events and carried out by historical actors.

In this paper I show (1) how the structure of self and other has changed over a long period; (2) how the reflexive structure, central to Japanese cosmology, may be tapped by the cultural meanings assigned to the monkey, a seemingly insignificant animal; (3) how changes in the cosmological structure of self and other correlate with changes in socio-political structures; and most importantly, (4) how to identify the nature of *transformation*—a term we too often use as if it provides an answer to our perennial question of *plus ça change*.[2] By comparing and contrasting these two types of transformation that took place at two different periods in Japanese history, I attempt to show how transformation represents structural stability on the one hand and constitutes historical change on the other. I use the term *history* to refer to our interpretation of the past on its own terms, elucidated as best we can.

Why the Monkey?

The monkey is a unique animal in Japanese culture, in that no other nonhuman being in the Japanese universe has been as closely

---

[2] I am indebted to Edmund Leach, who raised a warning flag while I was still content with the term *transformation*. As I worked through my Japanese material, his warning continued to nag me.

involved in the Japanese people's deliberations about who they are as humans and as a people.[3] The unique role played by the monkey in Japanese culture comes from its dual meaning—the monkey is simultaneously similar to, and yet distinct from, humans. It is precisely the similarities that the Japanese see between the monkey and themselves that force them to create distance and difference.

Perhaps the most important basis for the affinity which the Japanese see between themselves and the monkey is the fact that the monkey is a social animal, like humans as defined by the Japanese. The self in Japanese culture is defined in interaction with others, and interdependence, rather than independence, is valued. People who fulfill their own potential and develop their selves, not in isolation from others, but in the company of others, are ideal human beings. Therefore, even such a phenomenon as someone's illness becomes a culturally sanctioned means for the members of a Japanese social group to relate to each other through the expression of concern for one another's well-being (Ohnuki-Tierney 1984). An elaborate system of gift exchange, developed, it seems, to an extreme, may not make sense for an Economic Person in a highly developed capitalistic society unless one understands that the interpersonal relationship is at the symbolic locus of Japanese culture and society. Gift exchange is both an expression of interpersonal relationship and a means to reinforce this cultural value. Thus, a human being in Japanese culture is both dialogically defined in relation to others and dialectically defined in relation to society. The Japanese self as processually defined in relation to others is at the same time the socially defined *personage* and the morally and psychologically defined *moi*.[4] Therefore, the monkey, a group animal *par excellence*, is indeed an apt metaphor for humans.[5]

[3] I thank Marshall Sahlins, whose question during my talk on this research at the Department of Anthropology, University of Chicago, made me focus more precisely on the role of the monkey metaphor in the reflexive structure of the Japanese.

[4] For a recent treatment of interpretations of the category of the person in relation to the self, see Carrithers, Collins, and Lukes 1985.

[5] The concept of the human being presented in this section derives from an interpretation of various cultural institutions, such as illness and health care, gift exchange, the use of speech levels, and so on. I wish to emphasize here that my interpretation does not depict the Japanese as being always oriented toward the group's goal and in harmonious relations with one another. This view is held by some proponents of the *nihonjinron* (theories about the Japanese), a semischolarly genre of writing in which scholars, journalists, and others debate the question of the identity of the Japanese and their culture and in which some promote their "uniqueness" in a highly patriotic sense.

The affinity that the Japanese perceive finds its expression in the dominant characterization of the monkey as a mimic of humans—the monkey is capable of carrying on human behavior. On the other hand, perceiving the affinity between humans and monkeys, the Japanese attempt to secure a comfortable distance between the two, as is evident in animal folktales. Unlike the fairy tales by the brothers Grimm, in which animals may put on human attire but seldom become humans, Japanese tales frequently portray the metamorphosis of animals into humans. Furthermore, when humans become animals, which happens less frequently, their metamorphosis is depicted as a form of transcendence. Yet the Japanese are not comfortable with metamorphoses between monkeys and humans. Teiri Nakamura (1984) analyzed 134 tales from early historical periods, and in only 3 of the 42 cases involving a human metamorphosis into an animal does a human become a monkey. In all three cases, humans are transformed into monkeys as a form of punishment. Of the 92 cases in which animals become humans, again the monkey is involved in only 3 cases. In tales from the Early Modern period, the monkey is involved in only 2 of 156 cases in which animals metamorphose into humans. The monkey is involved in only 1 of 60 cases in which humans metamorphose into animals. The monkey thus differs sharply from other animals, such as the fox and the snake, that are also considered messengers of the deities and that frequently metamorphose into humans.

The Japanese definition of monkeys as "human beings minus three pieces of hair" expresses both the perceived affinity between humans and monkeys and the Japanese effort to keep the animal below them. By dangerously threatening to cross the line between humans and animals, the monkey constantly challenges the cherished throne on which the Japanese seat themselves, thereby prompting the Japanese to contemplate their identity.[6]

Historical Changes in Monkey Symbolism

The monkey as mediator in the early and transitional periods. The dominant meaning of the monkey during the Ancient period (250–1185) and throughout the Medieval period (1185–1603) was

[6] For a detailed discussion of the metaphorical predication of the Japanese self by the monkey, see Ohnuki-Tierney 1990.

that of mediator between deities and humans. One of the oldest sources of evidence to link the monkey with the role of mediator is Saruta Biko, the Monkey Deity, who is featured prominently in both the *Kojiki*, published in 712, and the *Nihongi*, published in 720—the two oldest Japanese publications that contain accounts of mythical-historical events of the early periods. Saruta Biko appears in an episode in which Amaterasu Ōmikami, the Sun Goddess, considered to be the ancestress of the Japanese, decides to send her grandson to earth to govern there. When the grandson, accompanied by several other deities, is ready to descend, a scout, who has been sent earlier to clear their way, returns to report on his encounter with Saruta Biko at "the eight crossroads of Heaven." The scout describes Saruta Biko as a deity whose nose is seven hands long and whose back is more than seven fathoms long; his eyeballs glow like an eight-handed mirror, and a light shines from his mouth and from his anus (Sakamoto et al. 1967: 147–48). Saruta Biko explains to the scout that he has come to greet the heavenly grandson.[7] This episode reveals that in the Japanese myth-history, Saruta Biko serves as the mediator between deities and humans, and between heaven and earth. His location at the eight crossroads is a spatial symbol of his mediation role.

Various factors identify Saruta Biko as the Monkey Deity. First, the term *saru*, which forms a part of his name, means monkey. Also, the deity has red buttocks, a prominent characteristic of Japanese macaques (Shimonaka 1941: 118). Furthermore, in the *Kojiki* Saruta Biko is said to have had his hand caught in a shell while fishing (Kurano and Takeda 1958: 131; Philippi 1969: 142)—a behavioral characteristic of macaques, who gather shellfish at low tide. A monkey with its hand caught in a shell is a frequent theme of Japanese folktales (Inada and Ōshima 1977: 392). Saruta Biko's shellfish gathering and his physical characteristics are cited by Minakata (1972: 401) as evidence for the unquestionable identification of Saruta Biko as an old male macaque. Others have suggested that since Saruta Biko welcomes the Sun Goddess just as Japanese macaques welcome the rising sun with their loud morning calls, he must be a macaque (Matsumae 1960: 44; Minakata 1972: 410–11).[8]

[7] For descriptions of Saruta Biko, see also Kurano and Takeda 1958: 127; *Kojiki*, 1969: 138, 140, 142; Shimonaka 1941: 118.

[8] Some scholars disagree with the identification of Saruta Biko with the monkey. Noboru Miyata (personal communication), for example, believes that the deity should

The monkey's role as a sacred mediator continued to develop throughout the Medieval period. In fact, some of the most unambiguous expressions of this role took place during the long transition between the Medieval period and the Early Modern period. Leaving aside much evidence from art, folklore, and folk religions, I present here only a few examples of the monkey as mediator during this period. One is the belief in the Mountain Deity, Sannō Shinkō. According to this belief, the monkey is referred to as the "monkey deity," or *saru gami*, whose function is to serve as a messenger to humans from various other deities, particularly the powerful Mountain Deity (Origuchi 1965: 299, 324–25; Yanagita 1982a: 333–40, 1951: 240). The mountains, where deities are believed to reside, constitute the most sacred places in the universe, and consequently the Mountain Deity is an extremely important deity in the pantheon of Japanese folk religions (Blacker 1975; Yanagita 1951: 642–44).

The belief in the Mountain Deity was prevalent toward the end of the Medieval period and the beginning of the Early Modern period. Toyotomi Hideyoshi, who in 1590 gained control over the entire nation, was nicknamed Kosaru (Small Monkey) or Saru (Monkey), not only because his face looked like a monkey's but also because he eagerly sought identification with the monkey in various ways (Ooms 1985: 285–87). Tokugawa Ieyasu, the first shogun, officially designated the Monkey Deity the guardian of peace in the nation, and the festival for the deity was elaborately observed in Edo (Tokyo) during his reign (1603–16) (Iida 1983: 65). Initially the festival procession was led by a monkey cart (*saru dashi*), although later a rooster cart came to take the lead.

Another conspicuous expression of the monkey as a sacred mediator is the monkey performance, during which a trained monkey performs to music that is either sung by the trainer or played on the three-stringed shamisen instrument or a drum (Ishii 1963: 39). Based on the belief that the monkey is the guardian of horses, the monkey performance originated as a ritual in the stables during which the monkey harnessed the sacred power of the Mountain Deity to heal sick horses and to maintain their welfare in general. Later it was performed in the streets and at the doorways of individual homes both

---

be identified as *tengu*, a mythical being of the mountains with a long nose. Yet another interpretation is that Saruta Biko represents a foreign people (*ijin*).

for entertainment and for religious reasons. Because the monkey is a messenger from the powerful Mountain Deity, the dance, wherever it was performed, symbolized the Mountain Deity's visit to the people to bless them with health and prosperity (see Oda 1980: 2).

While the *Ryōjin hishō* (1169–1179) is possibly the earliest description of the monkey performance, several sources from the mid-thirteenth century testify to the full development of the monkey performance by that time. The monkey danced and wore an *ebōshi*, the type of hat worn by aristocrats and warriors at the time, and which became a trademark for performing monkeys. The monkey also collected payment after each performance.[9]

Toward the very end of the Medieval period and the beginning of the Early Modern period we also see an additional role assigned to the monkey performance—the blessing of a new crop of rice. At this time a genre of paintings depicting rice harvesting emerged, and we find a dancing monkey in these scenes. The Mountain Deity is believed to become the Deity of the Rice Paddy in the spring; he descends to the rice paddies from the mountains, to which he returns in the fall. Therefore, the dancing by the monkey in harvesting scenes represents the blessing of the rice crop by the Mountain Deity. The monkey thus acts yet again as a sacred mediator between the Mountain Deity and humans.[10]

The monkey as scapegoat during the transitional period. The monkey's role as a scapegoat became dominant in the transitional period, while its role as a mediator gradually lost strength as the Early Modern period progressed. I use the term *scapegoat* broadly to refer to any innocent victim of ridicule or discrimination. The meaning assigned to the monkey as a scapegoat is most succinctly expressed in the Japanese saying that monkeys are "human beings minus three

[9] For an interpretation of the *Ryōjin Hishō* in regard to the monkey performance, see Yanagita 1982b: 336–37. The mid-thirteenth-century documents depicting the monkey performance include the *Nenjū gyōji emaki* (Kadokawa Shoten Henshūbu 1968; see also Fukuyama 1968); the *Azuma kagami*, dated 1245, and the *Kokon chomonshū*, dated 1254 (Tachibana 1966: 535–36); and the *Yūzūnenbutsu engi emaki*, dated 1391. For brief discussions of the monkey performance of this period, see also Miyamoto 1981: 82; Oda 1967: 49; Oda 1978: 15. A detailed historical development of the monkey performance is presented in Ohnuki-Tierney 1987.

[10] These paintings include those by Iwasa Katsumochi Matabei (1578–1650) and those by Kusumi Morikage (1620–90). For the relationship between the Mountain Deity and the Deity of the Rice Paddy, see Yanagita 1951: 642; Ouwehand 1964.

pieces of hair": The monkey lacks three pieces of hair—the essence of humanness—and yet unsuccessfully tries to be a human; it is a laughable creature.[11]

Perhaps the best-known expression of the monkey as a scapegoat is the three-monkey theme, which represents the self-portrayal of the common people during the Early Modern period. The people, who were deprived of any freedom and therefore resigned to neither seeing, hearing, nor speaking of societal evils, found a self-mocking expression in the three-monkey theme, which originally had a quite different meaning in Buddhism (Iida 1983; Ooms 1985).

Besides a number of folktales in which a monkey is depicted as a scapegoat, we see the expression in various genres of literature and art. One of the best-known examples is the proverb "*Tōrō ga ono, enkō ga tsuki*" (The forelegs ["axes"] of a praying mantis, a monkey and the moon). A praying mantis trying to chop the wheel of a cart with its forelegs is as ridiculous as a monkey that mistakes the reflection of the moon in the water for the moon itself and tries to capture it. Although the proverb originated in a Chinese story called *Sō-shiritsu*, its prevalence during the sixteenth century is signified by a famous painting entitled *Enkō sakugetsu* (Monkey capturing the moon) by Hasegawa Tōhaku (1539–1610).

Another expression of the same theme is found on a lacquerware stationery container made by an anonymous artist during the nineteenth century and now housed in the Freer Gallery of Art at the Smithsonian Institution. On the cover of the box three macaques, all wearing glasses, are opening a scroll while night falcons hover over them. Although no written message accompanies the picture, it carries a moral message: "Do not attempt things beyond your capacity." The monkeys, of course, do not have the ability to read, an ability that, to the Japanese, distinguishes humans from animals. While the monkeys are attempting the impossible, they are risking their lives by letting their chief enemies, night falcons, approach them; "nightjar" (*yodaka*) is also a euphemism for a prostitute. Here we see an iconographic equation of monkeys with prostitutes. That is, the low status of "the monkey scholar" is placed in prominent relief through the metaphorical linkage between the two.

[11] Hair is a metonymic symbol of the person in Japanese culture. See Ohnuki-Tierney 1990 for a discussion of metonym.

During the late Medieval period and the beginning of the Early Modern period, the meaning of the monkey seems to have been extended from undesirable copycat to all types of undesirables. In *Shinchōki* (a biography of the warlord Oda Nobunaga [1534–82] by Oze Hōan), a beggar is referred to as a monkey (Minakata 1972: 415). Minakata interprets the use of the term for monkey to suggest that some *senmin* ("base people," "outcasts") who were physically disabled and who resorted to begging were referred to as monkeys. During the Early Modern period, the expression "the monkey in the kitchen" (*zensho no saru*) was commonly used to refer to beggars (Hirose 1978: 303). Minakata (1972: 407, 414–15) also cites a number of publications from the early eighteenth century in which prostitutes and various other undesirables were referred to as monkeys.

The monkey is also depicted, although less negatively, as a scapegoat in a well-known *ōtsu-e*, a genre of folk paintings by anonymous artists that flourished from the late seventeenth to the early eighteenth century. In the painting, a monkey tries to subdue a slippery catfish with an equally slippery gourd—a foolish endeavor. During this period, the catfish was said to cause earthquakes (Ouwehand 1964). Therefore, the painting can be read as a monkey trying to do the impossible job of controlling an earthquake. Either way, the monkey is depicted as a fool.[12]

An even more specific example of the monkey's role as a scapegoat is seen in another seventeenth-century belief and associated practice whereby the monkey became a scapegoat for a human victim of smallpox. It was believed that the monkeys kept at Sakamoto Sannō Shrine suffered from smallpox when the emperors fell victim to the disease. In one instance, when Emperor Gokōmei (r. 1648–64) died of smallpox, the monkeys recovered; in another instance, Emperor Higashiyama (r. 1688–1713) recovered from smallpox when the monkeys died from it (Minakata 1972: 378–79). The belief in the monkey as a scapegoat for a human victim of disease has persisted for centuries. For example, around 1900 it was reported that people with eye diseases would pray at Tennōji Shrine in the belief that if the monkeys in the compound suffered from eye diseases, the human patients would recover from them (Minakata 1972: 378–79).

---

[12] Herman Oom of the University of California, Los Angeles, kindly pointed out to me that the painting expresses the Zen teaching of the impossibility of achieving *satori* (enlightenment) if one makes a voluntary effort to achieve it.

The monkey's meaning as a scapegoat continues to be the dominant one in contemporary Japan. Until recently, newspaper editorials often reprimanded the Japanese who engaged in "monkey imitation" of the West. Thus, the monkey continues to project the negative side of humans, although the strong moral message, which existed in the Early Modern period and which was used by the government for social control, is no longer present. Rather than conveying the order "Thou shalt not," most contemporary sayings simply ridicule people by the use of the monkey metaphor.

New meanings of the monkey in contemporary Japan. Although the monkey continues to be a scapegoat in contemporary Japan, two new forms have emerged recently. The first is the appearance of *bunkazaru* (cultured monkeys) (Miyaji 1973). Sold as souvenirs at parks and elsewhere, these figurines are carved with exaggerated gestures of seeing, hearing, and speaking. Sometimes called Shōwa *sanzaru* (the three monkeys of the Shōwa era, the era of the late emperor's reign), or *sakasazaru* (inverted monkeys), they endorse the attitude that one should examine, listen, and speak out—the attitude considered to represent the modern, progressive stance of new Japan. Like the clowning monkey discussed below, the *bunkazaru* represents a reflexive figure.

In the second place, the monkey performance, once discontinued, has been revived in a new form. The trainers who perform in Tokyo have developed the performance into a clown act, jointly put on by the trainer and the monkey. Amid the laughter of spectators the two make satirical commentaries on human assumptions of human superiority over animals and on the principle of hierarchy in Japanese society. The highlight of one performance, for example, is a cleverly staged act of disobedience by the monkey. It takes place during the act of jumping from block to block. When the trainer shouts the order "Go!" the monkey jumps onto the first block and hangs onto it with a miserable face. The spectators inevitably break into laughter at the sight of an animal defying a human, on the one hand, and a boss being defied by a subordinate, on the other.

The powerful presence of the monkey in the contemporary conceptual world of the Japanese is impressive when we consider that most urban Japanese see monkeys only in zoos, not in nature. In fact, a monkey trainer who performs in Tokyo told me that a kindergartner asked if the performing monkey was a stuffed monkey with remote control. It seems that the Japanese continue to be reflexive about themselves using the monkey as their means of deliberation.

Monkey as Mediator, Scapegoat, and Clown and Macrohistorical Changes

These historical materials indicate that the monkey has been assigned the meaning and power of a mediator, a scapegoat, and a clown. All of these meanings have been present since early times, but at any given time, just one meaning has been dominant, except during the two transitional periods, when two dominant meanings competed—mediator and scapegoat during the latter half of the Medieval period and scapegoat and clown in contemporary Japan.

In ethnographic literature, these meanings are assigned to so-called marginal or anomalous/ambiguous symbols and have received much attention from anthropologists. However, these studies have usually located a mediator here, a trickster there, and so on, either in separate contexts within a culture or even in different cultures. Ethnographic findings on these symbols, in short, have provided us with only a synchronic series of still photos, as it were, without systematically examining either ethnographic or conceptual relationships among them.

The data from Japanese culture demonstrate that all of these meanings are assigned to the monkey, which occupies a structurally marginal status. The very affinity that the Japanese recognize places the monkey on the periphery of their categorical schema. The monkey is a deity that is too close to humans to be a bona fide deity; hence, it is assigned a mediator role. In later history it is regarded as an animal that falls short of becoming human and thus is assigned the negative role of scapegoat (for different types of anomaly or marginality, see Ohnuki-Tierney 1981: 119–24).

Those categories of people, such as prostitutes and beggars, who were sometimes referred to as monkeys have also been assigned the same set of meanings; remarkably, their meanings have been transformed in exactly the same sequence and at the same time as those of the monkey. Most important, the same fate was shared by "the special-status people," who are at present called *hisabetsu-burakumin*. The special-status people constitute a heterogeneous group of people, including artistic and religious specialists, to whom various values and meanings have been assigned in different periods of Japanese history. All of these people, and women in general, have occupied a structurally marginal place in Japanese society and culture.

In short, the findings from Japanese culture testify that the meanings assigned to these symbols derive from their conceptual marginality and that there is a close relationship among these meanings. These findings are ethnographic-historical facts, rather than logical possibilities of a universal nature postulated in the abstract by anthropologists. The first order of business, then, is to examine the relationships of these meanings within the context of Japanese culture, lest the familiar terms remain hollow skeletons in our structural exercise.

Mediator, scapegoat, and clown in Japanese culture. We can understand the specific meanings and roles assigned to the mediator, the scapegoat, and the clown in Japanese culture by locating them within the context of a reflexive structure in which deities play a significant role. Certain Japanese deities called *marebito* are believed to reside outside a community or over the horizon. They are thought to have a dual nature—the peaceful and constructive soul (*nigitama*) and the violent and destructive soul (*aratama*). The Japanese manipulate these stranger-deities through rituals, whose primary function is to ward off the negative powers of the deities and harness the positive ones. These stranger-deities from outside have provided the model for interpreting outside forces, including foreigners, whose positive powers, such as Western technology, have been eagerly sought but whose negative powers have always posed threats. I propose here that the deities represent a transcendental self of the Japanese, who also see a dual nature in themselves. The deities mirror a purified transcendental human self. For this reason, I believe, in Japanese culture a mirror symbolizes a deity. The Japanese attempt to harness the creative power of the deities in order to replenish their lives, which otherwise become impure with stagnation. This is facilitated by mediators, who are assigned the crucial role in the effort to maintain the purity of self.

In relation to the reflexive structure, the meaning and function of mediator and scapegoat are exactly the same in Japanese culture, except that one constitutes an inversion of the other. The mediator brings in purity to the people from outside, whereas the scapegoat draws impurity onto itself, thereby removing it from the lives and selves of the people. Likewise, from the perspective of a classificatory system, the two carry the same function—facilitating the intercategorical traffic—but in different ways. The mediator is assigned the role of traversing the intercategorical boundaries, delivering to humans the message of blessing from the Japanese deities. The scapegoat facilitates intercategorical movements by being a "breakable taboo." I coin this term to refer to taboos that are breakable as long as offenders make amends by performing culturally prescribed rituals, formalized or nonformalized. If the system requires intercategorical transactions and yet must articulate boundary lines, it calls on breakable taboos and scapegoats to mark the boundary between purity and impurity. Taboos and scapegoats in fact highlight the boundary lines while facilitating traffic across them.

Whereas the mediator and the scapegoat work within the system, the clown is on the margin of or slightly outside it. Spectators laugh at the clown, unaware that they are mocking themselves or their culture and society. In the contemporary monkey performance, the trainer is offering himself and the monkey as a target of laughter—a sacrificial victim at the altar—while chiding the audience with his social commentary. The clown, too, derives its role from its structural marginality, but it is a positively reflexive figure, unlike the mediator and the scapegoat, which are not reflexive in themselves.

A closer look at the cultural representations of a monkey as mediator, scapegoat, and clown tells us of the intimate involvement of the monkey in the reflexive structure of the Japanese, as well as of the enormous complexity of the structure of meaning embodied in the symbolic representations of the monkey introduced earlier. We recall that the first appearance of the monkey in written sources is the Monkey Deity, Saruta Biko, who mediated between deities and humans at the time of the descent to earth of the grandson of the Sun Goddess. This deity's physical characteristics included eyeballs that glowed like mirrors and a mouth and an anus from which light shone. The symbolism of mirror and light clearly identifies the Monkey Deity as a reflexive agent. Yet the very same body part that symbolizes reflexivity, that is, the red rump, is selected as the symbol of the monkey's animality in Japanese culture; the association recurs again and again in songs and paintings in which the Japanese ridicule the monkey for its red buttocks.

According to some scholars, Saruta Biko represents shaman-actors in ancient Japan (see Matsumura 1948: 6–7, 32–36; 1954; see also Takazaki 1956). They argue that the unusual description of the physical appearance of Saruta Biko—with a long nose, mirrorlike eyes, and so on—is a depiction of a shaman-actor donning a mask and a disguise. They consider the term *saru* to mean "to play" or "to perform a comic act causing laughter." In the view of these scholars, the scene in which Saruta Biko's hand is caught in a shell represents a comical performance that at the same time had magical power.

Whether we link Saruta Biko to a *saru* (monkey), whose primary characteristic in Japanese culture is its ability to imitate, an important element of performance in ancient Japan, or whether we interpret Saruta Biko to be a shaman-actor in disguise, there seems to be a definite performance element in the meaning assigned to this mediator-god. Seen in this light, Saruta Biko is a reflexive symbol *par excellence*, whose meaning is expressed through its various physical characteristics as well as through its role as an actor-scapegoat-clown who is also a mediator. Saruta Biko therefore provides a concrete ethnographic case illustrating that the mediator, scapegoat, and clown derive from the same structure of meaning.

Likewise, the monkey reaching for the moon depicts not only a silly monkey striving for the impossible but a human striving for a transcendental self, symbolized by the mirror, that is, the moon.

Thus both cultural representations of the monkey show that mediator and scapegoat are reflexive agents at a higher level of abstraction. All of these meanings are almost always present in the representations of a monkey, but one is more articulated and overshadows the others (for further discussion of these symbols' multiple structures of meaning, see Ohnuki-Tierney 1987).

Micro-macro linkage. The finding that the transformations of the meaning of the monkey express the changing structure of reflexivity must now be placed in the broader context of Japanese society to determine the nature of the relationship of this microphenomenon with the macroscene. Toward that end, we must examine the historical context. Significantly, the two periods in which the changes in meaning took place—the latter half of the Medieval period and the present—coincide with the two major transitional periods in Japanese history.

Although Japan has often been thought of as an isolated country, its history is a series of conjunctures in Braudel's sense. Its earlier history was frequently affected by developments in northeast Asia; the transition from the Ancient period to the beginning of the Medieval period was a part of the dramatic transformation of northeast Asia at large. Japanese society then underwent a series of fundamental changes with the introduction of various ideas from China, including cash economy (Amino 1986). The transformation of society and culture became especially dramatic around the mid-thirteenth century, when the forces for change pushed for greater flexibility in the sociocultural system and for an emphasis on achieved, rather than ascribed, status.

Throughout the late Medieval period, these forces rocked Japanese culture and society from the bottom, most turbulently during the Muromachi period (1338–1573). They were most clearly manifested in the concept of *gekokujō*, which literally means "the below conquering the above." This concept, derived from the dualistic cosmology of yin and yang and the five elements, does not recognize the absolute supremacy of any particular element in the universe (La Fleur 1983; see also Putzar 1963; Yokoi 1980). This metaphysical-ontological perspective gave rise to a genre of literature called the *gekokujō no bungaku* (literature of the *gekokujō*), which enjoyed much popularity among the common people (Satake 1970; Sugiura 1965). The theme of *gekokujō* appealed to many Japanese, who translated and transformed it into a pragmatic philosophy of life, making it possible for a person of low social status to surpass someone above him. Also available were several institutionalized means whereby people with talent in religion and art could renounce their ascribed low status. These institutions freed many capable people from low status and contributed to an efflorescence of all forms of art.[13]

The inner dynamics were expressed outwardly as well. The Japanese during this period were open to outsiders—they were curious about foreign lands and cultures. They reestablished trade and cultural contacts with China in about 1342 under the direction of Zen monks (Putzar 1963: 287). They visited foreign countries in their ships and even founded Japanese colonies. Through extensive trade with other peoples, they brought in foreign goods that were endowed with positive symbolic meanings.

[13] These people were often of *senmin* status, indicating that they were of the special-status group, which at the time did not constitute a clearly marked group. These institutions did not really place them within the normal hierarchy of the society.

On the other hand, forces opposed to change were also at work during the Medieval period. These opposing principles and forces were already present during the Ancient period, during which Japanese society was already stratified. Even the basic structure of values, characterized by the symbolic opposition of purity and impurity, which has been dominant throughout Japanese history, had been well formulated (Ohnuki-Tierney 1984: 35–38). During the first transitional period, an emphasis on ascribed status, hierarchy, and the system of meaning that included purity and impurity as moral values was gathering intensity. It is in this period that we see the emergence of impurity as radical negativity (see Kuroda 1972).

Dynamism and fluidity were terminated, indeed quite firmly, with the establishment of Tokugawa government at the beginning of the seventeenth century. Externally, the government enforced the closure of the nation by restricting trade and closing ports to most foreigners. It tried to eliminate influences from outside, as manifested in the effective proscription of Christianity. Internally, the Early Modern period witnessed Japan's full development into a feudal society, which became hierarchically divided into four groups (warriors, farmers, manufacturers, and merchants, in descending order), plus two social categories outside the system—the emperor at the top and the special-status people at the bottom. The special-status people became outcastes also in the sense that conceptually they were placed outside Japanese society and took on the burden of impurity, which received a negative moral value. In addition, they were denied social mobility. The inauguration of the Early Modern period may be interpreted as a result of the conjuncture of internal development and foreign pressure. Unlike in the Medieval period, Japan responded negatively to the worldwide historical developments of the time.

The historical transition in Japanese society from the Medieval to the Early Modern period coincided with the transformation of the monkey and the special-status people from mediators to scapegoats. The parallel transformations offer a good fit. Symbolically, as noted earlier, taboos and scapegoats simultaneously fulfill the need to facilitate cross-categorical traffic and the need to mark the boundaries by embodying impurity. Japanese society and culture after the later Medieval period and especially during the Early Modern period indeed needed both functions simultaneously.

Taboos and scapegoats also met another need. The closure of the society to outsiders meant the elimination of foreigners, who, like the stranger-deities, supplied the vital energy of purity for the rejuvenation of the self. In their absence, another method of rejuvenation had to be found, hence the emphasis on scapegoats. In contrast to the rejuvenation accomplished by bringing in a positive element from outside, scapegoats provide a means for getting rid of negative elements (see Burke 1955 for an analysis of the Jews in Hitler's Germany). During this period, then, the increased rigidity within society and the elimination of outsiders paralleled the transformation of the meaning of the monkey, indicating that a significant change in the Japanese conception of self and other had taken place.

The end of the Early Modern period came with the Meiji restoration in 1868, which returned the emperor to the political center, at least nominally, and once again opened up the country. Again the major transformation signified by the Meiji restoration was a result of both internal forces and external pressures, exemplified by Commodore Matthew C. Perry's visit to Japan. Despite these dramatic changes and a strong push for more flexible structure(s), the basic character of the culture and society formed during the Early Modern period remained tenaciously intact. In particular, the Japanese conception of the self in relation to other peoples did not undergo a fundamental change. Just as the Japanese were awed by Chinese civilization during the fifth and sixth centuries, they were duly impressed by Western civilization when the country was reopened in 1868. The "others," represented by the Chinese and then by the Westerners, continued to represent the transcendental self of the Japanese.

An even more fundamental change in the reflexive structure did not take place until today, roughly since the 1970's. Although any assessment of change in contemporary Japan must be tentative, since waves and ripples have not settled yet for us to evaluate whether or not they are to have enduring impact upon the basic structure of the culture. Nonetheless, there is no doubt that the present is a period of transition and significant changes.

World War II ended with the first and only defeat the nation has ever experienced. Drastic changes were brought about by the Occupation, but they were imposed from without. Perhaps for this reason we see indigenous changes emerging only now, five decades after the war.

In many ways the contemporary period is similar to the latter half of the Medieval period. The fluidity of contemporary Japan is manifested both internally and externally. Internally, various opposing forces are at work. Externally, the Japanese public is exploring the outside. A phenomenal number of Japanese tourists travel all over the world, including the People's Republic of China—the country that provided the Japanese with a writing system, technology, a political structure, and a host of other vital cultural apparatus.

A particularly fundamental change, however, concerns the Japanese people's changing perception of the self as a result of their technological and economic successes in the world market. According to a survey conducted by the government in 1983 and reported in the November 17, 1984, *Asahi Shinbun*, the majority of Japanese then regarded themselves as superior to Westerners (Pyle 1987: 16). For the Japanese, science and technology had represented the superiority of the West. They symbolized the positive power of the stranger-deity. The Japanese had striven to excel in science and technology in their effort to emulate the transcendental order. Therefore, it is less economic success as such that has affected the concept of the collective self and more its symbolic nature—they have lost their transcendental self, which had supplied the psychological motivation to achieve in science and technology ever since the opening of the country at the end of the nineteenth century.

From the perspective of the structure of reflexivity, the present is a new era for the Japanese, who feel for the first time in their history that they have mastered the outside, the other, whose negative power devastated the country in 1945. Economic and technological success therefore requires a radical adjustment in their view of the self vis-à-vis the other. Therefore, while contemporary Japan is similar to the late Medieval period, from the perspective of the Japanese relationship to the *other* it constitutes an inversion of the traditional hierarchy between *self* and *other*. The inversion is a drastic change, happening for the first time in history. Again, this type of drastic change cannot be dismissed as simply a transformation.

The emergence of new meanings of the monkey—the three cultural monkeys and the clowning monkey—seems to reassure us of the central place that the monkey occupies in the Japanese structure of reflexivity. Since a clown in particular is a reflexive agent, the emergence of the monkey as a clown succinctly reflects the heightened sense of reflexivity of the contemporary Japanese.

Indeed, the monkey has sensitively expressed the thought processes of the Japanese throughout history. We can tap a significant part of the Japanese structure of meaning by examining the process of the transformation of the meaning of the monkey—a powerful metaphor for humans vis-à-vis animals and for the Japanese vis-à-vis foreigners.

Historical causality. Although there is no space to engage in an extensive discussion of historical causality, let me briefly introduce my basic perspective on mechanisms for historical changes insofar as they relate to the present discussion. My argument here is a subscription neither to assigning primacy to "external" factors nor to giving autonomy to the internal logic of the symbolic structure. Not only is there no simple historical causality, but neither social structure, political economy, nor any other single dimension of a culture holds primacy over the other dimensions (see the discussion of historical process in the Introduction to this book). Most important, causal agents of historical changes never work in monocausal fashion, as is illustrated by the changes in contemporary Japan. The concept of self and other had provided a model for Japanese economic behavior. To emulate the other, they strived in science, technology, and industry. Since they have succeeded in these areas, their concept of self is in turn undergoing changes. Thus, the conceptual realm and the economic realm are not separate, nor does one have primacy over the other. The meaning of economic behavior derives from the order of meaning in general, which in turn is affected by practice in the economic realm. Causal arrows always work in a reciprocal manner.

Japanese reflexivity has always involved other peoples, originally represented by the stranger-deities. It is in the interaction between the Japanese and other peoples that the transformations of the concepts of both self and society have taken place. Like the Hawaiians, the Chinese, and the Kwakiutl, all discussed by Sahlins (1989), the Japanese too have met the challenge of the world systems, economic and symbolic. At times they enthusiastically welcomed the other and used it to energize their collective self, but at other times they shunned it to protect and preserve their self. Or, a more accurate way of interpreting the phenomenon is that the Japanese attitude toward the other already had these two sides. At any rate, their reflexivity makes it a structural necessity to involve the other, as is defined in structure and in practice. This is the reason why the metaphor of the self is a strategic choice for examining historical transformations in Japan.[14]

Historical actors. It is almost a truism to state that historical transformations cannot be understood in terms of the structure of thought and historical events alone. Transformations are always mediated by the actions of people, who experience the various cultural and social representations and their changes with feelings and thoughts.

The monkey metaphor has served as a vehicle of contemplation both for the politically powerful and the politically peripheral. Toyotomi Hideyoshi and Tokugawa Ieyasu, the most powerful political leaders at a crucial period in Japanese history, both recognized the positive power of the monkey and incorporated it in their political rituals. Hideyoshi even strived to identify himself with the monkey. I know of no record that verifies the precise nature of his motive. We might guess, however, that it was not simply the positive power of the monkey but its ambiguous nature that attracted him. Like the monkey, which emulates a nobleman by wearing his hat, Hideyoshi rose from a humble origin to become the first leader to unify Japan.

A similar motive perhaps underlies various representations of the monkey by anonymous artists, such as the monkey scholars on the lacquerware box. Artists in general during the Early Modern period were of ambiguous status, and the choice of the monkey as their motif might not have been purely coincidental. Interpretations about past historical actors, however, are highly speculative.[15]

We have more information with which to assess the role of contemporary monkey trainers as historical actors. It is they who revived the extinct art and developed the monkey performance into a clown act. Clowning has a long tradition in Japanese culture, and the con-

[14]It may be a matter of degree, but Chinese cosmology and Chinese structure of reflexivity seem to have been self-contained. They have been "the central flower of the universe," as the first two characters of the name of the People's Republic of China signify. Sahlins (1989) notes that the Chinese were indifferent to European goods that the Hawaiians were only too eager to obtain.

[15]We may also speculate about Hideyoshi. It was he who in 1582 placed the ambiguously defined special-status people into two legally codified categories (Ueda 1978: 100–101). One might think that his own ambivalent social position drew him to the ambiguous animal but that identifying himself with humans whose position and meaning in Japanese culture were ambiguous was personally too threatening. But this interpretation may be overdetermined by the structure of meaning as I see it.

temporary monkey performance is related to, if not born of, this tradition. In fact, Murasaki Tarō, who stages monkey performances in Yoyogi Park in Tokyo, told me that he consciously followed the tradition of *manzai*, a genre of comic performance, as he was developing his repertoire. Though the particular form and content of his clown act are his creation, he did not have to give the meaning described above to the monkey performance. His own identity as a member of the special-status group may be responsible for the focus of his clowning—juggling the social hierarchy and the hierarchy between humans and animals, rather than gender inequality, for example, which is the focus of clowning in many societies.

These historical actors, however, do not dictate the course of history or the choice of meaning of a polyseme. While we seldom have enough historical data to understand these processes of negotiation in the past, scenes from contemporary monkey performances are illustrative. Thus, Murasaki Tarō told me that when he referred to the posture of the monkey as a sumo wrestler's, the spectators refused to respond. Only when he referred to it as Takamiyama's, that of a very popular sumo wrestler who was originally from Hawaii, did they react with spontaneous laughter. Needless to say, he henceforth changed his narration.

This is the kind of historical process duing which the meaning of the monkey as mediator, scapegoat, and clown is negotiated; a dominant meaning emerges as a result of negotiation, while always leaving some ambiguity typical of any communication via symbols.

In turning to the question of the power of the historical actor upon the course of history, we can say that a monkey trainer as a historical actor is not the same as Toyotomi Hideyoshi as a historical actor: The former represents the politically peripheral; the latter, the politically central. Their positions often determine the effectiveness of their actions on society. Murasaki Tarō does not directly or immediately affect the course of history. He neither negotiates his social position nor provokes spectators into action. His power as a historical actor must be evaluated in terms of its long-range effect: In the atmosphere of play, he gently prods spectators to contemplate their society and its received categories. I think his impact is like raindrops, which almost invisibly but steadily transform a huge rock onto which they fall. Therefore, a subtle but potentially powerful historical event is produced at the scene of action—created by a brilliant performing artist who acts on the structure of thought and the structure of society in the process of creating a metaphysical masterpiece.

On the other hand, we cannot overestimate the role of historical actors in the course of history. In particular, we must distinguish the intentionality of historical actors from the actual effect they have. There are several reasons for this. First, historical actors, like other members of society, are seldom fully cognizant of the meaning of their behavior. Such is the case with Murasaki Tarō. When I commented on the social commentary in his performance and pointed to the clowning element, he told me that he was quite unaware of those aspects. His role and power as a historical actor do not completely derive from his intentions. Second, the ambiguity and indeterminacy of polysemes often create a gap in the reading of symbols by the historical actors who use them and the people who interpret them. As I detail elsewhere (Ohnuki-Tierney 1987), two people may ascribe different meanings to a monkey without realizing it. For example, during a monkey performance in 1981, the trainers and the spectators assigned different meanings to the monkey, while the performance continued as usual. In communications using symbols, including linguistic symbols, people often talk past each other without realizing it.

Third, what I call the routinization of meaning takes place: The meaning of a symbol, including a patterned behavior, becomes taken for granted. The routinization of meaning sustains a situation wherein historical actors go about using the symbol or carrying on a patterned behavior without ever scrutinizing what it stands for; sometimes they keep using a symbol when they no longer accept the relationship between its form and its meaning. The symbol becomes "symbolic" and the behavior becomes a "tradition" or a "custom" in the popular sense of these words. For example, women who customarily wear a veil or a hat in a Christian church have rarely articulated its original meaning and purpose—to prevent contamination by the impurity of women, embodied in their hair.

In short, although it is necessary to recognize the role of historical actors and their intentionality in the course of history, it is also important to recognize their limitations. Communication between people—the stage of praxis—always involves a complex process in which polysemic symbols are used and interpreted by actors from diverse perspectives. The behavior of an actor is not always fully a product of his or her articulated intentions; further, polysemes can play such tricks on our communication that we often do not recognize the absence of communication.

Transformation as Historical Change

The advantage of studying a culture over a very long time is that it enables us to see the total picture of the system of meaning, in both its stability and its changes (cf. Braudel 1980). Like polysemes, Japanese culture has multiple structures, consisting of tendencies toward conceptual flexibility and social egalitarianism on the one hand and rigid and hierarchical tendencies, on the other.[16] These principles, as conceptual as they are social, underlie Japanese culture and society. In practice, the structure of meaning and the social principle interact with historical events, many of which had to do with forces outside Japan, and historical actors. At some times, as during the latter half of the Medieval period, both become conspicuous, since the two compete with each other. At other times, such as during the Early Modern period, one claims absolute hegemony over the other. Had we looked at one particular period of history, we would have had a snapshot of one phase of the total structure and process.

To gain insight into this complex historical process, I chose to focus on the reflexive structure. The structure of the collective self and other must lie at the heart of historical process, which moves with forces internal and external, since the self of the Japanese has always been dialectically and dialogically defined with respect to other, outside forces. There are a number of ways to tap the structure of reflexivity. I chose the monkey as metaphor as a window, since the Japanese have throughout history engaged in dialogues with the monkey, as it were, in their deliberations about themselves—as humans vis-à-vis animals and as a people vis-à-vis other peoples.

As a historical study, this research has yielded two findings. First is the persistent internal logic in the meaning system, in that the three meanings assigned to the monkey are logically related. Second is the

---

[16]Egalitarianism and hierarchy in the Japanese context are quite different from egalitarian and hierarchical principles as conceived and practiced in some Western societies.

historical regularity in the timing of changes: The historical transformations parallel the set of meaning assigned to the monkey and the
set assigned to the special-status group; further, these microtrans-
formations parallel macrotransformations of Japanese society and
culture. These two findings are closely related, and together they raise
questions about historical change. What is the nature of change when
a change in the form or the meaning of a symbol represents a transformation? Put another way, when does transformation represent
historical stability, and when does it represent historical change?

Theoretically speaking, change can be of three types: reproduction, random change, or transformation. Whereas reproduction signifies no change in structure, random change entails basic changes
that bear little relationship to the prior structure. These types of
change rarely occur. Although the term *transformation* (see Needham 1979: 38–47; Yalman 1967: 77) has been used too often to re-
tain a precise meaning, I continue to use it for the type of change that
opposes both reproduction and random change. It represents a
change that follows an internal logic in the structure. In this sense, the
changes in the meaning assigned to the monkey and in the structure
of reflexivity represent transformations.

If we view transformations as permutations of the basic structure,
then, the symbolic structure of Japanese culture has undergone little
change since the beginning of the eighth century. This is an astound-
ing finding, since the past 1,000 years have seen catastrophic wars,
famines, and earthquakes, the replacement of emperors by military
governments both during the Early Modern period and during World
War II, and even the conquest of other peoples and the conquest of
the Japanese by the Allied forces. These are major historical events
that rocked the very foundations of Japanese culture and society.

But to dismiss these changes in the meaning system of Japanese
culture simply as transformations of an unchanging basic structure
gives an illusion of a solution and thus discourages further scrutiny
of the nature of what these transformations represent. The internal
logic of the structure provides a range of possible directions for
change, but it does not dictate the choice of a given direction or meaning. The transformation from mediator to scapegoat and that from
scapegoat to clown both indicate profound shifts in the nature of the
basic conceptual structure underlying society and culture.

I propose that these transformations constitute historical changes in the following ways. First, a structure of thought that encourages mediation as a way of facilitating intercategorical traffic is of a radically different nature from a structure that must facilitate the traffic through breakable taboos and scapegoats. Such a change indeed signifies a basic historical change. Second, the monkey as mediator presupposes a belief in its supernatural power. People believed that the monkey had the power to maintain their health, cure illnesses in horses, and secure good crops of rice. A scapegoat figure, in contrast, is a secular figure, stripped of the sacred. The monkey as scapegoat is an object to be laughed at. It became a secular animal, that is, an animal inferior to humans. Thus the monkey's transformation from mediator to scapegoat represents a historical process of secularization.[17] Third, the changes in meaning from mediator to scapegoat to clown represent a change toward greater reflexivity, greater distancing, and greater self-awareness.[18] Although I do not espouse a unilinear cultural evolution of any kind, the particular development of Japanese reflexivity indicates a linear progression.[19]

In short, by shifting our attention away from a paradigm and its transformation, we are able to examine more closely the nature of transformation in order to understand historical change.

Acknowledgments

My theoretical arguments here are extensions of those in Ohnuki-Tierney 1987, which was a tripartite study concerned with the historical changes of the monkey metaphor, the special-status people (the so-called outcastes), and the monkey performance, which has been one of the traditional occupations of the special-status people.

I am grateful to Murasaki Yoshimasa, Murasaki Shūji, Murasaki Tarō, and other contemporary monkey trainers, and their friends and

---

[17]Elsewhere (Ohnuki-Tierney 1984), I argue that contemporary Japan is full of what I call "urban magic," if not religion, and argue against modernization theories that see the "disenchantment of the world" and "rationalization" (Weber), the "decline of magic" (Keith V. Thomas), the "mechanization of the world picture" (E. J. Dijksterhuis), and the decline of symbolic dimensions of people's behavior in general. Although the Japanese have used magic extensively throughout history, they show a definite tendency toward secularization.

[18]I am indebted to Yi-Fu Tuan of the University of Wisconsin for this insight.

[19]My statement here about increased reflexivity does not imply any sense of progress.

families, for their generosity in sharing their art with me. I am most appreciative of the support for this project provided by the John Simon Guggenheim Memorial Foundation, the Institute for Advanced Study at Princeton with a grant from the National Endowment for the Humanities, the Institute for Research in the Humanities of the University of Wisconsin, the Research Committee of the University of Wisconsin Graduate School, and the Wenner-Gren Foundation for Anthropological Research.

Discussions during our Fez conference contributed most usefully to my revisions. Insightful critiques and comments by Jan Vansina, Yi-Fu Tuan, Jerrold E. Seigel, and Simon Price all contributed greatly to my thinking at various stages of writing. Helpful comments were also offered by members of the anthropology seminar at the University of Pennsylvania, of a colloquium of the Department of Anthropology, Graduate Center, City University of New York, and of one held at New York University. I am grateful to all, but the shortcomings are of course my own.

6

Constitutive History: Genealogy and Narrative in the Legitimation of Hawaiian Kingship

VALERIO VALERI

> One knew that she worshipped the past, and that the instinctive wisdom the past can alone bestow had descended upon her—that wisdom to which we give the clumsy name of aristocracy.
>
> E. M. Forster, *Howards End*

The Legitimating Past

The world is not reinvented every morning. Growing up in a culture means learning, unreflectively for the most part, to replicate forms of behavior that already exist, that come from the past. This relationship with the past, however, may come to be partly intentional, and arguments for justifying it (or for rationalizing it) may be advanced. In many cultures an implicit or explicit argument for following the practices and knowledge inherited from the past is that they embody the experience of numerous generations. They have proved efficacious over time; their very duration shows them to be true. Other societies justify present practices by referring not simply to the generic idea of a past that is valuable as a body of accumulated wisdom but more specifically to its representation as a series of events, ordered in time, that are binding for the present. As Peel asks, How is it that "making history," in the sense of acting to realize a future, becomes interwoven with "making history, in the sense of giving accounts of the past?" (1984: 111). Peel's answer is that societies of any political complexity consciously hold on to their past and thus "strive to *make* history repeat itself," because unreflective habitus alone is not sufficient to ensure their "stereotypic reproduction" (p. 113).

That the development of reflective images of the past may go with an intentional striving to replicate it is undoubtedly true. But one should not take for granted that the past justifies stereotypic reproduction only. This view would be valid only if society represented its past as the stereotypic reproduction in time of the same models and thus as the mere duration of these models over time. But the past, or portions thereof, may be represented as a process, as a becoming; it may even offer precedents of innovation, of successful violation of the tradition. Thus one can find in the past arguments for change, not simply for changelessness. I would claim that both kinds of argument, and both kinds of representation of the past (as process and as mere duration), exist in every society of any complexity. In no such society is the past a monolithic system of models repeated identically in time. On the contrary, there are several, often conflicting, images of the past; and the past is often stratified and differentiated along the dimension of time. For instance, the Maori, whose society is less politically complex than Peel's Ijesha,

move into the future with their eyes on the past. In deciding how to act in the present, they examine the panorama of history spread before their eyes, and select the model that is most appropriate and helpful from the many presented there. This is not living in the past; it is drawing on the past for guidance, bringing the past into the present and the future. (Metge 1976: 70)

A past in which one is always able to find some precedent for some action, however new, in the present can hardly be linked to a tendency to "stereotypic" reproduction, unless the term loses all meaning. Indeed, Metge's description of the Maori attitude toward the past could also apply to the political use of history in the modern West (cf. Canfora 1982) or to the use of precedents in the English and American legal systems, neither of which is accused of reproducing itself stereotypically. Peel's attempt to relate stereotypic reproduction to both the exemplary character of the past and the intentional striving to repeat it is in line with a long tradition in British social anthropology. It is ultimately based on the view that social systems have a built-in tendency to maintain equilibrium, to reproduce themselves in a form as unchanged as possible, and thus to promote continuity in time as the supreme value (cf. Leach 1965: ix–xii).

Fortes, for instance, claims that "observation of the lineage system in action suggested that its distinguishing characteristic, as a regulating factor in the social structure, was its tendency towards equilibrium. This operated in such a way as to leave room for continual internal adjustments in the social organization without endangering its long-term stability" (1945: x). Fortes further argues that "if the equilibrium of Tale society is made possible by economic structure, and if the lineage system is the chief mechanism of social organization by which it is maintained, the system of religious values is undoubtedly the supreme sanction of its existence" (p. x). This equilibrium through time also "requires the assumption . . . that the social structure of to-day is the same as it was in the past" (p. 26). Thus the past must enshrine the image of the unchanging social structure: "All that matters in the past, which lies beyond the span of man's recollection, lives on in the social structure, the ideology, the morality, and institutions of to-day" (p. 24).

The problem with this argument is that it is largely circular: Because these societies retrospectively interpret their past as continuity, they are supposed to have a built-in tendency to changelessness, and this supposed tendency, in turn, is made to explain why they transform the past into the representation of a changeless social structure. The entire argument rests on the ignorance (or disregard) of these societies' actual history, but also, to a large extent, on Fortes's (or Evans-Pritchard's) lack of attention to the complexity and internal differentiation of these societies' representations of their past. Nobody would want to deny that the tendency to find in the past the justifications for the present is ultimately related to "social reproduction." But this ill-defined phenomenon cannot be treated as the ultimate cause of something that seems in fact to be one of its most important constituent features. We must search for less tautological reasons why present action is always to some extent inscribed in the past and receives its justification more from the past than from the present or the future.[1] Furthermore, the represented relationships between past and present can rarely be reduced to mere replication in any society that has developed a discourse about its past: They are far more complex

[1] Even in societies—such as modern Western societies—that have elevated means-to-end rationality and progress to ultimate values, the past still plays a considerable legitimating role, indicated by its use in political arguments and by the preservation or even "invention" of traditions (see Hobsbawm and Ranger 1983).

than that and often contain elements that contrast with the very idea of reproduction. The observations that follow attempt to map a few of these relationships and to delineate some of the more general reasons the past is legitimating (and memorable) for every society. The points made will then be illustrated by the analysis of a concrete case: the representations and uses of the past to legitimate and constitute power in eighteenth-century Hawaii.

In the course of the discussion, more with a view to economy of expression than to absolute conceptual precision, I will be describing some crucial relations among represented events as either syntagmatic or paradigmatic. Syntagmatic relations are established between events qua events, as defined by their position in the temporal chain. Paradigmatic relations are established between events as members of classes of action, that is, as instantiations of the rules (in Winch's 1958 sense) that govern or constitute them.[2] An event in the present can stand for one (or more) of the past and be treated as its sign or even as its ontological substitute, either metonymically (because they belong to the same syntagmatic chain) or metaphorically (because they belong to the same paradigm). Past events are conceived as constitutive and binding for present events because of either (but more often both) their paradigmatic and syntagmatic relations with them.

Gifts are good examples of the constitutive power of events as events and not simply as precedents. A gift is an event that creates an obligation that can only be fulfilled in time. Moreover, its fulfillment usually creates new obligations. The chain of events that forms becomes the major argument for justifying any further event: An event is legitimate because it is appropriate at that point in time, not simply because it corresponds to a precedent, and thus to a rule. Thus an event of the past may cast its constitutive shadow on successive events until the movement it has created is exhausted. This movement can only be apprehended with a notion of time as a cumulative process in which each successive event must be distinguished in its particularity.[3] It is strange that some have denied this notion of temporality

---

[2] See Searle 1969 on the distinction between governing (or, as he says, "regulating") and constitutive rules.

[3] Indeed Gernet (1976: 287) connects the origin of the category of time in Greek thought with the recognition of legally binding relationships between successive events.

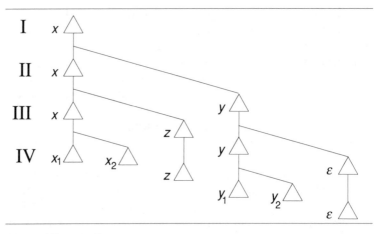

Fig. 6.1. The status lineage.

to traditional cultures, or reduced it to a universal, noncultural residue mysteriously coexisting with cultural notions (cf. Bloch 1977), for the legitimation of much social action is effected by culturally prescribed references to temporal chains, not only of gifts but also of feasts, of homicides, of wars. Of course this legitimation also has a paradigmatic dimension, since a gift given in the past must be equivalent to one in the present, or any action to some counteraction. But the point is that this paradigmatic dimension is not sufficient to account for the evaluation of the legitimacy of what is done, nor for the very evaluations of equivalences, which vary with time and context. The syntagmatic relations between events qua events is here constitutive, thus time is not eternal repetition, mere duration (cf. Bourdieu 1977: 6–7).

A predominantly syntagmatic relationship with the past is the constitutive principle of hierarchy in many systems. An example is a well-known system: the status lineage (cf. Gullick 1958: 69; Goldman 1970: 418–43), where rank depends on the cumulative effects of birth order over generations. For instance, in the lineage represented in Fig. 6.1, IVx_1 is senior to his brother, IVx_2, because he was born before him; but both brothers are senior to IVz because their father, $IIIx$, was born before $IIIz$, the father of IVz. This is so whether IVz was born before or after IVx_1 and IVx_2, since birth order in a previous generation overrules birth order in a later one. Clearly, the implication is that the system employs a cumulative notion of time. As a consequence, temporal proximity—genealogically reckoned—to a source-event (the founding of the lineage inscribed in an ancestor's procreation) determines status. Thus, for instance, IVx_1, as the firstborn son of a firstborn son ($IIIx$) of a firstborn son (IIx), is temporally closer to the founder of the lineage (Ix) than is IVx_2, who, as the younger brother of IVx_1, has a somewhat lesser rank because he has come later in the temporal process that structures the lineage. Even later, and therefore inferior, is $IV\varepsilon$, who is the son of the younger son ($III\varepsilon$) of the younger son (IIy) of the founding ancestor (Ix).

Of course, paradigmatic relations are built into this system, since the same principles of seniority are used in each generation, but these principles are fundamentally metonymic because they use the dimension of time for structuration. Differential temporal closeness to the founding ancestor implies differential power to metonymically stand for him and thus for the lineage generated and symbolized by him. Different positions in the temporal process that defines the lineage thus correspond to different parts/whole relations of which the hierarchical system properly consists. These metonymic equivalences are made explicit when positional succession (Cunnison 1957: 22ff.) prevails, as in Tonga (Bott 1982: 66–67; Valeri 1989). Then IVx_1 is named after Ix because he is metonymically identified with him and thus with the whole lineage he heads; IVy_1 is named after IIy and considered equivalent to him and to the lineage segment he founded, and so on.

This and other cases of using articulated time to construct hierarchical relations directly contradict Bloch's claim that the more hierarchical a system is, the more it will rely on "a timeless static past" (1977: 287). It is true that in the status lineage the present is a metonymy of a past, but it is so through a recognized temporal process. This system, by making time the principle of its organization, both recognizes history and triumphs over it. Of course it is customary among anthropologists ever since Robertson Smith (1903) to claim that the history embodied in lineage systems is purely fictitious. Evans-Pritchard, for instance, claims that "structural time," being a "conceptualization of the social structure . . . less a means of coordinating events than of coordinating relationships" (1940: 108), is "in a sense, an illusion, for the structure remains fairly constant and the perception of time is no more than the movement of persons, often as groups, through the structure" (p. 107). Maybe, but one should also entertain the possible accuracy of the native view that real events in real time determine present relationships, and not the other way round, as Evans-Pritchard, Fortes, and others dogmatically assert to justify their purely systemic and synchronic analysis (see, in particular, Bohannan 1952: 314). Because they claim to make history the basis of hierarchy, their systems may include actual historical events. Indeed, when it has been possible to compare the native representation of the history of a status lineage with independent written documentation (see, for instance, Fox 1971) or with the archeological record (see, for instance, Kirch and Yen 1982: 362–68), the historical veracity of the native representation has sometimes been vindicated.

These familiar facts should challenge the view that the relationship between represented past and present in traditional societies involves merely the replication of models enshrined in the past and thus a dissolution of temporality. The facts suggest that one way in which the past is recognized as founding the present is not incompatible with a historicizing view of the articulation of past and present, and indeed that such a way requires the differentiation of events qua events along the temporal chain. It remains nevertheless true that the paradigmatic (and thus tendentially detemporalizing) component of the relationship between past and present is the most important one. But the reasons for this go well beyond the ideal of stereotypic (or "complex," for that matter) reproduction of the past in the present. They have to do with a much more general phenomenon: Because the events of the remembered past are human actions, they exemplify rules—and it is as such that they are intelligible, relevant for present conduct, and thus memorable in the first place, even when they are not directly reproducible (cf. Winch 1958: 62).

All cultures with a historical tradition have maintained that the past offers a repertory of rules, of connections among types of action and types of consequences, in the form of concrete events that can be analogically related to present ones. Precisely because this relationship between past and present is analogical (and thus recognizes differences as much as similarities [cf. Canfora 1982: 27]) and because the repertory of rules contained in the past is often perceived as a set of possible choices, not of rules that must all be equally instantiated, the paradigmatic use of the past need not be correlated with an ideal of "reproduction," but simply with the idea of comparability of all human actions qua actions. In fact even modern professional historians, although they have broken with the tradition of "monumental history" (in Nietzsche's sense), claim that analogy (and thus the establishment of relationships of equivalence, of paradigmatic relations, among events) is the main organ of historiography (Droysen 1937; Engel 1956; Canfora 1982).[4] Since the relationship between past and present is analogical and not merely replicative, the past need not exactly replicate the present to function as its precedent. This undermines the extreme presentist thesis (derived from Malinowski 1954: 125), which postulates that the represented past needs to be a projection of the present in order to have legitimating effects. In formulating this thesis, extreme presentists are victims of the more overt, ideological aspects of traditionalism. Because traditionalism often emphasizes similarity over difference in the comparison of past and present, particularly whenever past events are used as explicit charters, they do not see that the perception of difference plays in fact a great role in that comparison. Furthermore, presentists do not see that a mere projection of present interests onto the past would defeat such a projection's purpose, because it would undermine the authority of the past by failing to live up to cultural standards of validation. These standards, however, are not simply the criteria of evidence and argumentation emphasized by some (e.g. Appadurai 1981; Peel 1984); they can also be performative criteria of felicity. With this qualification, I completely subscribe to Peel's point that the relationship between past and present is one of mutual, not unilateral, conditioning (1984: 113–14).

But however analogical and dialectical the relationship between past and present is, it remains asymmetrical. Whereas the principle of relevance for knowing and mobilizing the past is clearly in the present (since the rule content of past action is brought out by explicit or implicit analogies with the present, every statement about the past is in fact also a statement about the present), from an ideological point of view it is action in the past that legitimates its counterpart in the present. The present seems unable to justify, or to fully justify, itself.

---

[4] Veyne (1976: 38) notes that the comparability of past and present implies that, from a typological point of view, history repeats itself—that historical facts are individual but not singular.

Why is the value of past action greater than the value of present action? Why is such importance attached to finding the rules of the present embodied in the past? Why, in other words, is duration an argument for the validity of rules and thus a motive for their historical representation? The answer is to be found, I believe, in an argument that—as I have mentioned—is explicitly made in many societies: A rule's duration is a proof of its validity because it demonstrates its power to successfully resist the vicissitudes and challenges of history and to make society survive and prosper.[5] Duration is validating also because it implicitly multiplies the number of the believers in the rule: So many people could not have been wrong.[6] Furthermore, some were glorious heroes, whose actions further validate the rule by showing that its use was followed by exceptional success.

In sum, the association of rules with duration considerably expands their persuasive force by making past generations argue for them both quantitatively and qualitatively. Moreover, rules expressed in terms of duration allow the social group they define to magnify and thus legitimate itself by adding extent in time to its extent in space. Thus society and its rules mutually legitimate one another through one single powerful image: duration, as proof of "greatness," "potency," "vitality," "righteousness," "divine election," "predestination," "historical mission," "historical necessity," or whatever. In the end, by allowing a society to communicate with its image in time triumphing over time, its history (which includes its defining rules and their effects) constitutes that society and makes it endure. What Lévy-Bruhl says of myth and sacred history can be said of any representation of the past:

When a myth narrates the adventures, exploits, the good deeds, the death and resurrection of a civilising hero, it is not the fact that he has given the tribe the idea of fire-making, or cultivating corn, which, in itself, especially in-

[5] This view was found, for instance, in the Ancient City: "All these formulas and these practices had been transmitted by the ancestors who had tested their efficacy. It was not necessary to innovate. One had to rest oneself on what the ancestors had done, and the supreme piety consisted in acting like they did" (Fustel de Coulanges 1905: 197). Similar views were still expressed in the Venetian Senate in the eighteenth century, to oppose the suppression of an obsolete but traditional type of warship (Casanova 1960, 2: 177).

[6] This view was illustrated by the Hawaiian king Liholiho, who, when someone praised his wisdom, answered: "Why shouldn't I know, when it is a road often travelled by my parents?" (Pukui 1983: saying 2301).

terests and moves the audience. What occurs is rather that, as in sacred history, the group is able to participate in its own past, that it feels itself living, in a sort of mystical communion, with what made it what it is. In short, myths are, for the primitive mentality, both an expression of the solidarity of the social group with itself in time and with other beings in its environment, and a way of perpetuating and rekindling the feeling of this solidarity. (1912: 437)

The ability of past events to instantiate the rules that make them comparable to present events and thus relevant to them tends to vary with their distance in time. Events that have been directly experienced, whose memory does not come from tradition, manifest a greater resistance to analogical appropriation and thus to being reduced to the rule on which their analogy with other events is based. As a result, these events tend to be viewed less as tokens of a type than as events qua events. Thus, also, the syntagmatic component of their intelligibility is emphasized over the paradigmatic one. The opposite happens with more distant events, which are more malleable in memory and thus more easily typified.[7] This selectivity of memory is another reason why the distant past is able to carry a heavier ideological load than the recent past (cf. Barnes 1967: 120), but the effects of selectivity happily converge with the tendency to associate rules with duration in time and thus to embody them in past events.

Time is not only relevant as undifferentiated duration, however. Different degrees of distance from the present tend to correspond to qualitatively different levels of the past, which in turn correspond to different relations between those levels and the present. Two basic discontinuities can be recognized in many a culture's representation of its past. The first (as we have seen) is situated at the point in represented time where the paradigmatic apprehension of events becomes preponderant over the syntagmatic one, that is, where events are viewed more as instantiations of rules than as events. The second is situated at the point where the preoccupation with the analogical appropriation of the past by the present gives way to a preoccupation with explaining the origin of the rules and with making the society's existence unquestionable. The latter point marks the threshold between a past that is comparable (or directly comparable) to the pres-

[7]The most brilliant analysis of this process is still to be found in Granet 1926, 1: 171–225. See especially pp. 200–213.

ent and that founds it because it is exemplary for it, and a past whose principles of operation are no longer applicable to the present but explain the extraordinary events that made society and its institutions possible. The latter past often instantiates the more general principles that underlie the rules of the more recent past but are not immediately recognizable in them. The heterogeneity of this past with the present expresses the transcendental and unquestionable character of the image of society and of its fundamental institutions as the ultimate condition of the possibility of human relations. The past that is homogeneous with the present, and thus exemplary for it (but also questionable precisely because comparable to present experience), I call historical in the strict sense of the term; the heterogeneous, impossible-to-replicate (and thus beyond argument) past I call mythical.[8]

Contrary to the historical past, then, the mythical past justifies the rules but does not or does not directly embody them. Only insofar as myths are transformable into intermediary representations, which may or may not take the form of narratives, can they function fully as models. Otherwise, their legitimating power applies to both historical events and present ones through indirect, syntagmatic connections.[9] We therefore find that the relationship with the most distant past and with the most recent one are analogous in that they privilege the syntagmatic dimension over the paradigmatic one. The relationship between past and present thus turns out to be much more complex than it appears at first. Clearly, too, the represented past is rarely characterized by timelessness, or undifferentiated duration, alone, and its constitutive power for the present depends on a combination of detemporalizing and temporalizing aspects, on a play of discontinuity and continuity in time. This play—and even conflict— is particularly intense in hierarchical societies and perfectly illustrated by the Hawaiian case, to which I now turn.

[8] The many recent and not-so-recent attempts to define myth, most notably through the Greek origins of the notion (see Finley 1965; Kirk 1970: 39–40; Detienne 1981; Brisson 1982; Traube 1986), show that no absolute definition will do. The contrast I use here between mythical and historical modes of operation is often found in native ideology, particularly in societies with a developed historical literature. The Luapula, for instance, note that "the things which people of old could do, the men of to-day have not the power to effect" (Cunnison 1951: 21).

[9] As Bakhtin notes, toward a past that is "walled off absolutely from all subsequent times" (1981: 15) one can only have "the reverent point of view of a descendant" (p. 13).

Genealogies and Narratives

A major division characterizes Hawaiian society: that between no-bles (*ali'i*) and commoners (*maka'āinana*, lit. "people who attend the land" [Pukui and Elbert 1986: 224]). The nobles are people with a genealogy (*kū'auhau, mo'o kū'auhau*), people, then, who have a his-tory and whose identity is determined by relationships with the past. Commoners, in contrast, are not allowed to have genealogies (S. M. Kamakau 1961: 242; Apr. 20, 1896, article in *Ka Makaainana*, trans. in McKinzie 1983: 2): They are defined only by their present relations of subordination to the nobles who grant them the use of the land in exchange for products and services (Richards 1973: 22; Malo 1951: 61). Evidently for the Hawaiians an identity that does not en-dure in time has little value: It is not noble.

Noble genealogies do not automatically persist in time, though; they must be validated by a continuing relationship with a "core" line—the senior line, which is also by definition the ruling line. To be considered a noble, one must be able to trace, through either female or male links or both, a genealogical relationship with at least one ancestor appearing in that senior line within a ten-generation limit (Malo 1951: 192; S. M. Kamakau 1961: 243). Largesse, privileges, and particularly land (which is controlled by the ruler) are in theory distributed proportionally to the degree of closeness to the core line. The single-line (cf. Cartwright 1933: 3), mostly patrilineal dynastic core is thus surrounded, for a span of about ten generations, by a dense bilateral network that depends on that core for its reproduc-tion. In the genealogical, chanted panegyrics called *mele koihonua* this network is ignored and the dynastic line is represented as au-tonomous: It is allegedly reproduced by an inner virtue that comes from its divine past.[10]

[10] The most extended and most important genealogical chant is the Kumulipo (Lili-uokalani 1898; Beckwith 1951). The chant of Kūali'i contains another important ge-nealogical tree (Fornander 1916–20, 4: 370–73). Most one-line pedigrees written down in the nineteenth century seem to have been extracted from genealogical chants (see S. M. Kamakau 1961: 241). The most important may be found in the newspaper *Kumu Hawaii* 1835: 133 (reprinted in McKinzie 1983: ix–xv); in the chronicle *Mooo-lelo Hawaii* (1838); in Fornander 1878–80, 1: 184–96; and in Beckwith 1932: 191–92. The genealogy put together by the nineteenth-century Hawaiian historian Samuel Kamakau, and first published in the newspaper *Ka Nonanona* on Oct. 25, 1842, is much fuller than any of these, perhaps because of the antiquarian interests of its compiler (reprinted in McKinzie 1983: xix–xxiii, cf. 1).

The historical narratives (*mo'olelo*) and the informal, ambilateral, and even bilateral genealogies[11] that complete them tell a different story, however. They show that multiple-line networks and single-line dynasties are mutually dependent for their reproduction (Valeri 1985b) and, moreover, that the unilineal, indeed mostly patrilineal, characterization of the dynastic lines in the chants is largely illusory. The basic reason why this characterization is illusory is that the distinction between patrilineally inherited titular rank and bilateral personal rank that exists in Tonga (Bott 1981, 1982) is not found in Hawaii, where succession goes from father to son only if the son reproduces or increases the rank of the father. But since the son's rank depends on his mother as much as on his father, a dynasty can autonomously reproduce its rank only if its male members consistently marry their sisters. However, brother-sister marriage is allowed to happen only exceptionally; otherwise the collateral lines would steadily lose rank for lack of access to the rank of the senior line (Valeri 1972).

The dynasty must reproduce, then, by way of a trade-off between it and its collaterals: In exchange for political support, it gives the collaterals part of its rank through its women. But unless the ruling line periodically shuts itself off by making a few brother-sister (or uncle-niece) marriages, its rank becomes equal to that of some of its collaterals, who may then wrest the rule from the patrilineal successors. The historical narratives show that the collaterals frequently take control, thus belying the image of dynastic continuity presented in the genealogical chants. Moreover, the bilateral reckoning of rank creates another and more disruptive (from the dynastic point of view) possibility: A lowborn upstart who has mustered enough support and military power to take the kingship by force[12] is able to graft himself onto the royal line by marrying the sister or daughter of the defeated ruler. His children's rank will be increased by their mother's; and if his sons marry high-ranking women, their own children will bring the new ruling line to the high status that the displaced line pos-

[11] A published example is the Luluka genealogy in Ii 1963: 19. Many unpublished examples are found in the Bishop Museum Library and the Archives of Hawaii (cf. Sahlins 1985: 20 n. 18).

[12] "Sometimes the hereditary chief lost his land, and the kingdom was taken by force and snatched away by a warrior, and the name of 'chief' was given to him because of his prowess" (S. M. Kamakau 1964: 4, cf. 6, 9).

sessed.[13] Insofar as there is genealogical continuity in this case, it is through females and not males, contrary to what the genealogical chants, with few exceptions, claim. Indeed, the chants suppress the fact that even father-son successions are mediated by matrilateral relations and that the patrilineal reproduction of a dynasty depends on its ability to secure high-ranking wives. But while the prose narratives emphasize the centrality of these marriages and of the matrilateral relations they secure, genealogical chants include women mostly as appendages of their male spouses, very rarely as sources of relations.

Narrative representations of succession to kingship contrast with the genealogical chants' representations in another—and perhaps more fundamental—respect. They show that genealogically inherited rank is not the only criterion of succession and that other criteria may be equally—and sometimes more—legitimate. These alternative criteria are particularly prominent in the narratives that cover the period of ten generations or so from King Līloa to King Kamehameha I (who died in 1819) on the island of Hawai'i. As we have seen, a past ten generations deep is the most relevant for the internal organization of a kingdom and for political action in general. Not surprisingly, therefore, this is the temporal span best covered in the narratives and informal genealogical records, and also the one they account for in a manner very different from that of formal genealogical chants, which make no difference between it and earlier periods.

The tone for the period that begins with Līloa is set by the traditions concerning this king's succession. They stage a major paradox of Hawaiian political life: A high-ranking person may not act like one—be pious, generous, and valorous—whereas a low-ranking person may act like a high-ranking one. To understand how the paradox is resolved, we must keep in mind that rank is the expression of a divine potency (mana) acquired through descent from the gods, who are the ultimate ancestors. But mana may also be directly given by the gods to a person they elect, or it may be obtained by ritual, priestly

[13] This process (and the ensuing break in the dynastic continuity) is thus described by a native historian: "The branch of Keawe's line was broken by those below; those below climbed up to the peak and those above went down to the bottom. Hence the chiefs were now up, now down, like the olapa dance" (Kepelino 1932: 132). One understands why an appropriate blessing for a high chief is *e nī'aupi'o o ka lani*—may he and his descendants live on in purity of rank" (Pukui 1983: saying 359).

mediated means. However obtained, god-given mana is the true source of legitimacy, and its presence is demonstrated, in the last analysis, by the success of a person's endeavors. Therefore Hawaiians treated as divinely legitimate, indeed as divine, not only the highest-ranking nobles[14] but also those who, however low born, successfully conquered the kingdom (Remy 1862: 157; S. M. Kamakau 1961: 230; cf. Valeri 1985b: 95, 98).

All these points are illustrated by the story of Līloa's sons: 'Umi, who is very low ranking (his mother is a commoner) but who has all the chiefly qualities, and Hākau, whose high rank is unimpeachable but who behaves in a cruel, unchiefly manner. After a brief and unsuccessful period of joint rule imposed by Līloa, 'Umi is finally able to defeat Hākau and to become the only successor to his father because he obtains the support of some important priests and because his generosity and valor attract a number of faithful followers. While the genealogical chants present 'Umi as a legitimate successor to Līloa by descent, the narrative traditions openly present him as genealogically illegitimate (he is considered merely a *kanaka*, "servant" or "vassal," by his father and called *kauwā*, "slave" or "outcast," by Hākau [Fornander 1916–20, 4: 185; S. M. Kamakau 1961: 8]) but as legitimated by his very success, obtained by generosity and valor but also by violence and trickery (for instance, he pretends to have magical powers but has none [Valeri 1985b: 82]).

That these actions are considered legitimate and even legitimating (since they are successful) is indicated by the fact that they are also used to characterize other rulers' methods for rising in power. For instance, the parallelisms between the biography of 'Umi and that of Kamehameha have been emphasized by the latter's historians to justify his career. But the correspondences were not just constructed a posteriori: they were produced, in the first place, by Kamehameha's following the precedents set in the biographies of 'Umi and similar

---

[14] After having enumerated their taboos, Ī'i concludes: "So you see, our chiefs used to be gods" (Ii 1841). See also Valeri 1985a: 142–53. Those who still find unbelievable that humans could view themselves and be viewed as in some sense divine should meditate on the following passage from the Marcoses' interview in *Playboy* (Aug. 1987, p. 56):

Playboy. You think of yourselves as gods, then?

Imelda. Yes, because we are on a divine mission. . . .

Ferdinand. We are part of the achievement of being a god. That is what we are about now. An ordinary mortal would not be able to stand it.

rulers.[15] For instance, he probably used the analogies between his relationship with Kiwala'ō (the high-ranking son of his uncle, King Kalani'ōpu'u) and 'Umi's relationship with Hākau to feel allowed by precedent to liquidate Kiwala'ō (for these and other analogies, see Valeri 1982; S. M. Kamakau 1961: 209; Kuykendall 1938: 62). Another chief who clearly had 'Umi's precedent in mind was Boki, who, when he planned to rebel against Ka'ahumanu in 1827, started a huge farm to attract clients (Ii 1963: 153), precisely as 'Umi had done.

It appears, then, that while genealogical chants legitimate rulers by showing that divine potency flows to them in an uninterrupted descent from firstborn to firstborn, historical narratives legitimate rulers mostly by allowing them to demonstrate that their actions correspond to successful precedents. Thus genealogical chants legitimate through predominantly syntagmatic connections with the past, whereas historical narratives legitimate through predominantly paradigmatic ones. Of course, the two forms of legitimation may be combined. Rarely do successful upstarts have no genealogical connection at all with the past, nor can genealogically legitimate rulers succeed their fathers or maintain their rule without having recourse to the Machiavellian methods illustrated in the narratives. Furthermore, there are components of paradigmatic legitimation in the genealogical chants and of syntagmatic legitimation in the narratives.

One important paradigmatic component of the status lineage depicted in the genealogical chants is the contrast senior/junior, which correlates with certain expected behavioral traits: Junior lines are supposed to be unruly, more active than the senior ones, and so forth. From this point of view, the genealogies may be read as statements to the effect that one is predestined (and thus also legitimated) by birth to instantiate certain categories of action (cf. Sahlins 1981: 16).[16] However, the junior dynasties' attempts to demonstrate their connection with the senior ones, or even to take their place as seniors, show that the main thrust of the genealogical chants is to legitimate rulers by providing, not a justification for their modes of action through a connection with the appropriate ancestors, but the

[15] For a similar striving in eighteenth-century Java to follow a historical precedent and then to emphasize historiographically the correspondence between the precedent and its replication, see Ricklefs 1974: 74–76.

[16] This view receives some support from a few Hawaiian sayings (Pukui 1983: sayings 2418, 794–97, 817, 921, 1922).

closest possible connection with the senior line of the status lineage. Consequently, genealogical space is viewed as more homogeneous than heterogeneous; different hierarchical positions in it are identified more by the degree to which they metonymically instantiate a single form (thus by a scale type of classification [cf. Collingwood 1933: 60]) than by a logic of genus and species.[17] Examples of the tension between the two logics in the genealogies, but also of the preeminence of the former one in the Hawaiian as in all other status lineage systems (see supra section on the legitimating past) are provided by the dynasties of the islands of Maui and Hawai'i.

From the categorical standpoint, the activism of these dynasties fits their junior position in the status lineage (they belong to the junior Hema section of the junior Ulu branch [cf. Fornander 1878–80, 1: 190–94]). Yet their members have constantly attempted to counter this junior status by claiming connections with the most senior line, the Nanaulu (Fornander 1878–80, 2: 22, 48). For instance, the Kumulipo chant, which was composed for a noble of the dynasty of Hawai'i, bypasses that dynasty's genealogy altogether to trace his ancestry, through his mother's patriline, to the higher-ranking line of the island of Maui, which, via a crucial alliance, was connected with the ruling line of O'ahu and through it, with the "blue-blooded" (Beckwith 1940: 387) Nanaulu line (Kumulipo, ll. 2,092–2,102; Beckwith 1951: 137–39; Fornander 1878–80, 1: 189, 2: 83–87). While the connection with the Nanaulu is alluded to but not developed in the Kumulipo chant, it becomes the only one in another royal genealogy that exploits the same alliance (Fornander 1878–80, 1: 188–89). Analogously, some genealogies attempt to prove that King Keawe of Hawai'i and his half sister and wife, Kalanikauleleiāiwi, descend from the Nanaulu (Fornander 1878–80, 2: 204), although others

[17]Interestingly, the primary meanings of *mo'o*, the word that, alone or compounded with others (especially *kū'auhau*), designates "genealogical line," are "succession, series" (Pukui and Elbert 1986: 253). The word does not convey the notion of genus, which is so prominent in the English term genealogy, derived from the Greek *génos*, and in equivalent terms in many other languages (Tibetan is a particularly interesting case, although the notion of genealogy as a "chain" or "series" exists in it too; see Stein 1971: 537–45). Another indication that the "genus" aspect is less important than the "series" aspect in the Hawaiian notion of genealogy is that neither the "kinship I" (Johansen 1954: 36) nor positional succession with its frequent correlate, a title system (respectively a pronominal and a nominal reduction of all members of a line to a genus), is found in Hawaii, as far as I am aware.

stress their connection with the Ulu-Hema branch (Pogue 1858: 33–34; *Ke Kumu Hawaii* 1835: 133, reprinted in McKinzie 1983: xiv–xv; *Ka Nonanona*, Oct. 25, 1842, reprinted in McKinzie 1983: xxi–xxiii). No doubt, different connections were mobilized for different purposes, probably also reflecting the above-mentioned contrast between classification by scale or by genus and species. But we also know that certain shifts from junior to senior became exclusive and permanent. For instance, when Kamehameha, the most famous of the junior heroic rulers of the Hawai'i dynasty, conquered Maui, he stole the Maui dynasty's senior status relative to the Hawai'i dynasty by stealing their apical ancestor, Hanala'anui (Fornander 1878–80, 2: 27).

These attempts to show that the usurping juniors are in fact genealogically senior contrast sharply with the narratives' frank recognition that they are not and that the major sources of their legitimacy are not genealogical. The contrast is even more strident in the case of the mythical founder of the Hawai'i dynasty: Pili. Although the narrative traditions represent him as a usurper sponsored by a priest who brought him to Hawai'i from a distant land, the genealogies "piece him on to already existing Hawaiian lines" (Fornander 1878–80, 2: 27, cf. 33–38). Indeed, they transform him into a descendant of the ruler he displaced (Kapawa, known in the genealogies as Heleipawa [Fornander 1878–80, 1: 191; cf. Sahlins 1981: 10–11]). In sum, the dominant preoccupation of the royal genealogies is apparently to stress unbroken syntagmatic continuity with the founding past. Because this past's specific categorical content is left vague by them, it can be viewed as embodying a generic potentiality for actions whose models may be freely chosen rather than predetermined by heredity.

Even when genealogical chants such as the Kumulipo include narrative portions detailing certain formative events, they do not abandon the dogma of genealogical continuity and the correlative emphasis on the syntagmatic dimension of the relationship with the past. It is true that these portions have been interpreted by Beckwith (1951) as allegories of usurpation, as veiled references to the displacement of established lines by upstart ones. But I find little evidence in the text of the Kumulipo itself for these farfetched interpretations, most of which were suggested to Beckwith by modern Hawaiian informants.

Let us begin with the latest of these "usurpations." Beckwith

claims that the youngest of the four Maui brothers, the famous trickster (called Maui-a-ka-malo, "Maui of the loincloth," in the Kumulipo, l. 1,986), succeeds Kalapana (Beckwith 1951: 128). However, Beckwith must recognize (p. 116) that her claim is merely a hypothesis since the chant, contrary to other genealogies (see Fornander
1878–80, 1: 191), does not explicitly say that the Maui who succeeded Kalapana was the youngest one (see Kumulipo l. 2,049). But
even if we grant the hypothesis, we cannot accept Beckwith's further
claim that the youngest Maui was not the son of Kalapana but of some
god. Beckwith's thesis is based on the arbitrary conflation of the version of Maui's birth contained in the Kumulipo with the version in
the prose rendition of the myth. According to the latter, Hina, the wife
of Kalapana, finds a loincloth on a beach, puts it on, and as a result
conceives her youngest son. Kalapana recognizes him as the offspring
of a god (Beckwith 1940: 229). This divine origin qualifies him to
succeed Kalapana in violation of the rule of primogenitural succession. But the Kumulipo explicitly says on two occasions (ll. 1,987,
2,009) that the loincloth worn by Hina belongs to her husband, not
to a god. Thus, while the chant agrees with the prose version in saying
that the youngest Maui was not conceived in an ordinary way, it con-
tradicts it in stressing that he is his father's son nevertheless. In sharp
contrast to the narrative, then, the chant makes the ideology of descent triumph even if we accept the hypothesis that it is the youngest
and most extraordinary Maui who succeeds his father.

An earlier episode of the chant that Beckwith also interprets as
usurpation concerns Wākea's succession. Wākea begets a child with
the goddess Hina. In a very obscure passage the chant describes the
child as a cock perching on Wākea's back. According to Beckwith,
this means that "he usurps the normal succession upon the family
line" (1951: 99). However, the Kumulipo and all other genealogies
trace Wākea's descent through his firstborn son, Hāloa, not through
this pretended (and unnamed) usurper. The label usurpation applies
somewhat better to the earliest mythical episode in the Kumulipo.
The story is that a human, Ki'i, succeeds in impregnating his elder
sister, La'ila'i, before the god Kāne does. Because La'ila'i's firstborn
is a son of Ki'i and not of Kāne, Ki'i's descendants—"the long line of
chiefs of the forest upland enumerated in chant eleven" (Beckwith
1951: 103)—take precedence over the line of gods descended from
Kāne. In this sense, the humans have usurped the gods' preeminent

position. But they have done so by using the principle of genealogical seniority to their advantage, not by violating it. Furthermore, Ki'i himself is born before Kāne, who is his younger brother (Kumulipo, ll. 613–14). Thus the chant affirms the principle of genealogical legitimacy all the more strongly because he does so by way of a paradox; it shows that the principle overrules even the ordinary superordination of gods to humans. But this reversal does not occur again in the Kumulipo: It happens once and for all to explain why the royal lineage is divine.

In sum, the incorporation of narrative elements in the Kumulipo implicitly counters their possible paradigmatic use to justify usurpation. The chant attempts to demonstrate either that those mythical events do not involve genealogical discontinuity or that the usurpations depicted are only possible in the founding past, with which subsequent generations have had (and thus future ones must continue to have) only syntagmatic connections determined by descent, not paradigmatic ones.

As the genealogical chants may legitimate not only through the predominant syntagmatic relations but also through some paradigmatic ones, so narrative traditions may establish the legitimacy of certain events through their syntagmatic relations with antecedents, in addition to establishing it through the more usual paradigmatic relations. In fact the global image of history derived from the narrative tradition as a whole is that of a cumulative process in which later events presuppose earlier ones. Each event is a step in the formation of Hawaiian society. First Wākea establishes the taboo system, particularly the alimentary separation of the sexes and the separation of things impure from things pure. Then Haho institutes the 'aha ali'i, the system that sharply contrasts those who have genealogies and those who do not. At a later stage still, Pā'ao modifies the style of temple architecture and increases the frequency of human sacrifice (Remy 1862: 84–85; Fornander 1878–80, 2: 28, 33–38, 59; Valeri 1985a: 169–71). The process never seems to stop at a point where a complete structure, to be replicated in identical form in successive generations, is achieved; it continues down to the present and thus invites its further continuation by the invention of new institutions and practices. From this point of view, narrative history constitutes a precedent not simply for established practice but also for the establishment of new practices. This undercurrent of syntagmatic legitimation is particularly evident in the history of the ten generations or so from Līloa to Kamehameha (see details in Valeri 1990).

In sum, this comparison of narrative and genealogical history demonstrates that paradigmatic and syntagmatic dimensions coexist in both, although for purposes of legitimation, the paradigmatic one dominates in the narratives and the syntagmatic one in the genealogies. But it is also obvious that both syntagmatic and paradigmatic relations are much more complex in the realm of action depicted in narrative history than in the status lineage depicted in the genealogical texts.

The comparison also shows that however much one genealogical chant may differ from another chant, and one narrative from another narrative, their genres differ more because they correspond to different views of history. Narratives depict succession as a complex social process, which encompasses genealogical argument as only one (though extremely important) component and which takes a variety of forms that cannot be reduced to a single rule (cf. Valeri 1990). Genealogies, instead, represent succession as merely the instantiation of the rule of primogeniture and, with few exceptions, represent the first-born as male. They thus reduce the social history of kingship to natural history—to mere procreation. The effect is to make succession appear to be beyond human choice and intention and thus to make it unquestionable.

Some may object, however, that I am reading an ideological contrast where only a difference of purpose and complexity may exist. Genealogical chants attempt to validate the claim of a certain individual to high rank by following the most favorable line, not to depict the process of succession in all its complexity. They are selective, but not necessarily untrue, and they may in fact implicitly refer to the wider context described in narratives and other genealogies. But the chants' accounts of genealogical relations are not simply selective; they are often incompatible with the larger picture that they supposedly refer to. For instance, they treat king lists (lists of successors to kingship) as descent lines (Cartwright 1930: 46; Beckwith 1951: 149); they transform complicated consanguineal or affinal relationships into descent in the direct line;[18] they make elder brothers out of younger ones or, conversely, transform younger brothers into

---

[18] For instance, in the *Kumu Hawaii* genealogy, Kanaloakapulehu, the successor of Iwikauikaua, figures as his son, although he is his son-in-law.

sons of the elder brothers to whom they have succeeded;[19] they leave out defeated rulers, corulers (cf. Fornander 1916–20, 4: 364–65), and others. They do all these because their genre requires that all relevant ancestors be presented in single-line pedigrees to convey the idea of uninterrupted succession.

Whatever the compatibility or incompatibility in propositional content that may exist between a certain genealogical chant and a certain prose narrative, their true difference lies in the fact that their genres do not give propositional content the same importance to obtain their effects. The basic fact about the genealogical chants is that they are chants—compositions powerful because of their formal qualities—whereas the basic fact about the narratives is that they use prose, in which form retreats before content.

History as Magic and as Argument

The genealogical chants, the mele koihonua, have much in common with other chanted panegyrics that are the property of a high-ranking noble—*mele inoa* (chants [praising] the name), *mele ma'i* (chants [praising] the genitals), *mele hanau* (birth chants)[20]—in all of which the praised person is related to ancestral, divine, and cosmic entities together with their attributes. The mele koihonua differ from the other chants just mentioned in representing these relations in predominantly genealogical, and therefore metonymic, form. Indeed they make human dynasties the continuation of cosmic ones that include gods and natural species and that go back to the origins of life. The other chants, in contrast, present some of the same relations in predominantly synchronic and metaphoric form. In all cases, a high-ranking noble is praised as the epitome of the whole cosmos, its representative in human form, at the center of society. Even when the chants do not have a genealogical form, they indirectly exalt the genealogical principle.

While the mele hanau focus on birth as one's connection with an

---

[19] The *Kumu Hawaii* genealogy again provides an example: Most incongruously, it puts Kauikeaouli (Kamehameha III) in the position of son of his elder brother and predecessor, Liholiho (Kamehameha II). This example confirms that royal genealogies are often just king lists.

[20] "A birth chant is similar to a name chant. Both concern the origin and ancestry of a line of ruling chiefs. The main difference is that the birth chant, as the term suggests, concentrates at some point on the circumstances— cosmological, astrological, and by

ancestral line and ultimately with the cosmos, the mele ma'i celebrate one's ability to continue, through the act of procreation, that line and the cosmic process that encompasses it (Handy and Pukui 1972: 84).[21] Both therefore implicitly celebrate a line by explicitly celebrating the individual in which its generative potency is manifested at a given moment; both can potentially be expanded into genealogies. Reciprocally, genealogical chants proper can expand themes already contained in them to become birth chants or genital chants or name chants. Indeed, many chants combine these various aspects and may therefore be called by any of the names for the chants.

The Kumulipo, besides being the most elaborate mele koihonua extant, is also a mele hanau and a mele inoa. The genealogical framework of the chant is filled with various poetical developments that make it appropriate for use in a birth rite and as praise for Kalaninui'īamamao, the newborn noble for whom it was composed. One of many name and birth chants that, reciprocally, include genealogical sections or allusions is the mele inoa of Kūali'i, a king of O'ahu. It contains a long genealogical section (Fornander 1916–20, 4: 370ff.) that preserves the so-called Kumuali'i and Kumulipo genealogies, which is why Samuel Kamakau calls it a mele koihonua rather than a mele inoa (S. M. Kamakau in Roberts 1926: 59; cf. Stokes 1930: 26). The mele inoa of Pele'iohōlani is also a mele koihonua in that it includes the genealogical tree of Olōlo and Hāloa; and the mele inoa of Kamahanao includes the genealogical tree of Palikū and Punaimua (S. M. Kamakau in Roberts 1926: 59). One designation was probably applied to a chant in preference to another because of the context in which the chant was used at one particular moment. The very multivocality of their expression, the stratifications of meaning that they contain, and the multiple interpretations that they allow facilitate the use of the same chants for different purposes and even, it seems, for different people (cf. Pukui 1949: 255; Pukui 1983: saying 1621).

The chants' elaborate compositional forms are based on "name and term associations expressed through identities and antitheses"

---

necessity gynecological—of the actual begetting and bearing of the infant" (Pukui and Korn 1973: 198).

[21] Together the two types of chant imply that "the individual in old Hawaii viewed himself as a link between his long line of forebears and his descendants, even those yet unborn" (Pukui, Haertig, and Lee, 1972–79, 1: 182).

(Stokes 1930: 8), which create rhyming patterns. The chants also have a musical, particularly rhythmic structure that is subtly intertwined with their semantic component (Roberts 1926: 57–69). In addition, they are frequently choreographed (K. Kamakau 1919–20: 2–4; Malo 1951: 231; Handy and Pukui 1972: 84; Barrère, Pukui, and Kelly 1980: 21).[22] Chants, genealogical or otherwise, are thus "total works of art" and should be evaluated as such and not simply for their propositional content. But they are works of art that have magical, not simply aesthetic, effects (Handy and Pukui 1972: 93). For instance, mele hanau (such as the one composed for Kauikeaouli, the future Kamehameha III) are performed to facilitate birth or even to revive a stillborn child (Pukui and Korn 1973: 12–28). Also, panegyrics with ancestry included are chanted and danced during the pregnancy of a chief in order to protect the fetus against sorcery and to help its development (Malo 1951: 136; K. Kamakau 1919–20: 2–3; cf. Pukui and Korn 1973: 12; Valeri 1985a: 218). The Kumulipo was chanted, according to tradition, in connection with the birth of Kalaninui'īamamao and on the deathbed of one of his descendants (Liliuokalani 1898: introduction), probably because as a celebration of the life of the cosmos as embodied in a noble, it was believed to ward off a noble's death.

Panegyrics with genealogical and sexual elements (probably, thus, of the mele ma'i type) are also chanted and choreographed to bring "an enriching and empowering magic" (Handy 1931: 12) to the first union of a high-ranking noble (Malo 1951: 136). The magical character of all panegyrical chants is also indicated by the strict taboos that surrounded their composition and their composers (cf. S. M. Kamakau in Roberts 1926: 59–60) and particularly by the rule of auspiciousness that dictated the choice of the words employed in the compositions. Writes Pukui: "Carelessness in the choice of words might result in death for the composers or the person for whom it was composed. . . . Words and word combinations were studied to see whether they were auspicious or not" (1949: 247; cf. Pukui 1983: sayings 800, 2062). Samuel Kamakau stresses that the choices were meant to obtain definite effects: "Each word had to be studied for its

---

[22] The chants that were not danced to were called *oli*, properly speaking, especially if they had "prolonged phrases chanted in one breath, often with a trill (*'i'i*) at the end of the phrase" (Pukui and Elbert 1986: 285). But according to some, to distinguish oli from the other chants (mele) is not so easy (Emerson 1965: 254).

meaning, whether lucky or unlucky, and for its effect [in this particular connection], whether it suggested good or bad luck, a stingy or kind person, a grumbler or a brave one" (1961: 241).

Even the purely genealogical portions of the chants show that they are meant to achieve effects through poetic means, rather than through argument. Not only is "the whole meticulous structure" of these genealogies a rhetorical device whose purpose is to convey the idea of "unbroken inheritance" (Beckwith 1951: 143), but even the "genealogical" connections among ancestors (particularly the more distant ones) are in fact often based on name association and various other principles of poetic composition, whose purpose is partly incantational, partly mnemotechnic (cf. Stokes 1930: 8–12). The obsessive repetition of the same schemes—and ultimately of the genealogical one that unifies them all—is meant to capture the entire universe, the entire history of nature and humankind, and to bring it to bear on the noble whose name is put at the end of the chant. As Stokes puts it:

The charging of the divine chief with *mana* is made possible through the belief in the magic omnipotence of names. We find in the Kumulipo chant the name of every form or being apparently known to Hawaiians, arranged in progression from the state of chaos through all known and many other stages of growth, creation, evolution or generation, through gods and human beings, right down the line to the newborn chiefly babe. There is nothing which may be regarded as prayer. The mere recitation of names forms a chain along which the accumulated *mana* of ages untold may be moved into the recipient shell. I have observed fears among Hawaiians that *mana* may not go straight. The chain then becomes a verbal tube, the leaks of which are closed by the repetition of the innumerable name variations. (1930: 12–13)

Therefore, in comparing the narrative accounts of succession in the last ten (and, to a lesser extent, twenty) generations with their genealogical counterparts, one should not separate the latter from all that precedes them in the chants. For when they are viewed in their proper setting, these genealogical accounts cannot be considered simplified renderings that implicitly refer to the more detailed descriptions of the narratives; they refer, instead, to the rest of the chant and reflect its structure, which has little to do with that of the narratives. This autonomous structure was the main ground for evaluating the chanted genealogies, and on it we must base our understanding of their relationship with the narrative texts. Moreover, the contrasting

structures of the two genres must be related to their purposes, which are also to a large extent different.

The purpose of a genealogical chant is to obtain various effects (to facilitate birth, ward off death, promote procreative potency, or simply to glorify a name) by establishing a connection between the person who must benefit from the effect and the ancestral line (human and beyond a certain point cosmic) through which flows the life force that produces the effect. The question arises, Why should the chant *describe* that connection in order to make it efficacious for the particular goal it has in mind? Is birth not sufficient to establish a connection with the ancestral line and thus to obtain its potency? Is not membership in a noble line and the benefits, magical and otherwise, that come from it, a given?

We see it as a given, and yet we are told that the Kumulipo, for instance, is called *he pule ho'ola'a ali'i* (Liliuokalani 1898: 1), "a magic spell for the consecration of a noble [that is, for making one a noble—V. V.]" (Liliuokalani 1898: introduction; Beckwith 1951: 9). Why was the chanting of Kalaninui'īamamao's connection with his ancestral line at his birth a necessary condition for making him a member of that line and thus for "consecrating" him—making him into a sacred noble? We may surmise that in this case, as in the case of any other charm or prayer, the names of the ancestors must be recited to call them so that they can witness the birth of the new offshoot of their line and convey their potency to it.[23] The ancestors' acceptance is what really makes the newborn a descendant. This connection with the ancestors, and the flow of potency, of life, that it brings about, will have to be established again by the performance of the chant every time the noble is threatened by death, sickness, or simply the challenge of those who deny his or her noble ancestry (Pukui 1983: sayings 31, 231; Beckwith 1951: 36; Handy and Pukui 1972: 199). As in every Hawaiian royal ritual, divine and ancestral recognition is doubled by a less explicit, but no less crucial, recog-

[23]Going back in time is equivalent to reaching the other world, in which the ancestors continue to live. This other world is referred to by the same metaphor (*pō*, "night"), which is also used to refer to the distant, original past with which the Kumulipo chant begins. There is thus a clear parallelism between the memory of the Hawaiian chanter and the Mnemosyne of the archaic Greek chanter: In the *Theogony*, as in the Kumulipo, "The past appears as a dimension of the other world" (Vernant 1974, 1: 87).

nition that comes from a living human audience (cf. Valeri 1985a). The human spectators witness the successful evocation of the ancestors and gods (indeed of the entire universe, mobilized through the names of its components), and through their recognition the evocation becomes real, socially efficacious.[24] The ancestors' recognition thus presupposes the spectators' recognition—in fact it is the spectators' recognition in disguise and, so to speak, partly alienated from them. *Vox populi* presents itself as *vox deorum*.

That the audience is not a passive spectator of the power of the ritual chanting but an essential part of what constitutes it is explicitly recognized in Hawaii. Indeed Pukui reports that "the kaona of a chant was ineffective unless chanted before a gathering" (Pukui 1949: 249). The word kaona refers in general to the "inner meaning" (p. 247) and in particular to "words with double meanings that might bring good or bad fortune" (Pukui and Elbert 1986: 130). The idea that the magical force of the chant depends on the reaction it elicits in its audience and that this force is all the more powerful the more numerous the audience is, is illustrated by Pukui, who, after mentioning that birthday parties were a favorite occasion for performing such chants because they were attended by many people, reports the following anecdote:

A relative of mine, of my grandmother's generation, had a lover who was very dear to her. He came to Honolulu and forgot to return after finding another sweetheart in town. She promptly composed a poem in which she used many words meaning to bind, make fast, to nail down securely, and wove them into a poem for hula dancing. She chanted it at the first birthday party of a cousin, and so delighted her hearers that she was asked to repeat it several times. In the meantime, a feeling of restlessness came over her lover in Honolulu. A longing to see his Kau sweetheart seized him, and he took the first boat to Hawaii. He could hardly wait to marry her. (Pukui 1949: 249)

The notion that divine (and, implicitly or explicitly, human) recognition is necessary to make one a member of a noble dynasty—and that this recognition is the result of the very power of the verbal magic of chants—can have a narrow or a wide application. It has a narrow application when the thing to be recognized is actual birth. Here the performance of the chant allows the children of a royal couple who

---

[24] This view exists among other Polynesians. In Tikopia, for instance, "considerable importance" is attached to a ritual's "validation by consensus" (Firth 1970: 224).

are recognized as members of the dynasty to be discriminated from those children of the same couple (or of each spouse separately) who are not. By adding to mere descent another and more important quality (being *represented* as a descendant in a chant), the chants in effect *constitute* single-line genealogical trees while claiming merely to represent them. Far from being a simplified account implicitly demanding to be completed by the accounts of informal genealogies and narratives, then, genealogical chants stand in opposition to them. Indeed, they are the instrument for invalidating them, or rather, for making them irrelevant. What they implicitly say is this: The persons we exclude undoubtedly descend from that king, but the fact is irrelevant because it is unsung.[25] After all, commoners are also said to descend from kings, but they are forbidden to own genealogical chants or even informal genealogies that make that fact good (cf. S. M. Kamakau 1961: 19, 242). The *use* of genealogical chants thus belies their overt *content*: that birth alone is the principle of legitimate succession. Not birth alone, but the *representation* of birth as if it were alone. Therefore political rivals may fight one another by opposing the possession of chants to nonpossession (for an example, see Fornander 1916–20, 4: 280–89) and also, of course, by opposing one chant to another (cf. S. M. Kamakau 1961: 152–53).

But the constitutive, magical power of the genealogical chants may have a wider application than the validation of proper birth. The chants may be used to make one a member of the dynasty irrespective of proper birth or even, exceptionally, irrespective of birth altogether. The latter case is illustrated by the alleged chanting of the Kumulipo in Hikiau temple to confirm the identification of Captain Cook with

[25] The point is explicitly made in the traditional injunction to the junior relatives of a high-ranking noble not to publicly proclaim their genealogical connections: "Set aside the lesser genealogies and remain humble; let only one be elevated, that of the chief" (Handy and Pukui 1972: 199). Another saying ("Inside the house, the relationship may be mentioned but outside your chief is your lord") is thus commented upon by Handy and Pukui: "Those who served inside a chief's house were usually blood relatives of a junior line; they were taught from childhood not to discuss the relationship and always to address him as *ku'u haku* (my lord), *ku'u ali'i* (my chief), or *ku'u lani* (my heavenly one), and not by any relationship term" (p. 199). All this clearly demonstrates that there is a great conceptual and practical difference between publicly and formally proclaimed pedigrees and privately and informally recognized genealogical connections. The genealogical chant does not simply ignore collateral relations; it suppresses them in the public, political sphere, where the junior relatives are only called servants.

Lonoikamakahiki. This is the name of the god Lono when he arrives in Hawaii during the Makahiki festival; but in the Kumulipo, the name is also used to refer to Kalaninui'īamamao, probably because this noble was born during the festival. The name stands at the end of the chant that consecrates Kalaninui'īamamao as a member of the royal dynasty. It seems, therefore, that the performance of the Kumulipo equated Cook not only with Lonoikamakahiki the god but also with Lonoikamakahiki the member of the royal dynasty (cf. Liliuokalani 1898: introduction; cf. Sahlins 1981: 16). Since the latter Lonoikamakahiki was the father of Kalani'ōpu'u, who ruled at the time of Cook's visit, it would seem that Cook was also given the status of Kalani'ōpu'u's father! The eyewitness accounts of Cook's consecration in Hikiau temple mention that a chant was recited, but it is of course impossible to establish whether this was in whole or in part the Kumulipo (cf. Cook and King 1784, 3: 8). Furthermore, it is difficult to trust any of the Hawaiian traditions on Captain Cook. But the accuracy of the tradition matters less than the fact that it testifies to an idea: that chanting an ancestral line with the name of a person not born to it included in the line could transform that person into a member. At any rate, that usurpers from collateral lines such as Kanaloakapulehu could appear in genealogical chants as sons of their predecessors on the throne (*Ke Kumu Hawaii* 1835: 133) indicates that the successful performance of these chants was enough to make the usurpers members of the ruling line. The history of 'Umi says that his father, when he decided to recognize his son, directed him to undergo a rite in which he was symbolically reborn and incised again in order to be incorporated into the royal line (Fornander 1916–20, 4: 184–85). It is possible and indeed likely that this rite involved the chanting of the dynasty's mele koihonua, since birth rites for nobles (such as the one undergone by Kalaninui'īamamao [Liliuokalani 1898: introduction]) required this recitation (cf. also Fornander 1878–80, 2: 75 n. 1).

All these would tend to confirm the literal truth of Beckwith's claim that a genealogical chant is "in the nature of a charm" (1951: 36). What the chant describes—sometimes in connection with fictitious representations of birth and/or incision (both are referred to by the same expression, " 'oki ka piko")—is brought into existence by the mere act of describing it. More precisely, the description—of somebody's birth in a genealogical line, say, or simply of somebody's being

part of a line—brings about what it describes if it is approved by an audience that ideally consists of ancestors but in practice consists of living humans. The crucial question, then, is, What criteria guide public support? What prompts the audience to validate the chant's claims?

One answer is already implicit in my insistence that the chant is a total work of art. It seduces the audience with its beauties,[26] which can be perceived independently of its propositional content but which may rub off on what is minimally perceived of that content: that the person on whose behalf the chant is performed is the legitimate successor in a dynasty. Indeed, one may speculate that the symmetries, antitheses, and musical and gestural devices of the chant serve to put any other content into the background and are thus efficacious, not because their dazzle illuminates, but because it blinds.

Another answer seems more obvious and more important: Precisely because there is a belief that words chanted in the appropriate context and by appropriate persons do not simply communicate what already exists but are capable of validating and even bringing about what they communicate, the appropriate performance of an appropriate chant is considered by the audience as sufficient grounds for believing in its effects. Therefore the successful description of a ruler as a member of a dynasty will prompt the audience to believe that he or she has been successfully validated as such and thus to offer their support.[27] This support in turn brings about effects (political and military success, prosperity, etc.) that are interpreted as further signs that the ruler has been accepted by the ancestral gods as their legitimate successor. Belief is of course self-fulfilling: It brings about its content precisely because its content is a matter of belief.

However, this answer raises problems. It presupposes that every-

---

[26] "Genealogies were carefully memorized . . . because of pleasure in recitation" (Elbert 1951: 348).

[27] In this respect, Hawaiian panegyrics are functionally similar to the *laudes regiae* of medieval Europe. As E. H. Kantorowicz has brilliantly demonstrated, these panegyrics had a constitutive or "crypto-constitutive" meaning (1946: 76). "To 'acclaim' meant: to 'create' a new ruler and to recognize him publicly in his new dignity" (p. 77). The same is true of royal panegyrics in many other cultures. See also Marin's study of the role of kingly representation in the constitution of Louis XIV's power, where he concludes that "the power-effect of representation is representation itself" (Marin 1981: 11). One could say of the Hawaiian king, as of the French one, that "the king is really a king, that is, a monarch, only in his images" (p. 12).

body in the audience is equally able to understand and evaluate the performance. While most people are capable of evaluating whether certain minimal felicity conditions (time and place of the performance, status of the performer, uninterrupted utterance of the chant, proper rhythm, etc.) are met, few can probably evaluate felicity in the choice of words, antitheses, and parallelisms—all of which constitute, we are told, the most important sources of the efficacy of the chant. Moreover, because each individual does not react separately to the performance, the collective reaction cannot be viewed as the sum total of individual analyses and judgments, unaffected by the rest of the audience. On the contrary, the chanting is experienced together with the reactions of all those who witness it. Thus what weights an individual judgment is less its object (the chant) than the crowd's attitude toward it. In the extreme, the object may be fictitious—only the reaction to it gives it reality. This is particularly the case when one does not have the knowledge (and the interest) to judge for oneself. It seems likely, therefore, that the belief that the performance is felicitous forms less as a result of analytic evaluations of the performance itself than as the cumulative result of the influence that, in the course of the chanting, each interpretation of what others think has on each other.

In other words, in the absence of a real ability to interpret the performance, one will believe what all others (and those who are believed to be more knowledgeable in the first place) appear to believe. Belief forms in a play of mirrors, so that for this collective belief in the felicity of the chanting to form, it sometimes suffices that nobody shows disapproval. The collective approval that this abstention from criticism makes possible may eventually influence, *malgré eux*, even those who disbelieve the chant, perhaps because disbelief (like belief) cannot fully sustain itself without some public echo to it, without making some converts—particularly in a culture where truth cannot be easily differentiated from opinion, since historical information resides in living people, not in inert traces (documents) that appear independent of human relations and interests.

Thus, while disbelieving, one may yet believe. This paradoxical believing in disbelief and disbelieving in belief has often been remarked upon (see, in particular, Mannoni, 1969; de Certeau 1981; Valeri 1981; Veyne 1983). It may account for the strange coexistence of two attitudes toward the chanters and thus their products. On the one hand, chanters seem to have been viewed as seers who, precisely because they had the power of making the ancestral deities present in their performances, had access to a superior truth to which it was necessary to yield[28]—at least in the context of the performance—even when it contradicted what was actually remembered or known from purely human sources. On the other hand, the chanters were seen, more cynically, as distorters of historical truth in the interest of their masters. David Malo, for instance, reports that "genealogists were called the washbasins of the alii, in which to cleanse them" of any connection with lower-ranking people or even outcasts (1951:71). He notes that traditions were sometimes fabricated (pp. 1–2). Samuel Kamakau, analogously, remarks on the political function of the court genealogist: "He was like a premier in a foreign country who watched for trouble that might come to his ruler from without, and guarded him against those who spoke disparagingly of his rank and called him slave (*kauwa*)" (1961:242).

But it is not necessary to invoke the paradoxes of belief to account for the coexistence of assent and dissent vis-à-vis a chant's claims. Many clearly manifested their assent to the chant not so much because they believed or half-believed it as because to do so was a conventional sign of allegiance to the ruler who owned the chant or a mark of courtesy and of peaceful intentions toward a peer.[29] In fact, we must conclude that the chanters themselves did not quite believe in their lofty constructions, since they were usually also responsible for composing and transmitting the prose traditions that not infrequently contradicted them.[30] For many people, the performance of the chants was not very different from those rituals in which one engages just to show where one stands and where one belongs; the basic cri-

---

[28] Indeed the composition of the chants and accompanying dances "was not a matter of mechanical fabrication, but rather of inspiration: the *mele* and the *hula* were often given in a dream" (Handy and Pukui 1972:84; cf. S. M. Kamakau 1961:241). Inspired truth does not have to be argued, then: Like the *alētheia* of the archaic Greek seers, it is valid because it is asserted by a representative of the gods (cf. Détienne 1967).

[29] That genealogical claims could be tolerated, although recognized as fictive, is indicated by saying 151 in Pukui 1983.

[30] The *po'e mo'olelo* (historians) also composed genealogical chants (Kepelino 1932:134) and in the latter capacity were referred to as *po'e kū'auhau* as well (S. M. Kamakau 1961:242). They used both genres, history and chants, to establish their master's legitimacy (p. 242).

terion was owning a chant and being able to perform it, or have it performed, successfully when challenged to do so. A famous episode in the Hawaiian annals provides evidence for this point of view (although it refers to a mele inoa rather than to a genealogical chant proper). A king of Hawai'i visiting O'ahu is unexpectedly challenged by the king of that island to produce his mele inoa. The king of Hawai'i owns no such chant. As luck has it, however, he has spent the previous night with a visiting chief of Kaua'i and memorized her name chant in the course of their amorous exchanges. He now successfully meets the challenge by reciting this chant. Because the challenger is perfectly aware of the fact that the chant recited is not the king of Hawai'i's own but nevertheless accepts it as valid (Fornander 1916–20, 4: 280–89), we must infer that the ability to perform a chant, not its content, counts as a criterion of status legitimation in this case.

But of course genealogical chants may also be used as arguments in the controversies between rivals. Samuel Kamakau describes one such controversy between the cousins Keōua and Kamehameha:

The strife between the chiefs took the form of denying each other's pure descent from a line of high chiefs. Each was well-versed in genealogical lines, oratory, and minute details in the histories of chiefs, their birth-places, rules of government and the signs and omens that revealed their ranks as chiefs. Both sides also had composers of meles [chants—V. V.] who chanted the names of ancestors, the high and godlike rank of their own chief, and the mean ancestry of the other. This form of controversy between the two chiefs is well-known today and will be remembered for all time. (1961: 152–53)

Even when used in these controversies, however, the chanting was more effective performatively than argumentatively: It created a rallying point for the supporters of a contender, it added their strength to that of argument, and it thus weakened the adversary through more than words. The special emphasis on the performative dimension of chanting in contrast to other, more specifically argumentative forms of communication is revealed by what reportedly happened when Keōua, weakened by the force of words and rituals (cf. Valeri 1985a: 162–63), sought peace: He approached Kamehameha, uttering a chant in his honor, one that perhaps mentioned the exalted ancestry he had previously denied to him (Pukui 1983: 228). The choice of a chant instead of other signs of submission is evidently due to the belief in its superior constitutive power. While all speech putatively had a magical dimension (" *'olelo,* 'word' or 'speech,' was far more than a means of communicating. To the Hawaiian, the spoken word did more than set into motion forces of destruction and death, forgiveness and healing. The word was itself a force" [Pukui, Haertig, and Lee 1972–79, 2: 124]), chanting intensified it—as testified by the fact that most prayers or spells were chanted.

In contrast, prose deemphasizes the magical aspect of speech and emphasizes its descriptive, argumentative aspects. Indeed, it is nowhere said that the recitation of the prose chronicles in appropriate contexts and by appropriate persons has conventional (or expected) effects. One does not even have to follow the prescriptions applying to the stories about the gods, which are sacred and thus "told only by day and the listeners must not move in front of the speaker; to do so would be highly disrespectful to the gods" (Beckwith 1940: 1; cf. Pukui in *Hawaiian Ethnographical Notes* 1: 1602–5). Although not used ritually, prose narratives are nonetheless constitutive because, as we have seen, they provide arguments for the legitimacy of certain actions and for certain ways of obtaining power. They are constitutive through argument, not through magic. And while genealogical chants may be used as arguments reinforcing or complementing those contained in the narratives, ultimately the global picture of the reproduction of Hawaiian kingship that emerges from the narratives challenges the global picture offered by the genealogical chants. For the latter, kingship is the continuation in society of the procreative principle of nature: The royal dynasty perpetuates and sustains itself only through this principle, and all rulers are thus legitimated exclusively by their birth. For narrative history, however, dynastic continuity is not the hard natural core of society; it is a social fact itself, because it depends on successful social, rule-governed actions. Furthermore, dynastic continuity appears as a retrospective effect of another, deeper-running continuity (which may or may not occur): the continuity of power, where power is defined as the ability to make people act on one's behalf by the use of force, wealth, and persuasion. Of course, the narratives themselves show that one of the most potent of these persuasive means—and thus one of the most important sources of power, if not the most important one—is genealogical legitimacy. Genealogy gives no empty "prestige" (Kaeppler 1985: 128) in Hawai'i: Even conquerors yield to its power—in order to obtain it for their heirs—in the arms of the sisters or daughters of the kings they have defeated.[31] However important genealogical rank is as a source of power, it is not the only one: It is just a part of a complex whole whose functioning is revealed in the narratives. By showing this fact and revealing its consequence—de facto dynastic discontinuity retrospectively represented as continuity—narrative history ultimately accounts for its contrary: magical history. For it is in the chants that the supreme value of continuity is magically reproduced out of the discontinuities represented, and justified, by narrative history.

The coexistence of the two genres, and of the conflicting views of history that they enshrine, is thus explained by the coexistence of a dynastic ideal with the actual social conditions for its realization. To some extent, these conditions are such that the ideal can only be realized in representation, and becomes real only insofar as reality-producing powers are attributed to its representation in certain forms. What is particularly interesting is that the social conditions for the reproduction of kingship do not have a subterranean, tacit existence in Hawaii: They are legitimated by their explicit articulation in narrated precedents. Furthermore, the narrative genre as a whole enshrines and legitimates a singularly sober, occasionally almost instrumental view of history. In this history the gods are only allowed to intervene indirectly through human spokesmen or through humanly controlled rituals. It is a history made almost entirely human by divine kings, as if only they were powerful enough to banish the gods proper.

---

[31] The political importance of genealogical legitimacy (and its ideological supremacy) is well illustrated by the discussions on the criteria to follow in the succession of Kamehameha, an upstart king: "The chiefs disputed about the succession while Kamehameha was living, and Kamehameha asked the opinion of men skilled in genealogies and of the orators and those who knew about government in ancient days. Some of the chiefs and governors thought that the old standards should not count in the succession. But the skilled men told Kamehameha that in order to keep the kingdom united as he left it and prevent its falling to pieces at his death, he must consolidate it under one ruler and must leave it to an heir who was in the ruling line from his ancestors. He should therefore appoint Liholiho his heir and his younger brother, Kau-i-keaouli, to succeed him because, although they came [through their mother, Keōpūolani—V. V.] from the side of the defeated chiefs who were his enemies and not one of whom had aided him to gain the kingdom, they were *pi'o* chiefs [the highest ranking—V. V.] belonging to the line of chiefs who owned the rule from their ancestors" (S. M. Kamakau 1961: 429–30; cf. Fornander 1916–20, 4: 262–65).

Conclusion

Nietzsche, in his scintillating treatment of the use and abuse of history, humorously places the grazing cow, enclosed in the happiness of the eternal present, in silent dialogue with the human passerby, lamenting his inability to forget:

"Why do you not speak to me of your happiness but only stand and gaze at me?" The animal would like to answer, and say "The reason is I always forget what I was going to say"—but then he forgot this answer too, and stayed silent: so that the human being was left wondering.

But he also wonders at himself, that he cannot learn to forget but clings relentlessly to the past: however far and fast he may run, this chain runs with him. (1983: 60–61)

To be human, then, is to move forward into the future, constantly dragging the chain that binds one to the past. But peoples like the Nuer, the Tallensi, the Merina, or the Balinese are dehumanized by some of their ethnographers, who, by claiming that they live in a "timeless present" (Bloch 1977: 288) or "wholly in the present and the immediately recollected past" (Fortes 1945: xi), seem to suggest that they are not very different, as far as historical consciousness is concerned, from their cattle. It is true that one among these ethnographers, Bloch, claims that traditional societies, particularly hierarchical ones, think of themselves in a timeless present only when they have recourse to their culturally constituted concepts. He is generous enough to concede that they may escape from the fictitious world of culture into the real world of nature and social processes, thanks to an alleged natural "cognition system" (1977: 287), which remains identical in all societies and times. Bloch's generosity stops short of his colleagues', however; to them he refuses to explain how the intellect can be at one time so extraordinarily free from cultural constraints that it has a direct line of communication with the "infrastructure" and at another time so extraordinarily determined by them as to be unable to perceive any change or contradiction in society.[32]

[32] Note that this criticism applies to Bloch whether or not there is "a massive central core of human thinking which has no history" (as claimed by Strawson 1959:10). For if this central core exists, it is a "primary theory" (Horton 1982) applying to our basic perceptions of the physical world but hardly to our knowledge of social events and processes, which is inescapably evaluative and thus cultural (it is thus a "second-level theory" in Horton's terminology). On this question see also Valeri 1991.

In the Hawaiian case both a representation of history (such as the one contained in the genealogical chants) that stresses continuity between past and present and one that stresses discontinuity and change have their roots in the same culturally constituted social form. Far from lying outside the sphere of culture, the representation of history as a discontinuous and conflictual process is as culturally codified as the continuistic one. More importantly, it is used to give cultural legitimacy to the practices it represents. These often include usurpation, the liquidation of incumbents, successoral arrangements of extreme diversity, and such. Historical precedent may even be used to legitimate change. But even when it is not so used, the relationship between past and present is never conceived as one of mechanical replication. It is instead analogical and thus implies difference, not only similarity, between past and present. It implies, moreover, a choice between alternatives. This is precisely what is implied by my use of the term paradigmatic to describe its dominant mode.

Even the metonymic equivalence of past and present that is depicted in the mele koihonua implies a dimension of difference and does not suggest what Bloch calls their "total fusion" (Bloch 1977: 288), for these chants use the time dimension to differentiate individual ancestors and living people by the degree of their closeness to an origin point. Indeed, the most encompassing image of history, in the mele koihonua genre as in the mo'olelo genre, is one of progressive development, of time as a cumulative, not a repetitive, process. The genealogical image differs from the narrative one because the process is conceived in essentially procreative, indeed sexual, terms and not in terms of social action proper. History is naturalized in the genealogical chants, but not totally denied. Its presence is indicated, among other things, by the very infrequent repetition of proper names in the genealogies, so that each ancestor is pinned down to a specific time by a name that belongs to him or her alone.[33]

Finally, the Hawaiian case should undermine the simplistic view

---

[33] Pariente has noted that "proper names . . . present their bearers as different from all other things, but do not go so far as to specify in what this difference consists: they affirm it as such, but they do not make it reside in a specific predicate, thus leaving the mind of the receiver free to assign it any predicate that discourse may attribute to the named object" (1973: 69). One could say that genealogies are also a history of proper names, from which most (but not all) predicates have been eliminated, so that the listener is free to discover the appropriate predicates in each case.

that because a representation of history serves political interests, it is necessarily distorting or even fictitious. The implicit correlate is that only a "disinterested" history can adequately capture historical reality. But political interest may motivate a "realistic" attitude, a need to preserve the memory of past action *wie es eigentlich gewesen ist.* Because their political system rewarded successful action, Hawaiians had a vested interest in recording the actual successes or failures of political strategies. Furthermore, they had a vested interest in preserving the variety of the past because it provided them with the means for legitimating the variety of the present.

Ultimately, the most striking feature of Hawaiian narrative history, the escape of the past from a single reductionist scheme, both reflects and justifies the independence of the Hawaiian ruler from the constraints of a fixed and immutable system of rules.[34] Hawaiian rulers are to some extent free to invent, so their history records what escapes traditional custom, or perhaps even reflects, as in the case of succession (where we find a bewildering variety of solutions [see Valeri 1990]), a certain looseness of custom in the first place.

In sum, I would argue that since narratives of comparatively recent history (ten generations or so before Kamehameha) do not instantiate a single, timeless custom, since, rather, their content reflects the very complex dialectic of past and present that they serve to legitimate, they may therefore have a certain degree of historical veracity. I would further argue that this interest in history as it really was is very much a function of the workings of the Hawaiian polity. Those workings also explain, however, why the realistic image of history coexists with a magical counterpart.

I remain convinced, then, that what Bloch (1977) calls somewhat improperly the "social determination of knowledge" explains both false and authentic consciousness. Although all representations are cultural, they do not have the same representational power. And they

---

[34] On the autonomy of Polynesian rulers, see Sahlins 1985. On the autonomy of rulers in general, see Durkheim's famous page in *The Division of Labor in Society*: "Chiefs are, in fact, the first personalities that emerge from the social mass. . . . In dominating society, they are no longer forced to follow all of its movements. Of course, it is from the group that they derive their power, but once power is organized, it becomes autonomous and makes them capable of personal activity. A source of initiative is thus opened which had not existed before them. There is, hereafter, someone who can produce new things and even, in certain measure, deny collective usages" (1968: 195).

do not, in part, because different interests make different experiences possible, because they stimulate or block perception to go in different directions. Interest has more complex relations with representation than a distorting effect. But I must leave a fuller and more satisfactory discussion of this problem for another time.

Acknowledgments

This paper has been through several versions, successively presented to various audiences: to the participants of two conferences (the Wenner-Gren conference in Fez, held in January 1986, and the Finnish Academy conference on culture and history in the Pacific, held in Helsinki in January 1987) and to the members of two departments of anthropology (those at New York University in March 1986 and those at the University of Adelaide in August 1987). I thank them all, but I am particularly grateful to Jane Bestor, Nikolay Guirenko, Janet Hoskins, Edmund Leach, Emiko Ohnuki-Tierney, Marshall Sahlins, Jukka Siikala, and Annette Weiner.

7

Shaping Time: The Choice of the National Emblem of Israel

DON HANDELMAN AND LEA SHAMGAR-HANDELMAN

Of all histories, that of the
Jewish people has been the
most refractory to secularization because this history alone,
as a national history, was considered by all to be sacred to
begin with.

Yosef Hayim Yerushalmi

O Titus, Titus,
if only you saw
whose is the triumph, of
whom the songs of praise tell,
under the Arch you built
two soldiers from
Eretz-Yisrael.

"All Roads Lead to Rome"[1]

With the declaration of the founding of the state, on May 14, 1948, the legislators of independent Israel had to choose an emblem as an insignia of statehood. Before them was the problem of encompassing, in a single representation, that which the state signified to them and should signify to the wider public. The decision was to have been a speedy one for practical reasons, but discussions dragged on for months. The final preference—the seven-branched lampstand, the menorah, sculpted in relief and frozen for posterity in 81 C.E. on the triumphal Arch of Titus in Rome (Fig. 7.1)—signified choices about space and time, history and culture. In this paper we discuss how the choice was made and what factors entered into the selection.

The motifs that were offered for the emblem varied among the past

[1] This epigraph is a refrain from "All Roads Lead to Rome," a song written toward the end of World War II, lyrics by Yitzhak Yitzhak, music by Z. Ben-Yosef. Members of the entertainment troupe of the Jewish Brigade performed the song. The song became popular in the *yishuv*, the Jewish community of Palestine, and later among Israelis.

Fig. 7.1. Menorah in the bas-relief on the Arch of Titus.

informing the present, the present informing the future, and a combination of the two. The decision itself was only one of a multitude that came to form the experiential shape of the state. But the endurance required of the emblem, its summarizing qualities, and its conscious creation by the will of sovereign authority all set it apart from most other normative decisions, whose symbolic significance either was not evident or was understood to be malleable. In itself, the choice had no visible consequences. We have yet to know whether this choice was not one signpost to the future.

Those who selected the emblem, and those who commented on the various alternatives, referred frequently to tradition and to the history of ancient Israel. The ancient past—whether as myth, covenant, or source of culture—is inscribed and encoded in various modes in the Torah (the Pentateuch) and in the Hebrew Bible as a whole. A knowledge of the ancient past contained in these and other texts was integral, in varying degrees, to the lives of Jews. For the great majority the ancient past was part of their living present until the early twentieth century. Secular Zionists read the Hebrew Bible as history and culture, and on this reading they based their vision of a return to the Jewish homeland and statehood. The Zionist vision, in that it was messianic (Greenstone 1906; Ben-Gurion 1976:175; Katz 1971; Scholem 1971), ultimately pointed back to ontological coordinates that informed Jewish cultures in time and space. To the extent that Jews reacted to them on some level of being, such symbolic coordinates were not the detritus of time past, but the existential and experiential conditions of present and past informing one another. Therefore the subject of this essay is time through symbolism. The emblem encodes coordinates of time and space, historicity and place. In its visual composition the emblem construes the capacity to expand diachronically into a vision of the living of history, and living history, in a particular place. Other symbols and symbolic acts of modern Israel have the same capacity. Elsewhere (Handelman 1990, ch. 9), for example, a cognate argument is developed with respect to the three national days—Holocaust Day, Remembrance Day, and Independence Day—promulgated by the state after 1948. In their timing, as a set sequence of occasions, these days have the capacity to evoke narratives of Israeli Jewish historicity.

The choice of the emblem was made in the context of a new state just coming into being—one that was consciously experimental in certain of its institutions and deliberately revolutionary in certain of its experiments. But this state was the product of Jews. Whatever else they were—and they were deeply divided by ideology, politics, and way of life—they were almost unanimous in their axiomatic views of time and space. One historian has concluded that "the tie of the Zionist idea with Zion is not theoretical at all. It is an 'existential' reality, a historical fact which Zionism does not question but knows itself to embody" (Halpern 1969: 103). Thus Palestine was the sole existential and moral locus for the Jewish people, and this was inextricable from their history in this place. In other words, the decision about the emblem took place in the context of a pervasive Jewish culture.

The most enduring and influential template of Jewish culture was the Hebrew Bible, together with related commentaries, liturgies, legends, folk traditions, and festivals. These constituted a corpus of knowledge and experience, intellectual and commonsensical. Cultural axioms of space and time—crucial to any understanding of the significance of the emblem—are encoded in the Hebrew Bible. Since this encoding is of direct relevance to our discussion of the emblem, as it was to those who decided on its composition, it is outlined below.

We present this discussion because it is integral to the expressed thoughts of those who chose the emblem, and not because of any prior assumption on our part about the relevance of biblical texts to the enunciation of statehood. Following this necessarily schematic discussion, we take up the process of selecting the emblem as a sequence of issues and decisions. We then discuss, in more structural terms, the criteria of selection that came to inform this process. Finally, we consider some implications of the choice.

Space and Time, Exile and Return: Ontological Coordinates of Historicity

Our concern here is with cultural, ontological coordinates of space and time that together help to generate structures of historicity, of the existence of history. One such coordinate is the presence of a spatial center—cosmic, moral, social—within which the Israelites enjoy a special relationship with the divine. A second is the loss of this center and the condition of exile (*galut*). Together these coordinates contribute to the generation of cognitive structures, at times structures of desire, that often are enunciated as the need to return to this center—the singular place in which redemption (*ge'ula*) is sought for the nation as a whole.

Space and time in the Hebrew Bible are axes of the creation of the world and of the Jewish people. As the axes emerge, they become vectors of the structuring of history, which itself acquires paradigmatic shape. In other texts, this paradigm is expected to collapse back into the axes from which it emerged, and these axes themselves to be dissolved through eschatological processes. Proto-time and end-time are not homologous, but analogies can be made.

Humankind begins in the mythic space of Eden, a cosmic paradise (Genesis 2: 8–14). Eden is the omphalos that sustains all life, and from it radiate primal streams to the four quarters. In the center of this center grow the Tree of Life and the Tree of Knowledge of Good and Evil. Humankind here is at the midpoint of ordered space and in harmony with divine will (Fishbane 1974: 9; Meyers 1976: 135). But humans disobey God's commandment and are cast out, into exile. With this fragmentation of the perfection of cosmic unity and the disjunction of cosmic and human space, the periodicity of humankind begins in the dislocated space of exile.

The creation of the Israelites and of the nation of Israel follows this pattern of movement to and from a sacred center. God led Abraham from Ur of the Chaldees into the land of Canaan, prefigured as the sacred center and as the permanent abode of the Israelites (Judges 9–37), and there made His covenant with him. The offspring of Abraham, Isaac, and Jacob, enslaved in Egypt, were shepherded out into Sinai by Moses. Exodus marks the birth of the Israelites as a nation. From God, on His Holy Mountain in Sinai (Exodus 24–25), Moses received the Tablets of the Law (the Ten Commandments), the sacred order that signified the renewed Covenant, the compact between God and the People of Israel. God commanded Moses to build the Tabernacle, His dwelling place on earth and perhaps a model of its cosmic counterpart (Fishbane 1974: 17). The Tabernacle, which housed the Tablets within their Ark of the Covenant, was located in the center of the Israelite camp, the midpoint of the nation in its wanderings. The exile concluded when Joshua led the Israelites into the promised land, the sacred center of Canaan.

The uniting of the fragmented and warring nation of Israel created a permanent sacred center of centers. David made Jerusalem (Zion) the capital of the United Kingdom—a "matrix of covenantal order . . . valorized . . . as an Edenic center" (Fishbane 1974: 20; Psalms 46: 4; Psalms 48: 2–4, 12–14). Jerusalem was the "Mountain of Jahweh" set over the cosmic deep (Psalm 24), the Mountain of God and the entrance to the netherworld (Isaiah 29: 1), the location of the foundation stone (Isaiah 28: 16–17), the point of origin of the world.

David's successor, Solomon, further concentrated the sacred center in building the Temple, the permanent abode of the presence of God in the world (Weinfeld 1972: 196–97). In rabbinic literature, the Talmudic tractate *Yoma*, for example, the Temple Mount (or Mount Zion) was thought of as the primordial or protological center, the matter from which creation proceeded (Levenson 1984: 283). This sacred centricity is well brought out in a midrash (*Tanhuma*: Kedoshim 10) that depicts the Temple in the center of Jerusalem, the Great Hall in the center of the Temple, the Ark of the Covenant in the center of the Great Hall, and the Foundation Stone, the point of origins, before the Ark. The later Judeo-Hellenistic interpretations of Philo of Alexandria and of Josephus Flavius understood the Temple to be organized as a model of the cosmos, and Josephus noted that this knowledge was commonplace (Goodenough 1954: 81; Safrai

1976: 906). Jon D. Levenson suggests that this centricity in space had its counterpart of time: "The Temple is to space what the Sabbath is to time, a recollection of the protological dimension bounded by mundane reality" (1984: 298).

The biblical scholar W. D. Davies summarizes the relationship of the Temple and Jerusalem in stating that the Temple was the quintessence of Jerusalem, as the latter was the quintessence of the land (1974: 152–53). Both the Temple and Jerusalem became the crucible for the hopes of the land, and so of the people who, in biblical sources and later ones, often were depicted as a plant or shoot growing forever on the *axis mundi*, the cosmic Mountain of the Lord (Meyers 1976: 149; Childs 1960: 86–88; but see also Stone 1980: 77–81).

This bond between nation and land was not merely spatial, for centricity was ontological for that order of existence within which God-given morality would flourish. The Temple was the moral center of the world (Levenson 1984: 298), for space itself had no inherent sacred qualities (Childs 1960: 92). These existed always in relation to the presence of God, to that nexus of cosmic and human orders in which the latter was best able to realize the moral design of the former. And the landscape of Temple / Jerusalem / Land of Israel, more than any other, was imbued with divine sustenance. As Levenson puts it, this nexus of centricity "is not a point in space at all, but the point in relation to which all space attains . . . meaning. The center sustains the world" (1985: 139). A signal irony of Judaism is that the Jewish people are enjoined to strive for moral perfection, and so to enjoy the harmony and fruits of divine benefice—but such perfection is denied them, since ultimate perfection is an attribute only of God (Fredman 1981: 149). Therefore, times without number they fail to live up to the requirements of the law demanded of them by the Covenant. Exile from the center is the corollary of the struggle for perfection, and of failing in this struggle time and again. Exile is a moral condition of the nation as a whole. In biblical literature the weakness and laxity of humans produced the center in chaos, overrun and profaned, emptied of the divine presence. Or the Jews themselves, found wanting and futile, were cast out. Centricity led inevitably to the exilic condition.

The weakening of religious and national centricity (for example, the fragmentation of the United Monarchy) and worse—exile from the divine presence—signified again the disintegration of order and the unleashing of the chaotic human will. Unity, harmony, and blessing were dissipated, and people fell further from that physical and spiritual location that nurtured the true soil of potential perfectability. Historiography in the Hebrew Bible itself virtually stops with the rebuilding of the Temple after its destruction in 586 B.C.E. and the period of Babylonian exile. But the Second Temple period is punctuated by numerous depredations and invasions, all of which were colored by the bleakness of morality in exile, of the absence of God from his abode. The Second Temple period and Jewish independence ended with the Roman destruction of Jerusalem in 70 C.E. The sacred artifacts of the Temple were carried off to Rome and exhibited there in triumph—a scene depicted on the Arch of Titus, erected to commemorate the victory.

The corollary of absence from the center was the need to return there, to the focus of the divine presence, to the fount of all blessing and fruition, which eventually would harmonize the disjunctions of cosmic and human orders. The books of the Prophets in the Hebrew Bible are pervaded by such visions. This return came to be called redemption; and "the shape of redemption," argues Fishbane, "resumes the configuration of the exodus; that paragon of movements from disorientation and chaos to orientation and cosmos at a sacred center" (1974: 23). Thus the leaving of exile, and the return to Zion, is a return not only to the promised land but also to a desired moral condition for the nation as a whole.

The redemption of space was also that of time, for return was a signal index of the hoped-for attainment of a future golden age, of the intervention of God in history to end time—a new creation in the fullest sense. Although the ideal goals of redemption were metaphysical and existential, a return through metaphors of the spirit was not sufficient. If, on the one hand, "the history of [ancient] Israel is the account of God's redemptive acts occurring in space" (Childs 1960: 93), then, on the other, the nation of Israel would be granted redemption in that space made central for redemption. The hope of redemption required the presence of the people of Israel in that singular space. Moreover, just as the Israelites were defined as a nation by divine will, so redemption would come to the nation as a whole, and not as the salvation of individuals. The ideas of redemption almost always had a religious and national character, phrased often in the vocabulary of Israelite sovereignty (Werblowsky 1971: 30; Mowinckel 1959: 267).

Given the ultimately transcendent goals of return and redemption, the "salutary outcome of history" (Levey 1974: xix) was necessarily eschatological (see Stone 1982: 202–4); and this was, in a minor key, an eschatology of messianism. Eschatologies in the Hebrew Bible envisioned national restoration, independence, and kingship (Mo-. winckel 1959: 267). Later ones also emphasized the ingathering of the exiles (*kibbutz galuyot*) and their return to Palestine (the Roman name), the purification of the land, the restoration of the Temple and Jerusalem, peace and prosperity, and eventually the fulfillment of the vision of the End of Days (Levey 1974: xix). The later messianism, often apocalyptic, added the figure of the messiah, a king of David's lineage anointed by God, who either brought the golden age into being or signified its presence. However, themes of the moral centricity of singular space, of time as moral periodicity, and of the desired synthesis of disjunctions of space and time (which would lead to redemption and eternity) were common both to restorative eschatologies and to apocalyptic messianism.

R. J. Zwi Werblowsky notes that by the time of the great diaspora of the Jews, in the first and second centuries C.E., the Jews were equipped with messianic beliefs and hopes "too axiomatic to be questioned." Messianism, he adds, was "a permanent and ever-present feature, at times latent, at times manifest, of Jewish history" (1971: 37; cf. Greenstone 1906). Messianic eschatologies developed from the logic of restorative ones, and these in turn were predicated, in part, on the coordinates of centricity, exile, and return that are embedded in the Hebrew Bible.

Rabbinic or normative Judaism made the study of the scriptures and the performance of the Halacha (the rules for obeying divine law and its interpretations) the backbone of living in the diaspora. These were codes that in theory regulated all facets of life. Dislocated from moral space, Jews lived in gentile lands and in gentile time. But text and tradition contained their own rhythms and markers of temporality and spatiality. Yosef Hayim Yerushalmi (1982; see also Lewis 1975: 20–27) notes the paucity of Jewish historiography almost until the nineteenth century, even during periods when Jews were engaged actively in the humanities and sciences. Yet Jews thought of themselves as very much a people living in history. But in no small measure it was their own history of significance that was learned.[2] And although normative versions of Judaism emphasized that redemption would come to Jewry through that gradual perfection acquired from the study of the Torah and the performance of the Halacha, it was in the diaspora that messianic eschatologies really evolved, flourished, and were embellished. As Gershom Scholem notes: "The blazing landscape of redemption . . . concentrated in itself the historical outlook of Judaism" (1971: 35). In all of these theories of redemption, Jerusalem remained the temporal destination, signifying the morality of synthesis, completeness, perfect order, freedom, goodness, and light (Fredman 1981: 35).

Modern Zionism was the product of nineteenth-century Europe—of the Enlightenment, of emancipation from the ghetto, and of the rise of nationalism. It was predicated on the vision of Palestine as the national homeland, the center, for the Jewish people the world over. According to the Zionists, the lives of Jews in the diaspora were ones of degradation, diminution, stagnation, and persecution on the one hand or of assimilation and loss of identity on the other. Crucial to the Zionist vision was the mass return, or ascent (*aliyah*), of world Jewry to its only natural center. Ben Halpern (1969: 101–3) notes that Zionists of all ideologies and persuasions were in near unanimity that the locus of this ingathering of the exiles should be Palestine. This belief was subscribed to by many highly articulate and reflective humanists, philosophers, and ideologues. Yet they were least explicit in trying to explain why Palestine had to be the location, rather than other suggestions: Argentina, Uganda, and a homeland within the USSR. For the visionaries and pioneers of the Zionist movement, faith in the divine promise of redemption was replaced by belief in the historical inevitability of the ingathering of the exiles (Katz 1982: 38), but always with reference to the same spatial coordinate.

The idea of the temporal coordinate of redemption was also essential to the Zionist vision. Jacob Katz argues persuasively that modern Zionist national ideology was prefigured by, and was reinter-

[2] Thus, as W. D. Davies comments: "The Talmud has a communal national reference in its application of the Torah to the actualities of the Jews' existence. Its contents, formation, and preservation presuppose the continuance of the self-conscious unity of the people of Israel" (1982: 47). For example, generations of Jews studied the complicated laws of sacrificial rituals in the Temple centuries after the Temple was destroyed and the Temple-cult of sacrifice ended.

preted in relation to, traditional messianism (1971: 277). More recently, he suggests that only the messianic language of redemption has proven appropriate to encompass major events that helped to enunciate and to shape the origins and development of the Jewish state—from the Balfour Declaration of 1917 to the Six-Day War of 1967 and beyond (1982: 40; see also Aviad 1984).

Unlike versions of religious redemption, those of secular Zionism (the dominant thrust of the movement) emphasized the redeeming of the ingathered exiles and of their land through rational political and economic means. Secular Zionism, the Zionism of a resynthesized Jewish culture, as distinct from one whose premises were religious, envisaged an open-ended future of independence for the Jewish people and their progress through modern education and the rationalization of labor. But the new synthesis-in-the-making of Israeli Jewish culture was understood as well to have its sources in what was read as the literature and historiography of biblical writings. Through a host of activities, the secular Zionists transformed metaphorical relationships among land, texts, and Jewish presence into metonymic ones—through the revival of Hebrew as the language of daily use, through the giving of biblical names to places and persons, through the development of archeology as the science that objectified the historicity of the landscape, and so forth.

For pious Jewry the rise of Zionism constituted a severe metaphysical crisis about paths to redemption (cf. Aran 1986). For example, in 1937 the orthodox scholar Isaac Breuer asked an assembly of the ultraorthodox to decide whether the Balfour Declaration constituted "a divinely imposed task or a Satanic contrivance." No reply was forthcoming. Breuer himself argued that it was that rarest of occasions, a "historical-metahistorical miracle," which should not be passed over. For history "was concerned solely with the behavior of nations on their own soil, metahistory with the course of Divine Providence," and rarely did they conjoin. With exile, "Israel had been expelled from history and remained a purely metahistorical nation, waiting . . . for re-entry into history through restoration of the rule of its metahistorical constitution [the Torah] in its metahistorical land" (Marmorstein 1969: 85). For orthodox Jewry, the debates over the meanings of ingathering at Zionist initiative continue to rage. These had no overt impact on discussions over the emblem, for the representatives of the religious parties who participated in the choice were Zionists. But it is fair to state that they accepted the "historical-metahistorical miracle" as the tentative sign of redemption and did their best to imbue their influence with such significance.

Thus the demands made of the ideal emblem were complicated and at times contradictory. The state insisted that since Israel was the guardian of world Jewry, the emblem had to incorporate symbolism that spoke to Jews everywhere. For this, the touchstone could only be Judaism; and the common ground could only be ancient Israel, which was inextricably intertwined with Judaism as a religion. The emerging national culture of Israeli Jews tended to be secular, yet rooted in ancient Israel, and so again intertwined with religion. Therefore the emblem had to include symbolism of the ancient that would be understood clearly as a source of secular culture. But mainstream, secular Zionism also pointed to an evolutional future of modern progress, as distinct from the stagnant, involutional life of the diaspora. Therefore the symbolism had to bring to the fore this break with the past and this new beginning in the modern era. However, since modern Israel was posited as the political and moral center, one that demanded ingathering as the prerequisite of material and spiritual redemption, the symbolism also had to refer to these aspects, whose sources were again biblical. To further complicate this strained configuration of the desired, the politics of emblem pitted the Zionist religious parties against the primarily secular ones. In the end, after argument and compromise, the chosen emblematic visage gazed on only part of the Zionist dream and was blind to the rest.

Choosing the Emblem: The Sequence of Selection

With the declaration of statehood, the provisional government took office. Its legislative body was the State Council (SC), composed of 37 representatives of the major parties and organizations of the *yishuv*, the Jewish community in Palestine.[3] The provisional cabinet appointed the ministerial Committee on Symbols (MC), composed of four members of the cabinet, representing four parties, to choose the national flag and emblem.

[3] The provisional government was replaced by an elected parliament (knesset) in the spring of 1949.

Fig. 7.2. Modern and ancient—seven stars and the Lion of Judah.

Phase 1: The New and the Old (June 2–July 15, 1948). The MC convened on June 2. One of the motifs suggested for emblem and flag was seven golden stars. The stars were joined on the emblem by a rampant Lion of Judah (Fig. 7.2), considered an ancient symbol of Jewish kingship and statehood. The meeting protocol does not indicate with whom the idea of the stars originated, but its early presence was indicative of the desires of many.

In 1896, Theodor Herzl, the acknowledged visionary of the modern idea of a Jewish state, published *Der Judenstaat* (The Jewish State). Herzl was an assimilated Viennese Jew, a journalist who was shocked into a realization of the existence of anti-Semitism by the Dreyfus affair. His book is a cry for the founding of a Jewish homeland formulated by a liberal elitist who believed in the values of the Enlightenment—reason, progress, education, the rational use-value of labor, the paternalistic extension of social services, and so forth. It is also a secular utopian vision without a history, without tradition, and with a highly circumscribed role for religion (Herzl 1970: 100). One of the ideals in the book is the seven-hour workday, which to Herzl signified the rationalization of labor and social benefits (pp. 61–62). With regard to a national symbol, he wrote: "We have no flag. We need one. Anyone who wants to lead many men must raise a symbol over their heads. I am thinking of a white flag with seven gold stars. The white field signifies our new, pure life; the stars are the seven golden hours of our working day. For the Jews will move to the new land under the banner of labor" (p. 101). Of this motif, nothing came. Herzl himself became president of the First Zionist Congress in 1897 and was the leader of the movement for some years. In 1948 the bulk of the Zionist leadership agreed that Herzl had blazed a prophetic and charismatic trail, although the new state was not intended in the least to resemble his schematic outline.

The MC convened again on June 7. The proposed Lion of Judah was struck down, and the motif of the seven-branched lampstand, the menorah, joined that of the seven stars. The originator of this suggestion may have been the minister of transportation, the late David Remez of Mapai—the party of Ben-Gurion and the leading force in the government.[4] The MC proposed, pending cabinet approval, to solicit suggestions for the designs of emblem and flag from the public. On June 10 the provisional government declared a public competition for flag and emblem (*Davar*, June 10). The announcement requested that a seven-branched menorah and seven gold stars, each with six points, appear in the design, but stated that any proposal would be given consideration. The deadline for submissions was June 14; in response to protests it was later extended to June 25. The MC received 450 designs submitted by 164 persons. Of these, two for the flag and two for the emblem were selected for the consideration of the cabinet. The cabinet selections were put before the SC for ratification. The cabinet's choice for the emblem (Fig. 7.3) was seven 6-pointed golden stars on a band of white, beneath which was a white menorah on a field of light blue. By its stepped, octagonal base, the menorah is identifiable as an abstraction of that sculpted on the Arch of Titus panel.

According to Exodus (25: 40), God showed Moses the design of the seven-branched menorah on Mount Sinai and commanded him to make one like it. According to various legends (see Ginsberg 1968: 160, 219), the making of the menorah had connotations of both human work and divine intervention—in other words, of their intersection and (in a loose sense) their mediation through the menorah. The menorah was one of a complex of ritual artifacts with which Moses was enjoined to furnish the Tabernacle, the abode of God in

[4] Shlomo Kedar, in 1948 the government secretary to the MC, interview with the authors, June 28, 1985. However, a former legislator, Mordechai Ben-Tov, has stated that he suggested the menorah as the state emblem, having taken the idea from the menorah insignia awarded to members of the Warsaw Den of Hashomer Hatza'ir (the socialist youth movement) who left Poland for Palestine in the early 1920's (*B'Ma'aracha*, no. 299, 1985, p. 16).

Fig. 7.3. Modern and ancient—seven stars and an Arch of Titus menorah.

the Israelite camp. Passages in Exodus and Leviticus state that its lamps were to burn from dusk to dawn. The menorah accompanied the people of Israel on their wanderings in Sinai and Canaan. The First Temple contained ten menorahs (see 1 Kings 7: 49; 2 Chronicles 4: 7). The Second Temple contained a single one (*Encyclopedia Judaica* 1971), which Philo interpreted as a model of the celestial world and the soul, in which the light of God was reflected (Goodenough 1954: 86). In other words, the menorah is identified with the very birth of the Israelites as a nation and later with the pivotal Temple cult and statehood, blessed by the divine.

After the destruction of the Second Temple, Talmudic injunctions forbade the making of exact replicas of the menorah. Nonetheless, its schematic design flourished on synagogues, tombs, and various objects; the design spread rapidly throughout the Jewish world from the middle of the third century C.E. (Barag 1985).[5] In kabbalah mysticism, from the tenth century on, its design was thought to depict the *sefirot*, the luminous layered stages through which God descends and manifests His presence in the world. The menorah was often illuminated in medieval European manuscripts and was sometimes depicted as a Tree of Life (Namenyi 1957: 58; Yarden 1971; Sperber 1965). The menorah design became prevalent as synagogue decoration, often marking the *mizrach*, or eastern wall, the direction of

[5] Dan Barag argues strongly that it was only in this period that the menorah became a truly popular Jewish symbol, one that began to signify Jewish presence throughout the ancient world.

Jerusalem and the Temple.[6] In the twentieth century, Vladimir Ja-
botinsky took the menorah as the emblem of the Jewish Legion,
which fought with the British forces in World War I, and later as the
emblem of Betar, the revisionist youth movement he founded.

The emblem proposed by the cabinet juxtaposed a pervasive motif
of ancient lineage with one known to be invented in the recent past,
without pedigree, untried, but which connoted other values of enlightenment and progress that were central to the Zionist struggle in
the twentieth century. Moreover, both motifs signified light; and the
radiance and effulgence of light was probably a root metaphor of divine presence and the hope for redemption in traditional Judaism,
and of freedom, reason, and progress in secular Zionism (Liebman
and Don-Yehiye 1983: 114–15). Yet the juxtaposition of these motifs
was neither a synthesis nor even a conjunction, and this felt discontinuity festered and exposed fractures among conceptions of what the
state signified. Although these were mended through compromise,
the cost was the loss of any explicit recognition of progressive secular
Zionist values in the emblem.

The proposed emblem and the proposed flag were placed before
the SC on July 15, at its tenth meeting.[7] Their case was made by the

[6] The *hannukiah*, or lampstand of eight lamps, is probably a derivation of the menorah. The hannukiah is the major ceremonial artifact of Hannukah, the Festival of
Lights, which celebrates the Maccabean ouster of Hellenistic rule in the second century
B.C.E., the purification of the Temple, and the miraculous lighting of the lamps therein
for eight days, although there was sufficient pure oil only for one day.

[7] The design suggested for the flag was composed of seven six-pointed golden stars
on a white field, flanked above and below by blue stripes. The seven stars, of course,
were more prominent in this design than in that of the emblem. However, the Zionist
movement already had a flag, introduced at the First Zionist Congress in 1897. Its design consisted of a gold *magen david* (literally, Shield of David, the so-called Star of
David) on a white field, flanked above and below by light blue stripes. This flag had
accompanied the Zionist struggle throughout its existence. During the very period in
which state insignia were being selected, Jewish fighters were battling and dying beneath this flag. The magen david was also widely considered to be a Jewish symbol of
ancient lineage, regardless of the substantial evidence to the contrary unearthed by
archeologists and historians (see Scholem 1971). Moreover, it was the sign by which
the Nazis had marked the Jews and that had accompanied them to their death in the
Holocaust.

The MC's flag design, particularly the motif of the seven stars, bore the brunt of
much of the criticism of legislators, media, and public. It seems clear that at the time
it was inconceivable that the magen david should not signify the state of Israel in some
official way. Nonetheless, the foreign minister wished to distinguish the flag of the state
from that of the Zionist movement, and he consulted with Zionist organizations in

foreign minister, Moshe Shertok (later Sharett), who described the menorah as a "traditional" symbol but, according to the protocol, made no mention of the motif of the seven stars. The star motif came under scathing fire from members of the religious parties. The stars, they insisted, were a "new element" and therefore unworthy of inclusion. The minister of immigration and health, Moshe Shapira, of the Hapoel Hamizrachi party, expressed the tenor of debate in the coming weeks. His words were a sarcastic critique of the instability signified by a literal reading of the seven stars: "And as far as the seven stars symbolizing seven hours of work are concerned, perhaps there is someone in the State of Israel who is dreaming of six hours of work—and then how are we to explain why there are seven stars and not only six?" (*Hatzofe*, July 18). A motion to ratify both flag and emblem was defeated, nine votes to eight. The SC appointed a Flag and Symbol Committee (FSC) composed of sixteen of its members, including five ministers, to reconsider all suggestions. The composition of the FSC was explicitly intended to reflect the full political spectrum and included representatives of all the parties and organizations that were seated in the SC.

Phase 2: Lamplight and Starlight (July 16–October 26, 1948). The SC decision blew up a flurry of press comments raising issues that, according to protocols and press reports, had yet to be articulated by the legislators: the close relationship between the imagery of national symbolism and the formation of national life (Gershon Shocken, *Ha'aretz*, July 18) and the question of whether it was possible to invent national symbols or whether they "must grow organically with the historical creation of the nation" (Meir Troype, *Ha'aretz*, July 27). The archeologist Michael Avi-Yonah argued that the emblem should signify the scientific authentication of tradition. Therefore its motifs should be sought in the period of the last Jewish

---

North America, Europe, and South Africa. The general response was to keep the two flags similar. The deep and abiding sentiments that people had toward the magen david (see Eliav 1979) contributed to the defeat of the seven stars on the flag design and to the defeat of the design of the emblem (Fig. 7.3), which was paired with the former. Later on, the SC accepted the Zionist flag as the state flag, with minor distinguishing changes: the color of the magen david and the two flanking stripes was changed to dark blue. The presence of the magen david on the flag may have eased the way for the menorah to occupy the emblem.

The final decision about the flag was taken months before that about the emblem. The discussions about the emblem, although tempered by those about the flag, nonetheless had generated their own discourse between the menorah and the seven stars.

state. If this meant the acceptance of "a religious symbol as our political symbol," then Israelis were only following ancient Near Eastern practice (*Ha'aretz*, Aug. 6).

Except for some religious opposition (see Rabbi Z. N. Cooper-
stick, *Hatzofe*, Aug. 10), the idea of a menorah motif met with approval. But the motif of the seven stars was dismissed as an artificial
creation (Troype, *Ha'aretz*, July 27), and its creator, Herzl, as one ig-
norant of traditional Jewish symbols (G.S., *Ha'aretz*, July 20).

The FSC convened on July 28. The representatives of religious parties desired the motif of the Tablets of the Law, a proposal that encoded definitions of nationhood and statehood in relation to divine
compact and obedience to religious law. Aharon Zisling, the representative of the socialist Mapam party, retorted that the proposal
smacked of autocracy and that he would accept this motif only under
extreme duress. A religious member, Moshe Shapira, responded that
since the menorah incorporated religious elements, it was acceptable.
The committee voted, seven to three, to include a menorah motif in
the emblem, rather than one of the Tablets. The motif of the seven
stars was once again criticized by representatives of the religious parties, but the motion to include it passed, six votes to one. The questions were now of style and design; the FSC appointed a subcom-
mittee of experts (CE) to work these out.

These deliberations pointed to one criterion of choice. The major
motif was to be primordial and alive—to hark back to ancient origins
but simultaneously to be alive to the Jewish people in the present. To
this the CE—which included an archeologist, an artist, a graphic artist, and a printer—added a second criterion: the primordiality, or historicity, had to be validated by canons of modern science. The major
motif would not be the product of invention or theology. Elazar Sukenik, the archeologist, authenticated the menorah as an ancient Jewish motif but blocked an attempt to introduce into the emblem the
magen david (Shield of David)—a "doubtful symbol" (CE, Aug. 16).
He noted that in archeological finds the menorah motif was often accompanied by other motifs, such as those of the *shofar* (ram's horn)
and the *lulav* (date-palm frond), and he suggested that this authentic
configuration be kept in the emblem. Another member suggested that
the menorah lamps be lit.

The reconstituted emblem was wholly the product of the CE. The
shape of the field was closer to that of an ancient Middle Eastern

Fig. 7.4. Modern and ancient—the experts' proposals. The version on the left includes (left) the *lulav*, or palm frond, and the *etrog*, or citrus, and (right) the *shofar*, or ram's horn.

shield than to the "European" shield of the first proposal. The form of the menorah itself was an abstraction of details considered by experts to be Judaic. Thus the three-legged base was more in accord with the archeological record than was the Roman-Hellenistic base of the previous menorah. The menorah was lit in stylized fashion. One version (Fig. 7.4, left) contained the shofar and lulav on either side of the base. This was the version advocated by the experts, while the FSC members preferred the alternative (Fig. 7.4, right). In explaining the preference of the CE, David Remez told of their views on the necessary authentication of the historical record: "Facts have to be accepted as facts. . . . The committee did not invent anything here. Everything was ready, and not in the WIZO shop, but in the ancient existence of the nation. . . . Professor Sukenik insisted that if we chose the menorah as our symbol, it should be taken the way it is found in most of our antiquities" (24th meeting of the SC, Oct. 26).

The phrase beneath the menorah, "Shalom al Yisrael" (Peace unto Israel), was also suggested by Sukenik. It was taken from Psalm 128, which extols the blessings of labor, family, and Jerusalem, now and for generations to come. Apart from the stars, which either encompassed the menorah, complemented its light, or merely decorated the field (depending on one's point of view), the overall composition was an authentic Jewish one, according to canons of archeology and historiography.

The menorah of phase 1 had a particular lampstand as its model. But its design was an abstraction of that historical menorah, one whose historical predicate was removed, leaving an eternal form, as it were, but one without the substantive coalescence to make it also a significant marker of a people in relation to their own history. It was not referred to in terms of its historical referent. The menorah of phase 2 was a model of scientific accuracy. Yet once more, as an abstraction, it suffered from the same deficiency as the first, and it was even compared to a commercial imprint. Neither design succeeded in signifying the relationship of the people of Israel to the spatial center of their history and to their current presence there while simultaneously signifying that this place and their history had eternal qualities.

The words of the legislators and others show that they probably did not formulate their discomfort in such ways. They had not begun with a list of what they desired. They did not know quite what they wanted, but they recognized deficiencies in what they saw. Nonetheless, dimly and hesitantly, their struggle to formulate criteria produced a sense of the desirable. Yet as the search of the past loomed larger, the SC gradually lost sight of the vision connoted by the motif of the seven stars—an open, progressive future—and this motif became more vulnerable to its detractors.

The second proposal was discussed in the 24th meeting of the SC, on October 26. As before, the motif of a menorah met with general approval, although other suggestions were thrown into the discussion. Thus the minister of religious affairs, Rabbi Y. L. Fishman of the religious Mizrachi party, offered, "very simply, to draw a Torah scroll together with a Tree of Life"—indeed, a religious-messianic paradigm of first-time and end-time, from the creation of the Israelites as a religious nation to their future redemption and attainment of eternity through the study of Torah. "But," he exclaimed, "I know that this symbol will frighten many of you," and he seemed resigned to a menorah motif. A representative of the Hapoel Hamizrachi party, Zerach Warhaftig, himself a future incumbent of this ministry, preferred the Tablets of the Law, but he noted: "To my regret, when this suggestion came before the FSC, I heard that some said, and justifiably so, that such a symbol would be coercive for part of the yishuv, in spite of the fact that the Giving of the Torah [*Matan Torah*] was also coercion. But that coercion was the hand of God. But no person should coerce another." A third representative, David Zvi Pinkas, preferred the menorah because it was the holy artifact "that apparently is the most difficult to make. . . . Even Moses did not know how to make the menorah; and its original form . . . was given by God." The analogy here to the creation of the modern state, but one in accordance with divine design, was probably clear. In this forum the menorah motif met the criteria of holy primordiality and authenticity.

Most of the secular legislators stressed the importance of the emblem to the nation-state. These sentiments were expressed by Meir Grabovsky of the Mapai party. His speech, according to the documents we examined, marks the first explicit mention of the Titus menorah in an official forum, although it had been mentioned in the press and had probably been discussed in the committees.

There is no need to be caught up in too many explanations. I was tremendously impressed by the victory parade of Judea Capta on the Arch of Titus in Rome. I was in the Jewish Brigade [in World War II], and when for the first time we, as Jewish soldiers, came to this arch, we saw the menorah . . . carried by Roman soldiers, a symbol of an imprisoned Judea, Judea Capta. After the destruction of the state by the Romans, this menorah deserves to be taken by us as the symbol of our revived statehood. It will also be shown in Rome.

But the proposed emblem was not "a single, united symbol that immediately puts an imprint on your memory" (Mordechai Shattner, Mapai party), but one "more like a commercial trademark than the symbol of a nation" (Daniel Auster, General Zionists party). In summing up the debate, the speaker of the SC, Yosef Sprinzak of the Mapai party, asked the FSC to return with a menorah "that is also historical."

As the presence of the distant past filled the shape of the present, the seven stars came under increasing fire. This motif had advocates who saw in it "Herzl's heritage [which] symbolizes a very important social reform in the lives of working people" (Beba Edelson, Mapai party) and which "reminds us of the cherished element that we inherited from Herzl" (Auster). However, its detractors were the more numerous; and those of the religious parties, the most vociferous.

Rabbi Fishman, to widespread laughter, mocked the motif: "I would think that this is a symbol of the [recently promulgated] army order requiring seven days of work a week, an order I opposed [on religious grounds]." He called the motif a symbol of "hints" and reminded his audience of the Yiddish saying "Seven is a lie" (Zibn iz a lign) and that there were "seven elements in a golem," that magical, soulless being created from clay by the human hand, a figure in Yiddish legend.[8] (On apposite qualities of the number 7, compare Levenson 1984: 288; Fredman 1981: 109.)

As for Herzl, Fishman continued, "we trusted his talents, his political work, his power of organization, but we never asked Herzl about the Jewish symbol, especially as he did not know what a Jew was when he wrote that book." Shmuel Mikunis, the Communist representative, gibed, not without some validity, "Tonight Rabbi Fishman broke [the commandment] Thou shalt not kill. He murdered the symbol." Other members withdrew or qualified their support. Yitzchak Ben-Zvi (Mapai, and a future president of the state) commented: "Where there are seven shining stars, who needs the menorah? The light of the stars will suffice, and vice versa. If the light of the menorah is present, why stars? This is an unnecessary addition. The stars are totally unnecessary." And David Remez, perhaps the guiding hand in both the MC and the FSC, now stated: "This addition [the stars] doesn't connect nicely [with the menorah motif]. It isn't necessary to add seven stars to a seven-branched menorah, because the seven flames are like the seven stars." By a vote of fifteen to thirteen, the SC returned the emblem to committee.[9]

At the outset of the search for an emblem, the two major motifs of menorah and stars, of tradition and innovation, were intended to supplement and complement one another. But according to the available records, there were few initiatives to synthesize these two motifs or to replace the star motif with another of similar significance. Little by little the disjunction of menorah and stars came to be stressed, until each was opposed to the other.

[8] His attack was probably less against the number seven as such than against the stars themselves. In Judaic traditions, stars are associated with the signs of the zodiac; the phrase "workers of stars and signs" (*ovdei kochavim v'mazalot*) commonly denotes pagans and paganism, the very antitheses of Judaism and Jewishness. Such connotations probably gave to the stars a much more intense aura of opprobrium. Fishman's references to "hints," "lies," the golem, and Herzl's ignorance of matters Jewish all point to his indirect attack on the star motif itself. To have assaulted the stars directly as pagan signs would have been to offer the gravest of insults to the supporters of this motif (and to the memory of Herzl). Throughout this debate, and in other discussions, conflict was muted, and there was a strong emphasis on unity and compromise; at this time, and from late 1947 until late 1948, Israel was embroiled in intensive warfare with its neighbors.

[9] The design for the flag was ratified in the 24th meeting of the SC.

Fig. 7.5. Dominance of the modern—
the Shamir brothers' design.

Phase 3: In with the Old, Out with the New (October 27, 1948–February 10, 1949). The FSC reopened the competition for the emblem on the off chance that a new idea would emerge. By the deadline of December 10, an additional 131 suggestions had been received.[10] Still dissatisfied, the committee went back to a design submitted in the first round of competition by the brothers Shamir. Theirs was a menorah of a modern style with a star above each branch, flanked on either side by an olive branch (Fig. 7.5). The olive branches, said Gabriel and Maxim Shamir, symbolized the love of the nation of Israel for peace. In their view, certainly one of synthesis, the menorah itself was an ancient symbol, and therefore its form called attention to tradition, while its stylized design symbolized the age of modern Israel (*Ma'ariv*, Feb. 18, 1949). The FSC asked the artists to prepare three alternative versions of their design: a menorah, a menorah with seven stars and two olive branches, and a menorah with seven stars, two olive branches, and the word *Israel* beneath the base. It approved the third alternative (Fig. 7.5) over the opposition of its religious members. This was one of the few attempts, and the last, to develop a synthetic complementarity between the motifs of stars and menorah. In general, the star motif enjoyed more support in the FSC than in the SC. However, the FSC insisted that the Shamirs replace their stylized menorah with a detailed copy of that on the Arch of Titus. The emended design then brought together a historically true menorah, shaded to give a three-dimensional effect, and the visually flat and culturally arbitrary stars. This combination starkly confused genres of visual composition. It also appeared to contrast the truth and power of history with the weakness and lack of depth of the modern vision; the stars of Figure 7.5 must have looked like paper cutouts

[10] We will analyze the symbols offered in this corpus in a separate paper.

Fig. 7.6. Dominance of the ancient—
the official emblem of Israel.

attached to the lamps of the menorah of Figure 7.6. Faced with this
dissonance, the FSC insisted on retaining the Titus menorah and so
evicted the stars. In their confrontation the stars proved weaker than
the menorah, implicating both ontology and aesthetics, as we discuss
below. The final version (Fig. 7.6) was placed before the SC in its 40th
and final meeting, on February 10, 1949. There was no debate, and
the emblem was approved by unanimous vote.

Why this menorah? Grabovsky's explanation in the SC is amplified
by the following comments on the reasoning of the committees of
1948:

To bring it [the menorah] home. Although (*dafka*)[11] if the Romans, at the
time of the failure and the denigration of the Jewish people, took it as they
did, we will return it with our rejuvenation . . . revenge on the gentiles. The
menorah on the Arch of Titus is the symbol of the deepest demeaning of the
Jewish people. [Therefore] at this moment of the rise and resurrection of the
Jewish people, this [the emblem] has to commemorate and to resurrect that
very symbol that then symbolized our denigration. (Interview with Shlomo
Kedar, June 28, 1985)

This theme of returning the menorah is depicted, for example, by the
artist Abba in a drawing prepared for Independence Day 1951 (Fig.
7.7). The drawing shows the exiled Jews of the diaspora returning to
Zion, carrying before them the menorah from the Arch of Titus. The
drawing complements the words of the song with which this essay
opens, in which Jewish soldiers from Israel stand beneath the Arch

[11] *Dafka* is hardly translatable into English. It connotes "in spite of," but infuses
the term with a strong-willed "maverickness."

Fig. 7.7. *The Arch of Titus Menorah Returns Home.* Drawing by Abba (Fenichel), published in *Davar* on May 10, 1951.

of Titus. Together, these media well express popular sentiments toward the menorah symbol in 1948. The Titus menorah, unlike its predecessors, synthesized time (the last Jewish state), place (Jerusalem, Israel), the Jewish people, and qualities of the primordial and the eternal.[12] But the ratified emblem contained no motif that signified any of the innovative aspirations of modern Zionism for the future.

The Structuring of Significance

The motif of the seven stars was treated as a weak vehicle of meaning—its penumbra of potential significance was severely limited and contained, especially through interpretations that rarely went beyond the literal. But according to the record, one may also point to the small number of motifs, especially secular ones, that formed the corpus of deliberations,[13] and to the relative absence of attempts at innovation

[12] Charles Liebman and Eliezer Don-Yehiye claim that the menorah was chosen "because of its important historical associations as a religious symbol" (1984: 15). This statement is an oversimplification that ignores the polyvalent significance, in the modern world, of the menorah for secular and religious Jews and for those from opposite ends of the political spectrum. As noted, the menorah symbol was used by secular youth movements, areligious and even antireligious, of both the political right and left. The religious significance of the menorah was likely uppermost in the minds of the religious legislators; but, on the basis of the protocols, it seemed quite distant from the conscious significance given to it by secular ones.

[13] Apart from menorah and stars, these were the Tablets of the Law, the Lion of Judah, and the *sneh*-bush.

or at synthesizing the two major motifs (with the exception of the penultimate proposal discussed above). Such ideas were not lacking among the citizenry (Handelman and Shamgar-Handelman 1986), to wit, the following letter to the editor: "Let the fiery stars provide light within the menorah. . . . Just stick them onto the menorah. How symbolic it is that the eternal menorah will provide light from the eternal stars of fire" (A. Nahmani, *Ha'aretz*, July 19, 1948). In part, these absences may be due to the logic by which the participants organized that which they discovered to be of significance to them.

The previous section discussed the sequential emergence of choice and certain factors—ideology and compromise—that influenced it. Here we take up the criteria by which the legislators came to recognize a proper national emblem and what they wanted this one to signify.

Although parameters of comparison are lacking, there seems to be a paucity of symbolic objects in rabbinic Judaism. Religious injunction forbids graven images and hence an extensive range of plastic and pictorial representation (geometric design is permitted). Symbols are good to read, to hear, to think with, to speak, to smell, but less good to gaze on as static representations detached from (usually ritual) contexts. Symbolic objects in Judaism tend to have active use-values: to wear, to read, to hold, to cut with, to sound, or to contain various substances. They are artifactual extensions of symbolic action in ritual contexts. Their value is especially in their performance, as this is signified by context and in turn signifies it—a division of labor that continually highlights the active interdependence and reinforcement of form and function.[14] Here few signs signify the act of signifying; few symbols speak for themselves without immanent instrumental referents or functions. In other words, few signs are comparatively acontextual and autonomous, static and representational.

Such factors may have influenced the Zionist disinterest in static abstract representation. Socialist Zionists in particular were preoccupied in Palestine with the daily labor of working and building the land as symbolic action—thus inscribing in the landscape and in one another the realities of their beliefs (see Eisenstadt 1967: 17–19 on the symbol of the *chalutz*, the pioneer). The redemption of the land through labor sometimes neared the status of revered work, and labor itself, that of a religious act (see Don-Yehiye and Liebman 1981). The

[14] These points emerged from discussions with Shifra Epstein, to whom we give our thanks.

symbolic action of the pioneers, even part-time pioneers, also flourished through vigorous dance, through singing in concert, through innovative holiday celebrations, and through walking the landscape to become intimate with its contours. Again the focus was performative, on metonymic symbolism, on the creation of living symbols encoded with the actualities of living. In this, as in traditional Judaism, static representation had a minimal role.

In the quartet of major national symbols—the name of the state, the anthem, the flag, and the emblem—intended to be transcontextual to a higher degree, the emblem was the least performative, the most static, and the least emotive. Its use was as a sign of place, presence, and ownership, hardly given to nuance. By contrast, for example, the flag was alive to the rhythmic resonances of existence: unfurled and raised with first light, in mood with the weather, put to rest at dusk, diminished at half-mast.[15] There were precedents in the yishuv for the first three symbols, but not for the emblem.

The selectors, one could say, were working in a somewhat foreign medium. This they domesticated, slowly but incrementally, by developing criteria that thrust toward that historicity from which modern Zionism had evolved but which it tried to use for its own ends (see Halpern 1969: 75–76, 83). As noted, in the dominant view of participants, a motif had to be primordial to be significant; therefore, "the rule should be that the older is holier" (Warhaftig, FSC, July 28, 1948). Second, a significant motif had to be authentic; thus, "today the menorah is undoubtedly the most ancient Jewish symbol that can be identified with utmost assurance as a Jewish symbol" (Michael Avi-Yonah, Ha'aretz, Aug. 6, 1948). In the authentic there was no space for invention, innovation, or analogy. Thus, "the introduction of modern symbolism into the emblem should be avoided" (Avraham Elhanani, CE, Aug. 16, 1948); and, "there is no place for innovation. . . . We do not invent anything, but take everything from what already exists" (Warhaftig, 24th meeting of the SC). The authentic spoke for itself, without moderators. Third, to be significant, a motif had to be immutable, for "a symbol cannot be changed every day, it is decided on for generations" (Altman, 23rd meeting of the SC). Therefore qualities of endurance, and perhaps of the eternal, were

[15] On the summarizing and emotive qualities of flags, see Taylor 1981: 508–10; Firth 1973: 341–55; Hill 1982; Weitman 1973; and Sivan 1987.

essential. Fourth, the motif had to be unique to the Jewish people, singular and exclusive, unshared with other nations: "The committee [FSC] discussed the question of whether to add lions to the emblem, but decided against this, since lions exist in the emblems of many other countries" (*Ha'aretz*, July 29, 1948). These criteria of emblem as signifier all converged on the desire that "our emblem mirror everything that was sanctified in generations of tradition, and [that] this tradition be kept and be embodied in the emblem" (Edelson, 23rd meeting of the SC).

In the whole of the documented record there are but two voices that strenuously dissent from this emergent consensus. One argued for the inclusion of "an addition that expresses our life of labor in the city and in the villages" (R. Lubitsch, Mapai party, FSC, July 28, 1948). The other, Shmuel Mikunis, of the Communist party, wanted an emblem of landscape and labor. "We are," he said, "the People of the Book, but also the People of Work. We need this combination" (24th meeting of the SC).

These four criteria were intended to find their expression through representations that had the following compositional characteristics. There was to be no hint of discord or clash among motifs. Therefore the desired composition would best be expressed either through a single theme or motif or through a hermetic synthesis of compatible motifs. Second, the composition would be self-explanatory, imbued with a "recognizability" that "immediately creates the connection between the symbol and our subject [the ancient past]" (Avi-Yonah), but one that did "not lend itself to incorrect meanings" (Zisling, FSC, July 28, 1948). A minimum of exegesis was desirable. Of lesser relevance was the characteristic of beauty, necessarily modified by primordiality and authenticity: "We shouldn't look for developed art in our emblem. That is the image that our forefathers gave the menorah. That's what they saw and that's what they did. . . . I prefer the art of our forefathers of 2,000 years ago and more, even if it is not so beautiful . . . over the most successful art of our days" (Pinkas, 24th meeting of the SC).

In turn, the emblem as signifier, characterized by the preceding criteria of significance and composition, was oriented without equivocation to evoke the unified nation renewing and continuing its ancient past. History was not the backdrop to the choice, but pervaded and informed it, for the nation of Israel had been waiting 2,000 years to present itself again to the world (see Grabovsky and Fishman, 23rd meeting of the SC). Its symbolism encoded and condensed Jewish historicity. "We are not a new nation that has come to settle in a new country," wrote Avi-Yonah, "and we do not have to create for ourselves the traditional ancestry of our nationality" (*Ha'aretz*, Aug. 6, 1948); "the thought that should accompany us is that . . . we renewed a state that existed in past days" (Warhaftig, FSC, July 28, 1948). The historicity of the ancient was the existential raison d'être of "renewal" in the present. "It is only on the basis of that old history that we have the right to live in this country," Pinkas insisted, "for whoever denies this connection and our historical continuity has no moral right to demand the ownership of this piece of land for the people of Israel. In this symbol [the menorah] I see the sign of this right, on the basis of the connection of the nation with its past" (24th meeting of the SC). Just as there was no invention in the renewal of statehood, so there would be none in the emblem that signified this: "And if the state really is an ancient one, let us accept the symbol that has been with us for hundreds of years" (Warhaftig, 24th meeting of the SC).[16]

Even Mikunis, of the Communist party, for whom primordiality was deeply suspect, and religion (including the menorah motif) anathema, was caught up in the encoding of historicity. To stand, rampant, on his field of landscape and labor, he embraced the motif of the *sneh*-bush (suggested by Aharon Yaacov Greenberg, a member of the religious Hapoel Hamizrachi party), the burning bush that is not consumed, where God first revealed Himself to Moses and told him of the Covenant (Exodus 3: 2). Why? "Because we not only continue to live," said Mikunis, "but we even renew our youth. . . . We are creating a symbol in order to symbolize the 1948 of an old nation that is always fresh and alive and desires to be young. Don't drag it back 4,000 years" (24th meeting of the SC). He dealt with history by effacing it, yet was left with an ancient present and a living past, a version of the nation eternal.

The structuring of significance that these people developed closed in on itself. The sequence of selection, and the criteria of selection that emerged, both pointed unerringly in one direction—to the conjunc-

[16]On the significance of historicity and its authenticity, there was full agreement between the archeologists and the religious Jews, although their epistemologies and understandings were radically opposed and antagonistic.

tion of nation, state, and place in relation to a baseline of that last period of a nation at home to itself.[17]

"Judea Capta, Judea Resurrecta"

Does this process of choosing the emblem tell us something about the uses of history? Certain of these seem of limited relevance here. This choice was not the arbitrary splicing of present to past and the reinterpretation of their relationship, for the significant Jewish past—the historicity of the ancient—was integral to the Jewish present as both moved into the future. Neither was this the related "invention of tradition" (Hobsbawm and Ranger 1983), for it was taken for granted (and, of course, documented) that the ancient Jewish past existed and that it informed the present. Nor was this the retrieval of history lost (see Lewis 1975), although this rubric is relevant for certain aspects. Put otherwise, without a recognition of the element of enduring ontological coordinates in the way these Jews and others conceptualized their history, the Zionist enterprise makes little sense, except as the "invention of tradition."

Although, more generally, this position has conceptual merit, certain of its assumptions boil down to no more than a functionalism applied situationally to historical periods; in large measure tradition is created directly in response to changes in infrastructure, to legitimate ideology and to reproduce structures of power and interest. The "invention of tradition" is a simple response to the social "needs" of power and hegemony. Then, unless one also works with a perspective of ontological premises of culture—which in turn influence the shape of an emergent or consciously created tradition (see Ohnuki-Tierney 1987; Kapferer 1988)—social needs are reducible easily to one or another kind of psychologism, of "methodological individualism," cast as "culture" (Evens 1977).

Stripped of their metaphysical involutions and elaborations, these ontological coordinates stand forth starkly as a set of simple, generative axioms about time and place, in a sense as cultural first principles. So long as Jews, Zionists, and the choosers of the emblem be-

[17]Grace Harris's (1976) argument that the menorah is an "inward-looking" symbol, as distinct from the magen david, an "outward-looking" symbol, has a certain validity. But this pattern is more complex, as she notes, especially when their re-creation as national symbols is taken into account.

haved as if these cultural coordinates were axiomatic, were deeply imbued with common sense, and were reflexive to its presence, the abstract shape of Jewish historicity was infused with the paradigm of exile and return. Throughout Jewish history the meanings of these ontological coordinates, and of the paradigms they helped to generate, have shifted time and again between the metaphorical and the metonymic, depending on place, period, and circumstance. In the Zionist vision of the twentieth century, these coordinates have become strongly metonymic in their thrust of meaning. And so long as such axioms were not questioned (as, of course, they have been by numerous groups and persons), then social change was understood as some form of continuity.

Despite its often zealous pursuit of social change, these coordinates were, and are, foundation stones of the Zionist vision. By comprehending their own present in part through these coordinates, the Zionists thrust forward from past to present, toward living their history in the present as a continuous, unbroken structure of experiences of past and present. Their beliefs and actions resonated acutely with this structure of historicity from which their vision emerged and which, still on the most abstract of levels, informed their endeavor with certain crucial parameters of metonymic meaning. Their vision indeed involved the emendation of significant historicity. For example, there is no mention of the relevance of exilic history in committee and legislative discussions on the emblem, not even of the most recent catastrophe of the Holocaust. Yet so long as these coordinates fixed periodicity to place, from exile to return, the abstract shape of history remained, doing its shaping through the present. We are not arguing whether such cultural coordinates should be questioned; we are stating that, in this case, their influence and impact should be respected and that respect cannot be accorded without explicitly recognizing the coordinates for what they are (see Baer 1947; Paine 1983). Nor, most certainly, are we arguing that the shape of this history is deterministic. Neither was the shape of the emblem.

The central problem in anthropology's conceptualization of time as positional and directional may be the relationship between historicity and history—that is, between a people's formulation of their own perpetuated being and the formulations of others (such as anthropologists and historians), which enunciate the "objective" facts and influences of diachrony. For the anthropologist (of whatever persuasion) the most obvious yet complex point is that historicity and history are so informed by mutuality that to the analyst neither has much chance of making sense without the other. We do not deal in absolutes—in determinism or its utter absence. Therefore a wide range of relationships between historicity and history remains possible but not necessary. Neither history nor historicity encompasses the other, and therefore neither can inform us sufficiently to derive the other from itself. Again, we do not claim the autonomy of these formulations but their relational interdependence.

The idea of using the Arch of Titus menorah, the motif that finally ousted the stars, brilliantly complemented the structure of historicity discussed above. Earlier we noted the power of metonymic symbolism in Judaism and in Zionism. Like the ontological coordinates of time and space, the symbol of the menorah has shifted in meaning between the metaphorical and the metonymic on many occasions throughout recorded Jewish history. In 1948 the Titus menorah was more metonymic in its relationship to ontological coordinates, to the land and the people in Jewish history—for the biography of this menorah paralleled that of the Jewish nation. It was understood as a mirror image of the Second Temple menorah, of the singular centricity of the land of Israel. It too went into exile, paraded and degraded in the Roman triumph, enchained on a monument that commemorated the oppression of the Jewish nation. In secular Zionist views, the menorah was frozen on the arch—time stopped for the menorah, as, in a sense, significant time had stopped for the Jewish people, until their revival. Now the menorah returned, free, redeemed, reunited, as were the Zionists, with that place that offered the fruitful realization of nation and self. This menorah, then, denied the permanence of exile, as did messianic beliefs, and bore witness to the generations of absence by bringing them to a close. Viewed in this way, the choice of the emblem is a discourse on how time through symbolism made history itself into an unmediated visual symbol that encoded periodicity. This is evident if one looks seriously at the iconography of the ratified emblem in Figure 7.6.

Whether understood in secular or religious terms, this synchronic composition encodes diachrony in the relationship between coordinates of time and space. The base of the composition is the name (Yisrael/Israel) of the nation-state, a name that is an index of place. From this place the two olive branches extend or grow upward.

Standing on this place is the Titus menorah, its branches reaching upward, culminating in the apex of their lamps. Synchronically, this visual composition intimately relates the horizontal axis of the base, Israel, to the vertical axis, menorah and olive branches. But the visual encoding emphasizes the vertical axis of hierarchy, of lower and higher—moreover, of lower leading to higher. This is the only thrust that the menorah, as lampstand, can have. It must rest upright on its base, its branches must rise upward, and their lamps direct one's gaze even higher than themselves.

So far we can say that the emblem partakes of what Nathaniel Tarn (1976) called the "heraldic vision." Here parts and their whole are open fully to inspection; they continually index one another; and they always lead one to the other in a dialectic of the particular and the synthetic. That is, in the synchronic vision the parts are ideally related to the whole.

But more than this, the vertical axis encodes temporality, since "lower" and "higher" are integral to the vision of time—to a perpetual striving for the higher, a level that always is spiritualized in the epistemology of this vision. As we noted earlier, light, and the light of the menorah lamps, can signify on the one hand the striving for perfection through the practice of God-given law, or through messianic redemption, and on the other the striving for perfection through rationalism, social justice, secular knowledge, and progress. Therefore the emblem encodes process that must be temporal, since these procedural goals can only be attained through history. In this emblem, the horizontal axis encodes space, and the vertical, time. The emblem encodes the message that temporal process is to be actualized in the right place—thus the light of the menorah reaches toward the heights at whose base rests the support of Israel. This is the preeminent vision of this nation-state, whether in secular or religious terms.

At first sight the emblem may appear a highly allusive, synchronic image—adornment, but little more. However, this vision easily expands into one of temporal process, with the capacity to encode the meanings either of a general scheme of Jewish history or of particular segments of it. The iconography of the emblem shows its composition to be of profound signification that is understood in matter-of-fact ways by most varieties of Zionists. But the medium of signification—

the menorah, and especially the Titus menorah—is one with the deepest roots in religious Jewish culture.[18]

As it happened, the ratified emblem bore a remarkable resemblance to a vision of the prophet Zechariah, who knew exile in Babylon and who envisioned the then uncompleted Temple of Zerubbabel and Joshua. In his vision, Zechariah saw a golden menorah of seven lamps, flanked on either side by two olive trees (4: 3), or by two olive branches (4: 12), that through golden pipes supplied the lamps with oil. Zechariah asked what these olive branches were, and the angel replied: "These are the two anointed ones, that stand by the Lord of the whole earth" (4: 14). The vision is probably a messianic one. To our knowledge, no one has publicly noted its similarity to the emblem, and of course the resemblance may simply be happenstance.[19]

The ratified emblem has never been accorded an official exegesis. The first such attempt is found in a letter of June 13, 1952, from Ben-Tzion Eshel, coordinator of the Committee on Symbols, to the Department of Public Relations of the Ministry of Defense. This interpretation responded to the motifs wholly in terms of the coordinates of historicity discussed above, of the emblem closed in dialogue with past and present, directing attention more to one variety of future than to another. On the menorah he said: "The Temple menorah symbolizes the unity of our nation since it became a nation in the desert of Sinai, during its years of resting on its own land in the days of the First and the Second Temples and during all the days of its desire to return to Zion. The image of the imprisoned menorah, carved on the

[18] We suspect that the profound clash between the menorah and the stars was connected to the ways in which most of the submitted designs (like that of Fig. 7.5) visually related these motifs. The interaction of motifs tended strongly to make the seven stars into the flames of the menorah. We suspect that this was perceived inchoately by religious legislators as the ultimate triumph of the secular values signified by the stars. Perhaps they were unable to enunciate this because visual figuration was not central to their repertoire of experience. Elsewhere (Handelman and Shamgar-Handelman 1986) we discuss the logic of interaction between the motifs of menorah and stars in submissions for the emblem.

[19] This passage is part of a *haftarah* (a "conclusion"). Haftarot (the plural form) are selected chapters of the books of the prophets that conclude the Sabbath reading of a portion of the Pentateuch, the Torah, in the prayer service. This particular haftarah appears twice during the yearly cycle of reading the Pentateuch. One of these occasions is the Sabbath of Hannukah.

Arch of Titus, reminds of independence and the call for its renewal—
and in our days, the days of the arising, of the assembling of the exiles,
and of the unifying of the nation in its diaspora around the nation of
Israel." On the shape of the emblem: "The square form, that ends
with the point of a hero's shield, unifies the symbol of the past, the
present, and the vision of a future of total perfection."

Of fleeting reflections of starlight there was not a trace.

Acknowledgments

We are most indebted to the late Chana Even-Tov, of the Israel
State Archives, for her diligent help in the locating of documents. All
citations of government committees are to protocols in the archives.
We also are obliged, for their comments, to Dan Barag, Harvey Gold-
berg, Michael Lieber, Moshe Shokeid, Michael Stone, and Dick
Werbner. Figure 7.1 is reproduced courtesy of the Institute of Archeology, The Hebrew National University of Jerusalem. Figures
7.2–7.5 are reproduced courtesy of the Israel State Archives.

8

Aryan Invasions over Four Millennia

EDMUND LEACH

Problems of "culture through time," as I perceive them,[1] are posed by Marshall Sahlins's study of the historical circumstances surrounding the death of Captain Cook. For Cook and his companions the events were one-off, nonrecurrent; they took place in the world of here and now. For the Hawaiians they were ritual events, justified by mythology, potentially recurrent; they took place in the ambiguous zone between this world and the other, where gods and people may come face to face. To bring these two viewpoints together, the symbolism that is inherent in any description of past events has to be brought into the open. Some of us had hoped to discuss the problems which this entails. But we never got that far, so I must construct my own vocabulary.

Time, as we experience it, is continuous; it contains no discrete "events." The events are put there by reflection on the past. As the past becomes more remote the remembered events become fewer in number and more limited in kind. It is for psychologists to say just why we remember this and forget that, but at the end of the day, the remembered past reflects our interests. It makes us what we are *now*.

The same is equally true of the publicly shared experience that we describe as history. Eventually time past is reduced to a sequence of named happenings punctuated by major discontinuities: The Reformation, the French Revolution, World War I—each was, in its original occurrence, a blurred ambiguity without beginning and without end. Such history is based on records, residues from the past. But records do not become a part of history simply by happening to survive.

---

[1] Some features of this essay are influenced by its origination as a contribution to a conference funded by the Wenner-Gren Foundation and held in Fez, Morocco, during the third week of January 1986. The reader should bear that in mind.

Records are preserved because they provide a charter for what historians believe about the present. Different historians may believe different things, and the records are interpreted (and modified) accordingly.

In January 1986, on the way from Fez to Rabat, a party of people paid a hurried visit to the ruins of the Roman city of Volubilis. All members of the group must have noticed the prominent triumphal arch dedicated to the Emperor Caracalla and his mother, Julia Domna, though they may not have understood what they were seeing.

At the beginning of our era Volubilis was the capital of a local Hellenistic monarch, Juba II. Juba's son Ptolemy was murdered by Caligula, and in A.D. 44 Volubilis became the capital of a Roman province. The masonry was later plundered for the construction of nearby Moulay Idriss, and what then survived was mostly destroyed by the Lisbon earthquake of 1755. In 1911 the *Encyclopaedia Britannica* reported only that "four gates are still recognisable, and a triumphal arch erected in A.D. 216 in honour of Caracalla." The corresponding entry in the 1985 edition says: "Roman ruins are extensive. . . . Noteworthy are a forum, a 2nd-century-AD basilica, and the Arch of Caracalla." The reconstructions thus implied were carried out as an expression of Marshall Lyautey's highly personal view of the role of France in colonial North Africa. At the same time, the considerable artistic treasures surviving from Juba's city were removed to Rabat. With the withdrawal of the French, Volubilis reverted to its earlier status of an overgrown ruin. A modern English guidebook remarks that "[the arch] held no particular purpose beyond creating a ceremonial function for the principal street. . . . Its inscription records that it was originally surmounted by a great bronze chariot. This and the nymphs which once shot water into basins below are gone, though with its tall Corinthian columns [of imported marble] and unashamed pointlessness it is still an impressive monument." But is it really so pointless even in decay?

Colonial glory, whether Roman or French, may be a thing of the past, but the empty landscape on the horizon is still what it was 1,900 years ago. I was reminded of a surrealist vista by Magritte. Each of us creates out of the residues of time past whatever it is that we may wish to see.

The only serious historian of Volubilis, Carpocino (1943), concentrates on King Juba and the death of Ptolemy and never mentions the arch at all.

For my present purpose, the word *myth* has this iconic Malinowskian sense. A myth is a story about the past pegged to an identifiable relic and a place on the map. It serves as a charter for beliefs or actions in the present. The chronology of myth is at best ambiguous. Myth may be transmitted by oral tradition or in writing. By contrast, I use *history* to mean written history, a fixed text that explicitly claims to record what happened in the past in potentially datable sequence. For me the concept of "oral history" is misnamed. If an oral tradition happens to be concerned with events that we know (on other grounds) to be historical, this concern does not convert the tradition into history.

The cultural values of Western scholars of the twentieth century lead us to believe that "good" history *really* records what happened in the past while "bad" history does not, but the basis on which we can make this kind of distinction is always very insecure. "Bad" history is seldom constructed out of fantasy; it is simply that we tend to accept as good history whatever is congenial to our contemporary way of thinking. The good history of one generation becomes the bad history of the next.

From this point of view all history is myth. But the converse is not the case. Although some texts can function either as history or as myth, history and myth are, in a fundamental sense, categories of quite different kinds. History is anchored in the past; it is time-bound; it cannot be repeated. Myth is timeless; it is constantly reenacted in ritual performance. In days gone by, there have been many respected forms of historiography in which this formula could equally have been applied to history. History was thought to repeat itself as transformation. The authors of the Christian Gospels believed that they were writing history, but they wrote it in such a way that the individual stories were consciously presented as antitypes to the types encountered in the Old Testament. Such views have not been confined to religious authors. I will not pursue this matter; I simply wish to insist that when any of us who are anthropologists are presented with stories that purport to be history, we should be skeptical. We always need to ask: In whose interest is it that the past should be presented to us in this way?

In this essay I am mainly concerned with one particular case in which an oral tradition has been treated as if it were a datable written record and myth has been confused with history as it actually happened.

Until very recently most European scholars adopted an entirely different view of the relationship between myth and history from the one I have just presented. They have taken it for granted that the great majority of religious myths and secular legends contain elements of garbled history; for example, the Trojan War of Homer's *Iliad* and the Biblical Exodus both really happened, even though they did not happen quite as described. Ancient historians have regularly used such presumptions as part of their evidence. They have pieced together their picture of the cultural background of prehistory by combining the evidence provided by archeology with the evidence contained in religious texts. The basic principle seems to be "Always believe what the text says unless it is palpably quite impossible." Almost everything that passes for the history of the Jews prior to 600 B.C. is such a reconstruction.

In history writing of this sort the assertions that are made about vernacular speech and the details of everyday life are especially suspect. In our own highly literate environment, however, the evidence is all around us that the conventions of literature are quite different from the conventions of colloquial speech; we do not ordinarily talk as we write or write as we talk. But philologists who specialize in the decipherment of ancient scripts and the reconstruction of long-dead languages seem to imagine that once they have deciphered a written text they know the language that was spoken by the people who wrote that text. By claiming that the text in question was originally a transcription of an earlier oral tradition, they may even claim that they know how people spoke at a date far earlier than the written text itself. And from there they go on to discuss how languages were spread across the map by "movements of peoples." All studies of Indo-European language, culture, and literature are permeated with thinking of this sort.

Although there are admittedly some cases where language distributions are the end-product of movements of peoples, there are many other possibilities. The present-day distribution of Spanish, Portuguese, Dutch, and English speakers in non-European territories makes it very obvious that languages are sometimes dispersed across the map by military conquest and colonialism, but the process is never simple. No law of nature declares that the language of the conqueror will replace that of the conquered or that the invading conquerors need to be present in large numbers. Tupi rather than Portuguese could easily have become the national language of independent Brazil, for example; an English-based pidgin, not English or German, is the normal language of present-day Papua New Guinea. Within Europe itself the development of the Romance languages—Italian, Spanish, French—out of a merging of Latin with local dialects can be seen, in retrospect, as a consequence of political and social arrangements in the Roman Empire. But the development of Romance languages was not a response to any movement of peoples. Romans from Italy did not move in large numbers to the outer fringes of the empire. Trade and slavery and the administrative convenience of small numbers of bureaucrats had quite as much influence on who spoke what to whom as any form of migration. Modern English is not a simple lineal descendant of Celtic, or Latin, or Norse, or Anglo-Saxon, or Norman French, though it contains components from all these sources (and many others). The linguistic history of northern India is equally uncertain; it might contain all these confusing possibilities and many more.

Indeed, if the only evidence for a supposed population movement derives from the content and distribution of religious texts rather than from any real knowledge of who spoke what and when, then nothing can be inferred at all. We know that most documents originating in the British Isles between the fifth and seventh centuries A.D. were written in Latin. Under the influence of Christian missionaries the use of these texts became widely dispersed. But the status of Latin as a colloquial lingua franca was declining rapidly throughout this period, and insofar as there was a movement of peoples (as represented by the Anglo-Saxon invasions), it went from east to west, whereas the dispersal of the Latin texts went from west to east. Skepticism of this sort will seldom be encountered within the ranks of Indo-European specialists, most of whom claim that they can show not only how a (hypothetical) long-extinct parent language, Proto-Indo-European, evolved into the diverse and widespread language family that we now have but also how these modern languages came to be distributed across the map by historical movements of peoples. Religious texts provide a large part of the evidence on which these arguments are based.

One of my purposes in this paper is to take an anthropological look at the motivations that have led such scholars to think about these matters in the way that they do. In discussing this theme I shall use as my central example the Indo-Europeanists' doctrines concerning the Rig Veda. I am well aware that for an outsider to attempt to bring about a shift in this entrenched paradigm is like trying to cut down a 300-year-old oak tree with a penknife. But the job will have to be done one day.

It is now well over 100 years since European scholars first asserted that 3,500 years ago people in northern India spoke in the language of the Rig Veda. The idea is odd in itself, since the language of the Rig Veda is obviously religious, dramatic, and poetic rather than vernacular. We would not expect to be able to learn much about the colloquial speech and everyday customs of fourth-century Britain if the only available evidence was a copy of the King James version of the Bible. But it is the regular practice of Sanskritists and Indian prehistorians to use the text of the Rig Veda as a basis for their description of the culture of northern India around 1700 B.C. This is at least 1,200 years earlier than any written version of the text could possibly have existed.

Why has this curious scholarly tradition lasted so long? History is only true for the time being; each new generation of scholars rewrites the work of its predecessors. But such revisers rarely go back to the beginning and start from scratch. Instead they build uncritically on "generally accepted" foundations laid down by their predecessors. These traditional, established truths of history have a large symbolic component of which their exponents are usually unaware.

My case study is summarized in the following quotation from an authoritative work published in 1982:

In India the earliest written records so far available [apart from the still unread inscriptions of the Indus civilization] are the inscriptions of Asoka [third century B.C.], but there exists a body of earlier literature of very considerable size and variety which was composed and passed on for many centuries in oral form. This literature goes back to the oldest surviving text, the Samhita, or "compilation" of the hymns of the Rigveda. A reasonable estimate of the date of the compilation of the Rigveda is c. 1500–1300 B.C., and the composition of many of the individual hymns may be expected to have extended over several previous centuries. (Allchin and Allchin 1982: 288)

The title of the chapter in which this passage occurs is "The Arrival of the Indo-Aryan–speaking People and the Spread of the Indo-Aryan Languages." From this we must infer that prior to about 1700 B.C. the population of northern India spoke some quite different kind of language. It may well be so; but we cannot know. Even if the Indus-civilization inscriptions turned out to be written in some form of Dravidian or other non-Indo-Aryan language, we still would not know.

The beginning of the formulation of this story can be dated fairly precisely to 1786, when Sir William Jones announced his discovery of a close relationship between Latin, Greek, Sanskrit, German, and Celtic languages. The date is interesting. The English, having just lost most of their American colonies, were embarking on a vast, worldwide, colonial expansion. The details of the linguistic association among the various Indo-European languages had been fully worked out by 1833, when Franz Bopp published his *Vergleichende Grammatik* (Comparative Grammar). By the time Max Müller began to work on his translation of the Rig Veda around 1846, it was already being claimed that the text was extremely ancient. Max Müller himself spelled out the argument at full length in a lecture given in 1878 (1878: 145–67). As early as 1865 he had already proposed a dating that is very close to that given in my quotation from the Allchins: "We cannot well assign a date more recent than 1200 to 1500 before our era, for the original composition" (Max Müller 1880, 1: 13). With only slight variation, the general argument has been repeated over and over again, almost without criticism, so that it has now become a dogma.

I would have supposed that almost anyone looking closely at what Max Müller says would see that his reasoning is specious. There is no genuine evidence that the text of the Rig Veda existed in its present form before about 400 B.C., but no contemporary Indo-European scholar will admit as much. If you ask such a scholar for his or her evidence (as I have done on several occasions), you will find that the answer is simply a slightly tidied-up version of what Max Müller said in 1878.

But this is *not* the point at issue in my present paper. I am fully aware of all the arguments that have been put forward in favor of the belief that the text of the Rig Veda is substantially the same as an oral text that existed in remote antiquity. I do not myself believe that this is in the least likely to be the case, but that is irrelevant. The crux of my argument is that whatever the date of the Rig Veda text may be, absolutely no grounds exist for supposing that it refers to events that actually happened in "real" historical time. Equally, I consider it futile to suppose that the cultural environment that seems to be postulated by the Rig Vedan texts might be identified with any "real" cultural environment that might be reflected in the excavations of archeologists working in northern India.

Religious texts, whether oral or written, are almost invariably composed either in a language alien to the current vernacular (for example, Latin and Greek in medieval Christianity; Pali, a form of Sanskrit, by Theravada Buddhists in Burma, Thailand, and Sri Lanka) or in an "archaic" version of the current vernacular (for example, Old Church Slavonic in the Russian Orthodox Church). In the latter case we cannot assume that the religious language is necessarily a conservative survival of what had once been vernacular. The archaism is part of the code; it is a way of asserting that the content of the text is ancient and authoritative.

As Indo-European studies developed during the nineteenth century there was at first no fixed dogma about how the linguistic dispersion of the Indo-European language family had come about. Around 1850 Max Müller was still fairly vague. He wrote of the "Aryan" language, "spoken in Asia by a small tribe, nay, originally by a small family living under one and the same roof," as if it were the mother tongue of the human race, but prior to 1872 (and occasionally after that date) he was careful to distinguish the study of language from "ethnology," the study of the movements of peoples: "There are Aryan and Semitic languages, [but] it is against all rules of logic to speak, without an expressed or implied qualification, of an Aryan race, of Aryan blood, or Aryan skulls" (1880, 4: 223). But the last quotation comes from a lecture given at the Imperial University of Strassburg in May 1872, just after the annexation by Germany of Alsace (against the express wishes of the local German-speaking inhabitants). In the earlier part of the lecture Max Müller expressed his

Germanic pride in this reunification of the German nation. His distinction between language and race is clearly under strain. By 1878 he writes without equivocation about "the Aryans" as if they were a racial group moving outward from some central Asian homeland by a process of conquest. By the 1890's, the linguist Sir George Grierson was explaining all Indo-Aryan dialect distributions in northern India as due to past military conquest, a view that was repeated without criticism in the 1969 printing of the *Encyclopaedia Britannica*.

The history of European colonialism covers many centuries and takes diverse forms, but whereas the European explorers and conquerors of the Americas, Africa, and Oceania usually took it for granted that the local inhabitants could be enslaved or butchered or driven into the hinterland at the whim of the invaders, the literate nations of Asia were initially treated as peoples toward whom the courtesies of European diplomacy should be applied.

At the end of the day these Asian civilizations were likewise mostly subdued by force of arms, but such conquest needed some kind of moral justification, a mythical charter. The Rig Veda as interpreted by Max Müller and his contemporaries provided just such a myth. It had the following form: Away back, long before the dawn of true history, Aryan invaders (who spoke a proto-European language and were therefore close kin to the Greeks, Romans, and Persians, who were the acknowledged founders of European civilization) had brought the first civilization to India, establishing themselves as an elitist military aristocracy among a population of barbarian serfs. They followed the precepts of a morally pure religious system, "The Vedic Religion," which was very different from "the modern Brahmanic religion, as founded in the Puranas and Tantras, [which] consists in a belief in Vishnu, Siva and Brahma, and manifests itself in the worship of the most hideous idols" (Max Müller 1878: 154). After many centuries, during which the high culture of these original Aryans gradually decayed into gross immorality and superstition, a new wave of Indo-Europeans was now repeating the process. Once again the conquerors were establishing themselves as an elitist military aristocracy under the banner of a morally pure religion (Christianity).

Three elements in the argument are crucial. First, the hymns of the Rig Veda, which were committed to writing around 400 B.C. at the very earliest, had previously survived in the form of a word-perfect oral tradition for well over 1,000 years. Second, although these hymns are religious documents, they are also records of history. It was repeatedly and categorically asserted that we can infer the nature of Aryan society around 1700 B.C. from a close study of the Rig Veda. Third, the history thus recorded was the history of the beginning of civilization in India.

Essentially similar claims have frequently been made for the possibility of reconstructing the world of Odysseus from the pages of Homer or the world of the ancient Israelites from the pages of the Pentateuch. Only very recently have the radical skeptics in these matters begun to gain the upper hand, and it is still an open question as to whether skepticism or blind faith will end up victorious.

If we accept all this, then the Aryan invaders appear as a race of chariot-riding heroes who conquer a population of servile peasant barbarians, the Dasa (Dasyu). This is a familiar story. Crossland, writing as a skeptic about traditions concerning the origin of Greco-Roman civilization, remarks: "The role of the Indo-European peoples in the ancient world has been portrayed too often as the incarnation of northern virility sweeping down in massed chariots to bring new vigour to a decadent south" (1971: 826). Where India is concerned, the construction of this mytho-history was complete by 1920 and it was being written about as if it were fully authenticated history. It still is, though it deserves note that as early as 1914 a South Indian Brahmin scholar published in the pages of *Anthropos* a thoroughgoing criticism of the whole Max Müller enterprise (Iyengar 1914). So far as I can discover, this excellent article has been completely ignored in all subsequent Indo-Europeanist writings.

In 1922 archeologists started to turn up evidence of the Indus civilization. Mohenjo-daro and Harappa have had most of the publicity, but new discoveries are still being made all the time. Major engineering constructions similar to those recently discovered at Mohenjo-daro and dating back to around 2500 B.C. have now been discovered as far north as the Helmand and Oxus river basins in Afghanistan. The claim now is that the Indus civilization at one time "occupied an area larger than the cultures of ancient Egypt and Mesopotamia combined" (Norman Hammond, in the London *Times*, July 13, 1985, p. 10).

Common sense might suggest that here was a striking example of a refutable hypothesis that had in fact been refuted. Indo-European scholars should have scrapped all their historical reconstructions and started again from scratch. But that is not what happened. Vested interests and academic posts were involved. Almost without exception the scholars in question managed to persuade themselves that despite appearances, the theories of the philologists and the hard evidence of archeology could be made to fit together. The trick was to think of the horse-riding Aryans as conquerors of the cities of the Indus civilization in the same way that the Spanish conquistadores were conquerors of the cities of Mexico and Peru or the Israelites of the Exodus were conquerors of Jericho. The lowly Dasa of the Rig Veda, who had previously been thought of as primitive savages, were now reconstructed as members of a high civilization who were destined to subordination because of their dark skins. The Aryan invaders could still be considered the originators of Indian civilization because they wiped out by fire and slaughter whatever was there before.

In 1963 Thomas Burrow, a Sanskritist of great distinction, put the full weight of his authority behind this revamping of the Dasa. He claimed that the ruins of Harappan settlements are repeatedly mentioned in the Rig Veda and were viewed with religious awe by the Rig Vedan authors. He cites the following hymn to Agni as explicit evidence that the Rig Veda is in places a record of Aryan victories over non-Aryan Harappans: "Through fear of thee the dark coloured inhabitants fled, not waiting for battle abandoning their possessions, when O Vaisnavara, burning brightly for Puru and destroying the cities, thou didst shine, O Agni" (Rig Veda VII. 5.3, cited in Burrow 1963).

Burrow's interpretation has been widely applauded by specialists in Indo-European studies, but their approval was to be expected, since his matter-of-fact translation fits in with the proposition that myth is thinly disguised history. This can hardly be said of the version offered by Max Müller and Wilson a hundred years previously. In the Müller/Wilson sun-worship interpretation, the "dark coloured inhabitants" are seen as personified powers of darkness, while Agni is present not as the destroyer of enemy cities by conflagration but as the light of the sun triumphing over night. As an anthropologist I have no preference. Texts of this sort cannot possibly be interpreted (as distinct from translated) unless we have independent knowledge of the cultural background, which, in this case, is lacking. Even if bits and pieces of the text refer to "real" happenings, no modern scholar could possibly know what they are.

Moreover, if the Rig Veda is really a residue of a very early oral mythology, it is just as likely to derive from Harappa as from wandering bands of entirely imaginary chariot-riding conquerors. But it could also have been introduced into India at some quite indeterminate date by a few enterprising Persian missionaries. And there are many other possibilities. We know that the Indus cities traded northward to Central Asia and westward to Persia, Mesopotamia, and the Arabian Sea. They would have been as polyglot as imperial Rome, contemporary Jerusalem, or fifteenth-century Baghdad. All manner of religious cults would have been found there. Yet modern scholars have repeatedly asserted that the Rig Veda is only a slightly disguised account of an actual sequence of events, the Aryan invasions.

In 1950 Piggott, an archeologist of high repute, claimed without qualification that the god Indra "is the apotheosis of the Aryan battle leader . . . the victorious leader of the Aryans in their conquest of the hated ancient empire of the Punjab" (Piggott 1950: 260). He followed this up by saying that the identification of Vedic Dasa with Harappan is "something near to a certainty." A central feature of this thesis, in which Piggott was following Mortimer Wheeler, was that the Aryan invaders had completely obliterated the civilization of their Harappan predecessors. Since then whole books have been written on this theme (such as Shendge 1977).

We now know that Piggott's thesis is quite untrue. The Indus civilization did not come to an end suddenly but over a period of centuries. The primary cause of its decline was probably a geological catastrophe that led to a change in the course of the Indus, a failure of the irrigation system, and the collapse of waterborne trade. In the centuries that followed, the political and economic center of gravity moved eastward into the Ganges plain.

It is certainly possible that this is the period when Indo-Aryan languages first became dominant in this region, but we do not know. Moreover, even if it was the case, we cannot know why it would have happened. A rough survey of well-authenticated examples would suggest that, of the many possible reasons for a change in language distribution, political domination by a small minority is the most likely factor, while a mass movement of population is the most improbable.

Despite the enthusiastic fantasies that have been developed by Georges Dumézil and his followers, who claim that the post-

Harappan Vedic society of northern India had a form of social organization that was prototypical of the organization of all the Indo-European peoples (see, for example, Littleton 1982: 7–18), nothing in the archeological record suggests that the Ganges plain society was radically discontinuous from its Indus predecessor. Nor is there any independent *archeological* evidence for a massive intrusion of foreigners from the northwest. The suggestion in parts of the recent archeological literature (e.g. Allchin and Allchin 1982: 358) that such evidence does exist is quite misleading. The "Painted Grey Ware Culture" of these writers would never have been interpreted as such if they had not started out by treating the Rig Veda as a history book.

On my reading of the evidence, the firmly established parallels between north Indian society in the first millennium B.C. and societies in other parts of the Indo-European–speaking world are no closer than the parallels that existed in such non-Indo-European societies as China, Mesopotamia, and Egypt. Here is an example.

As part and parcel of the dogma that the Rig Veda was introduced into India by the Aryan invaders, we have the further dogma that the life-style of the divine beings of the Rig Veda was the life-style of the Aryan invaders themselves. In particular, the war chariots of Indra and his associates show that the Aryan invaders were lavishly equipped with war chariots, while the complex rituals of the Vedic horse sacrifice stem from the fact that the horse was "the supreme symbol of the victorious Indo-Europeans . . . whose domestication enabled the Indo-Aryans to conquer the Indo-European world" (O'Flaherty 1981: 85). This too is a fantasy, though it has been around a long time.

It is true that the two-wheeled chariot, in a crude form, is likely to have been invented in Central Asia. But the appearance of chariots as grave goods and the pictorial representation of chariots in other contexts suggest that it was a rare object, a ceremonial carriage rather than a piece of normal military equipment. The characters in the Rig Veda ride in chariots because they are divine beings.

And then there is the question of dates. Chariots were in use in Mesopotamia in the early third millennium B.C. They were known in Egypt by the middle of the second millennium and probably reached Minoan Crete and mainland Greece from the southeast rather than from the north. They were in use in Shang-dynasty China at about the same period. But in each of these archeologically verifiable cases, the context is that of a city-focused state with a well-organized army, and only the war leaders ride in chariots. Holocaust sacrifices of chariots and their horses and charioteers were a feature of royal funerals in both Mesopotamia and China at a very early date. Rig Vedan horse sacrifices seem tame by comparison. Admittedly, war chariots appear in the *Iliad*, but here again the author seems to regard them as prestigious rather than military objects. Chariots are used for racing and for transporting the heroes to the scene of battle, but that is about all. Hector's corpse is dragged in shame behind the wheels of Achilles' chariot, but the actual combat between the two heroes is on foot.

On the other hand, wild horses were common in all the more northerly parts of Eurasia from remote antiquity. They were probably hunted for meat long before they were domesticated for riding. Horse bones, carbon-dated to about 4400 B.C., have been identified in a "Kurgan culture" site in the Lower Dnieper region, but there is no evidence that they were from domesticated horses or that, if they were, the "Kurgan" people were the first to domesticate horses. And despite the current fashion among Indo-European scholars, there is no genuine evidence that the Kurgan people spoke any form of Indo-European language. Dates are uncertain, but all the ancient urban civilizations made extensive and quite early use of domesticated horses.

In other words, the prominent place given to horses and chariots in the Rig Veda can tell us virtually nothing that might distinguish any real society for which the Rig Veda might provide a partial cosmology. If anything, it suggests that in the real society (as opposed to its mythological counterpart), horses and chariots were a rarity, ownership of which was a mark of aristocratic or kingly distinction.

Likewise, the repeated assertion that Indra's victories over the Dasa can be confidently interpreted as a folk memory of real victories by real Indo-Aryan conquerors over their indigenous predecessors seems to me devoid of any plausibility. Of course nothing is impossible, but the likelihood is certainly slim. That the enemies of God should come to be identified with personal enemies is a phenomenon that is regularly encountered even in present-day warfare; but the converse proposition—that the mythical enemies of God always derive from badly remembered history—is fallacious, as should be obvious to anyone who has ever read Milton's *Paradise Lost*.

So I come back to my earlier question. Why do serious scholars persist in believing in the Aryan invasions?

At one time social anthropologists used to complain that their archeologist colleagues had no sense of the overall coherence of human societies. Now, under the influence of Dumézil, who was himself influenced by Durkheim and Granet, most of the prehistorians who have specialized in India and Pakistan and most of their Indo-Europeanist philological colleagues have become committed to a functionalism of a wholly naive sort. They seem to assume that cultural systems and language systems are bonded together and intrinsically stable over long periods of time. If societies are left alone, they stay put; otherwise, they roll across the landscape like impermeable billiard balls. If the archeological record shows that in fact changes have occurred, their occurrence is always explained as the consequence of a movement of population that carries with it the products (both material and immaterial) of a preexisting, alien, self-contained culture. As a rule, the alleged movement of people takes the form of a military conquest. The mythology of the Dorian invaders of ancient Greece who reduced their Ionian predecessors to serfdom matches point for point the mythology of the Aryan invasion of northern India.

I am not exaggerating the persistence of the "movement of peoples" doctrine. I quote again from the Allchins:

There seems to be general agreement that the Indo-Iranian languages . . . were originally spoken in the steppes of Eurasia, and that over a period of time they spread, undoubtedly largely through the medium of movements of groups of speakers, into the regions where they are later traceable through written records or where they are still spoken. . . . We would like to insist that the arrival and spread of the Indo-Aryan languages must have been associated with the movement of Indo-Aryan-speaking people, and that their relations with the populations they encountered must be conceived as a dynamic process of culture contact, producing a variety of cultural responses. This process must have continued over many centuries. Its result was to produce a cultural synthesis which we may refer to as culturally Indo-Aryan, that is, a synthesis of Indus or Indian, and Aryan elements. . . .
. . . Since 1871 there has been general acceptance that this early homeland [of the speakers of Indo-European languages] must have been somewhere on the steppes of Eurasia. (Allchin and Allchin 1982: 299–300)

The Allchins, in their archeological capacity, have consistently emphasized the continuity that links the residues of the Indus civilization with those of the later classical India in the Ganges basin and further south. Furthermore, they repeatedly emphasized that archeology provides no clear evidence of any mass movement of peoples from Central Asia into northern India. So why do they continue to pay deference to the "racist" notions of nineteenth-century philologists in this way? (Incidentally, there is no "general agreement that the Indo-Iranian languages . . . were originally spoken in the steppes of Eurasia.")

But we should note what is implicit in the Allchins' formulation. If the Indo-European languages were brought into India by a movement of population after the heyday of the Indus civilization, then the people of the Indus civilization did not speak an Indo-European language. The clear presumption is that they spoke a Dravidian language and were dark-skinned, like most of the present-day speakers of Dravidian languages. On the other hand, the speakers of Indo-European who arrived from "the steppes of Eurasia" are clearly presumed to be fair-skinned nomads. We have Max Müller plus Piggott and Mortimer Wheeler all over again.

Why is this sort of thing so attractive? Who finds it attractive? Why has the development of early Sanskrit come to be so dogmatically associated with an Aryan invasion? In some cases the association seems to be a matter of intellectual inertia. Thus Thapar (1969), who provides a valuable survey of the evidence then available, clearly finds the whole "movement of peoples" argument a nuisance, but at the end of the day she falls into line.

Where the Indo-European philologists are concerned, the invasion argument is tied in with their assumption that if a particular language is identified as having been used in a particular locality at a particular time, no attention need be paid to what was there before; the slate is wiped clean. Obviously, the easiest way to imagine this happening in real life is to have a military conquest that obliterates the previously existing population!

The details of the theory fit in with this racist framework. Just as each member of the total family of Indo-European languages is lineally descended from one or another of a number of extinct "protolanguages," so also are the speakers of these languages; hence the people who speak any particular language constitute an independent racial stock.

By an exercise of faith rather than common sense the language of the Rig Veda was long ago claimed to be very close to "proto-Indo-Iranian." It is thus supposed to be ancestral not only to the Sanskrit of the later Vedas but also to Avestan (the language of the Zoroastrian sacred books) and to Old Persian, bits of which are known from inscriptions of Darius the Great (sixth century B.C.). Written texts in Avestan date only from the fourth century A.D., but, as in the case of Rig Vedan Sanskrit, the philologists claim that it is a very ancient language preserved in secret by the pre-Zoroastrian priesthood over many centuries.

Because of their commitment to a unilineal segmentary history of language development that needed to be mapped onto the ground, the philologists took it for granted that proto-Indo-Iranian was a language that had originated outside either India or Iran. Hence it followed that the text of the Rig Veda was in a language that was actually spoken by those who introduced this earliest form of Sanskrit into India. From this we derive the myth of the Aryan invasions. QED.

Several more or less coincidental origin myths are involved. The origin myth of the Indo-European philologists calls for a lineage of wholly imaginary ancestral "protolanguages."

The origin myth of British colonial imperialism helped the elite administrators in the Indian Civil Service to see themselves as bringing "pure" civilization to a country in which civilization of the most sophisticated (but "morally corrupt") kind was already nearly 6,000 years old. Here I will only remark that the hold of this myth on the British middle-class imagination is so strong that even today, 44 years after the death of Hitler and 43 years after the creation of an independent India and independent Pakistan, the Aryan invasions of the second millennium B.C. are still treated as if they were an established fact of history.

It is relevant that in the Rig Veda the divine heroes have no relations with the indigenous Dasa other than those of war and contempt. Hostility is not mediated by marriage (see Thapar 1978: 229 n. 15). This attitude fit well with the prejudices of nineteenth-century English and German scholars, whose colonialist compatriots were committed to maintaining a system of sexual apartheid to separate the rulers from the ruled. It is also appropriate in the origin myth of a society that later evolved into a hierarchy of endogamous castes.

Practicing Hindus are not greatly concerned with how it all began because their view of cosmological time is cyclical. There was no beginning. Nevertheless, the Vedic texts are considered peculiarly sacred, the Rig Veda most of all, and this state of affairs seems to have prevailed for at least 2,500 years. What, then, is the mythical significance of the Rig Veda within India? This question has received surprisingly little attention. Yet here is precisely where anthropologists might make a useful contribution, if only their scholarly associates would stop thinking of the Rig Veda as a garbled history book.

When we look at the Rig Veda in context and try to understand just why it should have been regarded around 500 B.C. as a sacred text, several strange features become apparent. Received wisdom is that Vedic religion gradually evolved into Hinduism between the sixth and second centuries B.C. It should be noted, however, that Vedic religion is a fictional entity about which nothing whatever is genuinely known. The Vedas add up to a miscellany of undatable documents of unknown origin. Although the texts are preoccupied with the correct performance of sacrificial rituals of great complexity, especially the horse sacrifice, archeologists have so far failed to locate any site, apart from two horse burials in a non-Indian context in Swat, where such rituals, even on a reduced scale, might plausibly have been performed. A corpus of texts that is not associated with any clearly identifiable sequence of ritual performance does not constitute a religion.

At the present time, the spectrum of Indian religious doctrine and practice is very wide, but one important common component that is shared also by Buddhism and Jainism is the doctrine of the transmigration of souls, which is linked with the idea of *karma* (fate as determined by the merit or demerit of action during both present and past existences) and the goal of ultimate extinction (*mokśa* for a Hindu; *nirvana* for a Buddhist). This doctrine was already held by the Jains and Buddhists as early as the sixth century B.C., but nothing analogous is apparent in the text of the Vedas. Furthermore, the ambisexual nature of deity in which the feminine is usually the active principle, which is such a striking feature of modern Hinduism, is sharply contrasted with the model of deity represented in the Vedas, where active characters are masculine and females are subordinate and passive.

I think the puzzles have sensible anthropological solutions, but this is not the place to put them forward. The essence of the matter is that we must recognize that the standard Max Müller–derived story is wholly implausible. Instead, we should pay special attention to the likely state of affairs around 500 B.C. We should then recognize that the versions of Buddhism, Jainism, and Brahmanical Hinduism that were current at that time are best understood as contemporaneous structural transformations of a single system of ideas and ritual practices. Vedic texts may have a bearing on this system of ideas, but they are not primary in either a chronological sense or a theological sense. The Aryan invasions never happened at all.

Of course no one is going to believe that.

9

Form and Meaning in Recent Indonesian History: Some Reflections in Light of H.-G. Gadamer's Philosophy of History

JAMES L. PEACOCK

There are . . . many suspicions about the notion of "History as a Symbol Science."

Greg Deming, *The Bounty: An Ethnographic History*

We use what we have. That motto guides this exercise. What I offer as a way into Indonesian history is three stints of fieldwork there, and I start with them.

The use of ethnographic experience as a basis for constructing history implies a number of methodological and theoretical issues. As a way to focus on some of them, I follow my Indonesian analysis with a consideration of one of the more comprehensive (if not comprehensible) and anthropologically resonant philosophies of history, that set forth by Hans-Georg Gadamer in his *Wahrheit und Methode* (translated as *Truth and Method*). Finally, I consider the Indonesian analysis in light of this philosophy, and vice versa.

Three Symbolic Forms

I propose to concentrate on three symbolic forms, or so they might be termed, each of which was associated with one period of fieldwork and with one period in Indonesian history: *ludruk*, a working-class drama, was studied in 1962–63 in Surabaya, Java; Muhammadijah, a fundamentalist Muslim movement, was studied in 1970 throughout Indonesia but primarily in central Java; and Sumarah, a meditation club, was studied in 1979 in Surakarta, Java.

Ludruk. After two centuries of Dutch colonialism, Indonesian movements toward independence began in 1908 with a Javanese nativist movement. This movement, Budi Utomo, started in technical schools—a nativist quest for meaning stripped away by Western technology. Not long afterward came a Muslim movement, Sarekat Islam, which was then followed by, and for a time allied with, the Indonesian Communist Party (PKI). By the 1920's, then, had emerged the trio of forces that have dominated twentieth-century Indonesian history. The late President Sukarno called them NASAKOM: *NAS*, for nationalism, also implying nativism; *A*, for *agama*, religion, that is, Islam; and *KOM*, for communism.

Tutored by Tjokroaminoto, the head of Sarekat Islam, Sukarno created the Indonesian Nationalist Party (PNI) before World War II. He declared independence in 1945, won it by 1950, and had established so-called Guided Democracy by 1957. Guided Democracy was less democratic than guided—by Sukarno, who controlled a legislative machinery that was so huge and amorphous as to be powerless. The ideology of Guided Democracy was summarized by acronyms such as MANIPOL USDEK, which celebrated a social order based on "guided economy," "socialism à la Indonesia," and the "Indonesian personality." The guiding state was mythologized by a plethora of images, slogans, and ideologies. Sukarno named himself, certain regiments of the army, and epochs in history after characters and episodes in the sacral shadow plays. Malarial New Guinea was pictured in dance and song as an isle of paradise, inhabited by grass-skirted, black-faced savages and occupied by neocolonialists. A five-year plan, which Sukarno praised for its "symbolic richness," was divided into 8 sections, 17 subsections, and 1,945 sub-subsections to commemorate the date of Indonesia's independence. Buttressed by the nationalists, by the Indonesian communists (who by the 1960's were the second-largest communist organization in Asia), and by deeply rooted Javanese traditions, Sukarnoist Indonesia strove to create a mass political culture, a symbolic world that penetrated all levels of life.

A sense of the way Sukarno succeeded is suggested by a bizarre and extreme example. A Javanese laborer told me that he dreamed of a milk banana, *pisang Susu*, so named because of its firm, white, sweet tip, like a woman's nipple giving milk. In his dream he ate the banana, then realized it was Sukarno: "*Susu*," he said, meant "Sukarno." On the basis of this pun, he imagined that he had a direct, umbilical connection to the president, like a child to its mother. On this authority he proposed to create a communal utopia. Unfortunately, he chose a policeman as his audience and was confined to the Surabaya psychiatric hospital. The example illustrates a certain depth of infiltration by political culture into the consciousness of the masses.

Meanwhile, in the early 1960's material conditions were worsening. Rice prices were tripling monthly. Especially on crowded Java, life was desperate and miserable for many. In Surabaya, site of the ludruk plays, were an estimated 75,000 beggars. Even the poor, however, as in the *kampong* slum where my wife and I were living in Surabaya, were caught up in the cultural movements and forms that were part of Guided Democracy to a striking extent. The ludruk plays, for example, were produced and consumed entirely by the working class. In settings ranging from amusement parks to communist party meetings and to slum neighborhoods, one could see ludruk every night; on a weekend, perhaps 100,000 watched at once. Combining features of psychodrama, soap opera, and folklore, ludruk reveals something of the working-class consciousness during that period.

Owing to the ostensible communist affiliation of many ludruk troupes at this time, when 26 of 27 Surabaya districts were under communist control, some have assumed that ludruk parroted the party line. Sometimes it did, as in a play I saw at a PKI celebration. But in the 82 plays I saw, the majority of themes were not Marxist; in fact, the most frequent type of plot had a bourgeois emphasis. This type of plot took two forms, both of which involved a working-class heroine. (For a detailed discussion, see Peacock 1968.) The first type had a traditional Javanese setting, took 25 years or so of fictional time to unfold, and ended with the heroine failing in her effort to marry into the upper class. The second type, which was increasing in popularity while the first was dying out, had a modern setting, took only a few months to unfold, and ended with the heroine succeeding in marrying up. However, tensions and ambiguities marred this achievement. The success of the working-class heroine always entailed the violent destruction of another person. The person who married up was always a woman played by a man, a feature that might be interpreted as a signal of the illusory nature of the success, for the transvestite was generally a symbol of illusion. In any case, the vision was more bourgeois than might have been expected from a proletarian play in a communist city during Guided Democracy.

In addition to the working-class woman, the second character found in ludruk plays was the clown. The clown is a central figure in Java, one that the Marxist W. F. Wertheim (1965) has tried to interpret as an expression of the proletariat's rebellion against the ruling class. This was indeed true of ludruk clowns, but only to a point. More striking was the way a commitment to Javanese civilization shared by both upper and lower classes prohibited the mocking of upper-class values beyond certain limits. One clown was heckled, for example, when he went too far in ridiculing Javanese etiquette. Here a deeper cultural meaning overrode simple class loyalty, reminding us how Indonesian-style communism took on its own coloration.

The third character of the ludruk play was a transvestite singer and dancer who appeared between the scenes. While the clown was given the task of expressing proletarian gripes, the transvestite was given the task of singing slogans distributed by the Ministry of Information. He sang these in a peculiar way, with the form contradicting the content. The verbal message was usually active: Organize! But the style of music was a dreamy, slow chant, with an orchestral accompaniment customarily played while one character remembered his dead mother. Form apparently overrode content. One could hear these activist lyrics sung on the streets after midnight, chanted dreamily by beggar women as they sang their children to sleep.

These plots and characters illustrate how some of the grand themes and large forces of Sukarnoist Guided Democracy were translated into so-called mass culture, such as ludruk. Yet the translation was made in terms of the distinctive qualities and patterns of this particular subculture and sociocultural milieu.

Muhammadijah. On my second field trip to Indonesia, I arrived on New Year's Eve 1969 to join rowdy crowds celebrating the New Order. Following the "year of living dangerously," Sukarno had been replaced by Suharto after the massacre of half a million so-called communists—an event known as *Gestapu*. The economy was revitalized, at least for the wealthy capitalists. Pornography had arrived with imports of class Z (X-rated) Western movies. Rock and roll, banned by Sukarno, was back. A materialistic and hedonistic Westernization was replacing the exotic symbolism of Guided Democracy. In this bourgeois atmosphere, the second element of NASAKOM, the

Muslims—whose major party, Masjumi, had been banned by Sukarno in 1960—hoped for revival. Suharto allowed the Muslims to
reorganize, but their new party, Parmusi, lacked the strength of the
old Masjumi. Muhammadijah, the major Muslim reformist organization, was associated with the new Muslim party.

An organization of some 6 million, Muhammadijah has a missionary aim, to spread pure Islam, and is also active in social and ed-
ucational work. Muhammadijah runs thousands of schools, some
hospitals, and even business enterprises such as batik cooperatives.
Its headquarters are at the court city of Yogyakarta, but its more politically and economically oriented leaders are in Jakarta. It is not a
political party, though it has been allied with such Muslim parties as
Masjumi and Parmusi. It is not rabidly militant, though it has indulged in some terrorism. Its financial support, as well as many of its
members, comes from the indigenous business class from which it
originated, but increasingly its leaders are of the civil service class.
This trend is reflected in a certain bureaucratization of rhetoric and
ideology that is shared by Indonesian national culture.

"Muslim Puritans" was the phrase I applied to Muhammadijah in
a study that documented the ethos and psychology of Muslim re-
formists (Peacock 1978). I showed, for example, how Muhammadijans had rationalized the life cycle by deritualizing it, reducing rituals
that usher in birth and death as part of cosmic cycles and speeding
up the date of circumcision in order to get a boy more quickly onto
the straight and narrow. More telling than the statistics were certain
images that exemplified a kind of puritanism and Protestant ethic: the
Muhammadijan women who used ledgers to record and compute the
percentage of time they wasted each day in sin; the merchant whose
pride and joy was a specially constructed commode that flushed feces
away efficiently instead of permitting them to linger indefinitely in the
traditional fashion; the young men whose dirty jokes suggested a kind
of repressiveness very different from the cosmic obscenities of the ludruk. Muslim Puritanism in personal life was, however, being ov-
erlaid by a determined bureaucratization of collective life. Meetings
were opened by statements like "The first item on the agenda is a discussion of the agenda." Speeches were delivered explicitly in outline
form ("Now we proceed to part A") rather than in the subtle and rich
rhetoric of the old "fathers." Quasi-military uniforms became pop-

ular, even for civilians (this Muslim organization existed, of course, within a military regime).

Some of these themes are illustrated by a sketch of a Muhammadijah training camp. The last camp I participated in was an eighteen-hours-per-day, fifteen-day package of indoctrination with a bit of physical training. For branch leaders, the camp included sessions on Islamic history and doctrine, Muhammadijan history and politics, management terminology, discussions of such issues as whether the organization should establish a research branch (some joked I was it), discussions of discussion itself as a method, and testimonials that sometimes revealed an emotionality that I only dimly understood but that showed the relation between the psychological and the bureaucratic and ideological. One man, for example, began to weep after telling of his brothers, who were communists, being killed in the Gestapu massacre; but participants said he wept not for his brothers but because his mother had to suffer in raising them. However that may be, complex layers lurked beneath the schematic format of indoctrinational and organizational forms.

The last day of the camp began with a tour of development projects near the camp. At nine o'clock we were taken in a convoy of automobiles to the operations room of the regional head of government development projects, who happened to be Muhammadijan. With overlay maps and flashing lights, he showed planned developments, dams, roads, and farms, as well as 550 actual or planned mosques. After a lengthy school ceremony that was more Javanese than Puritan and put us two hours behind schedule, we visited some of these sites, described as Muhammadijan contributions to REPELITA, the national development plan. Through all of this, some of the camp instructors huddled in one of the cars, telling dirty jokes and rating the beauty of the women of Aisjijah, the women's auxiliary.

Night brought the camp's closing ceremony. Testimonies and awards climaxed in a speech by the military police commander of the region. As the stout and pompous general stepped to the podium, an aide picked up his spectacles and leather-bound notes and placed them on the podium. Two more aides marched forward, hung a colored chart, and handed the general a pointer. The general's chart represented *tauhid* (unity of God) as blue, *achlak* (ethics) as red, *ibadat* (pious action) as purple, and *ilmu* (knowledge) as green. The general spoke of the relationship of these elements, basic in Indonesian Islam: "You can't kill emotion [*nafsu*], but you can use these elements [ethics, knowledge, piety], which all come from God [tauhid], to channel emotion. Then it can even fire a rocket!" He warned, "False leadership bedazzles like shining gold teeth" (he smiled, showing his). "NASAKOM is *bohong* [bull]. Anyone who follows the old order is a fool!" Having dismissed Sukarnoism, the general also dismissed Christianity, Buddhism, and the Japanese way. He concluded, "Now, brothers, let Islam be your guide."

This last day had a comic-opera quality, which I suspect some of the other participants sensed too. This came, I think, not only from the pompous general but also from the abstract and schematic quality of the slogans and ideologies. Incompletely fused to the real lives of the participants, these often seemed silly caricatures of an alien order not yet grasped. But they could not be viewed very cynically, for they were part of a mood of hope and reconstruction as well as the result of military dominance.

What can be said of Muhammadijah in comparison to ludruk? Muhammadijah, unlike Sukarnoist political culture, did not succeed in affecting the full society. It was confined essentially to a bourgeois, rationalistic, ascetic, pious group of businessmen and bureaucrats. For this small group—6 million out of Indonesia's population of perhaps 175 million—Muhammadijah provided an orderly, disciplined, methodical way of life, somewhat isolated and sheltered from the chaos and tension that had characterized Indonesia since Sukarno, though, as the camp's last day illustrated, Muhammadijah was being drawn somewhat into the bureaucraticized development rhetoric of Suhartoist Indonesia. Still, Muhammadijah remained a sect. The term "Muslim Puritans" suggests a parallel to Weber's Calvinist capitalists. An important difference, however, is that the Protestant ethic became more than Protestantism; it was part of modernity, which infused whole societies. The Muslim reformation in Indonesia, and with it Muhammadijah, came too late, almost simultaneously with the coming of nationalism and communism at the turn of the century. In Indonesia, these other forces took over the role of creating a mass culture, while Islam flourished more as a sect for the pious minority, such as Muhammadijah.

Sumarah. On my third, brief field trip, in the summer of 1979, I attended meetings of the meditation society, Sumarah, in Surakarta,

Java (see Howe 1980). If ludruk was working class and Muhammadijah middle class, Sumarah was allied with the upper class, or perhaps, more precisely, with the *prijaji* subculture, a kind of white-collar stratum oriented toward classical Javanese arts, religion, and etiquette. Here was a new class context. Further, by 1979 a different political era had begun. PKI, the Communist party, had been crushed in the 1965 Gestapu massacre; PNI, Sukarno's nationalist party, had been destroyed in the 1971 elections, as had Parmusi, the Muslim party affiliated with Muhammadijah. Each of Sukarno's NASA-KOM forces had faded, so far as party representation was concerned; in fact, the only party that was a political force now was that of the military government, GOLKAR.

Sumarah teaches a way of resonating with *alam*, the deepest reality. Such resonance is achieved through meditation, by which one eliminates emotions, thoughts, and forms that obstruct. The result is not retreat from the world but tranquil living in the world as one comes to a state of mind from which all activity flows effortlessly. From *meditasi chusus* (special meditation) comes *meditasi harian* (daily meditation), in which one carries on life in a balanced state of mind. The dynamic local leader of Sumarah, Pak Wondo, who was also a banker and batik maker, always tried to run his bank and ride his motor scooter in such a meditative state.

The contrast between the worldviews of Sumarah, Muhammadijah, and ludruk participants is evident in the way members of each group narrate their life histories. The ludruk actors looked back nostalgically, recalling a mellow experience (usually a youthful love affair) in contrast to present bitterness. The Muhammadijan never narrated nostalgic memories but instead looked forward, describing life as a movement toward reform and good works, perhaps salvation. The Sumarah teacher Wondo emphasized neither past nor future but the continuity of experience, so that, as he says, his "teaching is still learning," his aging, still youth, and all is in resonance with the immovable and eternal, alam.

The three forms coincide with the three social classes of Java in relation to three eras of Indonesian history. Ludruk was part of the working-class experience of the 1960's during the Sukarnoist effort to construct a mass political culture. Muhammadijah was part of a middle-class revitalization during Suharto's regime in the 1970's, exemplifying not the creation of a mass culture but a bourgeois, though bureaucratized, sect, highly organized and rationalistic, to provide order and purpose for a restricted group in the midst of chaos, tension, and change. Sumarah was an upper-class, white-collar mysticism that was neither retreatist nor reformist. Sumarah, a way of sustaining a balanced inner state, has been part of Javanese civilization for a millennium but was perhaps especially suited for a time when outer reform through political activism was subdued, as it was when Suharto's regime moved into the eighties; such meditation societies seemed to be especially flourishing then, as was suggested not only by statistics but by the power of persons associated with them, including Suharto himself.

Native views. How might the Indonesians, or the Javanese themselves, interpret these patterns? There is no lack of Indonesian writing about the meaning of these forms in history. A ludruk director, for example, has written a metaphorical commentary about the play's meaning as a torch for the masses; a Muhammadijan historian has said that that sect signals a shift from inner mysticism to outer reform in Islam. But these comments pertain to the individual forms. I can only speculate about how Javanese or Indonesians might view their relationships.

An approach that a Javanese probably would favor, in this agreeing with the anthropologist, would be to treat all three as of the same cultural identity. All three are set within the basic Javanese structure of life, which is hierarchical, framed by classificatory cosmologies, and organized around norms of respect (*urmat*) and harmony (*rukun*). In ways that space does not permit me to explicate but that would be obvious to any Javanese, all three forms, ludruk, Muhammadijah, and Sumarah, are quintessentially Javanese, expressing three different aspects of an essentially unitary culture, as well as three epochs in a process that affects its material and organizational basis. Nor do Javanese lack schemas for categorizing the variations among the forms and epochs. Sukarno's NASAKOM, for example, does this nicely. *KOM* (communism) is represented by ludruk, *A* (agama, Islam) by Muhammadijah, and *NAS* (nationalism or nativism) by Sumarah. Here the three are seen not as epochs but as variant expressions of a triad within the deep structure of the society; the same forces erupt again and again, with new names but in enduring patterns. A more circumstantial example is suggested by the colored chart of the general, which can be compared to charts used by meditation groups similar to Sumarah to explicate their worldview. In one such chart, the difference between desire and spirituality is depicted as an opposition between black and white. The teacher explicating the chart saw black desire as destructive: "It can explode a bomb." Compare this to the general's chart, which depicted desire and spirituality as part of a spectrum from red to blue. He saw emotion as creative: it can "fire a rocket."

These examples treat the forms and epochs as variant types, but Javanese philosophies treat them as historical processes too. Some envision history as Hinduist cycles. Others see it as Malayo-Islamic sequences of epochs (*jaman*), which are, however, not so much nodes in a developmental process as types, rather like stages in anthropological schemes of cultural evolution. Further, folk notions incorporate complex ways of calculating time, based on calendrical cycles. Finally, there are prophecies. It was forecast long ago that the yellow men would come; they did, during the Japanese occupation. Then would come a just prince (*Ratu Adil*) to save the country; he did, in the form of Sukarno. Now, some might say, the yellow phase has returned with the Japanese business people under Suharto's capitalism.

Indonesians also boast Western-style historical interpretations, as well as the rationalistic interpretations of planners. These, however, sometimes show a glimmer of the cycles, jaman, and the rest as they are translated into folk theories and celebrations. Sukarno used to say that what Indonesia needs is a myth; Indonesians have an ample supply for use in interpreting history.

The difficulty with applying native interpretations to the relationships between these three forms is obvious. Indonesians have reflected abundantly on their history in general, on the periods and contexts in question, and on each of the three forms, taken individually. No one, however, has carried out this particular combination of researches—ludruk, Muhammadijah, and Sumarah—or shares my peculiar interest in putting the three together. It is, of course, always up to the ethnographer or the historian to interpret things in light of his particular experience and vantage point. The issues involved in doing so bring us to the philosophy of Gadamer.

Gadamer's *Truth and Method*

In *Truth and Method* Gadamer attempts to formulate a philosophical basis for "human" or "cultural" studies (*Geisteswissenschaft*). His aim in doing so is to emancipate the human sciences from the influence of positivistic natural scientific thinking, which reduces knowledge to a detached, analytic model that does not satisfy the "hermeneutical experience" (1982: xv). Attempting to retrieve the distinctive heritage of the humanities, Gadamer elucidates such notions as *Erlebnis* (experience [1982: 18]) and *Bildung* (maturation, as of one's cultural sensibilities [1982: 54]), which are as basic to humanistic understanding as the analytical concepts are to science.

Truth and Method treats hermeneutical approaches in three spheres: art, history, and language. Focusing on history, we note first Gadamer's arguments concerning art and language.

Art. Gadamer criticizes the differentiation of aesthetic from non-aesthetic consciousness that has resulted from the subjectivizing of the aesthetic in philosophical thought since Descartes. Gadamer asserts the principle of "aesthetic nondifferentiation" (1975: 112), which holds that hermeneutics must not focus on the art form alone but must grasp the world, the total mode of being, embodied in that form.

To communicate this world of the form, Gadamer uses the examples of play, festival, and drama. Play "plays itself" (1982: 111–12): It is a symbolic activity that takes on its own being, creates its own world, transcending the subjectivity of any player. Similarly, Gadamer asserts that drama takes on its own being each time it is performed, for each performance creates a world. The festival "is celebrated because it is there" (*feirert man das Fest weil es da ist* [1975: 118]); such a form "is known as a something" (*es wird als etwas erkannt* [1975: 109]). An art form is truly "there" and "something" because it is not mere sensuous surface but is an experiential world.

Manifesting being, art forms also embody becoming; they are placed in history and they represent history. "The aesthetic consciousness . . . constitutes itself as historical (as when architectural style of the nineteenth century indulged in continued stylistic reminiscence). . . . [This] shows the inner relation between the historical and aesthetic" (1982: 82).

Properly understood, the consciousness embodied in art can serve as a model for the type of understanding that the human sciences can achieve, in distinction to the positivist, analytic understanding of the natural sciences.

Language. Gadamer criticizes the philosophies that would differentiate linguistic from nonlinguistic consciousness just as he opposes aesthetic differentiation. Language is not a mere tool of communication but a world. It is more correct to say that "language speaks us than that we speak it" (*Sprache uns spricht, als daß wir sie sprechen* [1975: 421]).

If language is a world, then translation of a text is not a mechanical task but a mode of understanding (*Verstehen*), an experience of entering an alien world. When this world is penetrated and the text is fully understood, "we have, not translation, but speech" (1982: 346)—a complete and natural conversation between text and interpreter such that the text ceases to be an object and becomes part of the world of the interpreter. However, this kind of union—what Gadamer terms an "I-thou" relationship between interpreter and text—is never complete, for the text is always alien (1982: 430–31). Owing to the alien and abstracted character of the text, interpretation is a "secondary" endeavor, compared to the immediacy of communication between conversationalists or between poet and audience, but interpretation can approach such immediacy.

Understanding of art and of language—symbolic forms—epitomizes the kind of understanding central to the human sciences. Within this kind of understanding, Gadamer is especially concerned with the interpretation of texts, which is the task of hermeneutics.

Historical consciousness. History necessarily enters hermeneutics. Temporal distance always separates interpreter from text. Gadamer has in mind classical texts from the distant past, but inasmuch as a text must first exist in order to call forth interpretation, all texts are from the past in relation to their interpretations. And both text and interpretation exist in history.

Interpretation must work through the interpreter's "foremeanings" (*Vorbegriffen*) to apperceive "the things themselves" (*auf die Sachen selber*). Such a process is dialectical. Interpreters "project" (*entwerfen*) meanings for the text, then revise these projections—which of course entail foremeanings—as they penetrate more deeply. Such a process entails the interpreters' examination of both text and foremeanings (1982: 237; 1975: 251). The tension between these two means that interpreters will have "the experience of being pulled up short by the text" (1982: 237) as it violates their foremeanings. Such an experience forces them to "make them [the foremeanings] conscious, so as to check them and thus acquire right understanding from the things themselves" (1982: 239).

Foremeanings are not simply personal; more important, they are cultural. They embody tradition. To recognize one's foremeanings autobiographically is insufficient, perhaps even irrelevant, for a merely subjective understanding of one's foremeanings fails to recognize their "determination by the great historical realities of society and state. . . . History does not belong to us, but we belong to it" (1982: 245).

Prejudice (*Vorurteile*) is an aspect of foremeanings embodying tradition. To fail to recognize the role of prejudice in understanding is a flaw in rationalism; Gadamer criticizes the Enlightenment, whose "fundamental prejudice is the prejudice against prejudice itself" (1982: 240). Prejudice is not entirely unreasonable, for it is part of tradition, which entails the reasonable act of preservation (1982: 250). Gadamer rejects the antithesis between tradition, prejudice, and reason. Since understanding entails projection, one can only arrive at understanding by working through one's prejudices. Applying this argument to history, Gadamer rejects historicism. Historicism, as proposed in the Enlightenment, would set aside the prejudices of the present in order to reconstruct the past in its own terms. This, Gadamer asserts, is impossible. One can only reconstruct the past in terms of the present. Gadamer's argument also leads him to reject an antithesis between tradition and method. Instead, "the effect of a living tradition and the effect of historical study must constitute a unity" (1982: 251). What is the nature of this unity?

One aspect is in the process of understanding. Understanding is not to be thought of so much as a method of analysis but as "the placing of oneself within a process of tradition, in which past and present are constantly fused" (1982: 259). One does not dissect the text as an object, one surrenders to it, entering its world and joining that world to one's own. Such a process may sound mystical, but Gadamer insists that it entails "not a mysterious communion of souls, but a sharing of common meaning" (1982: 260). On the other hand, he asserts that this is not just a "method" but is "ontological" (1982: 261); that is, the process of understanding is itself a mode of being.

Present circumstances, which include tradition that preserves a past, affect understanding of a text, but understanding of a text also affects present circumstances. Interpretation alters the interpreter. Interpretation is itself part of history and affects history. These considerations lead Gadamer to emphasize that consciousness has historicity. He speaks of "historically effective consciousness" or "consciousness in which history is ever at work" (*Wirkungsgeschichtliche Bewußtsein* [1982: 249]). As part of such historical consciousness, understanding entails "thrownness"— it is thrown into time, being oriented to both past and future.

In joining their own historical consciousness to the meaning of texts, interpreters draw on experience—an openness to the "thou" of the text and to the "pain of growth and new understanding" (1982: 338). Yet interpretation is not empathy with the subjectivity of the other any more than it is a preoccupation with the subjectivity of the interpreters. The meaning of a text goes beyond its author (1982: 264); it is determined by "the objective course of history," just as the subjectivity of its interpreter is so determined. Accordingly, the joining of meanings that relates text and interpretation is not a union of the subjectivities of author and interpreter. Rather, it is a fusion of two historically determined worlds, two "horizons" in which personal meanings are only a small element.

If interpretation entails the fusion of two histories, then a framework more encompassing than either is required. Gadamer says interpretation requires "a higher universality that overcomes not only our own particularity but also that of the other" (1982: 272). Rather mystically, he asserts further that "it is the pantheistic enclosing of all individuality within the absolute that makes possible the miracle of understanding" (1982: 306). More empirically, he reasons on the basis of the hermeneutical circle—that one can understand a part only in terms of the whole, and vice versa—that history can only be universal, for we must comprehend detail in terms of the whole (1982: 176). However the argument is phrased, the direction is apparent; it would move interpretation away from the particularities of the worlds of text and interpretation, author and interpreter, toward a consideration of a frame that makes sense of both worlds.

Applications and Implications

We move now to consider Gadamer in relation to the Indonesian example. This exercise has several implications. Most broadly, Gadamer exemplifies the hermeneutical approach, which has recently gained considerable influence in sociocultural anthropology and ethnography, as well as in other social sciences and humanistic disciplines. An important emphasis of this approach is consideration of the observer or analyst in what is being observed or analyzed. Within the so-called first-person ethnographies (see Marcus 1980; Clifford 1983), for example, the ethnographer is treated as part of the ethnography—the messenger as part of the message, the data gatherer as part of the data. With respect to symbols through time, the concern of this book, this hermeneutical emphasis is brought to bear by Gadamer on the specific question of history; he leads us to ask about the place of the ethnographer as he or she extends the interpretive act through time. But before addressing Gadamer's approach to history, we need to ask the more general question of whether he is relevant to ethnography. If so, we can then explore the relevance of his kind of hermeneutics for ethnography applied historically.

Gadamer's aims appear to differ radically from those of ethnography. Gadamer claims to set forth an ontology rather than simply a method. Ethnography is conventionally considered a method. Yet ethnographers have long sensed that ethnography is difficult to treat as a method after the fashion of survey or experimental methods, for example. Ethnography is more than simply a procedure for gathering data; it is, in fact, difficult to outline as a procedure—a fact that confuses and frustrates scientists accustomed to research proposals that more readily outline procedures. What Gadamer identifies about the hermeneutical approach—that it is ontology as well as method—may in fact help identify the place of ethnography in intellectual history.

A second apparent difference between Gadamer's approach and ethnography is that for him the object of study is the text—or at least this is the metaphor he prefers in characterizing the object. Ethnography has traditionally referred to the object of study in terms that emphasize living rather than codified qualities—terms such as behavior or way of life. Attempts to draw direct analogies between ethnography and hermeneutics by treating "culture as text" (Geertz 1972: 36) have been illuminating but also distorting in that the analogy accentuates the intellectual and literary aspect of human experience at the expense of emotional and behavioral aspects. For the ethnographer of symbols, however, the metaphor of the text is a telling one. What Clifford Geertz's equation of culture and text accomplished was to strengthen anthropologists' appreciation of the symbolic aspects of experience so that they could open their discipline to the insights of literary criticism and other humanistic approaches to the symbol as a balance against the influence of positivistic approaches. We need not, as Geertz does, speak of culture as an "acted document" (1973: 10), thus drawing a direct parallel between culture and text. We need only recognize that texts join other phenomena as members of the category of symbolic forms—those efforts of humans to objectify consciousness, to distill from existence meaning that is expressed through some kind of crystallized form, of which verbal texts are one instance. Gadamer's textual focus is not, then, so foreign to ethnography.

A third apparent difference is that the distance between the interpreter and the object of interpretation envisioned by Gadamer is temporal while that envisioned by ethnography is cultural. But the issue of whether the distance is temporal, cultural, or both is less crucial than the larger principle, that there is distance. Again, Gadamer and ethnography are parallel.

Once the analogy to ethnography is made, much of Gadamer's philosophy is so similar to ethnographic common sense as hardly to bear repeating. The alienation of object from interpretation, the influence of foremeanings, the hermeneutical circle, the task of translation— these are all commonplace in the ethnographic experience, though identified with different terminologies and examples. What Gadamer adds is a principled analysis of the study of history. Ethnographers, such as myself, are bound to construct history through the lenses of their ethnographic experiences; if we use texts, we necessarily perceive them in terms of our experience with the living culture that produced or inherited such forms. To accentuate this point, I have restricted my own illustrative construction of Indonesian history to events that were part of my ethnographic experience in a direct way: they happened when I was there. Through this restriction I hope to explore directly the process by which the ethnography of symbols can be translated into an ethnographic history of symbols.

Gadamer reminds us that both the interpretation and the object of interpretation are located in history and that our task is to grasp the unity of these two historical configurations. To do this is to understand, yet the understanding is not given to us as a method but as an ontology. Gadamer does not tell us how to understand in the sense of setting forth a procedure; rather, he elucidates the nature of this experience of understanding once it is done.

Ludruk depicts social mobility by the lower class. Muhammadijah embodies a puritan ethic of the middle class. Sumarah distills cosmic and personal harmony for the upper class. The three forms and their contexts can be taken not only as symbolizing three rungs in the Javanese social ladder but as representing three phases in modern Indonesian history. Such is the "objective" pattern. Obviously, this pattern, though confirmable to a degree through data, is not entirely objective but is a product jointly of the interpreter's foremeanings and the thing itself. Following Gadamer's guidance, what kinds of relationships can we discern between this pattern and the horizons guiding the interpretation? I will not detail my intellectual history here, nor attempt a psychoanalytical introspection. Gadamer appears to advise against it, on the grounds that larger cultural forces are more significant than personal idiosyncrasies in constituting the horizons of the interpreter: Hermeneutics need not transform ethnography into autobiography.

It is also true that the symbols interpreted here are not as personal as one's dreams but are instead the creations of another culture and its history. Ludruk is still performed, even though my fieldwork is long finished. Muhammadijah still flourishes without my presence. Writing in the ethnographic present, I sometimes feel that the phenomenon studied existed only when I was there, so it is useful to be reminded of the obvious—that it goes on without me. What is true historically—that the symbolic form is independent of the ethnographer—is also true in situ. Ludruk was played to an audience, not to me; Muhammadijah had to operate under constraints—economic, governmental, theological, aesthetic—that transcended any my presence might have imposed.

In sorting out the influence of observer on observed, one should perhaps distinguish among the kinds of symbolic forms observed. When the form is the product of a dialogue between interviewer and interviewed, the influence of the interviewer is doubtless great; this point is cogently made by Vincent Crapanzano (1980) in his study of his relationship to the Moroccan Tuhami, a set of dialogues resulting in a jointly constructed life history. When the form is the product of large numbers of actors of which the ethnographer is only one, the ethnographer's influence should not be exaggerated. The comparison bears on the "first-person ethnographies" that endeavor to achieve a Gadamerian aim of joining the horizons of interpreter and object of interpretation by a confessional mode. Native acts and utterances are

seen as heavily influenced by the presence or viewpoint of ethnographers; hence ethnographers should reveal their background and
ideology—perhaps even their personal dispositions—so they can be
taken into account (Marcus 1980; Clifford, 1983; the personal emphasis is strongest in Riesman 1977). This is a necessary corrective
to the falsely positivistic style of older ethnographies. Still, the extent
to which the ethnographer needs to be factored in seems to vary with
the type of study: less, perhaps, in studies of collective performances
and movements like that of the ludruk and Muhammadijah than in
interviews like those between Crapanzano and Tuhami.

Whatever foremeanings would require elucidation in order to il-
luminate my interpretations of each of these forms, the primary interest here is with the construction of history; this I attempt by a
chronological-sociological juxtaposition of all three forms: ludruk,
Muhammadijah, and Sumarah.

Sequence: symbols through TIME. The chronology—ludruk to
Muhammadijah to Sumarah—is somewhat arbitrary from the standpoint of Indonesian history in that all three forms existed during all
three periods of my fieldwork. Gadamer would presumably admon-
ish me to ask, then, why this particular order was chosen. Two answers must be given. The first explains why each form was selected
for study at the time of fieldwork. The second explains why this sequence is selected for presentation now. The first answer entails introspective recollection. I was aware of all three forms before I began
fieldwork in 1962, for they are well-known representatives of the
three major strata of Javanese society that had already been noted by
Geertz (1960) and other observers. While doing fieldwork in
1962–63, I encountered all three tangentially. Why did I then choose
ludruk as the form for my 1962 study?—because the early 1960's featured Sukarnoism and his postrevolutionary mass-cultural fervor,
which attracted me. By 1970, on the other hand, the bourgeois new
order was on the rise and the reformist Muslims were attempting to
make a comeback, hence the appeal of Muhammadijah. One reason
to focus on each form was simply that its time had apparently come.

One can imagine other reasons. Was it accidental that a student
should focus on the lower class (1962), an assistant professor on the
middle class (1970), and a department head on the upper class
(1979)? I insist that this correlation is spurious. However, a system-

atic study of the relation between interpreter and object viewed historically should explore the question of such a correlation between the interpreter's life history and the object's history.

As for the explanation of why this particular sequence is presented now, the simple answer is that it follows the chronology of the fieldwork. But while the chronology of the fieldwork is given, my interpretation is not. To see Indonesian history as progressing from mass culture to restricted sects to personal search is neat but not necessary. Gadamer imagines one text with one author who, as a vessel for tradition, determines its arrangement. We encounter three forms that have many anonymous authors. Given the multiplicity of forms and the multiplicity and anonymity of the authors, the interpretation of the forms, including their arrangement into a sequence, is heavily determined by the interpreter—however much he may reflect (or refract) the culture history that produced these forms.

In Gadamer's terms, does such an interpretation sufficiently "surrender to the text"? In fact, the procedure is closer to structuralism or functionalism than to Gadamer; I isolate parts, then relate them according to logical or functional pattern, rather than becoming absorbed in the meaning of a single form. My structuralist/functionalist procedure is more analytic and manipulative than Gadamer's "understanding" of a text through constructing its particular experiential world.

Perhaps this contrast is overdrawn. I did not simply construct a chronological arrangement; instead, the meaning of that chronology is "read" by imputing to it a perceived trend in native history. The arranging is simply one way of reading that trend and its meaning. Nevertheless, the way of reading is different from that pictured by Gadamer. Instead of only two variables—text and reader—one has several: reader or ethnographer plus three texts or forms. Instead of a dialogue between reader and text, one has comparisons among forms—mediated by the reader, to be sure, but nevertheless shifting the emphasis away from the interplay of reader and text to that among texts themselves. If objectivity is not restored, at least the interplay between object and subject is rendered more complex through the addition of diachrony.

Forms: SYMBOLS through time. If symbols objectify consciousness, and if consciousness is historical, then symbols themselves embody history. The embodiment is explicit when Muhammadijans re-count their history, implicit when ludruk satirizes old forms within the framework of new, or vice versa, or a civil servant confessing at a Sumarah meeting epitomizes changes in the new order. Symbols construct histories. Time passes through symbols just as certainly as symbols pass through time.

The symbol sums up a world. Gadamer would emphasize this when speaking of the text, but it is also true of the world of the in-terpreter. Yet we speak as though interpreters bring to a particular symbol not their own symbols but a more abstract consciousness: concepts, attitudes, prejudices. Symbolic images of the thing itself are noted more often in religious visions than in science, though they are known there too. Gadamer asserts that understanding is not merely method but ontology—a mode of being. Perhaps symbolizing, as op-posed to conceptualizing, is a way for the analyst to shift from method to ontology.

Paradoxes are apparent in Gadamer's search for truth as opposed to method. He would draw away from science because it alienates interpreter from object. Yet much of Gadamer's advice would itself lead toward detachment, as is apparent in his interest in both symbols (for him, texts) and history.

We focus on symbols because they represent worlds; they are forms that distill meanings. Yet the forms are sufficiently detached from their contexts to supposedly be grasped in isolation—we can appre-ciate buildings without knowing their builders, paintings without knowing their painters, texts without knowing their authors. The un-derstanding of such forms is pursued in splendid isolation from living human creators and contexts; one contemplates forms, rather than becoming socially engaged. In this sense, Gadamer's focus—cultur-ological rather than sociological, symbolic rather than behavioral—encourages detachment in a way opposed to the ethnographic par-ticipant observation, even though Gadamer eschews the analytic de-tachment that is also identified with ethnography. Ethnographers' move in Gadamer's direction—toward a certain detachment—is ap-parent in the choice of symbolic forms as a way of embodying social forces.

A historical viewpoint also leads to detachment. This is obviously true when past is separated from present and when events are arranged in a sequence. To comprehend three forms requires a more comprehensive framework than to comprehend one. Inasmuch as constructing such an overarching framework requires detachment from the horizon of any one form, the kind of "surrender to the text" that Gadamer favors is lost through historiography.

Immediacy is partly regained when figures from one's past invade one's present—something not possible except in fantasy when the past under consideration is distant, as Gadamer imagines it. For the fieldworker this is possible; to leave the field does not necessarily mean it cannot follow. A son and a grandson of the family with whom I lived in Surabaya in 1962 now live in Durham, North Carolina, fifteen minutes away from my home. A Javanese teacher who was a friend of a friend in Yogyakarta has come to Chapel Hill, North Carolina, to study William Faulkner, giving body to old musings about parallels between Java and the South (Peacock 1981). These reentries, however restricted, of Javanese existence into my own existence reignite the struggle to encounter the other in terms of my own horizon, however conveniently that struggle is set aside in separating past from present.

Despite such ignitions, the sort of historical interpretation that ethnographers do remains method; only romantically can it be considered ontology. To whatever limited extent the sort of analysis presented here merges the horizons of the other and the interpreter, the process is very much controlled by the interpreter. The forms may, in fact, still flourish, but in the analysis they are dead and gone, by logical necessity. Conceivably we could resurrect them by applying their insights, as believers apply scriptures or lawyers legal documents; I do this obliquely, in teaching, in lecturing to the laity, even here, in this conventional ethnographic genre of writing for colleagues, this form of programmatic didactics. But here too it is the interpreter who controls the application, rather than the native Indonesians, who were the source.

In sum, a Gadamerian approach would indeed emphasize both symbols and time: a model for the interpretation of symbolic forms in relation to history. The most distinctive aspect of this approach is the emphasis on truth rather than on method, on understanding through a merging of the horizons of text and interpreter. As illustrated by this Indonesian example, even this kind of merging implies a degree of detachment.

Acknowledgments

I gratefully acknowledge comments by participants in the Wenner-Gren Conference "Symbolism Through Time," at Fez, Morocco, January 13–20, 1986, for which this essay was prepared, and by my colleagues Terence Evens and Steven Klein. I am also grateful to the Wenner-Gren Foundation and especially to Lita Osmundsen and Emiko Ohnuki-Tierney for their excellent work in organizing the conference and to Lita Osmundsen and Wenner-Gren for generous support and many kindnesses over the years.

IO

Historians, Anthropologists, and Symbols

PETER BURKE

History and Anthropology

In central London in the 1960's, two seminars dealing with problems of symbolism used to take place a few hundred yards apart while more or less ignoring each other's existence. Anthropologists frequented Mary Douglas's seminar at University College, in Malet Street, while historians of different kinds met at the Warburg Institute, in Woburn Place. Both the contiguity and the separation of the two seminars seem in retrospect to symbolize the relation between the two disciplines at that time, so near and yet so far. Yet this situation was beginning to change in Britain and elsewhere. The Association of Social Anthropologists held a conference at Edinburgh in 1966 on the theme "History and Anthropology" (Lewis 1968). Two studies in the history of English witchcraft, both heavily influenced by anthropology, appeared in 1970 and 1971 (Macfarlane 1970; Thomas 1971). On the continent of Europe and in the United States, a similar rapprochement between the two disciplines was under way. The present book represents one such encounter.

Like others, it reveals both convergences and divergences between historians and anthropologists, as well as raising awkward questions about the nature of culture and symbols and especially the modes in which, and the reasons for which, symbols change. The convergences of the last twenty years or so are obvious enough and may be illustrated by the increasing employment of the label historical anthropology to refer to a body of work that is of relevance to both disciplines (and indeed to others). The divergences between anthropologists interested in history (let us call them historical anthropologists) and historians interested in anthropology ("anthropological historians") have not received so much attention. In this relationship, each partner is attracted by an image of the other that the other finds difficult to accept. In the 1960's, for example, some historians previously unacquainted with the language of social function turned with enthusiasm to Emile Durkheim and Bronisław Malinowski, only to learn from their colleagues in anthropology departments that "we don't believe in all that any more."[1] In the 1980's, Anthropologyland, as it has been called, attracts historians partly because it allows them to practice description (as thick as possible) rather than narrative at just the moment that anthropologists are discovering the virtues of telling a story (it would be my turn to say, "We don't believe in that any more," were it not for what some historians call the "revival of narrative" [Cohn 1980; Stone 1979]). The two disciplines may, like two trains, be traveling past one another at high speed merely to change places. However, attempts at revival and at borrowing generally produce something unintended and unexpected, something new. A more appropriate as well as a more hopeful image of the encounter between history and anthropology might be that of the Japanese artists of the late nineteenth century who discovered and adapted to their own purposes the work of Toulouse-Lautrec and his contemporaries, apparently without realizing that this exotic Western art had itself been inspired by Japan.[2]

What is it that anthropologists and historians want from one another? From my own perspective as a practicing historian, the anthropologists' historical turn seems as simple as it is necessary: they obviously want to escape the limitations of the static analyses of the functionalists and of the structuralists who replaced them. On the other hand, the historians' anthropological turn seems to me not only the right thing to do at this point but also a complex, indeed a paradoxical maneuver. A group of people who define themselves as specialists in the past, often the remote past, somehow claims to draw inspiration from the work of another group that concentrates on, indeed writes in, the ethnographic present. Some historians of medieval and Renaissance Europe (myself included) study and cite monographs on remote parts of Asia and Africa, from Bali to Zandeland.

[1] Conversation at the University of Sussex between the author and Professor Freddy Bailey, circa 1966.

[2] I am thinking in particular of the work of Takeji Fujishima and Hanjiro Sakamoto. Cf. Smith 1983, nos. 8–9, 11–12.

What is it that has made anthropology so attractive to them? It is a combination of features, rather than a single trait; different aspects of anthropology appeal to different groups of historians at different moments (see Davis 1981). For cultural historians, the great value of anthropology is that this body of published work helps them first to notice and then to comprehend the "otherness" of the past. The knowledge of other cultures is of assistance in the opposite but complementary processes of defamiliarization and refamiliarization. In the first place, a knowledge of other cultures helps historians to view what is normally taken for granted as problematic, as requiring explanation, and thus to escape from what has been called "home blindness" (Löfgren 1981). In the second place, it helps them to solve the problem of cultural distance and "capture otherness" by placing it in a comparative context (Darnton 1984: 4).

For social historians, whose interest in anthropology is more recent, it offers a model for the study of small-scale communities in depth. In the 1950's and 1960's, social historians, following the example of their colleagues in economic history and sociology, tended to be concerned with the description of large-scale trends (urbanization, social mobility, and so on) on the basis of statistical data. The trouble with these homogenized descriptions was that they ironed out regional variation and failed to communicate any sense of the individual's experience of social change. The rise in the 1970's of what is now known as microhistory was a reaction to the defects of this approach. The remedy was to follow the lead of the social anthropologists and to focus on a community, as Le Roy Ladurie did in his *Montaillou*, or even on an individual person, such as Ginzburg's Menocchio.[3]

Social and cultural historians alike are becoming increasingly aware of the importance of symbolism in material culture and daily life. One recent illustration of this awareness is Robert Darnton's (1984) analysis of an incident in an eighteenth-century Paris printing

[3] Le Roy Ladurie (1975), citing as his model Ronald Blythe's *Akenfield*, an amateur community study of a Suffolk village; Ginzburg 1976. Ginzburg, in his introduction, presents his work as an attempt to undermine the history of mentalities practiced by the French. However, other works in the same series, edited by Ginzburg under the title of *Microstoria*, concentrate on social history, like Raul Merzario's study of "matrimonial strategies" in the diocese of Como, or F. Ramelli's monograph on weaving in a Piedmontese valley in the nineteenth century.

shop in which the apprentices carried out mock executions of a number of cats, including the favorite grey cat of their master's wife, a symbolic substitute for herself. Another recent example is Simon Schama's (1987) description of Dutch culture (in the wide, anthropological sense of the term *culture*) in the seventeenth century in which, following Durkheim and Mary Douglas, he interprets the notorious cleanliness of Dutch houses as one of the chief symbols of national identity.

The Study of Symbols

What is the relevance of this recent encounter between history and anthropology to the study of symbols? A short and simple answer to this question might be that anthropologists, having shown historians the importance and pervasiveness of symbolism, are learning from them to take change over time more seriously, not only from generation to generation but also over the long term.[4] A more precise and complex answer to the same question would have to extend well beyond two modern academic disciplines to include, at the very least, theology, philosophy, psychology, art history, and literary criticism. It would also have to go back much further than the 1960's.

In Western Europe, awareness of changes in symbols over time is not new. Systematic attempts to write the history of symbol systems go back at least as far as the early nineteenth century. The context in which these attempts were made was a religious crisis. One reaction to the Enlightenment critique of Christianity as myth was to present religious doctrines as symbolically rather than literally true and to argue that they were none the worse for that. As Schelling put it, myth has its own mode of reality. D. F. Strauss's *Life of Jesus* (1835), notorious in its own day, has become a classic example of this approach.

Robertson Smith, J. G. Frazer, and Lucien Lévy-Bruhl—writers on symbolism who have an important place in the history of anthropology, whether they are venerated or scorned—owe something to the eighteenth-century critics of Christianity and something to the Romantic reaction against those critics. From one group they learned to compare the symbol systems of medieval Christians with those of

---

[4]Lisón Tolosana 1966 includes an exemplary study of generations. Sahlins 1981 is an example of anthropological awareness of Braudel's ideas about the long term.

"savages"; from the other, to take symbolism seriously and to examine its change (especially its evolution) over time. Their ideas were important not only for the small group of people who then called themselves anthropologists but also for a larger circle of early-twentieth-century scholars who were working on the history of symbolism.

Many of these scholars were not historians in the professional sense of the term (a fact that should not surprise us, since the discipline of history was still dominated by the Ranke paradigm, according to which political events are the only fit subject for research). They included classical scholars and philosophers as well as specialists in art and literature. Their work was extremely diverse, and it was carried out in a number of different countries, including Germany, the Netherlands, France, Britain, and Russia.

What held it together was a common concern for a body of ideas formulated most clearly and explicitly by Lévy-Bruhl, whose "influence" (a clumsy term that I use as an umbrella to cover *model*, *catalyst*, and even *provocation*) deserves to be studied in detail. His name appears, for example, in the footnotes of studies as diverse as Jane Harrison on Greek religion (1912), Johan Huizinga on the later Middle Ages (1919), P. M. Bitsilli on medieval Russia (1919), Marc Bloch on the healing touch of medieval kings (1923), and Ernst Cassirer on mythical thought (1925)—to say nothing of the work of the psychologists Curt Koffka and Jean Piaget. Huizinga, for example, noted similarities between medieval and primitive thought and contrasted two mentalities, the "symbolic" and "causal" (or genetic), which according to him succeeded one another in the course of time.

The Cambridge of Jane Harrison and her fellow classicist Francis M. Cornford (author of *Thucydides Mythistoricus*) seems to have been a favorable milieu for this rethinking of the history of symbolism. So was the Strasbourg of Marc Bloch and his friend Lucien Febvre, who turned in the 1930's to the history of mentalities. Most important of all was Hamburg, the home not only of Cassirer but also of Erwin Panofsky, whose first important book dealt with perspective as "symbolic form"; of Percy Schramm, who devoted his life to the study of royal rituals and symbols in the Middle Ages; and of the master of them all, Aby Warburg, whose central concern was the history of the classical tradition but whose interests extended to anthropology (he learned to understand the Dionysiac element in the culture of ancient Greece by observing the serpent rituals of the Indians of Arizona and New Mexico).[5]

My reason for recalling the early twentieth century at this point is not just that it is good to be aware of one's ancestors: I believe that the promise of the 1920's was not completely fulfilled. Something went wrong. Lévy-Bruhl was not of course an ideal model for historians to follow, but the weakness in his description of "primitive mentality" was not the real problem.[6] The studies of symbolism that these groups produced were impressive in many ways, but they were, generally speaking, lacking in what might be called local or social depth. They emphasized grand trends over time, over the long term, at the expense of the local cultural, social, and political context. These defects are most obvious in the work of Cassirer and Panofsky, as in the tradition of *Geistesgeschichte* to which they owed so much.[7] They are also noticeable, however, in Huizinga, despite the seventeenth chapter of his *Waning of the Middle Ages*, which emphasizes the relation between mentalities and everyday life ("de Denkvormen in het praktische leven"). Marc Bloch and Aby Warburg, whose slogan was the divinity of detail ("Der liebe Gott steckt im Detail"), were more sharply aware of local context, but their example was not often followed.

In practice, most historians—not only in the 1920's but as late as the 1960's—virtually ignored symbolism, while some were literal-minded enough to use phrases like "mere ritual" and to find it rather odd that a schism should have developed in seventeenth-century Russia over questions such as whether to bless with two fingers or three, or that Louis XIV should have been able to reduce the French nobility to a "purely symbolic" role by creating Versailles. Those scholars who wrote on the history of symbol systems usually did so, whatever their discipline, without local or social depth. For their part, the anthropologists of the period who placed symbols in their social settings generally lacked historical depth. Fieldwork methods, no less than functionalist theory, militated against it. Even E. E. Evans-

[5] On Panofsky and Cassirer see Holly 1984. On Schramm see Bak 1973. On Warburg see Warburg 1939; Gombrich 1970.

[6] For traps into which Lévy-Bruhl led some historians, see Burke 1986.

[7] For a critique of Cassirer in these terms, see Lefort 1972, esp. p. 199. The work of Panofsky most vulnerable to this kind of criticism is his *Gothic Architecture and Scholasticism* (1951).

Pritchard—for all his interest in history—did not integrate it into his study of symbolism among the Azande.

The situation began to change in the 1960's, but the problem of combining historical with local or social depth has not disappeared. The late Victor Turner, for example, began his career with meticulous ethnographies of the Ndembu in the present and ended by making excursions into a broad comparative history of ritual, but he did not spend much time exploring the middle ground. Meanwhile, the historians' train has been proceeding in the opposite direction. They have discovered the pleasures and the insights of microhistory. The leading microhistorians—Emmanuel Le Roy Ladurie, Carlo Ginzburg, Natalie Davis, Rhys Isaac, Giovanni Levi—are well acquainted with social anthropology, and they have learned from Geertz, Turner, and others to place symbols in social context. They have not neglected change over time.

However, the concern with microhistory amounts, in many cases, to an evasion of what is perhaps the most important as well as the most difficult problem in history and anthropology alike, that of linking what is happening at a particular moment at the local level to the major trends in world history discussed by sociologists and historians in the Marxian and Weberian traditions. In the study of symbol making as in the study of other human activities, combining the microhistorical and macrohistorical approaches is surely necessary. The recent work of Marshall Sahlins on Oceania, and in particular on Hawaii (1981, 1985), offers an exemplary discussion of the relation between social and cultural change at the macrolevel, the level of capitalism and the World System, and at the microlevel, the level of the event and the local "cultural order." In other areas, however, a synthesis of this kind is sadly lacking.

Two Moments in the History of Symbols

To encourage such a synthesis, it may be useful (however temerarious) to make a few general macrohistorical points about changing attitudes to symbols in Western Europe since the end of the Middle Ages, points that can serve as some kind of framework for future local studies. In any case, these attitudes or assumptions underlie the approaches to symbols of twentieth-century Western anthropologists and historians. For example, Huizinga's influential account of late medieval symbolism is far from value free. Huizinga was at once fascinated and repelled by a culture in which, to quote one of his most famous examples, a man might cut his apple into three parts in honor of the Holy Trinity. He described the religious devotion of the late Middle Ages as "mechanical," taking over this term of contempt, without apparently noticing that he was doing so, from Erasmus and the Protestant reformers of the sixteenth century. It may be worth adding that Huizinga was descended from a long line of Protestant ministers.

This brief sketch will concentrate on two moments, the 1520's and the 1650's. The first is the moment of the Protestant Reformation, which was, among other things, a powerful critique of the symbol system of the traditional church. What might be called the practical criticism of the iconoclasts, such as Andrea von Karlstadt and Huldrych Zwingli, was accompanied by theoretical argument about idolatry.[8] The reformers made the point that in this sphere as in others the good old practices of the early or "primitive" church had been changed or corrupted in the course of the Middle Ages and that objects were receiving the devotion due solely to what they represented.[9] Martin Luther, Zwingli, and others discussed the problems of interpreting the term *is* in Jesus' words "This is my body," *Hoc est corpus meum*, arguing that these words had been taken far too literally in recent centuries. Zwingli was prepared to argue that the sacraments were mere rituals, lacking efficacy in themselves and performed simply as a commemoration of past events.

The reformers were not, of course, the first people to see symbols as problematic. As they well knew, there had been an iconoclastic controversy in Byzantium long before. The scholastic philosophers had devoted much energy to discussing the relationship between words and things, and Luther's studies with the nominalist Gabriel Biel were far from irrelevant to his later activities as a reformer. All the same, we may say that in the 1520's, a religious crisis both expressed and encouraged awareness of the complexities of the relation

[8] There is a substantial literature on Reformation iconoclasm. For overviews, see Freedberg 1977 and Eire 1986.

[9] Whether or not they were correct in this historical analysis is a question marginal to this essay, but one that has received some attention from anthropologically minded historians, notably Trexler 1972 and Bynum 1987, which notes the "late medieval concern with matter and physicality," notably in the cult of the Host (p. 252).

between words, images, and rituals and the spiritual reality they were supposed to symbolize. This relation might well be the focus for a future study of the anthropology of the Reformation.[10]

Clifford Geertz has floated the concept of "congruity" to describe the not uncommon situation where a society changes while its symbol system remains the same, long enough at any rate for some people to feel that the traditional symbols are empty of meaning (Geertz 1973; cf. Rabinow 1975). In this way he is able to link the observation of a microevent, a funeral in a town in Java, with a general discussion of social change. As an early modern historian, I find this idea of congruity an extremely helpful way of approaching the Reformation, which was, among other things, a crisis of symbolic representations in which emptiness was a charge frequently leveled against tradition by the reformers. All the same, the concept is not free from problems. What exactly is supposed to be incongruous with what? Does the concept imply the existence of a social infrastructure that changes first, to be followed, after a longer or shorter interval, by the superstructure? On the other hand, if symbols create social reality as much as they express it, how does perceived incongruity occur?

An alternative concept is that of the "invention of tradition," a concept itself invented by Eric Hobsbawm and one that has led to lively discussion among historians (Hobsbawm and Ranger 1983). It begs a lot of questions—about the nature of "genuine" traditions as opposed to invented ones; about the process of invention (conscious, unconscious, or something elusively in between); and about the situations in which invention takes place and the conditions under which it is acceptable, or at any rate accepted. All the same, it is a valuable corrective to what might be called traditional views of tradition as something handed down unchanging. The Reformation deserves to be reanalyzed in Hobsbawmian terms: in the first place, as a moment when Luther and others became aware of the conflict or discrepancy between the tradition of belief and worship they had inherited from the late Middle Ages and the older, "purer," more traditional tradition of the "primitive" church and, in the second place, as a time when spontaneous gestures of protest against corruption congealed or, as Paul Ricoeur would say, "sedimented" into a Protestant "tradition of the new" (1983–85).

[10] Swanson 1967 opens with a useful discussion of Reformation disputes about immanence.

The period around 1520 was an important moment in the history of European symbols and attitudes to symbols. The period around 1650 was another. Simplifying somewhat, as a brief account must, we might describe this second moment as a transition from a traditional worldview, in which symbols had an important place, to a modern worldview, in which their position is more ambiguous. This model is likely to remind anthropologists of Robin Horton's well-known account of changing worldviews in Africa (1967; cf. Horton 1982). Their sense of familiarity is hardly surprising, since Horton (like Michel Foucault in *The Order of Things*) drew, directly or indirectly, on a number of studies of intellectual change in the West written between the 1930's and the 1950's.[11] These studies contrast two images of the cosmos, two dominant metaphors. On one side is the traditional metaphor of the cosmos as an organism, a macrocosm corresponding to a microcosm, the "little world of man." On the other is the modern metaphor of the cosmos as a machine—the billiard-ball universe associated with Descartes. The metaphors describe a shift from a concrete, qualitative mode of thought to one more abstract and quantitative. Correspondences believed to be inscribed in things were replaced by analogies that were self-consciously subjective (Nicolson 1950: 108; cf. Harris 1966).

The "mechanization of the world picture," as Anneliese Maier and Dijksterhuis have called it, proved incompatible with traditional beliefs in magic. Educated Europeans found it increasingly difficult to believe that a man could cure the sick by touching them because he was a king or that an old woman could harm her neighbor by cursing him because she was a witch. The ruling class began to treat such beliefs as examples of popular credulity and superstition and as a confusion of the causal with the symbolic order. The disenchantment of the world necessarily involved a change in attitudes toward symbols (Huizinga had a point when he contrasted symbolic with causal thought). It was in the early modern period that educated Europeans first drew a firm distinction between what was real and efficacious on the one hand and what was "mere" symbol or ritual on the other.

The history of ritual has been studied rather less systematically than the changes in worldview. Douglas was surely wrong to assert

[11] Among the best-known of these studies are Willey 1934; Hazard 1935; Lovejoy 1936; Maier 1936; Dijksterhuis 1950; Nicolson 1950; Koyré 1957; Gouhier 1958.

that "ritual has always been something of a bad word" (1966). Ritual *became* a bad word in the course of the sixteenth, seventeenth, and eighteenth centuries. It was increasingly associated with the letter as opposed to the spirit, the shadow as opposed to the substance. Religious rituals were condemned on religious grounds by the pious (especially, but not exclusively, the Protestants) in the sixteenth century. Secular rituals, including modes of greeting, were rejected on religious grounds by the Quakers in the seventeenth century. The repudiation of ritual was reaffirmed by the worldly in the eighteenth century, this time on secular grounds, such as the need for spontaneity and sincerity (Burke 1987).

The change in attitudes toward witchcraft in the middle of the seventeenth century may be a useful example to discuss in a little more detail, since many anthropologists have written about witches and their work has inspired a number of historians (notably Thomas 1971). *Maleficium*, as it was called—doing harm by supernatural means, a charge brought against many witches—is a case of symbolic aggression. Burning or drowning witches was another symbolic act, the performance of a metaphor of purification (cf. Fernandez 1977). Another reason for choosing this example is that current controversies about the decline of trials for witchcraft in the course of the seventeenth century illustrate neatly both the actual clash and the potential compatibility between microsocial and macrosocial explanations.

In the late 1960's, two influential studies of witchcraft attributed its decline to major changes in European worldviews. Hugh Trevor-Roper's account of the end of what he called the European "witch-craze" attributed it to the rise of a "rival faith" in a mechanical universe and, in particular, in Cartesianism (1968: ch. 5). At much the same time, Robert Mandrou explained the decline of witch trials in France by a "new mental structure," a change in assumptions about the working of the universe in which it was no longer taken for granted that God and the devil made regular, direct interventions (1968: 554f).[12] In short, according to these historians, the skepticism about the efficacy of witchcraft was part of the major cultural trend that Max Weber long ago called "the disenchantment of the world."

A few years later, however, in a study of witchcraft trials in south-

---

[12] Paul Hazard had made similar suggestions a generation earlier.

western Germany, Erik Midelfort (1972) noted that the trials came to an end too soon, in the 1660's, for this kind of intellectual explanation of the decline to be satisfactory. His own view is that the decline of the trials in this region was in a sense the effect of their rise. The panic associated with mass trials "destroyed the trust in the tradition of magistrates and institutions that had permitted the hunts in the first place," while the magistrates themselves "lost faith in their judicial apparatus." This explanation is offered as an essentially local one.

How can we choose between the two kinds of explanation? Do we need to choose? Is it possible, or plausible, to combine them? This is what Keith Thomas did in his study of the English trials, suggesting that one explanation works for the ruling class, the other for ordinary people. The history of prosecutions in the courts "reflects the intellectual assumptions of the educated classes who controlled the machinery of the law courts," while the history of accusations, usually made by neighbors, "can only be explained in terms of the immediate social environment of the witch and her accuser" (1971: 583). A similar combination of local and general explanations was offered by William Monter in his account of the decline of witch trials in seventeenth-century Geneva, stressing the role played by a particular magistrate, Robert Chouet, who happened to be a Cartesian (Monter 1976: 37f, 61f). The case of witchcraft suggests that microsocial approaches by social historians and anthropologists are indeed compatible, at least on occasion, with the macrosocial emphases of sociologists and cultural historians of the traditional kind.

The Rise of Literal-Mindedness

The decline of witch trials and the repudiation of ritual were part of a much broader trend that I would like to call the rise of literal-mindedness. One day someone should write the history of this trend. Its protagonists include Martin Luther, Francis Bacon, Jeremy Bentham (a savage critic of "fictitious entities" such as the Crown, the Church, and the Law [1932]), Leopold von Ranke, and Herbert Spencer. Among the more important episodes in this long-running story are the Protestant emphasis on the literal interpretation of the Bible, the seventeenth-century scientists' dismissal of "occult" forces in nature, and the emphasis on realism and positivism in nineteenth-century philosophy, literature, sociology, and history ("what actually happened," "social facts," and all that).

If such a history were to be written, distinctions would of course have to be drawn. For example, some people seem to be more literal-minded than others in all periods, and the story told by Sir Thomas More about the priest who asked him how to get a benefice in Utopia has its twentieth-century British parallel in the radio listeners who write to the long-running pastoral drama *The Archers*, hoping to buy a house in its fictional location, Ambridge.

All the same, it does seem possible to discern major changes in attitudes to symbols over time. The Protestant reformers of the sixteenth century were literal-minded in their concentration on the literal meaning of the Bible, as opposed to its allegorical, analogical, moral, and other meanings (Caplan 1929). After the Council of Trent (1543–63), it was possible to find similar attitudes in Catholics as well. The cathedral chapter of Toledo objected to a painting they had commissioned from El Greco on the grounds that it represented the three Marys close to the tomb of Jesus, whereas the Bible described them as "far away." The theological opposition to Galileo argued that heliocentrism was incompatible with the literal interpretation of Scripture. In the field of biblical studies, the French Oratorian priest Richard Simon analyzed the Old Testament as a historical document, or rather, a collection of historical documents, in his *Histoire Critique du Vieux Testament* (1678; see Steinmann 1960). In the field of liturgical studies, the Benedictine abbot Claude de Vert (1706–13) rejected what he called "mystical" and "symbolic" interpretations of the rituals of the Mass and offered utilitarian and even functionalist explanations in their place. The thirteenth-century writer Guillaume Durand had suggested that lighted candles were placed on the altar because Christ is the light of the world. Vert dismissed this interpretation and explained that the custom follows the practice of the early Christians, who had used candles simply because they held their services at night.

Literal-mindedness has many achievements to its credit, from the steam engine to source criticism. It is hard to imagine how the systematic investigation of how (as opposed to why) things happen in the natural world could ever have developed without it, or indeed the systematic study of the past on the basis of documents. However, what might be called naïf realism and the repudiation of ritual, myth, and symbol associated with it create problems as well as solve problems.

In the first place, it creates political problems. The position of the king of France was politically weakened when people ceased to believe in the healing power of the royal touch, when the correspondence between the king's position in his kingdom and the sun's position in the cosmos came to be viewed as a mere analogy, and when the rituals of coronation and consecration could be described (as they were by members of the government in the 1770's) as a "futile game" (Haueter 1975: 339f). The French Revolution revealed the political danger of this demystification of the old regime.

One response to this problem was the invention of tradition (Hobsbawm and Ranger 1983).[13] The French revolutionaries themselves recognized the importance of what Jean Paul Marat once called the theater of the state. They created a number of new rituals, such as the Festival of the Federation and the Festival of the Supreme Being. They were well aware of what a recent historian has called the "symbolic forms of political practice," such as the tricolor cockade.[14] Indeed, the Revolution offers an excellent illustration of "the role of the sign in action" for historical anthropologists to study (Sahlins 1981). If the old regime had been lukewarm in its political devotions, the new regime was enthusiastic—a difference that could perhaps be explained in terms of the congruence between ritual and culture discussed above.

When the Bourbons were restored, so were their rituals. The ampulla, the container for the holy oil with which the kings of France were consecrated, had been solemnly, indeed ritually smashed by the revolutionaries in 1793, but it was put together again for the coronation of 1814 (Jackson 1984: 188–89). The clock of ceremony was put back. So was the clock of myth and symbol. The romantic medievalism of the early nineteenth century—Chateaubriand's *Génie du Christianisme*, for example, first published in 1802—was in part at least an attempt by writers and artists to reconstruct a symbolic world they had lost. Whether the clock of consciousness really could

[13] Hobsbawm himself emphasizes the importance of the late nineteenth century in this process; the examples that follow are intended to show that it has a longer history.

[14] This approach has been followed in recent historical studies on both sides of the Atlantic, such as Ozouf 1976 and Hunt 1984, ch. 2.

be put back is another matter. Today, Western Europeans (unlike the Tikopia or the Balinese, at least as these peoples are described in the anthropological classics) sometimes refuse to participate in rituals, sometimes perform them in an embarrassed or shamefaced way, and sometimes distance themselves from rituals while enjoying them as a survival or a peculiar custom that impresses visitors. Even if many people still take rituals seriously, even if television has to some extent remystified authority, a detached, indeed dismissive attitude toward ritual has become firmly rooted in Western culture.[15]

In the second place, literal-mindedness creates problems for historians, anthropologists, and other intellectuals today. Carlos Castaneda offered an engaging caricature of this mode of thought when he made his narrator ask Don Juan again and again, "Did I really fly? . . . I mean, did my body fly?" (1968: ch. 6). Literal-mindedness involves a kind of sophisticated incapacity to understand how other cultures can take symbols seriously—how medieval readers could enjoy allegories, for example, or how the Russian Old Believers could make such a fuss about blessing with two fingers or three. It also involves a more or less willful blindness to the presence of symbolic elements in works of history, anthropology, and other forms of what librarians call nonfiction. This blindness is particularly apparent among British historians, perhaps because they have swallowed a double dose of empiricism. Many of these historians still describe their task as presenting "the facts" and claim to see this task as intellectually unproblematic. They offer a strong resistance (in the literal as well as in the Freudian sense) to attempts to write the history of history and to suggestions (like Hayden White's) that historians employ rhetorical strategies, or that (as Edmund Leach likes to put it) historical writing is a form of myth (White 1973, 1987). They are generally blind to their own use of metaphors—the legal metaphors of detectives and judges, the hydrologist's metaphors of pure and contaminated sources, and so on.[16] The anthropology of history is only just visible on the horizon, and the craft is not crewed by historians.[17]

[15] This discussion follows the conclusion to my *Historical Anthropology* (see Burke 1987: 237–38).

[16] Among the rare studies of historians' metaphors are Barthes 1958 and Demandt 1978.

[17] Recommended in Sahlins 1985, it was the main theme of the conference of the Association of Social Anthropologists at Norwich in 1987.

This discussion of literal-mindedness raises large epistemological problems, problems that are not so much a conclusion of one paper as the opening of another. If there is an irreducibly mythical element in all historical writing, does anything go, are there no criteria for preferring one account or interpretation of the past to another? And what about the work of anthropologists? Is this also myth? Should there be an anthropology of anthropology, and if so, who would be qualified to write it?

References Cited

References Cited

1. Ohnuki-Tierney: Introduction

Bloch, Maurice
  1977   "The Past and the Present in the Present." *Man* 12 (2): 278–92.
Blu, Karen
  1980   *The Lumbee Problem: The Making of an American Indian People*. Cambridge: Cambridge Univ. Press.
Boon, James A.
  1977   *The Anthropological Romance of Bali, 1597–1972: Dynamic Perspectives in Marriage and Caste, Politics and Religion*. Cambridge: Cambridge Univ. Press.
Bourdieu, Pierre
  1982 [1972]   *Outline of a Theory of Practice*. Cambridge: Cambridge Univ. Press.
Bourdieu, Pierre, and Jean-Claude Passeron
  1977   *Reproduction: In Education, Society, and Culture*. London: Sage Publications.
Braudel, Fernand
  1980 [1958]   *On History*. Chicago: Univ. of Chicago Press.
Bucher, Bernadette
  1985   "An Interview with Claude Lévi-Strauss, 30 June 1982." *American Ethnologist* 12 (2): 360–68.
Clifford, James
  1983   "On Ethnographic Authority." *Representations* 1 (2): 118–46.
Cohn, Bernard S.
  1980   "History and Anthropology: The State of Play." *Comparative Studies in Society and History* 12: 198–221.
  1981   "Anthropology and History in the 1980's." *Journal of Interdisciplinary History* 12 (2): 227–52.

De Creamer, Willy, Jan Vansina, and Renée C. Fox

1976   "Religious Movements in Central Africa: A Theoretical Study." *Comparative Studies in Society and History* 18 (4): 458–75.

Errington, Shelly

1979   "Some Comments on Style in the Meanings of the Past." *Journal of Asian Studies* 38 (2): 231–44.

Fernandez, James W.

1982   *Bwiti: An Ethnography of the Religious Imagination in Africa.* Princeton: Princeton Univ. Press.

1986   *Persuasions and Performances: The Play of Tropes in Culture.* Bloomington: Indiana Univ. Press.

Furet, François

1972   "Quantitative History." In *Historical Studies Today*, ed. F. Gilbert and S. R. Graubard, 45–61. New York: Norton.

Geertz, Clifford

1973   *The Interpretation of Cultures.* New York: Basic Books.

1980   *Negara: The Theatre State in Nineteenth-Century Bali.* Princeton: Princeton Univ. Press.

1983   *Local Knowledge: Further Essays in Interpretive Anthropology.* New York: Basic Books.

1988   *Works and Lives: The Anthropologist as Author.* Stanford: Stanford Univ. Press.

Hobsbawm, Eric, and Terence Ranger, eds.

1986 [1983]   *The Invention of Tradition.* Cambridge: Cambridge Univ. Press.

Hunt, Eva

1977   *The Transformation of the Hummingbird.* Ithaca: Cornell Univ. Press.

Ingold, Tim

1986   *Evolution and Social Life.* Cambridge: Cambridge Univ. Press.

Leach, Edmund

1965 [1954]   *Political Systems of Highland Burma.* Boston: Beacon Press.

1967   "Virgin Birth." *Proceedings of the Royal Anthropological Institute* 1966: 39–49.

1982   *Social Anthropology.* Glasgow: Fontana Paperbacks.

Le Goff, Jacques

1972   "Is Politics Still the Backbone of History?" In *Historical Studies Today*, ed. F. Gilbert and S. R. Graubard, 337–55. New York: Norton.

Le Roy Ladurie, Emmanuel

1977   "Motionless History." *Social Science History* 1 (2): 115–36.

Lévi-Strauss, Claude
  1967 [1958] *Structural Anthropology.* New York: Doubleday.
  1983 [1976] *Structural Anthropology.* Vol. 2. Chicago: Univ. of Chicago
               Press.
Mintz, Sidney W.
  1986 [1985] *Sweetness and Power: The Place of Sugar in Modern His-
               tory.* New York: Viking.
Ohnuki-Tierney, Emiko
  1981   *Illness and Healing Among the Sakhalin Ainu.* Cambridge:
               Cambridge Univ. Press.
  1984   *Illness and Culture in Contemporary Japan: An Anthropolog-
               ical View.* Cambridge: Cambridge Univ. Press.
  1987   *The Monkey as Mirror: Symbolic Transformations in Japanese
               History and Ritual.* Princeton: Princeton Univ. Press.
Ortner, Sherry B.
  1984   "Theory in Anthropology Since the Sixties." *Comparative Stud-
               ies in Society and History* 26 (1): 126–66.
Ricoeur, Paul
  1980   *The Contribution of French Historiography to the Theory of
               History.* Oxford: Oxford Univ. Press, Clarendon Press.
Sahlins, Marshall
  1976   *Culture and Practical Reason.* Chicago: Univ. of Chicago Press.
  1981   *Historical Metaphors and Mythical Realities: Structure in the
               Early History of the Sandwich Islands Kingdom.* Ann Arbor:
               Univ. of Michigan Press.
  1983   "Distinguished Lecture: Other Times, Other Customs: The
               Anthropology of History." *American Anthropologist* 85 (3):
               517–44.
  1985   *Islands of History.* Chicago: Univ. of Chicago Press.
Said, Edward
  1978   *Orientalism.* New York: Pantheon.
Schneider, Jane
  1978   "Peacocks and Penguins: The Political Economy of European
               Cloth and Colors." *American Ethnologist* 5 (3): 413–47.
Siegel, James
  1979   *Shadow and Sound: The Historical Thought of a Sumatran
               People.* Chicago: Univ. of Chicago Press.
Skinner, Quentin
  1985   "Introduction: The Return of Grand Theory." In *The Return of
               Grand Theory in Human Sciences,* ed. Q. Skinner, 3–20. Cam-
               bridge: Cambridge Univ. Press.

Smith, Steven B.
  1984   *Reading Althusser: An Essay on Structural Marxism.* Ithaca:
           Cornell Univ. Press.
Thomas, Keith
  1971   *Religion and the Decline of Magic.* New York: Scribner's.
Thompson, E. P.
  1974   "Patrician Society, Plebeian Culture." *Journal of Social History*
           7 (4): 385–405.
Tuan, Yi-Fu
  1982   *Segmented Worlds and Self: Group Life and Individual Con-
           sciousness.* Minneapolis: Univ. of Minnesota Press.
Turner, Terry
  1977   "Narrative Structure and Mythopoiesis: A Critique and Refor-
           mulation of Structuralist Concepts of Myth, Narrative, and Po-
           etics." *Arethusa* 10 (1): 103–63.
Vansina, Jan
  1965 [1961]   *Oral Tradition.* Chicago: Aldine.
  1970   "Cultures Through Time." In *A Handbook of Method in Cul-
           tural Anthropology,* ed. R. Naroll and R. Cohen, 165–79. Gar-
           den City, N.Y.: Natural History Press.
  1984   *Art History in Africa: An Introduction to Method.* London:
           Longman.
  1985   *Oral Tradition as History.* Madison: Univ. of Wisconsin Press.
Wittgenstein, Ludwig
  1968 [1958]   *Philosophical Investigations.* New York: Macmillan.
Wolf, Eric R.
  1982   *Europe and the People Without History.* Berkeley: Univ. of Cal-
           ifornia Press.

2. Sahlins: Political Economy of Grandeur in Hawaii

Abbreviations

AH/F.O. and Ex.   Records of the Foreign Office and Exchequer, Hawaiian
           Kingdom. Archives of Hawaii, Honolulu.
BCP   British Consulate Papers, 1825–43. Typescript. Archives of Hawaii,
           Honolulu.
HC   Hunnewell Collection. Papers of James Hunnewell: Journal (Box 25);
           Letters. Baker Library, Harvard Business School.
LC   Lands Commission. Records of the Board of Commissioners to Quiet
           Land Titles in the Hawaiian Islands, 1846–54: FT, Foreign Tes-
           timony; NR, Native Register; NT, Native Testimony. Archives
           of Hawaii, Honolulu

MH *Missionary Herald*, various issues. Published by the American Board of Commissioners for Foreign Missions.

ML Marshall Letters: "Copies of letters rec'd from the Sandwich Islands & Canton," by Josiah Marshall (or by Marshall and Dixey Wildes), 1820–32. Ms Am W/63F, Houghton Library, Harvard University.

USCD Dispatches from U.S. Consuls in Honolulu, vol. 1. Microfilm (M-144) of originals at the U.S. National Archives, Washington, D.C.

Citations

Alexander, W. D.

1917 "Overthrow of the Ancient Tabu System in the Hawaiian Islands." *Hawaiian Historical Society 25th Annual Report* (for the year 1916): 37–45.

Arago, J.

1823 *Narrative of a voyage round the world . . . during the years 1817, 1818, 1819, and 1820. . . .* London: Treuttel et al.

Auna

Ms. Journal "Journal of Auna." Trans. William Ellis. Donald Angus Typed Manuscripts Collection. Hawaiian Historical Society, Honolulu.

Barnard, Charles H.

1829 *A narrative of the sufferings and adventures . . . during the years 1812 . . . 1816. . . .* New York: J. Lindon.

Barrère, Dorothy, and Marshall Sahlins

1979 "Tahitians in the Early History of Hawaiian Christianity: The Journal of Toketa." *The Hawaiian Journal of History* 13: 19–35.

Barrot, Théodore-Adolphe

1978 *Unless Haste Is Made: A French Skeptic's Account of the Sandwich Islands in 1836.* Kailua: Press Pacifica.

Beckwith, Martha

1970 *Hawaiian Mythology.* Honolulu: Univ. of Hawaii Press.

Beechey, F. W.

1832 *Narrative of a Voyage to the Pacific . . . in the Years 1825, 26, 27, 28.* Philadelphia: Carey and Lea.

Bell, Edward

1929–30 "Log of the Chatham." *Honolulu Mercury* 1 (4): 7–26; 1 (5): 55–69; 1 (6): 76–96; 2 (1): 80–91; 2 (2): 119–29.

Bennett, Frederick Debell

1840 *Narrative of a Whaling Voyage Round the Globe from the Year 1833 to 1836. . . .* 2 vols. London: Bentley.

Bennett, George
    1832   "Account of the islands Erromanga and Tanna, New Hebrides Group." *The Asiatic Journal,* n.s., 3: 119–31.

Bingham, Hiram
    1969   *A residence of twenty-one years in the Sandwich Islands.* Reprint of the 3d ed. of 1849. New York: Praeger.

Bloxam, Richard Rowland
    Ms. Narrative   "A Narrative of a Voyage to the Sandwich Islands in H.M.S. Blonde. 1824–1825–1826." MS 4255, National Library of Australia.

Bradley, Harold Whitman
    1968   *The American Frontier in Hawaii: The Pioneers 1789–1843.* Stanford: Stanford Univ. Press, 1942; Gloucester, Mass.: Peter Smith.

Bullard, Charles B.
    Letters   "Letterbook of Charles B. Bullard, Supercargo for Bryant and Sturgis at the Hawaiian Islands and Canton, March 20, 1821–July 11, 1823." Typescript copy at the Hawaiian Mission Children's Society Library, Honolulu.

Campbell, Archibald
    1822   *A Voyage Round the World, from 1806 to 1812 . . . with an Account of the Present State of the Sandwich Islands. . . .* 3d American ed. Charleston: Duke and Browne.

Chamisso, Adelbart von
    1981   *Voyage autour du monde.* Paris: Le Sycamore.

Corney, Peter
    1896   *Voyages in the northern Pacific: Narrative of several trading Voyages from 1813 to 1818. . . .* Honolulu: Thrum.

Cox, Ross
    1832   *Adventures on the Columbia River.* New York: Harper.

Cranmer-Byng, J. L., ed.
    1962   *An Embassy to China: Being the Journal kept by Lord Macartney during his Embassy to the Emperor Ch'ien-lung, 1793–1795.* London: Longman.

Dampier, Robert
    1971   *To the Sandwich Islands on H.M.S. Blonde.* Ed. Pauline King Joerger. Honolulu: Univ. of Hawaii Press.

Davenport, William
    1969   "The Hawaiian 'Cultural Revolution': Some Economic and Political Considerations." *American Anthropologist* 71: 1–20.

Daws, Gavan
    1968   *Shoal of Time.* New York: Macmillan.

Dibble, Sheldon
   1909   *A History of the Sandwich Islands.* Honolulu: Thrum.
Dixon, George
   1789   *A Voyage Round the World Performed in 1785, 1786, 1787, and 1788.* London: Goulding.
Dobel, Pierre
   1842   *Sept années en Chine: Nouvelles observations sur cet empire, l'Archipel Indo-Chinois, les Philippines et les Iles Sandwich.* Paris: D'Arnyot.
Ellis, William
   Ms. Journal   "Journal of William Ellis, Sandwich Islands, 1823." Journals (Box 5), LMS Collection, South Seas. SOAS Library.
   1828   *Narrative of a tour through Hawaii or Owhyhee. . . .* 4th ed. London: H. Fisher, Son, and P. Jackson.
Franchère, Gabriel
   1969   *Journal of a Voyage on the Northwest Coast of North America During the Years 1811, 1812, 1813, and 1814.* Trans. Wessie Tipping Lamb. Toronto: Champlain Society.
French, William
   Accts.   "Account book of William French, 1818–1819." MS 657F 88, Hawaiian Historical Society, Honolulu.
Freycinet, Louis Claude de Salses
   1978   *Hawai'i in 1819.* Trans. Ella L. Wiswell; ed. Marion Kelly. Pacific Anthropological Records, no. 26. Honolulu: Dept. of Anthropology, Bernice P. Bishop Museum.
Gast, Ross, and Agnes C. Conrad
   1973   *Don Francisco de Paula Marin.* Honolulu: Univ. of Hawaii Press, for the Hawaiian Historical Society.
Gifford, Edward Winslow
   1929   *Tongan Society.* Bernice P. Bishop Museum Bulletin no. 61. Honolulu: Bishop Museum Press.
Golovnin, V. M.
   1979   "Around the World on the *Kamchatka*, 1817–1819." Trans. Ella L. Wiswell. Honolulu: Hawaiian Historical Society and Univ. of Hawaii Press.
Hammatt, Charles H.
   Journal   "Journal of the residence of Charles H. Hammatt in the Sandwich Islands, 6 May 1823–9 June 1825." Bryant and Sturgis Papers. Baker Library, Harvard Business School.
I'i, John Papa
   1959   *Fragments of Hawaiian History.* Trans. Mary Kawena Pukui. Honolulu: Bishop Museum Press.

Ingraham, Joseph
    1918   *The log of the brig* Hope . . . *among the Sandwich Islands, May 20–Oct. 12, 1791.* Hawaiian Historical Society Reprints, no. 3. Honolulu: Hawaiian Historical Society.
Jarves, James Jackson
    1843   *Scenes and Scenery in the Sandwich Islands . . . 1837–1842.* Boston: James Munroe and Co.
Judd, Laura Fish
    1966   *Honolulu: Sketches of Life in the Hawaiian Islands from 1828 to 1861.* Chicago: Lakeside Press.
Kahananui, Dorothy M., ed
    1984   *Ka Mooolelo Hawaii* (The history of Hawaii). Honolulu: Committee for the Preservation and Study of Hawaiian Language, Art and Culture, University of Hawaii.
Kamakau, Samuel M.
    1961   *Ruling Chiefs of Hawaii.* Honolulu: Kamehameha Schools Press.
Kekauluohi[, M.]
    Journal   "Kekauluohi's Journal." M94, Lunalilo Collection. Archives of Hawaii, Honolulu.
Khlebnikov, Kyrill T.
    1976   *Kyrill T. Khlebnikov's Reports, 1817–1832.* Trans. Basisl Dmytryshyn and E. A. P. Crownhart-Vaughn. Portland: Oregon Historical Society.
Kirch, Patrick V., and Marshall Sahlins
    Forthcoming   *The Archaeology of History in an Hawaiian Valley.*
Korn, Alfons L.
    1983   "Shadows of Destiny: A French Navigator's View of the Kingdom of Hawaii." *Hawaiian Journal of History* 17: 1–39.
Kotzebue, Otto von
    1821   *A voyage of discovery into the South Seas . . . in the years 1815–1818.* 3 vols. London: Longman.
    1830   *A new voyage round the world in the years 1823, 24, 25, and 26.* London: Colburn and Bentley.
Kuykendall, Ralph S.
    1923   "A Northwest Trader at the Hawaiian Islands." *Oregon Historical Quarterly* 24: 111–31.
    1968   *The Hawaiian Kingdom.* Vol. 1, *1778–1854: Foundation and Transformation.* Honolulu: Univ. of Hawaii Press.
Ladd, William
    1838   "Remarks upon the Natural Resources of the Sandwich Islands." *The Hawaiian Spectator* 1 (2): 68–79.

Lafond, Gabriel
    1843–44   *Voyages autour du monde.* . . . Vol. 4. Paris: Dondey-Dupré.
Marin, Don Francisco de Paula (attrib.)
    Invoice   "Account of what King Kamehameha received from [torn] of Captain Winship in the year 1812. . . . " AH/F.O. and Ex., 1812.
Mathison, Gilbert Farquhar
    1825   *Narrative of a Visit to Brazil, Chile, Peru and the Sandwich Islands during the Years 1821 and 1822.* London: Knight.
Meares, John
    1790   *Voyages made in the Years 1788 and 1789, from China to the Northwest Coast.* . . . London: Logographic Press.
Meyen, F. J. F.
    1981   *A Botanist's Visit to Oahu in 1831.* Trans. Astrid Jackson. Kailua: Press Pacifica.
Morgan, Theodore
    1948   *Hawai'i: A Century of Economic Change, 1778–1876.* Cambridge: Harvard Univ. Press.
Morineau, M.
    Ms.   "Notice sur les Iles Sandwich, de 1826 à 1829." Memoires et Documents sur les Iles Sandwich, 1819–. Archives du Ministre des Affairs Etrangères, Bancroft Library, University of California, Berkeley.
Phelps, William Dana (attrib.)
    Ms.   "Solid Men of Boston." Bancroft Library, University of California, Berkeley.
Ralston, Caroline
    1984   "Hawaii, 1778–1854: Some Aspects of *Maka'ainana* Response to Rapid Cultural Change." *Journal of Pacific History* 19: 21–40.
Reynolds, J. N.
    1835   *Voyage of the United States Frigate Potomac . . . in the Years 1831, 1832, 1833, and 1834.* New York: Harper.
Reynolds, Stephen
    Journal   "Journal of Stephen Reynolds, November 1823–December 1843." Microfilm in Hawaiian Mission Children's Society Library of original script in the Peabody Museum, Salem.
Rocquefeuil, Camille de
    1823   *Journal d'un voyage autour du monde, pendant les années 1816, 1817, 1818, et 1819.* 2 Vols. Paris: Lebel.
Ross, Alexander
    1849   *Adventures of the first settlers on the Oregon and Columbia River.* . . . London: Smith, Elder.

Sahlins, Marshall

 1972   *Stone Age Economics*. Chicago: Aldine.

 1981   *Historical Metaphors and Mythical Realities: Structure in the Early History of the Sandwich Islands Kingdom*. Ann Arbor: Univ. of Michigan Press.

 1982   "The Apotheosis of Captain Cook." In *Between Belief and Transgression*, ed. Michel Izard and Pierre Smith, 73–102. Chicago: Univ. of Chicago Press.

 1985a   *Islands of History*. Chicago: Univ. of Chicago Press.

 1985b   "Hierarchy and Humanity in Polynesia." In *Transformations of Polynesian Culture*, ed. Antony Hooper and Judith Huntsman, 195–217. Auckland: Polynesian Society.

 1989a   "Captain Cook at Hawaii." *Journal of the Polynesian Society*. Forthcoming.

 1989b   "The Cosmology of Capitalism: The Trans-Pacific Sector of the 'World System.'" *Proceedings of the British Academy*. Forthcoming.

Schafer, Edward H.

 1963   *The Golden Peaches of Samarkand*. Berkeley: Univ. of California Press.

Shineberg, Dorothy

 1967   *They Came for Sandalwood: A Study of the Sandalwood Trade in the South-West Pacific, 1830–1865*. Melbourne: Melbourne Univ. Press.

Smith, Bernard

 1979   "Cook's Posthumous Reputation." In *Captain James Cook and His Times*, ed. Robin Fisher and H. Johnston. Seattle: Univ. of Washington Press.

Stewart, Charles S.

 1830   *Journal of a residence in the Sandwich Islands, during the years 1823, 1824, and 1825.* . . . 3d ed. London: H. Fisher, Son, & P. Jackson.

 1831   *A visit to the South Seas, in the U.S. Ship Vincennes, during the years 1829 and 1830.* . . . 2 vols. New York: Haven.

Thrum, Thos. G.

 1904   "The Sandalwood Trade of Early Hawaii." *Hawaiian Annual for 1905*: 43–74.

Tumarkin, D. D.

 Mimeo   "Materials of M. Vasilyev's Expedition: A Valuable Source for the Study of Culture Change and Inter-Cultural Contacts in the Hawaiian Islands."

Tyerman, Daniel, and George Bennet
  1831   *Journal of Voyages and Travels.* 2 vols. London: Westley and
          Davis.
Valeri, Valerio
  1972   "Le Fonctionnement du système des rangs à Hawaï." *L'Homme*
          12: 29–66.
  1982   "The Transformation of a Transformation: A Structural Essay
          on an Aspect of Hawaiian History (1809–1819)." *Social Analy-
          sis* 10: 3–41.
  1985   *Kingship and Sacrifice: Ritual and Society in Ancient Hawaii.*
          Chicago: Univ. of Chicago Press.
Vancouver, George
  1801   *A Voyage of Discovery in the North Pacific Ocean . . . in the
          Years 1790, 1791, 1792, 1793, 1794, and 1795.* New ed. 5 vols.
          London: Stockdale.
Whitman, John B.
  1979   *An Account of the Sandwich Islands: The Hawaiian Journal
          of John B. Whitman, 1813–1815,* ed. John Dominis Holt.
          Honolulu: Topgallant; Salem, Mass.: Peabody Museum of
          Salem.
Wyllie, Robert C.
  1856   *Supplement to the Report of the Minister of Foreign Relations.*
          Honolulu: Government Printer.

3. Ortner: Sherpa Religious Institutions

Aziz, Barbara Nimri
  1978   *Tibetan Frontier Families.* Durham, N.C.: Carolina Academic
          Press.
Bloch, Maurice
  1986   *From Blessing to Violence: History and Ideology in the Cir-
          cumcision Ritual of the Merina of Madagascar.* Cambridge:
          Cambridge Univ. Press.
Bourdieu, Pierre
  1977   *Outline of a Theory of Practice.* Trans. Richard Nice. Cam-
          bridge: Cambridge Univ. Press.
Braudel, Fernand
  1980   *On History.* Trans. Sarah Matthews. Chicago: Univ. of Chicago
          Press.
Burghart, Richard
  1984   "The Formation of the Concept of Nation State in Nepal." *Jour-
          nal of Asian Studies,* 44 (1): 101–25.

298   References Cited

Dozey, E. C.
   1922   *A Concise History of the Darjeeling District Since 1835.* Calcutta: N. Mukherjee.
English, Richard
   1985   "Himalayan State Formation and the Impact of British Rule in the Nineteenth Century." *Mountain Research and Development* 5 (1): 61–78.
Fernandez, James W.
   1974   "The Mission of Metaphor in Expressive Culture." *Current Anthropology* 15 (2): 119–45.
Fox, Richard G.
   1985   *Lions of the Punjab: Culture in the Making.* Berkeley: Univ. of California Press.
Funke, Friedrich W.
   1969   *Religioses Leben der Sherpa.* Innsbruck: Universitätsverlag Wagner.
Geertz, Clifford
   1973a   "Person, Time, and Conduct in Bali." In his *Interpretation of Cultures,* 360–411. New York: Basic Books.
   1973b   "Deep Play: Notes on the Balinese Cockfight." In his *Interpretation of Cultures,* 412–54. New York: Basic Books.
   1980   *Negara: The Theatre State in Nineteenth-Century Bali.* Princeton: Princeton Univ. Press.
Hobsbawm, Eric, and Terence Ranger, eds.
   1983   *The Invention of Tradition.* Cambridge: Cambridge Univ. Press.
Jerstad, Luther
   1969   *Mani Rimdu: Sherpa Dance-Drama.* Calcutta: Oxford Univ. Press and IBH Publishing Co.
Lévi-Strauss, Claude
   1969   *The Raw and the Cooked.* Trans. John Weightman and Doreen Weightman. New York: Harper and Row.
Macdonald, Alexander W.
   1980   "The Coming of Buddhism to the Sherpa Area of Nepal." *Acta Orientalia Academia Scientiarum Hungarica* 34 (1–3): 139–46.
March, Kathryn S.
   1977   "The Iconography of Chiwong Gomba." *Contributions to Nepalese Studies* 5 (1): 85–92.
   1979   "The Intermediacy of Women: Female Gender Symbolism and the Social Position of Women Among Tamangs and Sherpas of Highland Nepal." Ph.D. diss., Dept. of Anthropology, Cornell University.

Oppitz, Michael
 1968   *Geschichte und Sozialordnung der Sherpa*. Innsbruck: Univer-
        sitätsverlag Wagner.
Ortner, Sherry B.
 1970   "Food for Thought: A Key Symbol in Sherpa Culture." Ph.D.
        diss., Dept. of Anthropology, University of Chicago.
 1973   "On Key Symbols." *American Anthropologist* 75: 1338–46.
 1975   "Gods' Bodies, Gods' Food: A Symbolic Analysis of a Sherpa
        Ritual." In *The Interpretation of Symbolism*, ed. Roy G. Willis,
        133–70. ASA Studies 3. London: Malaby Press.
 1978   *Sherpas through their Rituals*. Cambridge: Cambridge Univ.
        Press.
 1983   "The Founding of the First Sherpa Nunnery, and the Problem of
        'Women' as an Analytic Category." In *Feminist Re-Visions:
        What Has Been and Might Be*, ed. Vivian Patraka and Louise
        Tilly, 93–134. Ann Arbor: Women's Studies Program, Univer-
        sity of Michigan.
 1984   "Theory in Anthropology Since the Sixties." *Comparative Stud-
        ies in Society and History* 26 (1): 126–66.
 1989   *High Religion: A Cultural and Political History of Sherpa Bud-
        dhism*. Princeton: Princeton Univ. Press.
 n.d.   *The Monks' Campaign and the Modernization of Sherpa Con-
        sciousness*. In preparation.
Paul, Robert A.
 1970   "Sherpas and Their Religion." Ph.D. diss., Dept. of Anthro-
        pology, University of Chicago.
 1982   *The Tibetan Symbolic World*. Chicago: Univ. of Chicago Press.
Regmi, Mahesh C.
 1978   *Thatched Huts and Stucco Palaces: Peasants and Landlords in
        Nineteenth Century Nepal*. New Delhi: Vikas.
Rose, Leo E., and John T. Scholtz
 1980   *Nepal: Profile of a Himalayan Kingdom*. Boulder, Colo.: West-
        view Press.
Sahlins, Marshall
 1981   *Historical Metaphors and Mythical Realities: Structure in the
        Early History of the Sandwich Islands Kingdom*. Ann Arbor:
        Univ. of Michigan Press.
Samuel, Geoffrey
 1982   "Tibet as a Stateless Society and Some Islamic Parallels." *Jour-
        nal of Asian Studies* 41 (2): 215–29.
Sangye Tenzing
 1971   *Shar-pa'i chos-byung sngon med tshangs-pa'i dbyu-gu*. (The un-

precedented holy scepter: A religious history of the Sherpa people.) Junbesi, Nepal, and Paris: n.p.

Schieffelin, Edward L.

1976   *The Sorrow of the Lonely and the Burning of the Dancers.* New York: St. Martin's Press.

Snellgrove, David L.

1957   *Buddhist Himalaya.* Oxford: Bruno Cassirer.

Turner, Victor

1974   *Dramas, Fields, and Metaphors: Symbolic Action in Human Society.* Ithaca: Cornell Univ. Press.

von Fürer-Haimendorf, Christoph

1964   *The Sherpas of Nepal.* Berkeley: Univ. of California Press.

1975   *Himalayan Traders.* New York: St. Martin's Press.

1984   *The Sherpas Transformed.* New Delhi: Sterling.

Waddell, L. Austine

1959 [1894]   *The Buddhism of Tibet, or Lamaism.* Cambridge: W. Heffer and Sons.

Wolf, Eric R.

1982   *Europe and the People Without History.* Berkeley: Univ. of California Press.

4. Fernandez: Enclosures in Asturia

Boas, Franz

1940   "The Aims of Ethnology." In his *Race, Language, and Culture,* 626–38. New York: Free Press.

Braudel, Fernand

1977   *Afterthoughts on Material Civilization and Capitalism.* Baltimore: Johns Hopkins Univ. Press.

Cela, Camilo José

1971   *Diccionario Secreto.* 2 vols. Madrid: Alfaguara.

1982   *Enciclopedia del Erotismo.* Barcelona: Editorial Distino.

Costa, Joaquín

1902   *Derecho Consuetudinario y Economía Popular en España.* Barcelona: Soler.

Díaz Cassou, Pedro

1980   *Tradiciones y costumbres de Murcia.* Murcia: Biblioteca Provincial.

Fabian, Johannes

1983   *Time and the Other: How Anthropology Constructs Its Object.* New York: Columbia Univ. Press.

Fernandez, James W.

1975   "Syllogisms of Association: Some Modern Extensions of Asturian Deepsong." In *Folklore in the Modern World*, ed. Richard Dorson, 183–206. Bloomington: Indiana Univ. Press.

1978 "African Religious Movements." In *Annual Review of Anthropology*, ed. Bernard Siegal et al., 7: 195–234.

1981 "The Call of the Commons: The Evolution of the Commons in Asturias (Spain) Since the Mid-Eighteenth Century. Decline and Recommitment." Paper presented to the SSRC Conference on Institutionalized Forms of Reciprocity and Cooperation in Rural Europe, St. Anthony's College, Oxford, September.

1982 *Bwiti: An Ethnography of the Religious Imagination in Africa.* Princeton: Princeton Univ. Press.

1985 "Signs out of Place: The Dynamics of the Religious Symbol." Paper read at The Hooker Symposium on the Religious Symbol, McMaster University, London, Ont., October.

1986 *Persuasions and Performances: The Play of Tropes in Culture.* Bloomington: Indiana Univ. Press.

Fonseca González, Ramón
1984 "El Régimen Jurídico de la Antojana." Oviedo: *Boletín del Instituto de Estudios Asturianos*. Vol. 2.

Freud, Sigmund
1963 *Dora, an Analysis of a Case of Hysteria.* New York: Collier Books.
1965 *The Interpretation of Dreams.* New York: Avon Books.

Frigole Reixach, Joan
1986 "La casa y el espacio doméstico tradicional y su sistema de representaciones." Unpublished ms.

García Alvarez, Benjamin
1963 *Concejos de parroquias (especial referencia a los de Aller, Asturias y Ordenanzas que regulan su organización y régimen).* Pola de Lena, Asturias: Gráfica Lena.

Goethe, Johann Wolfgang von
1951 *Faust.* Parts 1 and 2. Translated by Louis Macheice. Harmondsworth, Eng.: Penguin.

Hammond, John Lawrence, and Barbara Hammond
1911 *The Village Laborer.* London: Longman.

Harding, Susan
1984 *Remaking Ibieca: Rural Life in Aragon Under Franco.* Chapel Hill: Univ. of North Carolina Press.

Hobsbawm, Eric, and Terence Ranger, eds.
1983 *The Invention of Tradition.* New York: Cambridge Univ. Press.

Jovellanos, Melchor Gaspar
1753 *Informe de la Sociedad Económica de Madrid al Real y Supremo*

Consejo de Castilla en el expediente de la ley agraria. Madrid: Sociedad Económica.

Jung, Carl G.
1956   *Symbols of Transformation.* Princeton, N.J.: Bollingen.

Lisón Tolosana, Carmelo
1973   "La Casa en Galicia." In his *Ensayos de antropología social,* 109–64. Madrid: Editorial Ayuso.

Malinowski, Bronislaw
1984 [1922]   *Argonauts of the Western Pacific.* Prospect Heights, Ill.: Waveland Press.
1936   *Coral Gardens and Their Magic.* 2 vols. London: Macmillan.

Marx, Karl
1946   *Capital: A Critique of Political Economy.* Trans. Samuel Moore; ed. Frederick Engels. New York: Modern Library.

Ohnuki-Tierney, Emiko
1981   "Phases in Human Perception/Conception/Symbolization Processes: Cognitive Anthropology and Symbolic Classification." *American Ethnologist* 18 (3): 451–67.

Prieto Bances, Ramón
1977   *Obra Escrita.* Vol. 1. Oviedo: Facultad de Derecho, Universidad de Oviedo.

Ruiz de la Peña, Juan Ignacio
1981   *Las "Polas" asturianas en la Edad Media.* Oviedo: Universidad de Oviedo.

Sarandeses, Francisco
1966   *Heráldica de los apellidos asturianos.* Oviedo: IDEA.

Singer, Milton
1984   *Man's Glassy Essence: Explorations in Semiotic Anthropology.* Bloomington: Indiana Univ. Press.

Turner, Michael
1984   *Enclosures in Britain, 1750–1830.* London: Macmillan.

Vico, Giambattista
1976   *The "New Science" of Giambattista Vico.* Ed. T. Bergin and M. Fisch. Ithaca: Cornell Univ. Press.

Wagner, Roy
1981 [1975]   *The Invention of Culture.* Rev. ed. Chicago: Univ. of Chicago Press.

Wallace, A. F. C.
1957   "Revitalization Movements." *American Anthropologist* 58 (2): 264–81.

Werbner, Richard
1985   "The Argument of Images: From Zion to the Wilderness in Af-

rican Churches." In *Theoretical Orientations in African Religion*, ed. Wim van Binsbergen and Matthew Schoeffelers, 253–86. London: KPI Press.

5. Ohnuki-Tierney: Monkey as Self

Amino, Yoshihiko
1986   "Ajiya to umi no butai o haikei ni" (Against the background of Asia and the sea). *Asahi hyakka: Nihon no rekishi* (Asahi encyclopedia: Japanese history), 1: 2–3. Tokyo: Asahi Shinbunsha.
Blacker, Carmen
1975   *The Catalpa Bow: A Study of Shamanistic Practices in Japan.* London: Allen and Unwin.
Braudel, Fernand
1980   *On History.* Chicago: Univ. of Chicago Press.
Burke, Kenneth
1955   *A Grammar of Motives.* New York: Braziller.
Carrithers, Michael, Steven Collins, and Steven Lukes, eds.
1985   *The Category of the Person.* Cambridge: Cambridge Univ. Press.
Fukuyama, Toshio
1968   "Nenjū gyōji emaki ni tsuite" (Notes on the scroll paintings of annual events). In *Nihon emakimono zenshū* (A collection of Japanese picture scrolls), ed. Kadokawa Shoten Henshūbu, 24: 3–23. Tokyo: Kadokawa Shoten.
Hirose, Shizumu
1978   "Nihonzaru o meguru animaru roa no kenkyū" (Research on the animal lore of Japanese macaques). In *Shakai bunka jinruigaku* (Socio-cultural anthropology), ed. T. Katō, S. Nakao, and T. Umesao, 287–334. Tokyo: Chūōkōronsha.
Iida, Michio
1983   *Mizaru kikazaru iwazaru—sekai sanzaru genryūkō* (No see, no hear, no speak—sources of the three monkeys in various cultures of the world). Tokyo: Sanseidō.
Inada, Kōji, and Tatehiko Ōshima
1977   *Nihon mukashibanashi jiten* (Dictionary of Japanese folktales). Tokyo: Kōbundō.
Ishii, Ryōsuke
1963 [1961]   *Zoku Edo jidai manpitsu* (Essays on the Edo period). Vol. 2. Tokyo: Inoue Shoten.
Kadokawa Shoten Henshūbu, ed.
1968   *Nenjū gyōji emaki* (Scroll paintings of annual events). Vol 24 of

Nihon emakimono zenshū (Collection of Japanese scroll paintings). Tokyo: Kadokawa Shoten.

Kojiki
1969   Trans. Donald L. Philippi. Princeton: Princeton Univ. Press; Tokyo: Univ. of Tokyo Press.

Kurano, Kenji, and Yūkichi Takeda, eds.
1958   *Kojiki Norito* (Kojiki and Norito). Tokyo: Iwanami Shoten.

Kuroda, Toshio
1972   "Chūsei no mibunsei to hisen kannen" (Social stratification during the early medieval period and the concept of baseness). *Buraku mondai kenkyū* 33: 23–57.

LaFleur, William R.
1983   *The Karma of Words: Buddhism and the Literary Arts in Medieval Japan.* Berkeley: Univ. of California Press.

Matsumae, Takeshi
1960   *Nihon shinwa no shin-kenkyū* (New research on Japanese mythology). Tokyo: Ōhūsha.

Matsumura, Takeo
1948   *Girei oyobi shinwa no kenkyū* (Research on ritual and myth). Tokyo: Baifūkan.
1954   *Nihon shinwa no kenkyū* (Research on Japanese mythology). Tokyo: Ōhūsha.

Minakata, Kumakusu
1972 [1971]   *Minakata Kumakusu zenshū* (Collected essays by Minakata Kumakusu). Vol. 1. Tokyo: Heibonsha.

Miyaji, Denzaburō
1973   "Shōwa sanzaru" (Three monkeys of the Shōwa period). *Monkī* 17 (2): 12.

Miyamoto, Tsuneichi
1981   *Emakimono ni miru Nihon shomin seikatsushi* (Life of common people in Japan as depicted in scroll paintings). Tokyo: Chūōkōronsha.

Nakamura, Teiri
1984   *Nihonjin no dobutsukan—henshintan no rekishi* (Japanese views of animals: History of tales about metamorphoses). Tokyo: Kaimeisha.

Needham, Rodney
1979   *Symbolic Classification.* Santa Monica, Calif.: Goodyear.

Oda, Kōji
1967   "Sarumawashi no fukei" (Data on roadside performing artists during the Early Modern period: The history of monkey trainers). *Geinō* 9 (9): 48–53.
1978   "Nihon geinōshi eno atarashii hikari" (New light on the history of Japanese performing arts). In *Suō no sarumawashi* (Monkey

performances at Suō), ed. Suō Sarumawashinokai Jimukyoku, p. 15. Hikari City, Yamaguchi Prefecture: Suō Sarumawashinokai Jimukyoku.

1980   "Suō ni okeru sarumawashi" (Monkey performances at Suō). In *Suō sarumawashi kinkyū chōsa hōkokusho* (Report on the urgent investigation of monkey performances at Suō), ed. Yamaguchiken Kyōiku Iinkai Bunkaka, 3–29. Yamaguchi: Yamaguchiken Kyōiku Iinkai.

Ohnuki-Tierney, Emiko

1981   *Illness and Healing Among the Sakhalin Ainu—A Symbolic Interpretation.* Cambridge: Cambridge Univ. Press.

1984   *Illness and Culture in Contemporary Japan.* Cambridge: Cambridge Univ. Press.

1987   *The Monkey as Mirror: Symbolic Transformations in Japanese History and Ritual.* Princeton: Princeton Univ. Press.

1990   "Monkey as Metaphor?: Transformations of a Polytropic Symbol in Japanese Culture." *Man* (n.s.) 25: 399–416.

Ooms, Herman

1985   *Tokugawa Ideology: Early Constructs, 1570–1680.* Princeton: Princeton Univ. Press.

Orikuchi, Shinobu

1965   *Orikuchi Shinobu zenshū* (Collected works by Shinobu Orikuchi). Vol. 2. Tokyo: Chūōkōronsha.

Ouwehand, Cornelius

1964   *Namazu-e and Their Themes: An Interpretative Approach to Some Aspects of Japanese Folk Religion.* Leiden: Brill.

Putzar, Edward D.

1963   "The Tale of Monkey Genji, *Sarugenji-zōshi.*" *Monumenta Nipponica,* 1–4: 286–312.

Pyle, Kenneth B.

1987   "In Pursuit of a Great Design: Nakasone Betwixt the Past and the Future." *Journal of Japanese Studies* 13 (2): 243–70.

Sahlins, Marshall

1981   *Historical Metaphors and Mythical Realities: Structure in the Early History of the Sandwich Islands Kingdom.* Ann Arbor, Michigan: Univ. of Michigan Press.

1985   *Islands of History.* Chicago: Univ. of Chicago Press.

1989   "The Cosmology of Capitalism: The Trans-Pacific Sector of the 'World System.'" *Proceedings of the British Academy.* Forthcoming.

Sakamoto, Tarō, Saburō Ienaga, Mitsusada Inoue, and Susumu Ōno, eds.

1967   *Nihon shoki.* Vol. 1. Tokyo: Iwanami Shoten.

Satake, Akihiro
 1970 [1967]   *Gekokujō no bungaku* (Literature of the Gekokujō). To-
    kyo: Chikuma Shobō.
Shimonaka, Yasaburō, ed.
 1941   *Shintō daijiten* (Encyclopedia of Shintō). Vol. 2. Tokyo: Hei-
    bonsha.
Sugiura, Minpei
 1965   *Sengoku ransei no bungaku* (Literature of the turbulent world
    during the cyclical conquest). Tokyo: Iwanami Shoten.
Tachibana, Narisue
 1966 [1254]   *Kokon chomonshū* (Stories heard from writers old and
    new), ed. Y. Nagazumi and I. Shimada. Tokyo: Iwanami Shoten.
Takazaki, Masahide
 1956   "'Hina' no kuni" (The country of "hina"). *Kokugakuin Zasshi*
    56 (5): 4–26.
Ueda, Kazuo
 1978   "Kinsei hōken shakai to mibunsei" (The feudal society of the
    Early Modern period and the hierarchical system). In *Buraku
    mondai gaisetsu* (Introduction to buraku problems), ed. Bu-
    raku Kaihō Kenkyūsho, 100–118. Osaka: Kaihō Shuppansha.
Yalman, Nur
 1967   "'The Raw:The Cooked: :Nature:Culture'—Observation on
    Le cru et le cuit." In *The Structural Study of Myth and Totem-
    ism*, ed. Edmund Leach, 71–89. London: Tavistock.
Yanagita, Kunio
 1982a [1968]   *Teihon Yanagita Kunioshū* (Collected writings of Kunio
    Yanagita). Vol. 6. Tokyo: Chikuma Shobō.
 1982b [1969]   *Teihon Yanagita Kunioshū* (Collected writings of Kunio
    Yanagita). Vol. 8. Tokyo: Chikuma Shobō.
Yanagita, Kunio, ed.
 1951   *Minzokugaku jiten* (Ethnographic dictionary). Tokyo: Tō-
    kyōdō.
Yokoi, Kiyoshi
 1980   *Gekokujō no bunka* (Literature of the *gekokujō*). Tokyo: Tokyo
    Daigaku Shuppankai.

6. Valeri: Hawaiian Kingship

Appadurai, Arjun
 1981   "The Past as a Scarce Resource." *Man*, n.s., 16: 201–19.
Bakhtin, Mikhail
 1981   *The Dialogic Imagination*. Austin: Univ. of Texas Press.

Barnes, John A.
 1967 "Genealogies." In *The Craft of Social Anthropology*, ed. A. L. Epstein, 101–27. London: Tavistock.
Barrère, Dorothy, Mary Kawena Pukui, and Marion Kelly
 1980 *Hula: Historical Perspectives*. Pacific Anthropological Records no. 30. Honolulu: Bishop Museum Press.
Beckwith, Martha W.
 1940 *Hawaiian Mythology*. New Haven: Yale Univ. Press.
 1951 *The Kumulipo: A Hawaiian Creation Chant*. Chicago: Univ. of Chicago Press.
Beckwith, Martha W., ed.
 1932 *Kepelino's Traditions of Hawaii*. Bernice Pauahi Bishop Museum Bulletin no. 95. Honolulu: Bishop Museum Press.
Bloch, Maurice
 1977 "The Past and the Present in the Present." *Man*, n.s., 12: 278–92.
Bohannan, Laura
 1952 "A Genealogical Charter." *Africa* 22: 301–15.
Bott, Elizabeth
 1981 "Power and Rank in the Kingdom of Tonga." *Journal of the Polynesian Society* 19: 181–212.
 1982 "Tongan Society at the Time of Captain Cook's Visits: Discussion with Her Majesty Queen Salote Tupou." *Memoirs of the Polynesian Society* no. 44. Wellington: Polynesian Society.
Bourdieu, Pierre
 1977 *Outline of a Theory of Practice*. Cambridge: Cambridge Univ. Press.
Brisson, Luc
 1982 *Platon, les mots et les mythes*. Paris: Maspéro.
Canfora, Luciano
 1982 *Analogia e storia*. Milan: Il Saggiatore.
Cartwright, Bruce
 1930 "Note on Hawaiian Genealogies." *Hawaiian Historical Society Annual Report for 1929*, 45–47.
 1933 "Some Aliis of the Migratory Period." *Bernice Pauahi Bishop Museum Occasional Papers* 10 (7): 1–11.
Casanova, Jacques
 1960 *Histoire de ma vie*. 12 vols. Wiesbaden: Brockhaus.
Collingwood, Robin George
 1933 *An Essay on Philosophical Method*. Oxford: Clarendon Press.
Cook, James, and James King
 1784 *A Voyage to the Pacific Ocean*. 3 vols. Dublin: Camberlaine.

Cunnison, Ian

1951   *History on the Luapula: An Essay on the Historical Notions of a Central African Tribe.* The Rhodes-Livingstone Papers, no. 21. London: Oxford Univ. Press.

1957   "History and Genealogy in a Conquest State." *American Anthropologist* 59: 20–31.

de Certeau, Michel

1981   "Faire Croire." In *Modalités de la diffusion et de la reception des messages religieux du XIIe au XVe siècle.* Collection de l'Ecole Française de Rome, no. 51. Rome: Ecole Française de Rome.

Detienne, Marcel

1967   *Les Maîtres de la vérité dans la grèce ancienne.* Paris: Maspéro.

1981   *L'Invention de la mythologie.* Paris: Gallimard.

Droysen, Johann Gustav

1937   *Historik: Vorlesungen über Enzyklopädie und Methodologie der Geschichte.* Munich: Oldenbourg.

Durkheim, Emile

1968   *The Division of Labor in Society.* Trans. G. Simpson. New York: Free Press.

Elbert, Samuel H.

1951   "Hawaiian Literary Style and Culture." *American Anthropologist* 53: 345–54.

Emerson, Nathaniel B.

1965 [1909]   *Unwritten Literature of Hawaii: The Sacred Songs of the Hula.* Rutland, Vt.: Tuttle.

Engel, Joseph

1956   "Analogie und Geschichte." *Studium Generale* 9 (2): 96–107.

Evans-Pritchard, E. E.

1940   *The Nuer.* London: Oxford Univ. Press.

Finley, Moses I.

1965   "Myth, Memory, and History." *History and Theory* 4: 280–302.

Firth, Raymond

1970   *Rank and Religion in Tikopia.* London: Allen and Unwin.

Fornander, Abraham

1878–80   *An Account of the Polynesian Race, its Origin and Migrations and the Ancient History of the Hawaiian People to the Times of Kamehameha I.* 3 vols. London: Truebner.

1916–20   *Fornander Collection of Hawaiian Antiquities and Folk-Lore.* Memoirs of the Bernice Pauahi Bishop Museum, nos. 4–6. Honolulu: Bishop Museum Press.

Fortes, Meyer
    1945   *The Dynamics of Clanship Among the Tallensi.* London: Oxford Univ. Press.
Fox, James J.
    1971   "A Rotinese Dynastic Genealogy: Structure and Event." In *The Translation of Cultures*, ed. T. O. Beidelman, 37–77. London: Tavistock.
Fustel de Coulanges, Numa Denis
    1905   *La Cité antique.* 19th ed. Paris: Hachette.
Gernet, Lucien
    1976   "Le Temps dans les formes archaïques du droit." In *Anthropologie de la Grèce antique*, 261–87. Paris: Maspéro.
Goldman, Irving
    1970   *Ancient Polynesian Society.* Chicago: Univ. of Chicago Press.
Granet, Marcel
    1926   *Danses et légendes de la chine ancienne.* 2 vols. Paris: Alcan.
Gullick, John M.
    1958   *Indigenous Political Systems of Western Malaya.* London: Athlone.
Handy, Edward S. C.
    1931   *Cultural Revolution in Hawaii.* Honolulu: Institute of Pacific Relations.
Handy, Edward S. C., and Mary Kawena Pukui
    1972   *The Polynesian Family System in Ka-'u, Hawai'i.* 2d ed. Rutland, Vt.: Tuttle.
Hawaiian Ethnographical Notes
    Typescript Vols. 1–3   Bernice Pauahi Bishop Museum Library, Honolulu.
Hobsbawm, Eric, and Terence Ranger, eds.
    1983   *The Invention of Tradition.* Cambridge: Cambridge Univ. Press.
Horton, Robin
    1982   "Tradition and Modernity Revisited." In *Rationality and Relativism*, ed. Martin Hollis and Steven Lukes, 201–60. Cambridge: MIT Press.
Ii, John Papa
    1841   "John Ii's speech, delivered at Rev. H. Bingham's church on Thanksgiving Day, January 1, 1841." *The Polynesian* 1 (May 5): 186–87.
    1963   *Fragments of Hawaiian History.* 2d ed. Honolulu: Bishop Museum Press.
Johansen, J. Prytz
    1954   *The Maori and His Religion in Its Non-ritualistic Aspects.* Copenhagen: Munksgaard.

310   *References Cited*

Kaeppler, Adrienne
    1985   "Hawaiian Art and Society: Traditions and Transformations."
            In *Transformations in Polynesian Culture*, ed. A. Hooper and
            Judith Huntsman, 105–31. Wellington: Polynesian Society.
Kamakau, Kelou
    1919–20 "No na Oihana Kahuna Kahiko." In Fornander 1916–20,
            6: 2–45.
Kamakau, Samuel M.
    1961   *The Ruling Chiefs of Hawaii*. Honolulu: Kamahameha Schools
            Press.
    1964   *Ka Poʻe Kahiko: The People of Old*. Honolulu: Bishop Museum
            Press.
Ka Nonanona
    1841–54 Honolulu.
Kantorowicz, Ernst H.
    1946   *Laudes Regiae: A Study in Liturgical Acclamations and Me-
            dieval Ruler Worship*. University of California Publications in
            History, vol. 33. Berkeley: Univ. of California Press.
Ke Kumu Hawaii
    1834–39 Honolulu.
Kepelino, Kaho-aliikumaieiwakamoku
    1932   *Kepelino's Traditions of Hawaii*. Ed. Martha W. Beckwith.
            Bernice Pauahi Bishop Museum Bulletin no. 95. Honolulu:
            Bishop Museum Press.
Kirch, Patrick V., and Douglas Yen
    1982   *Tikopia: The Prehistory and Ecology of a Polynesian Outlier*.
            Bernice Pauahi Bishop Museum Bulletin no. 238. Honolulu:
            Bishop Museum Press.
Kirk, G. S.
    1970   *Myth*. Cambridge: Cambridge Univ. Press.
Kuykendall, Ralph S.
    1938   *The Hawaiian Kingdom*. Vol 1. Honolulu: Univ. of Hawaii
            Press.
Leach, Edmund
    1965   *Political Systems of Highland Burma*. 2d ed. Boston: Beacon
            Press.
Lévy-Bruhl, Lucien
    1912   *Les Fonctions mentales dans les sociétés inférieures*. 2d ed.
            Paris: Alcan.
Liliuokalani
    1898   *An Account of the Creation of the World according to Hawaiian
            Tradition*. Boston.

Malinowski, Bronislaw
    1954   *Magic, Science, and Religion.* New York: Doubleday.
Malo, David
    1951   *Hawaiian Antiquities.* 2d ed. Bernice Pauahi Bishop Museum
            Special Publication no. 2. Honolulu: Bishop Museum Press.
Mannoni, Octave
    1969   "Je sais bien, mais quand même. . . . "In *Clefs pour l'imaginaire
            ou l'autre scène,* 9–33. Paris: Seuil.
Marin, Louis
    1981   *Le Portrait du roi.* Paris: Minuit.
McKinzie, Edith Kawelohea
    1983   *Hawaiian Genealogies Extracted from Hawaiian Language
            Newspapers.* Vol. 1. Laie: Institute for Polynesian Studies.
Metge, Joan
    1976   *The Maori of New Zealand, Rautahi.* 2d ed. London: Routledge
            and Kegan Paul.
    1838   *Mooolelo Hawaii.* Lahainaluna: Seminary Press.
Nietzsche, Friedrich W.
    1983   *Untimely Meditations.* Trans. J. R. Hollingdale. Cambridge:
            Cambridge Univ. Press.
Pariente, Jean-Claude
    1973   *Le Langage et l'individuel.* Paris: Armand Colin.
Peel, John D. Y.
    1984   "Making History: The Past in the Ijesha Present." *Man,* n.s.,
            19: 111–32.
Pogue, John F.
    1858   *Ka Mooolelo Hawaii.* Honolulu: Government Press.
Pukui, Mary Kawena
    1949   "Songs (*Meles*) of Old Ka'u, Hawaii." *Journal of American
            Folklore* 62: 247–58.
    1983   *'Olelo No'eau: Hawaiian Proverbs and Poetical Sayings.* Bernice
            Pauahi Bishop Museum Special Publication no. 71. Honolulu:
            Bishop Museum Press.
Pukui, Mary Kawena, and Samuel Elbert
    1986   *Hawaiian Dictionary.* Rev. ed. Honolulu: Univ. of Hawaii
            Press.
Pukui, Mary Kawena, E. W. Haertig, and Catherine A. Lee
    1972–79 *Nānā i ke Kumu* (Look to the source). 2 vols. Honolulu: Queen
            Liliuokalani Children's Center Publications.
Pukui, Mary Kawena, and Alfons Korn
    1973   *The Echo of Our Song: Chants and Poems of the Hawaiians.*
            Honolulu: Univ. of Hawaii Press.

Remy, Jules
  1862   *Ka Mooolelo Hawaii: Histoire de l'Archipel Hawaiien.* Paris:
          Franck.
Richards, William
  1973   "William Richards on Hawaiian Culture and Political Condi-
          tions of the Islands in 1841." Ed. Marshall Sahlins and Dorothy
          Barrère. *Hawaiian Journal of History* 7: 18–40.
Ricklefs, Merle C.
  1974   *Jogjakarta Under Sultan Mangkubumi: A History of the Di-
          vision of Java.* London: Oxford Univ. Press.
Roberts, Helen H.
  1926   *Ancient Hawaiian Music.* Bernice Pauahi Bishop Museum Bul-
          letin no. 29. Honolulu: Bishop Museum Press.
Sahlins, Marshall
  1981   *Historical Metaphors and Mythical Realities: Structure in the
          Early History of the Sandwich Islands Kingdom.* ASAO Special
          Publications no. 1. Ann Arbor: Univ. of Michigan Press.
  1985   *Islands of History.* Chicago: Univ. of Chicago Press.
Searle, John R.
  1969   *Speech Acts: An Essay in the Philosophy of Language.* Cam-
          bridge: Cambridge Univ. Press.
Smith, William Robertson
  1903   *Kinship and Marriage in Early Arabia.* 2d ed. London: Black.
Stein, Rolf A.
  1971   "Du Recit au rituel dans les manuscrits tibétains de Touen-
          Houang." In *Etudes dédiées à la mémoire de Marcelle Lalou,*
          479–547. Paris: Maisonneuve.
Stokes, John F.
  1930   "An Evaluation of Early Genealogies Used for Polynesian His-
          tory." *Journal of the Polynesian Society* 39: 1–42.
Strawson, Peter F.
  1959   *Individuals.* London: Methuen.
Traube, Elizabeth
  1986   Review of M. Détienne, "L'invention de la mythologie." *History
          and Theory* 25: 75–87.
Valeri, Valerio
  1972   "Le Fonctionnement du système des rangs à Hawaii." *L'Homme*
          12: 29–66.
  1981   "Pouvoir des dieux, rire des hommes: Divertissement théorique
          sur un fait hawaiien." *Anthropologie et Société* 5 (3): 11–34.
  1982   "The Transformation of a Transformation: A Structural Essay
          on an Aspect of Hawaiian History (1809–1819)." *Social Analy-
          sis* 10: 3–41.

1985a   *Kingship and Sacrifice: Ritual and Society in Ancient Hawaii.*
         Chicago: Univ. of Chicago Press.
1985b   "The Conqueror Becomes King: A Political Analysis of the Ha-
         waiian Legend of 'Umi." In *Transformation of Polynesian Cul-
         ture*, ed. A. Hooper and Judith Huntsman, 79–103. Wellington:
         Polynesian Society.
1989   "Death in Heaven: Myths and Rites of Kinship in Tongan King-
         ship." *History and Anthropology* 4: 209–47.
1990   "Diarchy and History in Hawaii and Tonga." In *Culture and
         History in the Pacific*, ed. Jukka Siikala. Helsinki: The Finnish
         Ethnological Society.
1991   "Relativisme culturel." In *Dictionnaire d'ethnologie et d'an-
         thropologie*. Paris: Presses Universitaires de France.

Vernant, Jean Pierre
1974   "Aspects mythiques de la mémoire." In *Mythe et pensée chez les
         Grecs*, ed. J. P. Vernant, 1: 80–107. Paris: Maspéro.

Veyne, Paul
1976   *L'Inventaire des différences.* Paris: Seuil.
1983   *Les Grecs ont-ils cru à leurs mythes? Essai sur l'imagination
         constituante.* Paris: Seuil

Winch, Peter
1958   *The Idea of a Social Science and Its Relation to Philosophy.* Lon-
         don: Routledge and Kegan Paul.

7. Handelman and Shamgar-Handelman: National Emblem of Israel

Aran, Gideon
1986   "From Religious Zionism to Zionist Religion: The Roots of
         Gush Emunim." In *Studies in Contemporary Jewry*, ed. Peter Y.
         Medding, 2: 116–43. Bloomington: Indiana Univ. Press.

Aviad, Janet
1984   "The Contemporary Israeli Pursuit of the Millennium." *Reli-
         gion* 14: 199–222.

Baer, Yitzhak F.
1947   *Galut.* New York: Schocken.

Barag, Dan
1985   "The Menorah as a Messianic Symbol in the Late Roman and
         Byzantine Periods." Paper read to the Ninth World Congress of
         Jewish Studies, Jerusalem, Aug. 4–12. (In Hebrew.)

Ben-Gurion, David
1976   *Like Stars and Like Dust.* Tel-Aviv: Massada. (In Hebrew.)

Childs, Brevard S.

  1960   *Myth and Reality in the Old Testament.* London: SCM Press.

Davies, W. D.

  1974   *The Gospel and the Land: Early Christianity and Jewish Territorial Doctrine.* Berkeley: Univ. of California Press.

  1982   *The Territorial Dimension of Judaism.* Berkeley: Univ. of California Press.

Don-Yehiye, Eliezer, and Charles S. Liebman

  1981   "The Symbol System of Zionist-Socialism: An Aspect of Israeli Civil Religion." *Modern Judaism* 1: 121–48.

Eisenstadt, S. N.

  1967   *Israeli Society.* London: Weidenfeld and Nicholson.

Eliav, Mordechai

  1979   "The Story of the Zionist Flag." *Tziunim* 3: 49–59. (In Hebrew.)

Encyclopedia Judaica

  1971   Vol. 11, s. v. "Menorah." New York: Macmillan.

Evens, T. M. S.

  1977   "The Predication of the Individual in Anthropological Interactionism." *American Anthropologist* 79: 579–97.

Firth, Raymond

  1973   *Symbols: Public and Private.* London: Allen and Unwin.

Fishbane, Michael A.

  1974   "The Sacred Center: The Symbolic Structure of the Bible." In *Texts and Responses,* ed. M. A. Fishbane and Paul Flohr, 6–27. Leiden: Brill.

Fredman, Ruth Gruber

  1981   *The Passover Seder: Afikoman in Exile.* Philadelphia: Univ. of Pennsylvania Press.

Ginsberg, Louis

  1968 [1928]   *The Legends of the Jews.* Vol. 3. Philadelphia: Jewish Publication Society of America.

Goodenough, Erwin R.

  1954   *Jewish Symbols in the Greco-Roman Period.* Vol. 4. New York: Pantheon.

Greenstone, Julius H.

  1906   *The Messianic Idea in Jewish History.* Philadelphia: Jewish Publication Society of America.

Halpern, Ben

  1969   *The Idea of the Jewish State.* Cambridge: Harvard Univ. Press.

Handelman, Don

  1990   *Models and Mirrors: Towards an Anthropology of Public Events.* Cambridge: Cambridge Univ. Press.

Handelman, Don, and Lea Shamgar-Handelman
1986 "Imagining the Nation-State: Visual Composition in the Emblem of Israel." Paper read to the 85th annual meeting of the American Anthropological Association, Philadelphia, Dec. 3–7.

Harris, Grace
1976 "Inward-Looking and Outward-Looking Symbols." In *The Realm of the Extra-Human: Ideas and Action*, ed. A. Bharati, 301–9. The Hague: Mouton.

Herzl, Theodor
1970 *The Jewish State*. Trans. Harry Zohn. New York: Herzl Press.

Hill, Alette
1982 "Hitler's Flag: A Case Study." *Semiotica* 38: 127–37.

Hobsbawm, Eric J., and Terence Ranger, eds.
1983 *The Invention of Tradition*. New York: Cambridge Univ. Press.

Kapferer, Bruce
1988 *Legends of People, Myths of State*. Washington, D.C.: Smithsonian Institution Press.

Katz, Jacob
1971 "The Jewish National Movement: A Sociological Analysis." In *Jewish Society Through the Ages*, ed. H. Ben-Sasson and S. Ettinger, 267–83. New York: Schocken.
1982 "Israel and the Messiah." *Commentary* 73 (3): 34–41.

Levenson, Jon D.
1984 "The Temple and the World." *Journal of Religion* 64: 275–98.
1985 *Sinai and Zion: An Entry into the Jewish Bible*. Minneapolis: Winston Press.

Levey, Samson H.
1974 *The Messiah: An Aramaic Interpretation—the Messianic Exegesis of the Targum*. Cincinnati: Hebrew Union College.

Lewis, Bernard
1975 *History Remembered, Recovered, Invented*. Princeton: Princeton Univ. Press.

Liebman, Charles S., and Eliezer Don-Yehiye
1983 *Civil Religion in Israel*. Berkeley: Univ. of California Press.
1984 *Religion and Politics in Israel*. Bloomington: Indiana Univ. Press.

Marmorstein, Emile
1969 *Heaven at Bay: The Jewish Kulturkampf in the Holy Land*. London: Oxford Univ. Press.

Meyers, Carol L.
1976 *The Tabernacle Menorah: A Synthetic Study of a Symbol From*

the Biblical Cult. ASOR Dissertation Series, no. 2. Missoula, Mont.: Scholars Press.

Mowinckel, Sigmund
1959   He That Cometh: The Messianic Concept in the Old Testament and Later Judaism. Oxford: Blackwell.

Namenyi, Ernest
1957   The Essence of Jewish Art. New York: Thomas Yoseloff.

Ohnuki-Tierney, Emiko
1987   The Monkey as Mirror: Symbolic Transformations in Japanese History and Ritual. Princeton: Princeton Univ. Press.

Paine, Robert
1983   "Israel and Totemic Time?" Royal Anthropological Institute News (Dec.) 59: 19–22.

Safrai, S.
1976   "The Temple." In The Jewish People in the First Century, ed. S. Safrai and M. Stern, 2: 865–907. Philadelphia: Fortress Press.

Scholem, Gershom
1971   The Messianic Idea in Judaism. New York: Schocken.

Sivan, Emmanuel
1987   "The Arab Nation-State: In Search of a Usable Past." Middle East Review 19 (3): 21–30.

Sperber, Daniel
1965   "The History of the Menorah." Journal of Jewish Studies 16: 135–59.

Stone, Michael E.
1980   Scriptures, Sects and Visions: A Profile of Judaism from Ezra to the Jewish Revolts. London: Collins.
1982   "Reactions to Destructions of the Second Temple." Journal for the Study of Judaism 12: 195–204.

Tarn, Nathaniel
1976   "The Heraldic Vision: A Cognitive Model for Comparative Aesthetics." Alcheringa: Ethnopoetics, 2 (2): 23–41.

Taylor, Simon
1981   "Symbol and Ritual Under National Socialism." British Journal of Sociology 32: 504–20.

Weinfeld, Moshe
1972   Deuteronomy and the Deuteronomic School. Oxford: Clarendon Press.

Weitman, Sasha R.
1973   "National Flags: A Sociological Overview." Semiotica 8: 327–67.

Werblowsky, R. J. Zwi
    1971   "Messianism in Jewish History." In *Jewish Society Through the Ages*, ed. H. Ben-Sasson and S. Ettinger, 30–45. New York: Schocken.

Yarden, L.
    1971   *The Tree of Life: A Study of the Menorah—the Seven-Branched Lampstand*. London: East and West Library.

Yerushalmi, Yosef Hayim
    1982   *Zakhor: Jewish History and Jewish Memory*. Seattle: Univ. of Washington Press.

8. Leach: Aryan Invasians

Allchin, Bridget, and Raymond Allchin
    1982   *The Rise of Civilisation in India and Pakistan*. Cambridge: Cambridge Univ. Press.

Burrow, Thomas
    1963   "On the Word *Arma* or *Armaka* in Early Sanskrit Literature." *Journal of Indian History* 41: 159–66.

Carpocino, J.
    1943   *Le Maroc antique*. Paris: Gallimard.

Crossland, R. A.
    1971   "Immigrants from the North." Chap. 28 of *Cambridge Ancient History*. 3d ed. Vol. 1, part 2: 824–76. Cambridge: Cambridge Univ. Press.

Iyengar, P. T. Srinivas
    1914   "Did the Dravidians of India Obtain Their Culture from Aryan Immigrants?" *Anthropos* 9: 2–15.

Littleton, C. Scott
    1982   *The New Comparative Mythology: An Anthropological Assessment of the Theories of Georges Dumézil*. 3d ed. Berkeley: Univ. of California Press.

Müller, F. Max
    1878   *Lectures on the Origin and Growth of Religion*. London: Longman, Green.
    1880   *Chips from a German Workshop*. 4 vols. 2d ed. London: Longman, Green.

O'Flaherty, Wendy Doniger, ed.
    1981   *The Rig Veda: An Anthology*. London: Penguin.

Piggott, Stuart
    1950   *Prehistoric India*. London: Penguin.

Sahlins, Marshall
    1985   *Islands of History*. Chicago: Univ. of Chicago Press.

Shendge, Malati J.
   1977   *The Civilized Demons: The Harappans in Ṛgveda*. New Delhi:
           Abhinav.
Thapar, Romila
   1969   "The Study of Society in Ancient India." Reprinted in Thapar
           1978: 211–39.
   1978   *Ancient Indian Social History*. Delhi: Orient Longman.

                    9. Peacock: Indonesian History

Clifford, James
   1983   "On Ethnographic Authority." *Representation* 2 (Spring):
           118–46.
Crapanzano, Vincent
   1980   *Tuhami: Portrait of a Moroccan*. Chicago: Univ. of Chicago
           Press.
Deming, Greg
   1988   *The Bounty: An Ethnographic History*. Victoria, Austral.:
           Dept. of History Monographs, University of Melbourne.
Gadamer, Hans-Georg
   1975   *Wahrheit und Methode: Grundzüge einer philosophischen Her-
           meneutik*. Tübingen: J. C. B. Mohr.
   1982   *Truth and Method*. Trans. and ed. Garrett Barden and John
           Cumming. New York: Crossroad.
Geertz, Clifford
   1960   *Religion of Java*. Glencoe: Free Press.
   1972   "Deep Play: Notes on the Balinese Cockfight." *Daedalus*
           101: 1–37.
   1973   "Thick Description: Toward an Interpretive Theory of Culture."
           In his *The Interpretation of Cultures*, 5–32. New York: Basic
           Books.
Howe, David G.
   1980   "Sumarah: A Study of the Art of Living." Ph.D. diss., University
           of North Carolina, Chapel Hill.
Marcus, George E.
   1980   "Rhetoric and the Ethnographic Genre in Anthropological Re-
           search." *Current Anthropology* 21 (4): 507–10.
Peacock, James L.
   1968   *Rites of Modernization: Symbolic and Social Aspects of Indo-
           nesian Proletarian Drama*. Chicago: Univ. of Chicago Press.
   1978   *Muslim Puritans: Reformist Psychology in Southeast Asian Is-
           lam*. Berkeley: Univ. of California Press.

1981   "Traditionalism and Reform: Constancy and Climax in Java and the South." In *Perspectives on the American South*, ed. Merle Black and John Shelton Reed, 207–16. New York: Gordon Breach.

Riesman, Paul
1977   *Freedom in Fulani Social Life: An Introspective Ethnography.* Chicago: Univ. of Chicago Press.

Wertheim, W. F.
1965   *East-West Parallels.* Chicago: Quadrangle Books.

10. Burke: Historians

Bak, János
1973   Medieval Symbolology of the State: Percy E. Schramm's Contribution." *Viator* 4: 33–63.

Barthes, Roland
1958   *Michelet.* Paris: Seuil.

Bentham, Jeremy
1932   *Theory of Fictions.* Ed. C. K. Ogden. London: Routledge and Kegan Paul.

Bitsilli, P. M.
1919   *Elements of Medieval Culture.* Odessa. (In Russian.)

Bloch, Marc
1923; trans. 1973   *The Royal Touch.* London: Routledge and Kegan Paul.

Burke, Peter
1986   "Strengths and Weaknesses of the History of Mentalities." *History of European Ideas* 7: 439–51.
1987   "The Repudiation of Ritual in Early Modern Europe." In his *The Historical Anthropology of Early Modern Italy*, 223–38. Cambridge: Cambridge Univ. Press.

Bynum, Caroline
1987   *Holy Feast and Holy Fast.* Berkeley: Univ. of California Press.

Caplan, Harry
1929   "The Four Senses of Scriptural Interpretation." *Speculum* 4: 282–94.

Cassirer, Ernst
1925; trans. 1955   *Mythical Thought.* New Haven: Yale Univ. Press.

Castaneda, Carlos
1968   *The Teachings of Don Juan.* Berkeley: Univ. of California Press.

Cohn, Bernard
1980   "History and Anthropology." *Comparative Studies in Society and History* 22: 198–221.

Cornford, Francis M.
  1907   *Thucydides Mythistoricus*. London: Edward Arnold.
Darnton, Robert
  1984   *The Great Cat Massacre*. New York: Basic Books.
Davis, Natalie Z.
  1981   "The Possibilities of the Past." *Journal of Interdisciplinary History* 12: 267–75.
Demandt, A.
  1978   *Metaphern für Geschichte*. Munich: Beck.
Dijksterhuis, E.
  1950; trans. 1956   *The Mechanisation of the World Picture*. Oxford: Oxford Univ. Press.
Douglas, Mary
  1966   "The Contempt of Ritual." *New Society*: Mar. 31. Reprinted in her *In the Active Voice*, 34–38. London: Routledge and Kegan Paul, 1982.
Eire, Carlos
  1986   *War Against the Idols*. Cambridge: Cambridge Univ. Press.
Fernandez, James W.
  1977   "The Performance of Ritual Metaphors." In *The Social Use of Metaphors*, ed. J. D. Sapir and J. C. Crocker, 100–131. Philadelphia: Univ. of Pennsylvania Press.
Foucault, Michel
  1966   *Les Mots et les choses*. Paris: Gallimard. Translated as *The Order of Things*. London: Tavistock, 1970.
Freedberg, David
  1977   "The Structure of Byzantine and European Iconoclasm." In *Iconoclasm*, ed. Anthony Bryer and Judith Herrin, 165–77. Birmingham, Eng.: Centre for Byzantine Studies.
Geertz, Clifford
  1959   "Ritual and Social Change." Reprinted in his *Interpretation of Cultures*, 142–69. New York: Basic Books, 1973.
Ginzburg, Carlo
  1976   *Cheese and Worms*. English trans., 1981. Trans. Ann and John Tedeschi. Baltimore: Johns Hopkins Univ. Press.
Gombrich, Ernest H.
  1970   *Aby Warburg: An Intellectual Biography*. London: Warburg Institute.
Gouhier, Henri
  1958   "Le Refus du symbolisme dans l'humanisme cartésien." In *Umanesimo e simbolismo*, ed. Enrico Castelli, 65–74. Padua: Liviana.

Harris, Victor
    1966   "Allegory to Analogy in the Interpretation of Scripture." *Philological Quarterly* 45.
Harrison, Jane
    1912   *Themis*. Cambridge: Cambridge Univ. Press.
Haueter, A.
    1975   *Die Krönungen der französischen Könige in Zeitalter des Absolutismus und in den Restauration*. Zurich: Juris Druck.
Hazard, Paul
    1935   *La Crise de la conscience européenne*. Paris: Boivin.
Hobsbawm, Eric, and Terence Ranger, eds.
    1983   *The Invention of Tradition*. Cambridge: Cambridge Univ. Press.
Holly, Michael Ann
    1984   *Panofsky and the Foundations of Art History*. Ithaca: Cornell Univ. Press.
Horton, Robin
    1967   "African Traditional Thought and Western Science." *Africa*.
    1982   "Tradition and Modernity Revisited." In *Rationality and Relativism*, ed. M. Hollis and S. Lukes, 201–60. Oxford: Blackwell.
Huizinga, Johan
    1919; trans. 1924   *The Waning of the Middle Ages*. Reprint. Harmondsworth, Eng.: Penguin, 1955.
Hunt, Lynn
    1984   *Politics, Culture, and Class in the French Revolution*. Berkeley: Univ. of California Press.
Jackson, Richard A.
    1984   *Vive le roi!*, Chapel Hill: Univ. of North Carolina Press.
Koyré, Alexandre
    1957   *From the Closed World to the Infinite Universe*. Baltimore: Johns Hopkins Univ. Press.
Lefort, Claude
    1972   *Machiavel: Le travail et l'oeuvre*. Paris: Gallimard.
Le Roy Ladurie, Emmanuel
    1975   *Montaillou*. London: Scolar Press.
Lewis, I. M., ed.
    1968   *History and Social Anthropology*. London: Tavistock.
Lisón Tolosana, Carmelo
    1966   *Belmonte de los Caballeros*. Oxford: Oxford Univ. Press.
Löfgren, Orvar
    1981   "On the Anatomy of Culture." *Ethnologia Europea* 12: 26–46.
Lovejoy, Arthur O.
    1936   *The Great Chain of Being*. Cambridge: Harvard Univ. Press.

Macfarlane, Alan D.

1970 *Witchcraft in Tudor and Stuart England.* London: Routledge and Kegan Paul.

Maier, Anneliese

1936 *Die Mechanisierung des Weltbildes.* Leipzig: Mainer.

Mandrou, Robert

1968 *Magistrats et sorciers en France au 17e siècle.* Paris: Plon.

Midelfort, H. C. Erik

1972 *Witch Hunting in Southwestern Germany.* Stanford: Stanford Univ. Press.

Monter, E. William

1976 *Witchcraft in France and Switzerland.* Ithaca: Cornell Univ. Press.

Nicolson, Marjorie

1950 *The Breaking of the Circle.* Evanston, Ill.: Northwestern Univ. Press.

Ozouf, Mona

1976; trans. 1988 *Festivals and the French Revolution.* Cambridge: Harvard Univ. Press.

Panofsky, Erwin

1951 *Gothic Architecture and Scholasticism.* Reprint. Latrobe, Penn.: World Publishing Co., Meridian Books, 1957.

Rabinow, Paul

1975 *Symbolic Domination.* Chicago: Univ. of Chicago Press.

Ricoeur, Paul

1983–85 *Temps et récit.* 3 vols. Paris: Seuil. English trans. by Kathleen McLaughlin and David Pellava. Chicago: Univ. of Chicago Press, 1984–.

Sahlins, Marshall

1981 *Historical Metaphors and Mythical Realities.* Ann Arbor: Univ. of Michigan Press.

1985 *Islands of History.* Chicago: Univ. of Chicago Press.

Schama, Simon

1987 *The Embarrassment of Riches.* London: Collins.

Smith, L.

1983 *The Japanese Print Since 1900.* London: British Museum Publications.

Steinmann, Jean

1960 *Richard Simon et les origines de l'exégèse biblique.* Bruges: Desclee de Brouwer.

Stone, Lawrence

1979 "The Revival of Narrative." *Past and Present* 85: 3–24.

Swanson, Guy E.
  1967   *Religion and Regime*. Ann Arbor: Univ. of Michigan Press.
Thomas, Keith V.
  1971   *Religion and the Decline of Magic*. London: Weidenfeld C. Nicolson.
Trevor-Roper, Hugh R.
  1968   *The European Witch-Craze*. Harmondsworth, Eng.: Penguin.
Trexler, Richard
  1972   "Florentine Religious Experience: The Sacred Image." *Studies in the Renaissance* 19: 7–41.
Vert, Claude de
  1706–13 *Explication simple, littérale et historique des cérémonies de l'Eglise*. 4 vols. Paris: Delaulne.
Warburg, Aby
  1939   "A Lecture on Serpent Ritual." *Journal of the Warburg and Courtauld Institutes* 2: 277–92.
White, Hayden
  1973   *Metahistory*. Baltimore: Johns Hopkins Univ. Press.
  1987   *The Content of the Form*. Baltimore: Johns Hopkins Univ. Press.
Willey, Basil
  1934   *The Seventeenth Century Background*. London: Chatto and Windus.

Index

In this index an "f" after a number indicates a separate reference on the next page, and an "ff" indicates separate references on the next two pages. A continuous discussion over two or more pages is indicated by a span of numbers. *Passim* is used for a cluster of references in close but not consecutive sequence.

Library of Congress Cataloging-in-Publication Data

Culture through time : anthropological approaches / edited by Emiko Ohnuki-Tierney.
   p.   cm.
Includes bibliographical references and index.
ISBN 0-8047-1792-3 (alk. paper) — ISBN 0-8047-1791-5
(pbk. : alk. paper)
   1. Ethnohistory.   2. Ethnology—Philosophy.   3. Historiography.
4. Culture.   I. Ohnuki-Tierney, Emiko.
GN345.2.C85   1990
306—dc20

90-36662
CIP

♾   This book is printed on acid-free paper